To Judy Mabro and Ka...

Begun : 6 September 1976.

Finished :

From left to right

Top row	*Bottom row*
Kautsky	Hilferding
Bukharin	Schumpeter
Hobson	Fanon
Engels	Trotsky
Marx	Rosa Luxemburg
Lenin	Galiyev

**Studies in
the theory of
imperialism**

EDITED BY ROGER OWEN & BOB SUTCLIFFE

Longman

LONGMAN GROUP LIMITED
London
*Associated companies, branches and representatives
throughout the world*

First published 1972
Second impression 1975

ISBN 0 582 48752 8 cased
     0 582 48753 6 paper

Printed in Great Britain by
J. W. Arrowsmith Ltd., Bristol

Contents

Acknowledgements

We would particularly like to thank the following people for their assistance in the preparation of this book: Thomas Hodgkin, Olga Nicholson, Ursula Owen and Patrick Seale; Judy Mabro—who typed almost everything; Pat Moss—who also typed; John Harrison, Rick Brandon, Joris de Bres and Don Filtzer—for their work on the bibliography; James Hamilton-Paterson—for editorial assistance; Bernard Reaney—for his assistance in compiling the index; and all the contributors to our Oxford *Theories of Imperialism* seminar, including those who gave papers which we were unable to use. We would also like to thank Tom Kemp whose own book *Theories of Imperialism* was the original stimulus both to the seminar and to this present volume.

Introduction

by Roger Owen

In recent years there has been a great revival of interest in theories of imperialism. It is not difficult to see why. Just as the first wave of interest took place during the early decades of this century when the world was finally being divided up among the empires of the European powers, so too the second wave, beginning in the 1950s, was in large measure a reflection of the new situation produced by the dismantling of these same imperial structures. To some people this was an occasion to look back at the world they had lost, to others the main features of the post-colonial period—the internal divisions inside movements of national liberation, the problems facing third world countries seeking rapid economic development, the wars in the Congo and Vietnam —were best seen as part of a single historical process, one which could only be understood properly in terms of the long history of Europe's relations with the nations of Africa and Asia and Latin America.

The revival of interest has taken a number of forms. Among British historians debate has tended to centre round the arguments put forward by J. Gallagher and R. Robinson in their article, 'The imperialism of free trade' (1953).[1] This was an attempt to stand a number of the assumptions of the models of economic (or capitalist) imperialism, developed by Hobson and Lenin, on their head. Instead of agreeing with Hobson that the expansion of Europe had entered a new phase after 1870, Gallagher and Robinson argued that, at least

1. For reference to the works of all the authors mentioned in this Introduction, see Bibliography.

as far as Britain was concerned, there was no sharp change of policy at this period. Again, unlike Hobson and Lenin they maintained that the 'scramble' for Africa in the 1880s was triggered off not by developments in Europe but by movements which had their origin in Africa itself. A second line of attack on the Hobson and Lenin models was opened up by the same authors in their *Africa and the Victorians* (1961) in which they asserted that the partition of Africa was undertaken for strategic rather than economic motives. Later, there was further criticism of Hobson and Lenin's theories by D. K. Fieldhouse who was instrumental in resurrecting the political approach to imperialism of W. L. Langer and others in which the division of the world after 1870 was seen as dependent on diplomatic rivalries within Europe.

During this same period interest in economic theories of imperialism also began anew. Michael Barratt Brown, Harry Magdoff and others attempted to account for the 'new imperialism' after 1870 not so much in terms of the export of surplus capital from Europe (as Hobson had done) but more as a function of increasing international competition leading to an intensive search for protected markets and for access to vital raw materials. Again, a number of political economists, P. A. Baran and A. Gunder Frank among them, drew attention to the process by which the development of Afro-Asian and Latin American countries had been inhibited, if not actually prevented, by the way in which they had been incorporated within the world economic system. There was also fresh interest in the hypothesis that the drive for overseas expansion in the late nineteenth century was largely the result of the need of the advanced industrial nations to cope with the strains imposed on their societies by periods of irregular, unstable economic growth. Exponents of this particular concept of what has been called 'social imperialism' include W. Lafeber in America and H.-U. Wehler in Germany.

Finally, in recent years there has been an effort to reverse the traditional Eurocentricity of theories of imperialism based on an analysis of the drive for expansion inside the advanced industrial nations by concentrating on what Georges Balandier has termed 'the colonial situation',[2] that is, the effect of colonisation on the society of the colonised. Undoubtedly the most influential works in this field have been those of Frantz Fanon.

But for all this new interest in imperialism, discussions between exponents of rival theories have usually tended to produce greater

2. *Sociologie actuelle de l'Afrique noire* (Paris, 1955 and 1963), trans. by D. Garman as *The Sociology of Black Africa*, (London, Deutsch, 1970).

confusion than clarity. For one thing there is no general agreement about the meaning of the word itself, or about the phenomenon it is meant to describe. For some the subject matter of a theory of imperialism is all empires at all times, for others the formal colonial empires of the nineteenth and twentieth centuries, for others again just that situation of 'competing' empires which Hobson described as being characteristic of the world after 1870. Even by Marxists the word is often used ambiguously, being given both a technical meaning—the final stage of the development of capitalism (and thus the system of relationship between states of all types)—and a colloquial one—the relations between the advanced capitalist countries and the third world.

A second source of confusion lies in the disagreement about the nature and purpose of theory. Whereas even the most empirically-oriented British historians of empire have come to believe that some theory of imperialism is desirable (if only to disprove the theories of other people) there is a wide range of opinion about how such a theory should be tested, how general it should be, and how it ought to be used. Must a theory of imperialism by expected to explain all the phenomena labelled 'imperialist' or just the most important? What is to count as proof of its truth or falsity? How might it relate to theories of other types? These are all questions which Marxists and non-Marxists, historians and economists, academics and political activists, have tended to answer in different ways.

One of the best examples of disagreements of this kind concerns historians writing on imperialism, on the one hand, and economists (and, to some extent, economic historians), on the other. As a rule the former are more interested in the particular than the general. Their primary concern is with why something happened when it did. In the case of imperialism these preoccupations lead naturally to a concern with how policy is made and with the motives of particular policy-makers. Moreover, most British historians are shy of theory; they use it only rarely, and even then its utility is judged not so much in terms of its explanatory power but, rather, according to whether it raises interesting questions and suggests fruitful hypotheses. Against this, economists and economic historians concerned with the study of imperialism are bound to see it in relation to an already existing body of theory. They are interested, too, in the general more than the particular, in the effects of policies rather than how and when they are made. For all these reasons discussions between historians and economists usually break down early. Like the two women shouting across a street in Sydney Smith's illustration of a situation in which agreement is impossible, they are arguing from different premises.

A last, and very important, source of confusion has arisen from the context in which theories of imperialism have been made and from the different political positions of the various protagonists. It could hardly have been otherwise. Given the fact that the authors of the first theories of imperialism, whether liberals like Hobson or Marxists like Lenin and Rosa Luxemburg, were concerned not merely to analyse or explain the phenomenon, but also to find ways of ending it, it was inevitable that the debates which followed were more than simple academic exercises. Those who attacked the theories developed by critics of imperialism were often concerned either to defend the possession of empire or, more generally, to demonstrate that if radical or Marxist thinking was wrong in this area it must be wrong about everything else. Later, when historians and economic historians began to use particular theories to assist them in their studies they too were drawn into a debate which was also implicitly, if not explicitly, about contemporary politics. Even today when scholars discuss the empire-building of the past it is often with the passions of the present. Polemics abound; rival theories are parodied to the point of absurdity in order to demolish them the more quickly; frequently there seems to be an almost deliberate disregard for the complexity of an opponent's position.

For all these reasons it is necessary to spend time in a preliminary attempt at analysing the character of the various theories. This is the more important as it is impossible to classify the different approaches to the subject of imperialism in terms of a set of simple polarities: Marxist and anti-Marxist, economics and history, theory and practice, nineteenth century and twentieth century, the certainty that imperialism is dead and the knowledge that it is still alive. These are not mutually exclusive categories; the boundaries between theories are rarely so distinct. A preliminary attempt at analysis is also necessary if the study of theories of imperialism is to progress beyond the stage at which each writer on the subject is forced to introduce it with an identical explanation of all the traditional sources of misunderstanding.

It was with these thoughts in mind that the editors decided to organise a seminar on theories of imperialism at which a number of papers would be presented, either outlining various theories or demonstrating how such theories might be used to assist research into particular historical or economic problems. Our aim was threefold. First, we wanted to take a new look at existing theories and at the nature of the differences between them. In particular we were anxious to discover in what way these differences were based on different assumptions about the phenomenon of imperialism itself and about the nature and purpose of theory. The second aim of the seminar was to attempt some assessment of the utility of each theory by seeing how it could be applied to concrete historical situations. To this end we asked for a number of case studies by economists, economic historians and historians with very different ideas about the role of theory in the study of imperialism. Our third and last aim was to isolate some of the areas in which further research seemed particularly useful. The result, we hoped, would be a better understanding of the nature of the debate between rival theories which would allow ourselves and others to push on with the study of imperialism without constantly having to go over the same ground again and again.

In the event the papers presented to the seminar (held at Oxford in 1969/70), as well as the discussions which followed, allowed some, but by no means all, of these aims to be achieved. One obvious shortcoming was that certain influential theories were hardly touched on. These included the diplomatic and political theories of Langer and Fieldhouse, the strategic theory relating to Africa of Gallagher and Robinson, and the sociological theory of J. A. Schumpeter. Furthermore, even with the theories which were discussed it was not always possible to isolate their essential characteristics or, more importantly, the differences between them. In the latter case what made the task particularly difficult was the fact that these differences involved questions of aim, of approach, of method, and thus had to be examined on a number of separate levels. Moreover, in some cases, disagreements between rival theorists turned on the interpretation of evidence which is by no means clear, for example the whole question of the role of the export of capital in the economic development of Europe (a subject which is dealt with at greater length in the Conclusion). On the other hand, we feel that the analyses and the case studies do allow a better understanding of the utility of particular theories. Again, the papers and discussions each raised a variety of important topics which require further research, some of the most important of which are examined in the Conclusion of this book.

The exposition of various theories of imperialism is contained in Part One. To begin with T. Kemp gives a presentation of the Marxist Theory. Here the most important point to note is that, for Marxists, 'imperialism' is a word taken by Lenin to describe the last, monopoly, stage of capitalism which began round about 1900 and which continues until the present day. This at once places it in a very special category. On the one hand, the theory has very little to do with the possession of empire as such, or with capitalism as a world system before 1900. On the other hand, it can be used to analyse the entire development of American and European capitalism (including the important questions of its relations with the non-European world) during the twentieth century. Confusion is inevitable if this point is forgotten.

Nevertheless, having made this basic assertion, it should also be noted that it has been common practice to abstract certain of Lenin's ideas (as well as some of Marx) in order to produce a 'Marxian' account of the expansion of Europe in the late nineteenth century. This, in essence, is what M. Barratt Brown has done in his 'A critique of Marxist theories of imperialism', although in his case he tends to rely more on some or Marx's ideas and less on those of Lenin, in particular the former's emphasis on the tendency of capitalist development to lead to a greater and greater concentration of capital. It was this, in Barratt Brown's opinion, which was responsible for one of the most important characteristics of the new imperialism of the late nineteenth century, the drive for markets overseas by competing European industries backed by competing European states. It was this, too, which provides an important part of the explanation of why the expansion of Europe was accompanied by a polarisation of wealth on an international as well as a national scale, and a widening of the gap between the level of development of the industrial countries and the rest. Against this, Barratt Brown is critical of one of the central tenets of the Leninist theory, its emphasis on the importance of the export of European capital.

Another type of theory of imperialism, social imperialism, is discussed by H.-U. Wehler in his 'Industrial growth and early German imperialism'. The belief that expansion overseas could be used to cope with social tension at home was a commonplace among politicians in Europe and the United States in the late nineteenth century. As Wehler demonstrates, this belief was particularly important in Germany where the unstable economic growth of the 1870s and 1880s, bringing with it a vast increase in support for the Social Democrats, seemed to threaten the whole social basis of the new German state. It was this reason, above all, which lay behind Bismarck's pursuit of a policy of state-directed commercial expansion. Further, given the fact that competition was increasing so fast among the leading industrial powers it was more or less inevitable that this expansion should, in part, take the form of a search for colonies.

Lastly, there are two papers outlining partial theories which stand in opposition to the Eurocentric approach of the great majority of European theorists. One, T. Hodgkin's account of 'Some African and third world theorists of imperialism', is a reminder that Africans and Asians have had their own particular contribution to make to an analysis of the phenomenon. He notes their concern with what for them is the central fact of the age of imperialism: their nation's defeat and loss of sovereignty at the hands of Europe. He notes too their insistence that any general theory must be comprehensive enough to include an analysis of the nature of the colonial relationship and of its effects on the society of colonisers and colonised alike. Equally important, Hodgkin points out how the work of third world theorists stands as a continuing challenge, not only to the arguments put forward by apologists of imperialism, but also to the position of those Marxists or Marxist parties which rests on the assumption of the alleged 'superiority' of 'higher' societies or cultures.

The other paper, R. E. Robinson's 'Non-European foundations of European imperialism', presents a totally different attack on the Eurocentricity of traditional theories. Its author is concerned not with the effects of Europe's control over the rest of the world but with the method by which it was exercised. Assuming that the general purpose of this control was to reshape non-European societies in the image of Europe, he goes on to explain the particular forms it took in terms of a changing relationship between the Europeans and local collaborating or mediating groups. In most Afro-Asian countries there was a three-stage process. To begin with Europe attempted to lever local regimes into the collaboration necessary to open their countries to trade and commerce, from the outside. This soon proved unsatisfactory, however, and one European power or another assumed direct political control, though still using native collaborators to see that its policies were carried out. Finally, as local independence movements grew strong enough they were able to destroy the existing collaborative mechanism and the colonialists had to leave. In this way Robinson seeks not only to describe how imperialist control was exercised but also when and why the nature of this control changed over time.

The five papers in Part One by no means exhaust the great variety of theories of imperialism. But they do illustrate something of their range, of the phenomena they seek to analyse or explain, and, above all, of the scope they offer for disagreement and debate. With the possible exception of the fact that the protagonists of these theories see imperialism as in some way related to the growth of capitalism in nineteenth-century Europe it is difficult to find much else about which they agree. Three separate areas of disagreement are of particular importance:

1. *The phenomenon to be explained*   Whereas for Wehler and Barratt Brown the main phenomenon to be explained is the expansion of Europe after 1870, Hodgkin and Robinson are primarily occupied with the relations between European states and their colonies throughout the nineteenth and the first half of the twentieth century. Kemp, for his part, concentrates on the development of capitalism since 1900.

2. *Type of approach*   While Wehler's and Hodgkin's theories depend on an understanding of a complex set of relationships between economic, social and political factors, Robinson is concerned chiefly with the political and social levels and Kemp and Barratt Brown with the economic.

3. *The purpose of theory*   For Wehler and Barratt Brown the main purpose of a theory of imperialism is to explain how and why Europe expanded in terms of changes within Europe itself, while Robinson seeks to answer the same questions but through an emphasis on events in the non-European world. Hodgkin, on the other hand, asks for a theory which, though concerned with the expansion of Europe, also attaches primary importance to an analysis of the effects of the colonial relationship on the societies of both Europe and those it conquered. Lastly, Lenin's theory, as described by Kemp, seeks to isolate the basic characteristics of capitalism in its final stage.

In addition it should be noted that whereas Barratt Brown, Wehler and Robinson see theory as, primarily, a tool of the historian, Kemp and Hodgkin are anxious to underline the point that it must also lead to action. In Hodgkin's case too there is a fear that the study of theories of imperialism itself may be used as a retreat from political responsibility.

Part Two contains papers illustrative of the way in which one particular theory, the Marxist, can be used to assist in the analysis of the nature of the relationship, past and present, between the advanced industrial countries and the rest of the world. In the first, 'Imperialism without colonies', H. Magdoff examines the way in which this relationship has developed from the late nineteenth century onwards, while the second, 'Imperialism and industrialisation in the third world', B. Sutcliffe poses the question: Can contemporary capitalism lead to a fully independent industrialisation anywhere in Afro-Asia or Latin America? Both authors begin with an analysis of various arguments put forward by earlier Marxist writers before concentrating on those which they think are of particular importance. In the case of Magdoff, for instance, he rejects the idea that the sharp rise on the export of European capital in the late nineteenth century was due to a superabundance of capital in the industrial economies, seeing it rather as a natural consequence of (1) the development of capitalism as a world economic system and (2) the increasing international competition between industries during the last quarter of the nineteenth century. Sutcliffe, for his part, demonstrates how the present consensus among Marxists that contemporary capitalism is an insuperable obstacle to further industrialisation in the third world goes against the spirit, and often the letter, of a good deal of Marxist thinking in the past.

Finally, Part Three contains six case studies, each designed to illustrate some aspect of the relationship of theory to a particular historical problem. To speak very generally, this relationship is conceived of in two different ways: in some studies an existing theory is employed to guide the analysis of the problem, in others the analysis of the problem is used to test a theory.[3] Hence whereas R. Owen ('Egypt and Europe'), P. Patnaik ('Imperialism and the growth of Indian capitalism') and R. W. Johnson ('French imperialism in Guinea') are concerned to approach their subject within the general context of the theory of capitalist imperialism, J. Stengers ('King Leopold's imperialism') and S. Kanya-Forstner ('French Expansion in Africa') seek to demonstrate that the agents of imperialism, whether the King of Belgium or the French military, were able to act autonomously, without influence from the economic system of the state to which they belonged. D. C. M. Platt ('Economic imperialism and the businessman') makes a related point: for him businessmen can only be considered as agents of imperialism if they were able to exercise control over the economies of the countries in which they worked.

Enough has been said to show the basic contrasts between the

---

3. This point is discussed at greater length in the Introduction to Part Three.

different theories under discussion and the different ways in which they can be used. Nevertheless, even if the various papers have so little in common as far as aim and approach and method are concerned, this does not mean that there were not certain general themes running through the majority of them. The first concerns the so-called 'new imperialism' of the 1870s. For most contributors European expansion in the last quarter of the nineteenth century differed qualitatively from that of earlier periods. In this they were all in disagreement with the position taken in respect of Britain by Robinson and Gallagher in their 'The imperialism of free trade'. Reasons for this disagreement varied, but there was some support for the view that the 'new imperialism' was caused, in part, by the fact that Britain's predominant position in world markets was then beginning to be challenged by industrial rivals like the Germans and the Americans. The result was an accelerated competition for the remaining markets in Asia and Africa, the majority of which were placed under the direct political control of one or other of the powers in order to prevent their own goods from being excluded.

A second area of more or less general agreement concerned the effects of capitalist imperialism on the economies of non-European countries. With much of the indigenous industry destroyed and all their resources concentrated on the production of a few agricultural products—or minerals—for export, such economies became little more than markets for European industrial goods and a source of raw materials. Once established, this pattern was difficult, if not impossible, to break. Thus, as far as these economies were concerned, the end of colonisation made little difference; most of the old barriers to industrialisation and the diversification of exports remained.

A third theme relates to the fact that many theories of imperialism were seen as Eurocentric in that they focused attention on changes within European society and had little to say about their effect outside Europe. Thomas Hodgkin's eloquent plea for a theory which would take account of the disruption which imperialism had caused in Africa and Asia found a strong response. On the other hand, there was some disagreement about the relative weights to be attached to the study of the European as opposed to the non-European world. This in turn raised the more general question of whether the growth of capitalism in nineteenth-century Europe would have been possible without the rest of the world to exploit and whether the present capitalist system could survive if it was deprived of its African and Asian markets and sources of raw materials.

Finally, there was a continuing discussion of the relationship between economics and politics. Once again the point was made with particular clarity in Thomas Hodgkin's paper. Even though the third world theorists he describes believe that imperialism is, at root, a system of economic exploitation, a more important fact for them was that their peoples had actually been politically subordinate to a foreign power. To be colonised was to be subject to an intolerable experience of political domination: this, in their eyes, was the essential reality of the era of imperialism.

PART ONE

Theories of

imperialism

It is Marxist writing, and in particular that of Lenin, which dominates the question of imperialism. Tom Kemp gives here a survey of the origins of the Marxist theory in the economic analysis of Marx in *Capital* (section 2), specifically the realisation problem, the tendency of the rate of profit to fall and the concentration and centralisation of capital. He goes on to outline its development by Lenin to whom imperialism was virtually synonymous with the epoch of monopoly capitalism (sections 3 and 4), and finally its contemporary relevance and the ways it might be tested and developed (section 5).

Two points which he makes must be kept in mind throughout any discussion of imperialism. First, Marxists use the term imperialism to mean something different from and usually a good deal broader than, what is meant by other writers, especially historians (section 2). This is the source of constant misunderstandings, both accidental and deliberate. Second, a true Marxist theory of imperialism, or of anything else, cannot be conceived apart from its relevance to a political struggle for socialism (section 5); and that in the end is the criterion by which a Marxist would have his theory tested. To reveal the truth about the world is to lay a foundation for changing it.

Some of the terminology of section 2 may be unfamiliar to some readers. It is more fully explained in Tom Kemp's book *Theories of Imperialism* (chapter 2), but a very brief explanation may be helpful here. In Marx's analysis of the capitalist mode of production the value of a commodity is composed of: first, the value of the constant capital (c), that is, the machinery and raw materials used up in production; second, variable capital (v), the amount of labour used—measured in terms of the wages paid to keep the workers alive; and, third, surplus value (s), the excess of a value of a commodity over its costs of production ($c + v$).

The capitalists have a problem of realising this surplus value: in the process of circulation (of commodities and money) they must find a market for their products. Not only must the market for goods in general be sufficient to sell all that is produced, but of course there must also be sufficient demand for both consumers' goods and producers' goods (what Marx meant by the two departments of the economy). The conditions for this proportionality in demand in both a static and a growing economy are to be found formally stated in the reproduction schema in Volume II of *Capital*.

Technical progress in Marx's view tended to raise the organic composition of capital (c/v) in production, reducing the amount of labour needed relative to capital. With the class struggle tending to keep the rate of surplus value, or rate of exploitation (s/v), constant, it follows that there is a tendency for the rate of profit in Marx's sense $\frac{s}{c+v}$ to fall.

I

The Marxist theory of imperialism[1]

Tom Kemp

The attempt of an older conservative school of historiography to banish the term 'imperialism' from the scholar's vocabulary has conspicuously failed. Whatever content is given to it, whether it is approached with the intention of finding a general explanation or with an entirely sceptical attitude towards theory, there is now broad agreement that it embraces recognisable phenomena which have to be explained. Since the term can no longer be brushed aside the need for greater precision becomes more imperative. And therefore the challenge of the Marxist, or Marxist-Leninist, theory—despite all the vicissitudes which Marxist theory has been subject to—makes itself felt with renewed force. The debate has tended to shift to one about this theory. More or less consciously, even in the academic havens of the Anglo-Saxon countries, work in this field, whether by historians or by economists, is seeking to disprove, and more rarely to test or verify, what this theory asserts or is assumed to assert. The prevailing academic orthodoxy is necessarily hostile to Marxism in these countries and is unlikely to be converted. But this is not necessarily true of younger scholars and students who are dissatisfied with the subjectivism, idealism and ideological loading of most establishment

1. Within the space limitations laid down for this paper it is not possible to give an adequate exposition and defence of the Marxist theory of imperialism and to deal with its different variants. The reader is therefore referred to the same author's *Theories of Imperialism* (London, Dobson 1967) where some of the points considered here are dealt with more fully. The present essay follows the lines of an earlier article which appeared in *Labour Review*, **7**, no. 3, 1962 and in *Partisans*, no. 13, Dec. 1963–Jan. 1964.

scholarship and are aware of its inability to grasp or understand the real processes at work in shaping our epoch. The interest in the problem of imperialism shows that. What, then, does the Marxist theory consist of?

1. Questions of method and interpretation

The Marxist theory of imperialism forms part of that theoretical whole known as Marxism which is grounded in dialectical materialism, includes its own political economy and provides the tactics and strategy of proletarian revolution. It has suffered from the vicissitudes of the Marxist movement in this century and particularly from the revisions and perversions of Stalinism.[2] As a result those who claim to be Marxists today have serious differences about the theory of imperialism, as about other aspects of theory and practice. Rather than deal with these differences, what follows will make the claim to be in the authentic Marxist tradition and will leave others to contest it if they please.

This being said it may be added, although the point is obvious enough, that the Marxist theory of imperialism was not devised as an aid to the study and writing of history as practised in the universities. It had, and still has, a definitely operational character as a guide to policy-making and action. Nevertheless Marxists do study and write history and do claim that in skilled hands their method enables the historical record to be more fully understood.[3] It is therefore necessary at the outset to say something, however briefly and inadequately, about historical materialism.[4] Marxism traces the dynamic of social activity and historical development to its roots in the production and reproduction of the means of existence. It is on the material base, itself continually changing as men establish greater powers of control over their environment, that the superstructure of culture, institutions, laws and political systems arises. While these superstructural forces may and do assume an autonomy of their own and react upon the material base they are, in the last analysis, referable to it. It should be emphasised that the materialist conception of history is not the crude kind of 'economic' interpretation which it is sometimes assumed to be by ill-informed or dishonest critics. Nor does it see human development as the product of separable 'factors' of which the economic is

2. *Theories of Imperialism*, ch. vii *passim*.
3. See the quotation from Franz Mehring in *ibid.*, p. 10.
4. *Theories of Imperialism*, pp. 8–15 and the references there cited.

the determining one. It assumes the totality of human relationships, traces out their interrelationships and seeks the source of historical change not in motives, not in ideologies but in the material basis of the society in question. The study of imperialism thus begins with the economic structure and finds there the forces which set in motion 'great masses, whole peoples and again whole classes of people in each people', as Engels put it. For Marxism imperialism is not a political or ideological phenomenon but expresses the imperative necessities of advanced capitalism.

For Marxists, therefore, the explanation of such aspects of imperialism as colonial expansion and power struggles between states has to be sought in material conditions rather than in ideology and politics. The subjective or psychological explanation of imperialism has been most cogently expressed by Joseph Schumpeter—perhaps the only non-Marxist thinker to provide an all-embracing theory—but elements of it pervade most, if not all, non-Marxist theories.[5] While not denying the influence of forces which are mainly superstructural, the Marxist theory rejects the view that the course of history can be explained in terms of power drives, love of war, desire for glory and the influence of outstanding personalities. In particular, it denies that the massive technological and economic forces of advanced capitalism have been somehow geared to imperialist drives, contrary to their inherent tendencies, by statesmen, military leaders, aristocratic castes or even whole peoples. It begins with the capitalist mode of production in its state of movement and sees what it defines as 'imperialism' as being the expression of the working out of its immanent laws. The complexity of the forms in which these laws work themselves out, their interaction with forces in the superstructure and the infinite variety of actual historical situations make the task of actual historical explanation no less and in some ways more difficult for the Marxist historian than for the non-Marxist.

2. What is imperialism?

The Marxist theory of imperialism sets out to explain the characteristics displayed by the capitalist mode of production in its latest, most advanced stage as a result of the working out of its 'laws of motion' discovered by Marx. It thus uses the term 'imperialism' in a technical

5. *Ibid.*, ch. vi *passim.*

sense which has to be carefully distinguished from the variable meaning attached to it by historians and others. For the latter it generally means principally or exclusively the relationship between the advanced, imperial country and the colonial or semicolonial areas falling within its formal or informal empire. The Marxist theory does more than this. It uses the term to describe a special stage of capitalist development and, by extension, it speaks of the epoch of imperialism in which this has become the dominant form and stresses the new, distinguishing features of this stage. Since it deals specifically with the capitalist mode of production it is not concerned with a more general and comprehensive theory of imperialism in a wider sense. If the same term is applied to other periods, or in a sense which is closer to its etymological origins, there can be no objection in principle as long as the differences are made clear and confusion avoided.

Although Marx left no theory of imperialism, the analysis he made of the capitalist mode of production provides the starting point for the Marxist-Leninist theory. In *Capital* Marx was at pains to show that the capitalist mode of production was governed not by the satisfaction of human needs but by the drive to extract surplus value from a class of wage-labourers, to realise this surplus value by finding a market for the commodities in which it was embodied and to capitalise this surplus value in new means of production. The theory of imperialism deals with the special phenomenal form which this process takes at a particular stage in the development of the capitalist mode of production. Marx's own work in political economy required the construction of a model of 'pure capitalism' at a relatively high level of abstraction. The theory of imperialism, dealing as it must do with the actual working out of the 'laws of motion' which Marx discerned, tries to give greater concreteness to the way in which they have expressed themselves in history. Lenin, in particular, began with the new developments in capitalism which had to be explained.

Those parts of *Capital* which are most relevant to explaining the new stage of the capitalist mode of production, imperialism, are as follows:

(a) *the reproduction schemas* in volume ii which deal with the problem of how the surplus value extracted from the working class is realised. We thus have what is known as 'the realisation problem', a problem of markets, as well as that of the maintenance of the proportions between the two main departments of production (that concerned with means

of production and that concerned with means of consumption).
Rosa Luxemburg was mainly preoccupied with these aspects.[6]
(b) *the tendency for the rate of profit to fall* which follows from technical
change which increases the proportion of constant to variable capital,
of crystallised 'dead' labour to living labour, in other words bringing
about a rise in what Marx called the organic composition of capital.
For Marx this law was a law of tendency: it was counteracted by
other forces and by the efforts of capitalists to find ways of maintaining profitability despite the law. It is dealt with in the manuscripts
which went into volume iii of *Capital*.
(c) *the concentration and centralisation of capital* as an inevitable outcome
of the competitive struggle. This is referred to in volume i and
returned to more specifically in volume iii, where it is linked with the
structural changes in capitalism already visible and which were preparing the way for 'monopoly capitalism' as Marxists were later to
use the term. See, for instance, Marx's observations on the rise of the
business company and the 'managers', the role of the stock exchange
and the banks. These trends are also dealt with briefly in Engel's
Anti-Duhring.

   The component parts of Marx's analysis of capitalism were part of
an, albeit unfinished, model intended to reveal the 'laws of motion' of
this mode of production in its whole development. Marx's method of
abstracting one aspect for close examination was a necessary part of
this task. To build a theory on one part of the total structure, as Rosa
Luxemburg did with the reproduction schemas of volume ii, can
lead to serious error. It is also necessary to be clear about the distinction
between the characteristics of the 'pure capitalism' of the model—
e.g. the existence of only two classes, capitalists and workers—and the
real world which the theory ultimately has to explain. Thus, for
example, no amount of sophisticated analysis and model-building
based on Marx's schemes of reproduction can completely represent the
dialectical and contradictory character of actual economic relations
in their specific, historically derived context. Account has to be taken
of the character of the superstructure and its interaction with the
economic base. This applies particularly to the national state, the
form of governmental organisation within which the capitalist mode
of production took shape.
   The productive forces released by the capitalist mode of production

---

6. *Theories of Imperialism*, ch. iv *passim*.

could not be contained within the geographically confined areas of the old dynastic states of Europe. The rise of capitalism, and the industrialisation of the advanced countries to which it led, brought into being a world market and an international division of labour. It was through their relationship with the world market that the national capitalist states acquired their specific physiognomy and that the less developed areas, as they were brought into contact with the world market, assumed a position of dependence. By the end of the nineteenth century most of the world had been carved up into empires and spheres of influence of the dominant powers. Apart from the countries of European settlement only Japan was able to develop independently on capitalist lines.

At the same time, the bourgeoisie, the capitalist ruling class, established itself politically through the national state and thus there grew up a system of states which embodied different national interests. The state defined itself in the economic sphere through its own laws, monetary system, tariffs and restrictions on the movement of the factors of production. There was, therefore, a contradiction between the international unifying tendencies of the new technologies and the constricting influence of the national state. This expressed itself in rivalries and tensions between the main powers, in colonial expansion, in alliances and preparations for war and finally in war itself. By the end of the nineteenth century, Marxism claims, the progressive role of capitalism as a whole had come to an end: the epoch of imperialism had begun.

Relations and conflicts between states provide much of the stuff of political history. In appearance political, diplomatic and military questions predominated, and much of the historical writing about the period after, say, 1870, pays little or no attention to the economic forces which were at work below the surface. At the same time, most academic economic history is written as though the outbreak of the First World War bore no relation to the subject matter of the discipline.[7] For Marxism this dichotomy is entirely unreal and springs from the fact that much academic study of modern history is ideo-

7. David S. Landes has dealt more realistically with Anglo–German rivalry and states than 'In the reaction against Marxist slogans (*sic*) of "imperialist war" and "the last stage of capitalism", scholars have leaned over backwards to expunge the slightest taint of economic determinism from their lucubrations. Yet doctrine was never a valid guide to knowledge, at either end of the ideological spectrum, and this effort to rule out material considerations as causes of the World War betrays *naïveté* or ignorance about the nature of power and the significance of power relations for the definition of national interests', *The Cambridge Economic History of Europe*, vol. vi, Part i (Cambridge, Cambridge Univ. Press, 1965), p. 554.

logically loaded. For the Marxist theory a connection clearly exists *Yes, but* between the changes which took place in the structure of capitalism *what ?* in the leading countries during the period after 1870 and the new *=* forms of interstate rivalry and the carving up of the world into colonial empires and spheres of influence which marked the beginning of the epoch of imperialism. It follows from the application of historical materialism that in their main direction the political trends *?* of the so-called 'new imperialism' expressed the working out of economic laws and reflected the contradiction between the development of productive forces and the national state.

Returning then to the section of Marx's *Capital* which are relevant here, the following brief points can be made. Firstly, capitalist enterprises in the advanced countries sought to expand their markets (to realise surplus value) and keep up profits by pushing into the world market. They did so, where possible, with the aid and support of their governments and/or by using their own superior bargaining power in trade with weaker partners, in obtaining concessions and so on. Secondly, other areas of the world were linked economically to the centres of advanced industry, thus making possible the acquisition on favourable terms of primary products which entered into the process of circulation, as variable and constant capital, and thus helped to counteract the tendency for the rate of profit to fall. Thirdly, this required the export of capital to undeveloped areas to build railways and ports, opening up their interiors and thus bringing sections of their economies into dependence on the world market. Fourthly, these developments of the international division of labour, determined by the needs of the advanced countries, were accompanied by and were the expression of those structural changes—notably the growth of monopolies—whose beginnings had been noted by Marx and Engels but which had now become, or were becoming, the dominant forms of the capitalist mode of production in its highest stage. These characteristics, especially the fourth, were the starting point for Lenin's analysis of imperialism which will be examined later.

Numerous problems arise here which can only be touched on. They all depend on whether a connection can be established between on the one hand the politics of 'imperialism', its ideologies and colonial expansion, and on the other the changes in the economic structure which Marxists claim were, in the last analysis, the driving forces in the new historical epoch. It may be admitted that to formulate the theory appropriate to this stage in Marxist terms carries no conviction with those who do not accept the same postulates. It remains difficult to see what 'proof' they require or would accept. Within the confines of the present study, therefore, it seems best to proceed by making clear what they have to refute.

3. Monopoly capitalism and imperialism

To take up the problem from a different angle, it can be said that most non-Marxists who employ the term 'imperialism' do so in a political rather than an economic sense.[8] They mean the relationship established between the advanced metropolitan countries and their colonies, or they may extend it to include other dependencies, the 'informal' empire. As a consequence, some writers have concluded, somewhat disingenuously, that with the end of colonial rule imperialism has come to an end. The term is also sometimes used in a less precise way to describe expansionist policies in all epochs and the political and military subjection of some peoples by others. It may thus be claimed that 'imperialism' begins with the rise of organised states engaged in conquest. Without contesting such usages in the proper context, as has already been pointed out, the term, for Marxists, has a definite technical or scientific meaning. The Marxist theory, which uses it in this sense, cannot therefore be refuted by importing into the discussion some other meaning or, indeed, by juggling with definitions. To come to the point, then, Marxists mean by imperialism a special stage in the development of capitalism which began in the latter part of the nineteenth century and which defines the nature of the current epoch of history. In Lenin's words: 'If it were necessary to give the briefest possible definition of imperialism we should have to say that *imperialism is the monopoly stage of capitalism*' (emphasis added).

By monopoly Marxists do not mean literally the occupation of each industry or branch of enterprise by a single firm. They use 'monopoly capitalism' to indicate the passage of capitalism from its earlier stage of more or less free competition to one in which giant firms, trusts and cartels dominate the market.

Marx and Engels were among the first students of capitalist economy to recognise that the laws of the market themselves tended to make competition between producers inherently unstable. As Marx put it, 'One capitalist kills many'. They arrived at this conclusion not from a study of actual market situations (which in their day were still predominantly competitive), but from a combination of condi-

8. *Theories of Imperialism*, ch. viii for a review of some of these theories.

tions—technical, economic, financial—which assisted the successful capitalist in increasing the size of the capital he employed and enabled him to drive out or absorb his less successful rivals. By the process which Marx called *centralisation* of capital a smaller number of large capitals tended to dominate the market in each field of business ('oligopoly'). At the same time, by the process of *concentration*, separate individual capitals were amalgamated into larger units with the same effect (mergers, takeovers). These larger capitals made it possible to embark on the increasingly costly outlays required to set up in business at all where technology required a big initial expenditure on plant and machinery. The need for huge blocks of capital to start up a business protected existing firms from new entrants. Further, the successful large-scale firm not only had larger amounts of its own capital at its disposal but it was also able to acquire fresh money capital from the banks and the stock exchange on favourable terms. The whole process was indeed linked historically with the rise of joint stock companies and the growth of large deposit and investment banks and financial institutions which centralised the financial reserves of the system as a whole.

These trends, to which Marx and Engels had drawn attention in sections of their writings which have a particularly modern ring, began to interest those professional economists with an institutional approach in Germany, the U.S.A. and other countries from about the end of the nineteenth century. Marxists began to take up the study of actual developments and Hilferding, the most impressive writer on the question, gave currency to the term 'finance capital' to describe what was now becoming a dominant trend. Those economists who were primarily concerned with market situations were slow to recognise what was new in these developments and continued until the 1930s to work on the assumption that there is perfect competition.

An important characteristic of the new trends was their unevenness between countries. They were most strongly marked in the industrial latecomers, and most of all in Germany. Marxists tended to generalise from these cases—as Lenin himself did—and on the basis of the considerable technical literature which had accumulated. In Britain, on the other hand, competitive individualism was still pronounced in industry where old-established, family firms, well provided with capital, resisted amalgamation. Industrial 'retardation' was accompanied, in any case, by continued predominance in shipping, international investment and financial services, and the possession of the major world empire. The newcomers, leaping over several stages, went more directly to modern forms of industrial-financial organisation. They also came into conflict with entrenched British interests in markets and colonies. This was an aspect of what Marxists call the law of uneven development.

how?

In the Marxist theory the expansionist drives of advanced capitalism are associated with the emergence of large amalgamations of capital both in the industrial form and in money form in the hands of banks and giant financial institutions. It was for these concerns, in particular, that the confines of the national market became too narrow. A conspicuous part was played by the firms, most of them large-scale, which operated in heavy industry, producing means of production and of destruction, whose growth invariably exceeded the limits of

when?

the internal market. Continuing accumulation and the maintenance of profitability therefore demanded a large and growing market. Government contracts at home and abroad, such as arms orders and railway concessions, became indispensable for such concerns. In the same way, the big banks, assembling the spare funds of the investing public into ever larger blocs, sought new investment outlets—and not least the profits of promotion itself—abroad and in the colonies. Divisions of opinion inevitably appeared within the capitalist class: some interests encouraged, others opposed these external drives, expressed in colonial expansion and in an active foreign policy. In particular colonialism had to show some prospect of returns to the interests directly involved before business gave its support. Furthermore, at first sight, the most active exponents of expansionism seemed to be flag-wagging nationalists drawn mainly from the middle class or headed by old-style patriots from the land-owning aristocracy. And in the cabinet room, as well as in the field, decisions had finally to be made by politicians, proconsuls and military chiefs who had no direct contact or necessary sympathy with the monopoly capitalists, the magnates of heavy industry and the bankers and stock-jobbers who personified the new forces of capitalism.

These complex historical situations undoubtedly pose difficult problems in establishing the facts, working through the interconnections from the material base to the superstructure and detecting the source of the dominating impulses in development. A whole sociological explanation is required which must reflect the great complexity and variety of actual situations. The Marxist theory will obviously not convince its critics by assertions; but it is by no means clear what 'proof' these critics require. Further, it is when they put forward their own alternative explanation or theory that their own weaknesses stand revealed. Their own position assumes, in most cases, the predominance of just those ideological and political factors which Marxist would call the 'superstructural' forces.

Confronted with such situations, the Marxist theory holds fast to its starting point which lies in the analysis of changes in the material base as reflecting themselves, in however a complex and contradictory way, in the superstructure. It seeks to trace out the origins of the new forces released by the capitalist mode of production in its development, forces which could not be contained within the old forms but which nevertheless, to some degree, had to operate through them. The growth of monopoly and finance capital was irrepressible; capitalism could not be fixed in its earlier competitive shape. The expansionist drives which they generated within the national states carried government with them. Politicians, general staffs, ideologists, public opinion, constituted so many interrelated layers reflecting different pressures and interacting with each other in complex ways. An enormous variety of patterns resulted from these crisscrossing influences.

The nub of the question is really this. Given the scope and power of the technological and economic drives of advanced capitalism, represented by powerful firms and financial institutions which owned and controlled the main means of production, the sources of wealth and power, can it really seriously be maintained that the determining and decisive role in world development was played by those forces which Marxists call superstructural? As a theoretical hypothesis, judged in relation to the compelling power of the dynamics of production, circulation and accumulation which govern the operation of the capitalist mode of production, it seems most implausible. Properly and skilfully used, therefore, the Marxist method of historical materialism is the most likely to provide an objectively valid, scientific account of the epoch of imperialism.

In summary it can be said that in the countries of advanced capitalism, those in which the structural changes characteristic of 'finance capital' and 'monopoly capitalism' were taking place, in which the pressure to find new markets and sources of raw materials, to open up wider investment fields, was building up, a keener interest began to be taken in an active foreign and colonial policy. Although colonies were still being acquired and held for 'old' reasons, political and strategic, and were often economically disappointing, colonial expansion was only one part of the outward thrust in which the big banks and large scale industry in the advanced countries engaged. In doing so they engaged their governments; or, indeed, governments may have taken the lead in the hope that economic benefits would follow. The process of expansion into the world market inevitably assumed an internationally competitive character because of the national state form in which the dominance of the bourgeoisie as a ruling class expressed itself. It therefore took place beneath a cover of nationalism and patriotism; it found ideological spokesmen and involved politicians and military men over whose words and decisions industrial and financial interests did not necessarily exercise much, if any, control. On the surface politics and ideology ruled; deep down it was the imperative necessities of the capitalist mode of production which exercised the determining role.

4. The contribution of Lenin

The Marxist theory of imperialism derives not directly from Marx but from Lenin's application of Marx's method to a study of the economic and political developments which brought about the First World War in his famous work *Imperialism: the Highest stage of capitalism.*[9] While other Marxists of his generation made important contributions to the theory, it is undoubtedly to Lenin's work that supporters and critics must alike turn if they wish to understand the nature of the Marxist theory.

The publication in recent years of the notes which Lenin made while writing his book shows the wide range of material which he consulted.[10] Much of the literature he used was in German and was about developments in Germany, and that has undoubtedly left its mark on the book. While it is true that British capitalism was still resisting the trend towards 'monopoly capitalism' and 'finance capital', Lenin has been proved right in seeing what was happening in Germany as typical of the direction in which all the capitalist countries were moving.

Lenin, it must be remembered, was not writing an academic treat-

9. *Imperialism, the Highest Stage of Capitalism*, written in 1916 with an eye to the tsarist censorship. Lenin wrote a new preface in 1920 in which he said that his aim was to present 'a *composite picture* of the world capitalist system in its international relationships at the beginning of the twentieth century—on the eve of the first world imperialist war'. There are innumerable studies of this work and the centenary of Lenin's birth has produced a new crop of articles. See *Theories of Imperialism*, ch. v *passim* for a fuller discussion. Also the paper read by Georges Labica at the Algiers colloquium on imperialism in 1969 in *La Pensée*, no. 146, August 1969.
10. V. I. Lenin, *Collected Works* (London, Lawrence & Wishart, 42 vols, 1969), vol. 39, *Notebooks on Imperialism*.

ise but a tract for the times whose purpose was to explain to the international socialist movement the nature of the forces which had brought about the war and, at the same time, the collapse of the Second International. The events which followed its appearance, notably the Bolshevik Revolution, have ensured for the book an authoritative place in Marxist literature and a status which would no doubt have surprised Lenin himself in view of the limitations, imposed and self-imposed, on its scope.

When Lenin wrote *Imperialism* he was not thinking of it as the last word on the subject. The reader will note that his claims are modest and carefully qualified. At the same time he was trying to characterise fully and yet succinctly, pedagogically so to speak, what he considered to be the distinguishing features of the latest stage in capitalist development to which, following a growing practice, he gave the title 'imperialism'. It is important to underline that for Lenin as for other Marxists the term was used in a special, scientific sense. Lenin worked out his own definition in some detail and it is to this meaning and to none other that the Marxist theory now generally refers.

In the first place Lenin combined the dominant tendencies in capitalism observable in a number of countries into a composite picture of 'monopoly capitalism'. This may be seen as a development and extension into a more finished conceptual form of those traits about which Marx and Engels had written some decades before when they first began to appear. Lenin stressed that monopoly capitalism was a necessary outgrowth from the old style competitive capitalism, that it took over in a very uneven way and produced new antagonisms and contradictions. He associated these new forms of capitalism, arising within the nation-state, with the division of the world into empires and spheres of economic influence and hence with the international rivalries and tensions which had produced the war. He thus drew together the principal economic and political trends of the period in order to define the nature of the epoch of imperialism.

A close reading of *Imperialism* will confirm that Lenin did not claim to have a completely worked out theory of imperialism. It should also show that some of the objections to his theory are based upon a mistaken idea of its intention and the claims he made for it. Lenin saw his own contribution as part of a joint investigation with other Marxists, notably with his own collaborators Zinoviev and Bukharin, both to be victims of Stalin's purges.[11] It is evident that he

11. Lenin wrote the preface for Bukharin's *Imperialism and World Economy* (1929) which later fell into undeserved oblivion.

largely took for granted that his readers would be familiar with *Capital* and other Marxist classics. He did not consider at all the reproduction process, which had been at the core of Rosa Luxemburg's celebrated work, and the 'realisation problem' arising from it to which he had made an important contribution in some of his own earliest theoretical writings.[12] As can be seen from the *Notebooks*, Lenin made an exhaustive empirical study of the latest structural changes in the advanced capitalist countries which showed the growth of monopolistic practices and the integration of industry with the banks. He did not try to bring up to date Marx's model of the reproduction process to take account of these changes, because this was no part of his purpose. It is implicit, however, that the phenomena he investigated reflected the efforts of the capitalists to evade or ward off the tendencies towards crisis inherent in the reproduction process: the need to realise surplus value, to preserve proportionality between the different departments of production and to fight off the tendency for the rate of profit to fall.

From this point of view Lenin is concerned with effects rather than with causes and with the lessons which the socialist movement had to draw from the passage of capitalism into the monopoly stage. According to him, 'Imperialism emerged as the development and direct continuation of the fundamental characteristics of capitalism in general'. In the course of defining imperialism he referred to the following five basic features. Despite the fact that they are so often quoted it is worth returning to them, both in order to show that Lenin's theory of imperialism put the emphasis on the structural changes in capitalism rather than upon the relations between the metropolitan countries and their colonies, and to suggest that they still accurately characterise the dominant features of capitalism today.

While drawing attention to 'the conditional and relative value of all definitions, which can never include all the connections of a fully developed phenomenon', his definition runs as follows:

(*a*) 'The concentration of production and capital has developed to such a high stage that it has created monopolies which play a decisive part in economic life'. The evidence for the persistence of this trend is overwhelming; few branches of economic activity have escaped it.
(*b*) 'The merging of bank capital with industrial capital, and the

12. See the first four volumes of his *Collected Works* where this is one of the major questions taken up in his critique of the Narodniks.

creation, on the basis of this "finance capital", of a financial oligarchy.' While there is room for different interpretations of the relationship between industry and the banks, and for discussion about where control really lies—this can only be settled by empirical enquiry—the dominant role of a recognisable 'financial oligarchy' can hardly be questioned.

(*c*) 'The export of capital as distinguished from the export of commodities acquires exceptional importance.' Here again, the role of the export of capital from the U.S.A. in particular has been of fundamental importance in the development of capitalism in recent decades. The controversy about the 'American challenge', the weakening of the dollar and the crisis in the international monetary system are bound up with this characteristic.

(*d*) 'The formation of international monopolist capitalist combines which share the world among themselves.' The names of these giant corporations will be familiar to any reader of the business pages of the press. Their increasingly dominant role has placed them at the centre of presentday controversy.

(*e*) Indeed, it is only about the last point, 'the territorial division of the whole world among the biggest capitalist powers is completed', that there can be serious argument. The old territorial empires of the European capitalist states of which Lenin was thinking no longer exist. The United States, which displays the other characteristics of 'imperialism' in the most advanced form, has never possessed colonies of any importance. Instead, American imperialism rules over 'an empire without frontiers' which has no parallel in the past.

Lenin was himself cautious about this definition which, after a further sixty years or so of turbulent history, is open to refinement and extension. But this will be to take in the new forms which imperialism has assumed, not to change the essence of the matter. What he called 'parasitic and decaying capitalism' has taken a lot longer to die than he expected, not because of its inherent strength but as a consequence of the crisis of leadership in the socialist movement. In the meantime the antagonisms, contradictions and unevenness of development which Lenin stressed as inseparable from the epoch of imperialism have manifested themselves to the full.

vive Trotsky!

The fate of Lenin's work at the hands of the 'epigones' and the criticisms made of it by opponents or revisers of Marxism would require more detailed treatment than can be accorded here. A theory must be judged as a whole: to take passages from their context and then claim that the point he makes has been invalidated, as some critics do, does no damage to the essentials of Lenin's model. The attempt to belittle his contribution by emphasising his acknowledged debt to Hobson and Hilferding in particular hardly deserves attention. In any case Lenin's position was completely different from that of the underconsumptionist, Hobson, and he had serious political differences with the Austrian school of Marxism to which Hilferding belonged.

Deriving its strength from the interpretation of much fresh economic data, Lenin's work was not intended as a contribution either to economics or to history. It sought to characterise the nature of the epoch, define the tasks of the working-class movement and isolate those false theories and leaders responsible for the betrayal of 1914. On the whole, however, Lenin was not concerned with the general repercussions of imperialism in the fields of ideology and politics. Nor, in his economic studies, did he deal with the reproduction process and the realisation problem or investigate the connection between imperialism and the tendency for the rate of profit to fall. These aspects are implicit rather than explicit. He did not examine in detail the relationship between militarism and arms production and imperialism, which had interested Rosa Luxemburg. The question of the nature of the state under conditions of imperialism was to be taken up more fully in later writings. The fact that there has been little specialised Marxist study of such problems in the decades since the publication of *Imperialism* means that there is a constant challenge now to continue and carry forward the work begun by Lenin and his collaborators when they were obscure exiles in Switzerland in the early part of the First World War of the imperialist epoch.

5. Imperialism today

The significance of Lenin's contribution lies in his ability to bring together all the contradictory features of advanced capitalism under a single head. He found the term 'imperialism' at hand to suit his purpose and it is difficult to see how he could have invented a better one. The Marxist theory of imperialism rests on this definition. It is, of course, open to anyone to define and use the term 'imperialism' in some other sense or to show that Lenin was completely wrong or stands in need of correction on this or that point. What is at issue, however, is not the interpretation of certain episodes in history or merely the explanation of colonial policy, but the appropriateness of the term to describe a phase in the development of capitalism and of a whole historical epoch. Whether he had this point in mind or not, the anony-mous reviewer who said that 'imperfect as Lenin's diagnosis certainly was, nobody has since really carried the argument any further on the theoretical plane, whether by way of reinforcement or refutation' was not far from the truth.

In the epoch of imperialism the forces realeased by modern tech-nology continue to beat against the constricting limits of the old state forms which enshire the political dominance of the bourgeoisie and preserve the social relations upon which it depends. The attempt to establish a European Economic Community shows that the capitalists themselves now realise the limitations of the national state. The capitalist world market is increasingly dominated by a small number of giant firms closely interrelated with powerful financial institutions. The intimate relations established between the big private corpora-tions, including those of a 'multinational' character, and the state makes it increasingly difficult to tell where the sphere of private capital ends. The state is drawn directly into the arena, not merely to defend the general legal conditions for private ownership and com-modity production but also actively to assist the process of accumula-tion. The contradiction between the socialisation of production and the private ownership of the means of production, and thus of the social surplus, becomes more manifest.

As a result of the Second World War great changes have taken place in world capitalism.[13] The leading position of the United States has been reinforced; the imperialist world system now has its centre in North America. The forms of imperialist domination of the dependent countries have changed considerably. Direct rule has almost everywhere been abandoned: a strategic retreat but a retreat nonetheless. Part of the world has been closed to it. Over the 'Free World' American imperialism exercises an uneasy dominance. The great international corporations, mainly American, control the principal resources of this area of the globe. The demands of tech-nologically advanced industry cannot be met without combing the world for raw materials.

Meanwhile, outside a few favoured areas poverty and hunger stalk the world's millions, perhaps to a greater extent than ever before.

13. In this context such works as P. Jalée, *The Pillage of the Third World* (New York, Monthly Review Press, 1969) and *L'Impérialisme en 1970* (Paris, Maspero, 1970), H. Magdoff, *The Age of Imperialism* (New York, Monthly Review Press, 1969) and C. Julien, *L'Empire Américain* (Paris, 1968), despite their limitations and short-comings, indicate a revival of purportedly Marxist studies of imperialism. What these works chiefly lack is a satisfactory *theoretical* basis and a tendency to remain at the level of surface impressions and empiricism.

And, while material standards stagnate or deteriorate, the sense of deprivation spreads and intensifies. The politically independent states of Latin America, Asia and Africa remained tied to the world market in a position of economic dependence. There seems no possibility of their following the same path to industrialisation as was taken, historically, by the presentday advanced countries. Their economic destinies are decided not by the politicians who may from time to time struggle with insuperable problems but by giant foreign corporations and banks and their native allies. The break up of the old colonial empires, the accession of dozens of new states to political independence, has changed the forms of imperialist domination much more than the substance. Large areas of the world, which lack resources or potential for profitable investment and development by international capital, are condemned to stagnation and decline. American imperialism is only concerned with them so far as they may become breeding grounds for revolution and thus upset the precarious equilibrium with the Soviet bloc on which the maintenance of its world military position depends.

All these and other features of contemporary imperialism offer a challenge to students of Marxism to develop and refine their theory to take account of a constantly changing situation. There is nothing to suggest that the postwar developments undermine or contradict the Marxist theory of imperialism.[14] On the contrary, they appear to offer a striking confirmation of its essential critique of a world system which has turned the conquests of modern technology into frightening means of mass destruction and condemns millions to poverty and slow death through malnutrition.

This statement of what the Marxist theory of imperialism endeavours to do is necessarily no more than a beginning. It does not solve the type of problem in which the participants in an academic discussion of history or economic development will be mainly interested. The general validity of the theory will scarcely be acceptable to those who reject the claims of Marxism as a whole. In any case it is the responsibility of Marxists themselves to test and develop the theory in contact with concrete facts, historical and contemporary. The explanation of the nature of the epoch, the tracing out of the operation of the laws of motion of the capitalist mode of production,

14. There is no space here to deal with the crop of theorists, Strachey, Kidron, Barratt-Brown *et al* (the spectrum is wide but the method similar) who claim that imperialism has come to an end or has changed fundamentally. Some of their views are dealt with in *Theories of Imperialism*. The works quoted in the previous note are useful in opposing their pretensions.

the extension and refinement of theory provide a continuous chal- lenge. The Marxist theory of imperialism is more than an indispens- able tool for the understanding of the course of world development in our epoch. It is also part of a body of theory which is designed, consciously, to change the world: a practical task which requires that it should become the theory of the only objectively revolutionary class in capitalist society, the proletariat or working class. Separated from its striving to connect with the struggles of the exploited class and to raise its political consciousness until it becomes a class for itself, any part of Marxist theory will be seen merely as an interesting academic concept or a piece of dogma with no further significance.

DISCUSSION

Eurocentricity? Kemp acknowledged that a great deal of explanatory work on the workings of imperialism remained to be done, especially in relation to the third world, since Lenin had viewed the question more or less from the standpoint of the advanced countries. Some dissatisfaction was nonetheless expressed about what was described by one questioner as the 'eurocentricity' of the speaker's approach. This began an argument which reappeared in various ways throughout the series of seminars: most of the elements of it first showed themselves in this discussion.

Third world theorists. There were four questions raised and discussed, all of which related in some way to the alleged eurocentricity of some presentations of the Marxist theory. The first was the contribution to the theory of imperialism made by writers and theorists in the third world (taken up more fully in the paper by Hodgkin below). Kemp felt doubtful if Frantz Fanon, for instance, could be integrated into the mainstream of Leninist theory, although one participant thought that Fanon's analysis of the political factor in the changing nature of imperial control, especially of the national bourgeoisie in the third world, was important. Kemp thought that similar points had been made by Trotsky who had already seen the role of imperialism in retarding the industrial progress of backward countries; Marx famous remark, that in the developed country the underdeveloped one could see the image of its own future, was obsolete. The same development was no longer possible.

Industrialisation under imperialism? This then was the second issue raised about imperialism from the standpoint of the third world: whether an independent capitalist industrialisation was possible during the imperialist epoch. Throughout the seminar there was little disagreement on this ques- tion; it was generally agreed that the possibility was no longer open. (It is more fully discussed by Sutcliffe below.)

Economic importance of the third world. There was more disagree- ment on the third issue. Kemp took issue with some professed Marxists who claimed that the countries of the third world were no longer of great economic importance to imperialism. In response to a doubt expressed about the severe temporal disjuncture between political control in the colonies and the export of capital to them, he said that it was a fallacy to base analysis of imperialist relations on the balance of payments and the calculations of profit and loss. Profits are made by corporations and banks; but it may be the taxpayer who foots the bill for imperialist annexation and control. One speaker added in support of this that an apparent fall in United States foreign investment in the third world, or the fact that there was negative United States net investment in Latin America, might be illusory since investment out of retained profits often failed to appear in the available figures. (There is further discussion of these points in, Conclusion, section 4.)

How important are third world revolutions?   The fourth question was more contentious: it was the role of third world revolutions in the struggle against capitalism and imperialism, an issue which emerged naturally from the others and from the general Marxist view that the purpose of analysing imperialism was to see how to end it. Kemp's position was that the crisis now building up in imperialism has its centre in the advanced countries; hence they must be politically central. The people of the third world were in fact suffering the consequences of the incompleteness of revolution in the advanced countries. Third world struggles, he argues, are important but not decisive.

China.   This view was challenged by a number of participants. One disagreement centred on China where, it was argued, the peasantry had played a dominant role in a socialist revolution based on a proletarian ideology. Kemp insisted that the peasantry was an amorphous class not capable alone of changing society in a socialist manner; in China the revolution had been made by an alliance of the proletariat and the peasantry under the leadership of a party which had its origins in the urban areas; it had neither a peasant leadership nor a peasant strategy.

Vietnam.   A second instance was Vietnam. One participant argued that the Vietnam war had seriously weakened the structure of American capitalism. Kemp thought it of some importance but not decisive; it was a running sore but not an intolerable burden. The war after all had coincided with a period of growth in the American economy.

India.   On one country, India, there was more agreement. While sticking to his position that a condition of definitive success of third world revolution was the success of revolution in the advanced countries, Kemp acknowledged that India might have special significance. A large scale uprising there could be of such direct and immediate concern to imperialism that it might produce a chain reaction in other third world countries, its impact spreading even to the advanced countries themselves.

II

A critique of Marxist
theories of imperialism
Michael Barratt Brown

Theoretical writings on imperialism have travelled from Marx by various routes and contemporary writers do not always look to the same aspect of Marx's picture of capitalism for the origins of their own theory. In this survey and critique of the Marxist theory, Barratt Brown, like Kemp, locates the starting point of the Marxist theory of imperialism in Marx's economic model in *Capital* (sections 3 and 4). But he lays more emphasis than Kemp on Marx's view of foreign trade and less on the tendency of the rate of profit to fall; and while they both stress the realisation problem Barratt Brown is more sceptical of the importance of the centralisation and concentration of capital, at least for some periods and countries. (For an explanation of these terms see introduction to Kemp.) These differences in emphasis result from the fact that they are looking for the origins of two somewhat different conceptions of the Marxist idea of imperialism (see Conclusion, section 3). Going on to trace the theory through Hilferding, Rosa Luxemburg and Lenin (sections 5, 6 and 7), Barratt Brown looks at the question particularly of how capital accumulation and development (the build-up of the forces of production) in the advanced countries has been and is associated with underdevelopment in the rest of the world, a question which is taken up again later in the book (see, Sutcliffe, VII, and Patnaik, IX).

Section 8 contains a number of pieces of evidence which, Barratt Brown argues, demand new explanations to be developed by Marxists. For the period up to 1939 these include the fact that property income exceeded capital export. Before 1914 this capital export was in any case not direct investment by monopolies but portfolio investment; it had no higher rate of return than domestic investment and it did not go mainly to colonies. In addition there was the fact that the arrest of colonial industrialisation was no help to the metropolis. The apparent inconsistency between Hobson's and Lenin's emphasis on capital export in relation to imperialism and the fact that normally the inflow of profits in any period has been higher than the outflow of capital was mentioned frequently during the seminar and to many people was a source of difficulty (see Magdoff, VI.2 and Conclusion, 4). Barratt Brown mentions it once again as one of the pieces of problem evidence in the period since 1945. The others are: most capital export is now by monopolies in subsidiaries but, like trade, it mostly flows to other developed countries; its rate of return has been higher than domestic investment for the U.S. but not for British companies.

Polarisation in the world economy continues and grows as a consequence of cumulative causation (section 10); and Barratt Brown looks at the consequences of this for revolutionary potential in the third world (section 9); see also the discussion of the paper by Kemp, I, and Hodgkin, IV, and for the potential economic development of the third world (see also Sutcliffe VII).

1. A note on theories in general and Marxist theories in particular

To write about theories of imperialism is already to have a theory. Indeed until very recently it would have been widely assumed that theories of imperialism would be Marxist theories. Just to use the word was to tie a label to what was said. This was not simply because the word had emotive associations as a catchall for those who regarded United States foreign policies as being guided by something less than altruism. Much more important for our purpose here, the word —like capitalism—implied a theory of social and political economic systems and epochs which can be clearly identified and analysed; and which, since more than one can be identified in human history, are presumably subject to some laws of change, even to rapid not to say revolutionary change. For those who prefer things to remain much as they are, or to change very slowly, this was disturbing. A steady continuum with no such clear distinctions would be more reassuring.

Now all this has changed and it is not a solecism to speak of capitalism and imperialism. In part, no doubt, this is because increasing numbers of people have come to question what motives the United States can have for doing what it is doing in Vietnam; more important it is the result of a new approach to Marxism in academic circles. Marxism can no longer be ignored, thanks to a more critical generation of students; but words and concepts which were developed within the Marxist tradition are looked at and given new meanings. True followers of the Marxian tradition should be grateful; the Marxist view had been narrowed down into a dogma, excluding a great wealth of theory which the tradition had created. What follows is a critique of Marxist theories of imperialism by one who stands within the Marxian tradition; it is certainly not limited to the one received theory in the canon, and if it is critical it certainly does not reject the whole tradition.

I have spoken here of the Marxist tradition; I could have spoken of the Marxist system of ideas or the Marxist general theory of society. Any general theory of society like Marxism provides a way of looking at the facts and ordering our collection and classification of them. The collection of facts that have a certain similarity (as in the natural sciences with rocks, or plants, or animals) reveals certain regularities and sequences and certain discontinuities which all require explanation. These suggest hypotheses which we test to provide possible theories within our general theory. The nature of such subtheories will depend of course on the original decision to collect certain facts together, in one box so to speak. We may find that our theories give satisfactory explanations and there are no relevant facts outside the box; or we may find that there are important facts which we did not include in our original collection. This is a question of judgment of what is relevant. In the natural sciences we can make precise predictions, once we have isolated certain factors in a situation, about how these factors will interact. We can do somewhat the same in the social sciences, but the process of isolation is more difficult. The writings of social scientists are punctuated with the words 'other things being equal'.

In history we have to rely for our tests mainly on retrodiction, on looking to see if what happened is what we should have expected to happen. Sometimes, as in the case of Marx, we can test what the writer said would happen against what actually happened. The problem here is not that men are less predictable than natural forces but that we stand inside the social system ourselves and can take avoiding action when dire calamities are forecast for us. The value of a general theory as E. H. Carr has emphasised is the fruitfulness of the hypotheses it suggests.[1] The point was made in criticism of Professor Popper's attack on the usefulness of the predictions that may be made from history. But Popper himself had been arguing that all social scientists start from some theory or hypothesis. No one goes out to collect the facts with an open mind.[2] There are far too many facts for this; some

1. E. H. Carr, *What is History?* (London, Macmillan, 1961), p. 101.
2. K. Popper, *The Poverty of Historicism* (London, Routledge, 1957; 2nd edn. 1960).

preliminary classification has to be made. Popper suggests that this is done by the need to solve a specific problem; Marxists believe that this is the use of a general theory.

The general theory of Marx is well known and is most succinctly formulated in the Preface to the *Contribution to the Critique of Political Economy* (1859). Social formations in successive epochs can be distinguished by their modes of production; the latter depend on a certain level of technology (what Marx calls the 'forces of production'), to which the economic structure of society corresponds. This in turn is 'the real foundation on which rise legal and political superstructures and to which correspond definite forms of social consciousness'.[3] Revolutionary changes occur when the advance of technology comes into conflict with the existing economic structure, however much this conflict may appear to be fought out in ideological terms. Therefore Marxists will tend to collect facts about societies in different epochs according to the economic or property relations that are to be found, and not according to the ideas that men had about them. They will not, however, forget Marx's insistence that it is as men become conscious of the conflict between the forces of production and the economic relations which contain them that revolutionary changes are made; and it is classes of men having a special relationship to the new and the old forces of production that fight it out.

2. The relation of imperialism to capitalism

Imperialism has undoubtedly been developed as a Marxist theory. As such it was used to describe and explain the spread of British and later of other European capitalism throughout the world in the nineteenth century. The word did not enter the English language until the 1850s and 60s (although 'imperialist' had been used for much longer as an adjective to describe earlier imperial powers). In origin, however, it was not a Marxist word and does not appear in the writing of Marx or Engels. It was used to describe the views of those who wished to strengthen the links between Britain and the British Empire as it was emerging in the 1870s. Who were these men? They were Disraeli and Carnarvon in the 1870s, the Liberal Imperialists in the 1880s, Chamberlain, Rhodes and Hewins in the 1890s, writers like Froude and Seeley, Tennyson and Kipling, a few trade unionists and a group of men like

3. K. Marx, Preface to *Contribution to the Critique of Political Economy* (Univ. of Chicago Press, 1904 edn.), p. 11.

Torrens who were themselves colonials, i.e. Australians and Canadians.[4]

It seems a rather mixed bag of names. What they had in common was first an interest primarily in the self-governing colonies (the dominions). These newly developing territories had a great need for capital, for technical know-how and for skilled artisans from Britain. Second, they were all powerfully conscious of the tensions inside English society. Schumpeter,[5] who set out to criticise the Marxist interpretation of imperialism, spoke of Disraeli taking up imperialism in 1872 merely as a catch phrase for winning elections;[6] may be, but it won elections; it was a successful catch phrase, people were caught. Consciously, at least in the case of Disraeli, Rhodes and Hewins, unconsciously perhaps with others, the view developed that what was needed after the concession of the franchise in 1867 was an overlaying of class tension by a sense of national belonging. Nationalism in Britain was fostered not by a war of liberation, nor even by wars of domination (though there were to be several of these), but by glorification of the Empire and of the common interest of the British people in it. Disraeli's emotive appeal has died hard.

For J. A. Hobson[7], who wrote the first major critique of imperialism at the turn of the century, the 'economic tap root of imperialism' lay in the export of capital in search of investment opportunities that were declining at home.[8] In fact, as I have argued elsewhere, the export of British capital to which Hobson drew attention, did not go mainly to the territories newly added to the British Empire. The opening up of mineral and raw material production in them was of undoubted importance and it replaced the declining flow of investment to India, but it failed to-raise the share of British overseas investment in the dependent Empire. The dominions and South America received the major flow, and between the 1860s and 1913 their share of the total rose from a third to over a half.[9]

Schumpeter, aware of this British trend, concluded in 1919 that the connection between capitalism and imperialism was not substantiated. Lenin, unaware of the trend, and drawing upon the facts of capital export from European countries other than Britain enthus-

4. For all these see C. A. Bodelsen, *Studies in Mid-Victorian Imperialism* (London, Heinemann, 1960).
5. J. A. Schumpeter, *The Sociology of Imperialism* (1919; New York, Kelly, 1951), section 2.
6. *Ibid*, p. 10.
7. J. A. Hobson, *Imperialism; a study* (London, 1902, Allen & Unwin, 1938).
8. *Ibid*, 1938 edn., p. 81.
9. M. Barratt Brown, *After Imperialism* (London, Heinemann), Table V, p. 110.

iastically endorsed the chief elements in Hobson's analysis.[10] This only goes to show how important it is what facts you choose to collect together in the box marked 'Imperialism'.

The class of event we are seeking to explain under the concept of imperialism is the claim of the leaders of advanced industrial countries in the last quarter of the nineteenth century and thereafter to privileged positions in other countries. Many who made the claim asserted that these positions were of great economic importance. However, they may have been deceiving themselves and others. The real motive in Britain *may* have been 'jobs for the boys', as Schumpeter suggests, for an otherwise decaying military aristocracy and for an under-employed and inflated middle class. Rhodes *may* have been driven in fact by his own self-importance, Chamberlain by political calcula-tions and Hewins by the mystical aim of a catholic empire. But in that case similar explanations have to be found for French and Belgium empire building in Africa, French and Dutch colonialism in South East Asia, Russian expansion into Central Asia, United States pressure on South America, Japan's war on Russia and the German *drang nach Osten*. Only if we can discover certain factors that all the colonial powers had in common in the last quarter of the nineteenth century can we talk of a causal connection. Although a decaying military aristocracy and an underemployed middle class was a com-mon feature of Britain, Japan, Austria and Germany and perhaps of France, it was not a feature of the U.S.A. or Russia, Belgium or the Netherlands. Again there were similar sociological structures in other countries that showed no sign of outward expansion to obtain privileged positions in other lands: China provides an obvious example. What all those that did expand had in common was a certain level of technological development—some more advanced than others— and the driving force in this technological development of a capitalist class. It is from the special circumstances of this class and the economic relations that it established that Marxist theories of imperialism start.

3. Marx's economic model

Hobson was not a Marxist, but attempts to apply Marxist analysis to the question of imperialism had already been made by Hilferding and Luxemburg before Lenin. To understand them it is necessary,

10. V. I. Lenin, *Imperialism, the Highest Stage of Capitalism* (1917; Moscow, Progress Publishers, 1966).

first, very briefly to summarise Marx's model of capitalist economic structures. Its essence is contained in the formula M–C–M' (money-commodities-money). Owners of money (capital) turn it into commodities for the purpose of making more money. This is the rationale of private capital ownership: in industrial capitalism money is made not through hoarding or extravagant consumption but by setting labour to produce commodities for sale at a profit. An essential part of this model is the competition of private firms for new capital. It follows that firms must maximise their profits to generate their own new capital or to attract capital from the profits of others; for this they must keep up their investment in new equipment, and for this in turn they must expand their markets to obtain the economies of larger scale operation. The limits to the growth of scale in production have proved much wider than Schumpeter anticipated. For the most technically advanced producer free trade is wholly beneficial. The less advanced must protect themselves behind tariffs until they can compete on equal terms. In any one free trade area (and indeed in the whole world once it was opened up to capitalist trade) there will be a limit to the expansion that is possible. The competitive pressure for profit maximisation will create a surplus of capital seeking profitable opportunities for investment. Since every increase in profit is at least relatively at the expense of the current purchasing power of the mass of the people, crises of over-production will regularly occur throughout the capitalist world. Thus not only are cycles of boom and slump inevitable, but a steady polarisation of wealth and poverty will occur throughout the capitalist world.

> On the one hand, therefore, the additional capital formed in the course of accumulation attracts fewer and fewer labourers in proportion to its magnitude. On the other hand, the old capital periodically reproduced with change of composition, repels more and more of the labourers formerly employed by it.[11]

> Accumulation of wealth at one pole is, therefore, at the same time accumulation of misery, agony of toil, slavery, ignorance, brutality, mental degradation at the opposite pole, i.e. on the side of the class that produces its own product in the form of capital.[12]

This is the essential Marxist economic model, but as we saw earlier Marx's general theory of society went beyond the analysis of the

11. K. Marx, *Capital* (1867), vol. i, ch. xxv, section 2.
12. *Ibid.*, section 4.

conflict between the advances of technology and the economic relations of private capital ownership to embrace a whole super-structure, as he called it, of political, military, legal and religious forms which corresponded to and supported the property relations. He allowed, moreover, for the presence of remnants of the super-structures of past social formations and equally for the embryos of the superstructure of future social formations, from all of which man's social consciousness derived. When Schumpeter emphasised the role of monarchs and aristocrats in the development of capitalism he is not contridicting Marx. The old forms are used and transformed by the new capitalist class which for long existed side by side and interlocked with an older ruling class. Nevertheless at a certain stage it can be said that the central driving force of society is the private ownership of capital and machinery and not of land and associated military power.

It is with the aid of this central model that Marxists have approached an understanding of international relations over the last century. We may list the relationships that have seemed to them central in their definition of imperialism as a stage of capitalism:

(*a*) the (widening) gap in economic development between indus-trialised European (and European settled) countries and those restricted to primary production;

(*b*) the outward movement of labour and capital (especially capital) from the more developed countries to the less;

(*c*) the annexation of territories all over the world by the more developed nations in a competitive scramble for supposed strategic and economic advantages, especially in the last quarter of the nine-teenth century;

(d) the growth of international economic rivalries and of a series of arms races leading to two world wars and threatening a third;

(*e*) the emergence of the international firm and the continuation of attempts by the more economically developed nations to maintain and extend their political, military or economic power over the less, even after the ending of direct colonial rule.

It is to be hoped that the phrasing of these statements of observed events, and particularly the association of economic and military actions and intentions in (*c*), (*d*) and (*e*), may not seem to beg too many of the questions that have to be answered. Few will deny that

economic and military acts have occurred side by side at the same time
and to state the fact does not imply a causal relationship.

After these rather lengthy preliminaries the procedure to be followed here is a brief review of the main Marxist theories of imperialism, both in their original form, and in that of their followers. After
reviewing each theory, there will follow some discussion of the main
criticisms that have been made of them. At the end there will be a
summary of what remains both of Marxist theories and of their
critics' theories, and on the basis of this some suggestions of the general
form which an acceptable theory of imperialism would have to take.
I shall distinguish first Marx's own views, then in succession those of
Hilferding, Rosa Luxemburg and Lenin, and finally the followers of
each of these and their critics. A note on Soviet imperialism leads the
essay to certain predictions that may be made about the future of
relations between the developed and underdeveloped world.

4. Marx's view of foreign trade

Marx's view of the expansion of Britain's worldwide military and
political power, including colonial expansion, was that this was an
essential part of freeing the trade of the world to the products of the
most advanced industrial producer. For such a producer, free trade,
not protection or privilege, was the key to increased profit. This does
not mean that Marx ignored other forces that were at work. His views
are most explicitly stated in his writings on India but they have to
be supplemented by what he says on foreign trade in volume iii of
Capital, and understood in relation to his general view of capitalist
accumulation, viz that this tends to be a polarising process with wealth
centralised in fewer and fewer hands and poverty and misery growing
at the other end of the scale. This follows from the fact that capital is
not hoarded but laid out in setting labour to work in order to increase
the amount of the capital and that the process by which this is effected
is, in Marx's view, one of extracting surplus value from the labourers
who are set to work. Despite the competition of capitals, the relationship between owners of capital and owners of labour power is an
unequal one and there is a tendency for the inequality to become
cumulative.

New technology is assumed to be labour-saving so that capital
equipment used in production increases in relation to labour used in
production. A 'reserve army of labour' is replenished with each new

advance in technology and the rate of profit tends to fall.* There are, however, counteracting tendencies. Technology might be capital saving, exploitation might be stepped up and wages depressed, but above all foreign trade might provide new opportunities for expanding the capitalists' surplus.

Thus writings in 1853 about the East India Company Marx says:

> At the same rate at which the cotton manufactures become of vital interest for the whole social frame of Great Britain, East India became of vital interest for the British cotton manufacture. Till then the interests of the moneyocracy† which had converted India into its landed estates, of the oligarchy who had conquered it by their armies, and of the millocracy who had inundated it with their fabrics, had gone hand in hand. But the more the industrial interest became dependent on the Indian market, the more it felt the necessity of creating fresh productive powers in India, after having ruined her native industry. You cannot continue to inundate a country with your manufactures, unless you enable it to give you some produce in return. The industrial interest found that their trade declined instead of increasing . . . by 1850, they were exasperated at depending on America, instead of deriving a sufficiency of raw cotton from the East Indies.[13]

In the third volume of *Capital* Marx writes in the following way of foreign trade as one of the counteracting forces to the tendency of the rate of profit to fall.

> Foreign trade permits an expansion of the scale of production. . . . The expansion of foreign trade which is the basis of the capitalist mode of production in its stages of infancy, has become its own product in the further progress of capitalist development through its innate necessities, through its need for an ever expanding market . . . an advanced country

---

* This follows logically because the rate of profit in Marx's equation is the relation of surplus value to capital laid out on equipment and labour i.e. $\frac{s}{c+v}$ (when s = surplus, c = capital laid out on equipment and v = wages). But this is the same as

$$\frac{\frac{s}{v}}{\frac{c}{v}+\frac{v}{v}}$$

that is to say that the surplus (s) in relation to wages (v) depends on the relation of capital laid out on equipment (c) to that laid out on wages (v). If c rises in relation to v, then for the rate of profit $\frac{s}{v}$ to remain the same the surplus (s) in relation to wages (v) must rise in the same proportion. This is possible, although Marx thought it improbable for various reasons including the action of trade unions.

† By moneyocracy Marx seems to mean merchants, financiers and the aristocracy—see his article in the next day's issue of the *New York Daily Tribune*.

13. Marx, *New York Daily Tribune*, 11 July 1853 (reprinted in Marx and Engels, *On Colonialism* (Moscow, Foreign Languages Publishing House 1960, p. 48).

is enabled to sell its goods above their value even when it sells them cheaper than the competing countries. . . .

On the other hand, capital invested in colonies etc., may yield a higher rate of profit for the simple reason that the rate of profit is higher there on account of the backward development, and for the added reason that slaves, coolies etc., permit a better exploitation of labour. . . . The favoured country recovers more labour in exchange for less labour, although this difference, this surplus is pocketed by a certain class, as it is in any exchange between labour and capital . . . this same foreign trade develops the capitalist mode of production in the home country.[14]

In these quotations, and in the context that the second is set, there are implied four stages of imperial expansion. *First*, the combined interest of merchants, army and aristocracy in the East India Company —a combination which Schumpeter saw as the central explanation of the sociology of imperialism.

Second, the growing interest of the British capitalist mill-owners in expanding the market for their products which would not be absorbed at home because of the low wages paid to workers at home. At this stage the East India Company's sales in Britain of Indian textiles had to be stopped by high tariffs to protect the infant British manufacturing industry; but the Company's control of the Indian market was crucial to the expansion of large-scale production by British industry.

Third, having mopped up the Indian market with the by then cheaper Lancashire products, and ruined the handicraft workers of India in the process, this market declined. Keynesians' criticism of Marx's analysis, which seems to them to ignore the crucial expansion of the market in his emphasis on advances in technology and capital accumulation as explanations of economic growth, are thus forestalled. It was for Marx by mopping up existing markets first in Europe, then in North America and Central America, then in South America, then in India, then in China that British capitalism developed.

Fourth, as each of these markets declined, something was left behind which sustained a continuation of trade. In most areas this was a new worldwide division of labour in which Britain produced the manufactured goods and the rest of the world the raw materials. In the second volume of *Capital*, in writing of the cotton trade, Marx comments:

A new and international division of labour, a division suited to the

14. *Capital*, vol. iii, pt. iii, ch. xiv, section 5.

requirements of the chief centres of modern industry, springs up and converts one part of the globe into a chiefly agricultural field of production for supplying the other part which remains a chiefly industrial field.[15]

In such a division of labour bargaining power was strongly on the side of the more advanced economy. At first new opportunities opened up for the investment of capital that was meeting a falling rate of profit at home. Capital piling up in Britain began to flow out into railway building, port installations, plantations and mines overseas and the return on this investment was steadily ploughed back in further investment. But if Marx was right about the exploitation of the colonies this could hardly be expected to last and once again we must ask with the Keynesian critics: Where were the fields for such investment once the existing wealth had been mopped up and raw material production established with the maximum return of profit to the investing country?

The answer is that Marx undoubtedly envisaged a further stage in this process of expansion. We can see this in another of his *New York Herald Tribune* articles:

England has to fulfil a double mission in India: one destructive, the other regenerating—the annihilation of old Asiatic society, and the laying of the material foundations of Western Society in Asia. . . . The political unity of India . . . was the first condition of its regeneration . . . . The free press . . . is a new and powerful agent of reconstruction. . . . From the Indian natives . . . a fresh class is springing up, endowed with the requirements for government and imbued with European science. . . . The millocracy have discovered that the transformation of India into a reproductive country has become of vital importance to them, and that, to that end, it is necessary, above all, to gift her with means of irrigation and of internal communication. . . .

I know that the English millocracy intend to endow India with railways with the exclusive view of extracting at diminished expenses the cotton and other raw materials for their manufactures. But when you have once introduced machinery into the locomotion of a country, which possesses iron and coals, you are unable to withold it from its fabrication. You cannot maintain a net of railways over an immense country without introducing all those industrial processes necessary to meet the immediate and current wants of railway locomotion, and out of which there must grow the application of machinery to those branches of industry not immediately connected with railways. The railway

15. *Capital*, vol. ii, pt. iv, ch. xv, section 7.

system will therefore become, in India, truly the forerunner of modern industry.[16]

This was almost precisely what did not happen, at least for a hundred years. Of course, Marx was cautious enough to add:

> The Indians will not reap the fruits of the new elements of society scattered among them by the British bourgeoisie, till in Great Britain itself the now ruling classes shall have been supplanted by the industrial proletariat or till the Hindus themselves shall have grown strong enough to throw off the English yoke altogether.[17]

But it is clear that, in the words of one of his followers he supposed that:

> The general direction of the historical movement seems to have been the same for the backward echelons as for the forward contingents.[18]

In the Preface to the first volume of *Capital* Marx warned his German colleagues '*De te fabula narratur*' — You next. 'The country that is more developed industrially only shows to the less developed the image of its own future'.[19] Yet while Marx was right in anticipating the bringing of the whole world into the capitalist mode of production, and with it the increasing centralisation of capital, it was only in certain 'favoured' lands of Europe and of European settlers and in Japan that industrialisation took place and there not as a result of free trade but, precisely, because they immunised themselves from the effects of free trade behind protective walls of tariffs and monopoly. Elsewhere the distortion of economic development which we call 'underdevelopment' was what followed.

5. Hilferding's study of finance capital

It was the response of other nations in Europe and North America to Britain's industrial supremacy that required some revision of Marx's conclusions among those who accepted his general analysis of capitalism. Between the publication of *Capital* in 1867 and the end of the century, both the United States and Germany surpassed Britain in industrial production. Other European nations and lands settled by Europeans, and the Japanese also, were busily catching up

16. *New York Herald Tribune*, 6 Aug. 1853 (reprinted in *On Colonialism*, p. 19).
17. *Ibid.*, (*On Colonialism*, p. 80).
18. P. Baran, *The Political Economy of Growth* (New York, Monthly Review Press, 1957), p. 40.
19. *Capital*, vol. i, Preface to the first (German) edition.

on Britain's head start. As we saw earlier, they all did so with state assistance and behind tariff walls to protect their own markets, while all across the world they challenged British industry in the markets that British military (or naval) and economic power had opened up.

Rudolf Hilferding, basing his work on Otto Bauer's study of the *National Question and Social Democracy* in Austria, started from Marx's emphasis on the centralisation of capital that takes place as the scale of production increases and as the control of big capitalists extends beyond the limits of their ownership of capital. Hilferding saw in Germany and the United States that the banks were taking the leading role in extending and controlling industrial capital and conceptualised this in the title of his book *Finance Capital*. No such role was played by the banks in Britain at that time, but the merging of finance and industrial capital is a process that has since occurred in every advanced capitalist country in this century.

Hilferding's argument was that these monopoly positions of capital in its own national market were created by state protection and developed into foreign expansion.

> The old tariff policy had the task . . . of accelerating the growth of an industry within the protected borders. . . . With the development of the [state] subsidy system, protective tariffs completely change their function even turn into its opposite. From being a means of defence against foreign conquest of domestic markets they become a means of conquering foreign markets, from a weapon of protection for the weak they become a weapon of aggression for the strong.[20]

Hilferding saw imperial expansion as the requirement of the monopoly capitalists in each nation state for new areas to be brought under the jurisdiction of the capitalist state to develop raw material production, safeguard capital investment and guarantee markets for each national monopoly capitalist's output. The free trade and open markets of the British who had been first in the field had to be challenged; in responding to this challenge the British too extended their imperial power. The export of capital then flowed into government guaranteed loans for public works, railroads, public utilities, ports and raw material production creating the conditions for the development of local industry, as Marx had expected.

What Hilferding emphasised was the national development of capitalism and the growing conflict of national monopolies in what he called in the subtitle of his book 'the latest phase of capitalism'.

20. R. Hilferding, *Das Finanzkapital* (Vienna, 1923), pp. 384–9.

Finance capital needs a strong state which recognises finance capital's interests abroad and uses political power to extort favourable treaties from smaller states, a state which can exert its influence all over the world in order to be able to turn the entire world into a sphere of investment. Finance capital finally needs a state which is strong enough to carry out a policy of expansion and to gather in new colonies.[21]

National monopolies might sign cartel agreements dividing up the world, but these should not be taken as implying more than an uneasy truce, a temporary agreement to be abrogated as soon as any one monopoly saw the opportunity of advancing its position. The economic rivalry of the great nation states was thus seen as leading inevitably to war. But Hilferding carried over into his thinking something of Marx's belief in the regenerative role of capitalism in the backward areas of the world:

In the newly opened lands themselves the imported capitalism . . . arouses the ever growing opposition of the people awakened to national consciousness, against the intruders. The old social relations are completely revolutionised, the agrarian thousand year old unity of the 'nations without history' is rent asunder. . . . Capitalism itself gradually gives to the oppressed peoples the means and the method of achieving their own liberation.[22]

Hilferding, moreover, expected the whole process, by reducing competition, to equalise profit rates and, by promoting exports to backward countries, to equalise economic development and maintain the viability of capitalist accumulation, even though increasingly undermined by the threat of world war. It was from these conclusions of Hilferding's that the rather different lines of Marxist thought developed in Rosa Luxemburg and Trotsky on the one hand and in Lenin on the other. Hilferding's finance-capital explanation of nationalism both in the advanced and in the backward countries was accepted by Lenin and later by Hilferding's followers like Paul Sweezy.[23] It raised doubts in the minds of those Marxists rather more closely involved in the clashes of central European national feeling, as it had raised doubts in Hobson's mind.[24]

---

21. *Ibid.*, p. 300.
22. *Ibid.*, p. 406.
23. P. M. Sweezy, *Theory of Capitalist Development* (New York, Monthly Review Press, 1942), esp. chs. xiv, and xvi.
24. Hobson speaks of 'aggressive Imperialism' not only 'fostering animosities among competing empires' but 'stimulating a corresponding excess of national self-consciousness' in the 'peoples who were too foreign to be absorbed and too compact to be permanently crushed' (*Imperialism*, p. 11).

6. Rosa Luxemburg's view of nationalism and militarism

Rosa Luxemburg's theory of imperialism is generally dismissed rather contemptuously by Marxists and others as being quite simply based on a mistake. She sought to prove that 'in a closed capitalist system' capital accumulation becomes actually impossible, because she assumed that consumption does not increase as investment increases. In fact, of course, it increases through increased productivity and in other ways: and Marx was usually careful to make clear that both the disproportions between investment and consumption and the over-production of means of production were tendencies leading to regular crisis and not absolute necessities of the system. Rosa Luxemburg could prove that capital accumulation resulting from increased consumption was impossible because she had assumed from the start that consumption would not increase.

Part of Rosa Luxemburg's 'mistake' arose through continuing to treat the national and world economy as a self-regulating system. It was reasonable for Marx to do this when governments in fact barely intervened if at all, in its regulation. What Hilferding had been describing, however, was a situation in which active state intervention could stabilise the economy while causing highly dangerous insterstate rivalries. The value of Rosa Luxemburg's work lay in reminding people that the tendencies to crisis in the economy were still there, behind the management by national states. Her description of the process by which the advanced powers mopped up the markets of the still remaining non-capitalist world and left them poorer than they found them was true to Marx's views as we reported them earlier in his essays on India. Rosa Luxemburg's 'mistake' was to suggest an inevitable mechanical breakdown in the system rather than, as Marx had suggested, a tendency to polarisation of wealth and poverty which could lead to breakdown.[25] Her great virtue was to suggest that this polarising process was occurring on a worldwide scale, the rich nations getting richer and the poor getting poorer, a process we can recognise very easily today.[26]

The conflict between the thinking of Hilferding and of Rosa Luxemburg was not so great as appears. They were describing different processes occurring at the same time. Hilferding was des-

25. Rosa Luxemburg, *Accumulation of Capital*, ed. Joan Robinson (London, Routledge, 1951); see especially Robinson's introduction, pp. 14–19.
26. *Ibid*, pp. 348ff.

cribing a genuine process of capitalist economic expansion where movements of capital (and labour) to underdeveloped lands in Europe and lands of European settlement overseas led to the building up of industry in these lands with the help of state protection behind tariff walls. Rosa Luxemburg was describing the failure of expansion, partly because of the tribute to the advanced powers, but mainly because movements of capital to underdeveloped non-European and non-European settled lands did *not* lead to local industrial development. The reason was that these lands were held by free trade in an artificial world division of labour as primary producers forever.

Shorn of its mechanical and dogmatic under-consumptionist elements, Rosa Luxemburg's theory emphasised the continuing contradiction between the ends of production as a technical process of producing goods for human consumption and the ends of capitalism as a historical system for expanding capitalist surplus value. Paradoxically we may see that this emphasis requires no breakdown theory to sustain a belief in socialist answers to capitalist contradictions, in the advanced countries at least. War and the arms race between these countries provided for Rosa Luxemburg the supreme example of capitalist contradictions. It was she who first saw that the intensified militarism and navy building of the years before 1914 had a crucial economic function. In this she anticipated much later thinking.

The central element in Rosa Luxemburg's thought must now be revealed: her preoccupation with nationalism as in every way an antisocialist force.[27] She shared with Hilferding his fear of nationalist economic rivalries leading to war. She did not share with him his faith in the revolutionary potential of exploited colonial peoples. She expected them, as Hobson had, to develop a nationalist rather than a socialist consciousness; perhaps as poor nations they might revolt against the rich nations, but in the process national consciousness would certainly overlay class consciousness. It was an extraordinarily perceptive vision of what was to come; but she had seen it all in Central Europe. Socialism was nothing for her if it did not overcome the narrow limitations of the nation state. For was not the nation state the very essential political form of capitalism? The strength of the desire for self-determination of the peoples in the Russian and Austrian empires, which Marx and Engels had encouraged and Lenin had to contain, were for Rosa Luxemburg a diversion from central loyalty to the working class.

27. See J. P. Nettl, *Rosa Luxemburg* (London, Oxford Univ. Press, 1966), vol. ii, App. 2.

Rosa Luxemburg was defeated in the arguments among the Russian, Polish and German communists. She was defeated also by events. Nationalism grew from strength to strength, as much in Russian communism as in German national socialism. The colonial peoples after 1945 added fifty new names to the so-called United Nations. Only her followers with total consistency held to Rosa Luxemburg's principle that the socialist revolution must be international or nothing. Lenin was quite happy to compromise with nationalism for his political ends, but such a compromise implied recognition of nationalist consciousness as a force that was independent of the capitalist development of the nation state. When he came to examine imperialism however, Lenin did not make allowance for any distinction between its nationalist and capitalist roots.

7. Lenin's *Imperialism*

Lenin's *Imperialism* was written in Zurich early in 1916 in the middle of the carnage of the First World War and on the eve of the Russian Revolution. It was designed, in his own words, to prove 'that the war of 1914–18 was on both sides an imperialist (i.e. annexationist, predatory and plunderous), war for the partition of the world and for the distribution and redistribution of colonies, of "spheres of influence" of finance, capital etc'.[28] It was an appeal for the support of the 'billion oppressed people, i.e. for more than half the population of the earth in the subject countries and for the wage slaves of capitalism in civilised lands'.

> Capitalism [he wrote] has grown into a world system of colonial oppression and financial strangulation of the overwhelming majority of the people of the world by a handful of advanced countries . . . of particularly rich and powerful states which plunder the whole world . . . and out of their enormous super profits . . . bribe the labour leaders and an upper stratum of the labour aristocracy.[29]

The 'proof' consisted of a combination of Hilferding's analysis of finance-capital and the analysis of J. A. Hobson. For Hobson, though a non-Marxist, was claimed by Lenin to have understood what Hilferding (and Kautsky) neglected, viz. that imperialism was not only internecine but also parasitical and decadent. Hobson's view was that a perfectly proper nationalist pride in nation had become

28. *Imperialism, the Highest Stage of Capitalism*, Preface, section 2.
29. *Ibid.*

distorted by the pressures of the monopolists of capital. These men were forced by their search for new markets for their goods and capital to

> use their governments in order to secure for their use some distant undeveloped country by annexation and protection. . . . It is admitted by all businessmen that the growth of the powers of production in their country exceeds the growth in consumption, that more goods can be produced than can be sold at a profit, and that more capital exists than can find remunerative investment. It is this condition of affairs that forms the tap-root of imperialism.[30]

It was Hobson's emphasis on the need to export capital that Lenin took up. Hence although the need for foreign trade in goods is typical of the early capitalism of free competition, it is the export of capital that is typical of monopoly capitalism and that requires the division and redivision of the world, the partition of Africa and China among the great powers.

We can quote Lenin's own words in explanation of this need to export capital:

> As long as capitalism remains capitalism, surplus capital will never be used for the purpose of raising the standard of living of the masses, for this would mean a decrease in profits for the capitalists; instead it will be used to increase profits by exporting the capital abroad, to backward countries. In these backward countries profits are usually high, for capital is scarce, the price of land is relatively low, wages are low, raw materials are cheap. The possibility for exporting capital is created by the entry of a number of backward countries into international capitalist intercourse, the main railway lines have either been built or are being built there, the elementary conditions for industrial development, have been assured, etc. The necessity for exporting capital arises from the fact that in a few countries capitalism has become 'over-ripe' and, owing to the backward stage of agriculture and the impoverishment of the masses, capital lacks opportunities for 'profitable' investment.[31]

Lenin takes Hobson to task for supposing that the consuming capacity of the people could be raised under capitalism. But fundamentally he appears largely to share his underconsumptionist view. As he puts it:

> It goes without saying that if capitalism could develop agriculture, which today lags far behind industry everywhere, if it could raise the standard

30. Hobson, *Imperialism*, p. 81.
31. Lenin, *Imperialism*, ch. iv.

of living of the masses which are still poverty stricken and half-starved everywhere in spite of the amazing advance of technical knowledge, then there could be no talk of a surplus of capital. . . . But then capitalism would not be capitalism.[32]

Those who have followed Hobson like John Strachey have seen the *End of Empire*[33] precisely in capitalism's ability to develop agriculture and raise the standard of living of the masses through the provisions of the 'welfare state'. Leninists are forced to argue that what has been done in a few advanced welfare states has been necessarily at the expense of the masses in the poorer parts of the world. Their poverty is in other words still essential for capitalist accumulation.

8. A review of the evidence

The continuing and indeed widening gap between the wealth of the advanced capitalist nations and the poverty of the poor nations within the capitalist sphere do provide circumstantial evidence of the Leninist view. Certain crucial facts about the export of capital, however, have to be taken into account here. The facts may be briefly summarised as follows:[34]

(a) In the period up to 1939
(i) Property income from British overseas investment was in excess of the outflow of capital throughout most of the nineteenth century and up to 1914. It in fact financed a part of each year's trading deficit on goods and services incurred by Britons as well as financing new British investment. It did nothing to reduce the 'plethora' of capital at home, although it may have kept up the rate of profit.
(ii) By far the greater part (over threequarters at least) of British capital exports before 1914 and again between the wars, did not consist of exports of capital by monopoly capitalist companies to overseas subsidiaries but rather of loans to governments and government guaranteed public utilities. The emergence of monopolistic firms in Britain was slow before the 1920s, yet most of the foreign capital in the world, at least before 1914, was British.
(iii) The rate of return on British capital invested overseas was not markedly higher than that invested at home except in the quite

32. *Ibid.*
33. J. Strachey, *The End of Empire* (London, Gollancz, 1959), pp. 98ff.
34. See Barratt Brown, *After Imperialism*, where the evidence is supplied for these statements.

small investments in colonial plantations and mines, and then only in years of booming demand for primary products.

(iv) By far the greater part of British capital exports before 1914 and again between the wars went to independent countries. Only about 20 per cent was invested in the British colonies including India and another 20 per cent in South America. The main investment was, as Hilferding suggested, in other capitalist countries mainly in Europe and North America which were rapidly overhauling Britain in absolute and *per capita* wealth.

(v) The arrest of industrial development in the colonies largely through the working of free trade, while disastrous for the colonies, was not advantageous to Britain. Although shareholders in some foreign mines and estates received a high return on their capital, and although imported colonial food and raw materials were cheap in the 1930s, the resulting impoverishment of the colonial peoples worked back in high unemployment rates on workers in Britain's export industries. The advantages to be derived from capital export did, as Hilferding suggested, come rather from the real economic development of European lands and European-settled lands in North America etc., which supplied expanding markets for British goods and the base for increases in productivity.

(b) In the period since 1945

(i) The income from overseas investment in undeveloped lands both by the U.K. and U.S.A. has generally exceeded the outflow of private capital to these lands, but both have been declining in relative importance.

(ii) The new post-1945 wave of capital export from the United States and from Britain has consisted primarily in the export of capital by monopolistic firms in establishing overseas subsidiaries.

(iii) The greater part of this capital has not, however, gone into the poorer underdeveloped or ex-colonial lands, despite the huge investments in oil and certain minerals but has consisted of a kind of cross-investment of giant manufacturing enterprises in each other's markets.

(iv) The comparative rate of return on capital invested overseas compared with that on investment at home has been higher in the case of the United States but not in that of Britain. Overseas investment is, however, forced upon British firms if they are to keep up in the world market.

(v) International trade, like international investment, has become increasingly concentrated in exchanges betweeen the advanced industrial lands and, despite the provision of aid of various sorts, the underdeveloped lands have been largely left out of the rapid growth in international movements of goods and capital.

These recent developments go far to account for the widening gap between the rich and poor countries in the capitalist world, but they are the result rather of the withdrawal of capital than of the export of capital. This has to be explained in some new way which embraces the emergence of the international firms' cross-investments in each other's home markets. With the exception of oil and mineral investment, and not even most of that, the continued exercise of economic power by the advanced countries over the underdeveloped is still not explained in terms of capital exports. New explanations have therefore been sought by Marxists.

9. Neo-Marxist explanations of imperialism

The first explanation to be considered is that of Harry Magdoff.[35] He argues firstly that the outflow of capital even to rich developed countries involves a form of imperialism (over smaller companies and countries) that we in Britain should very well understand. It still provides a crucial outlet for the plethora of U.S. capital generated at home. There is an evident measure of truth in this, but it does not explain the continuing concern of U.S. policy in maintaining U.S. control over the underdeveloped lands, and this is our main concern. Magdoff's second argument is that the quantity of investment in underdeveloped lands may now be relatively small, but it is of crucial importance for U.S. capitalism because it is involved in the control over key strategic raw materials that are no longer available in the United States. Since most underdeveloped lands are only too anxious to sell these materials (it is generally all they have to offer on the world market), what is involved here is a battle between the giant companies for control rather than a direct struggle between the advanced industrial countries and those that are underdeveloped. This inter-capitalist competition must certainly form a major element in any understanding of imperialism today as it did in the imperialist rivalries at the end of the nineteenth century.

The central explanation of imperialism in the thinking of modern Marxists like Paul Baran and P. M. Sweezy, lies in the challenge of the

35. H. Magdoff, *The Age of Imperialism* (New York, Monthly Review Press, 1966), esp. pp. 50ff.

Soviet Union and of communist inspired revolt. The challenge is to capitalism. The competition of rival capitalist nation states has to be contained in face of this challenge to all. This picture dovetails with the emphasis on the latest stage of the centralisation of capital, the emergence of the multinational firm as a more powerful entity than the nation state. The new empires are of the giant corporations. Nation states are their tools. The aim may still be:

> *monopolistic control* over foreign sources of supply and over foreign markets, enabling them (the monopolists) to buy and sell on specially privileged terms, to shift orders from one subsidiary to another, to favour this country or that depending on which has the most advantageous tax, labour and other policies—in a word they want to do business on their own terms and wherever they choose . . . with allies and clients not trading partners.[36]

Competition with other capitalist powers has become secondary to competition with Soviet power. The competition between firms remains, albeit now a world battle of giants, and provides the necessary link in the causal chain of Marx's thinking that connects private capital ownership and capital accumulation. But the firms are now international. Moreover, on this view 'the revolutionary initiative against capitalism, which in Marx's day belonged to the proletariat in the advanced countries, has passed into the hands of the impoverished masses in the under-developed countries who are struggling to free themselves from imperialist domination and exploitation'.[37]

We are back to Hilferding's belief in the revolutionary potential of the poor nations, which Rosa Luxemburg doubted. But the existence of a centre of anticapitalist power in the Soviet Union, according to the Neo-Marxist view, provides the sinews of strength and encouragement for the 'wretched of the earth' in underdeveloped lands. The export of capital to underdeveloped lands is no longer regarded, in this view, as helping to solve the problem of surplus capital accumulation. Annual income from postwar overseas investment of U.S. companies is recognised as having been in excess of the annual capital outflow, in the same way that U.K. property income from overseas was in excess of capital exports before 1914. 'One can only conclude', say Baran and Sweezy, 'that foreign investment, far from being an outlet for domestically generated surplus, is a most efficient device for transferring surplus generated abroad to the investing

36. P. Baran and P. M. Sweezy, *Monopoly Capital* (New York, Monthly Review Press) p. 201.
37. *Ibid.*, p. 9.

country'.[38] The rate of return on U.S. investments abroad may be higher than that on U.S. investments at home but the problem of absorbing the surplus remains.

Up to the Second World War the surplus of capital accumulated in the advanced industrial lands of capitalism created, according to Marxist explanations, the periodic crises of the system, most notably in 1929 and 1937. The vast demands of military spending by the state mopped up the surplus after 1937, but the crisis reappeared in the late 1940s in the U.S.A. Thereafter, it is argued, military spending by the U.S.A. combined with the space race maintained a fairly steady if slow rate of growth of the whole economy, and from 1963 onwards a much increased military spending generated a much more rapid rate of growth. A question remains as to whether the giant companies, having developed a certain kind of technology, wished the U.S. Government to buy that technology for the arms and space race, and if necessary for war, and then found good reasons for persuading the government to fulfil their wishes; or whether the giant companies really feared the advance of communism and socialism and invoked state protection on their side.

The question is important for us to decide because, if it could be shown that the fear came first and this could be removed by Soviet assurances and by successful competitive coexistence, then presumably the United States Government would spend less on arms and more on improving the conditions of life of its poorer citizens and the economic development of poorer nations. The giant companies could then sell more goods to them. Although Baran and Sweezy themselves reject the idea that the Soviet Union is aggressive, they evidently believe that the giant corporations have real reasons for fearing the spread of socialism in the world.

The expansion of United States military and political power in the world is thus seen as being very similar to that of British military and political power at the end of the nineteenth century. It is the result of pressures from industrial and financial capital to obtain guaranteed privileged markets for goods and capital and sources of raw materials against the threat to these from economic rivals. There are two differences today: one is that the major rival is what Baran and Sweezy call a 'world socialist system as a rival and alternative to the world capitalist system'. [39] The other is that the giant industrial firm itself now provides the finance capital from its own capital accumulation

38. *Ibid.*, pp. 107–8.
39. *Ibid.*, p. 183.

and towers over most nation states in resources and international connections. Baran and Sweezy repeatedly point out that, if the giant corporations wished only to increase their trade with the 'socialist world system' (or for that matter with the poorer part of the United States population), they could do this without military expenditure or privileged control of markets and raw materials.[40]

That they do not do so implies both a fear for their own power and a fear of losing the source of their own capital accumulation in the low levels of earnings of workers and primary producers the world over. Provision of government aid to poor countries and equally of Keynesian welfare measures at home are therefore limited to those which leave the accumulating power of the giant corporation intact. Marx's prediction of increasing misery proved wrong only to the extent that a section of the workers had to be allowed to increase their consuming power. Other sections remained to generate the accumulation of capital.

It is suggested by economists like Kenneth Boulding that since 'one can now get a hundred dollars out of nature for every dollar that one can squeeze out of an exploited man . . . the pay-offs of empire have been radically reduced and the pay-offs of the "milorg"* likewise'.[41] This view was even endorsed by a United Nations Committee on the Economic and Social Consequences of Disarmament 1962, including Soviet Russian, Polish and Czechoslovak members. The problems of transition from military to civilian spending were regarded as difficult but not impossible. A perhaps more realistic view is taken by the author of the fake-official 'Report from the Iron Mountain'. The 'waste' of war production has the great advantage in his view that it not only becomes obsolescent quickly but 'is exercised entirely outside the framework of the economy of supply and demand. As such it provides the only critically large segment of the total economy that is subject to complete and arbitrary central control. . . . It is production that would not otherwise have taken place'.[42] Yet the author, while remaining doubtful about the efficacy of any welfare or aid programmes in providing a substitute for arms expenditure did believe that the space research programme could provide the necessary expansionary element for the

40. *Ibid.*, pp. 192ff.
41. K. Boulding, *Disarmament and the Economy* (New York, Harper & Row, 1963), p. 17; United Nations, *The Economic Consequences of Disarmament* (New York, 1962).
42. L. C. Lewin, ed., *Report from the Iron Mountain* (New York, Dial, 1967), pp. 67–8.

* 'milorg' is the word Boulding uses for the whole complex of national military organisation.

economy. This seemed much less likely after the successful moon landings in 1969.

We need not, anyway, perhaps take too seriously the arguments of what was designed as a propaganda hoax, but the questions raised about the possible substitutes for the functions of war serve to remind us that the commitment of ten per cent of world industrial output to preparation for war is the result of a complex of economic, political, sociological, ecological, cultural and scientific pressures, which are not so easily reduced to a single economic cause, even one so powerful as the engine of capital accumulation in a number of giant international companies. It cannot be doubted that, while arms production has the great advantage of quick obsolescence and effective central control, it does also apparently meet the least resistance from wide groups of people as being an acceptable form of state spending out of taxation. But it leaves the Marxists uncomfortably facing its equal and opposite manifestation: the military and space race budgets of the Soviet Union and other communist-ruled nations. Even less comfortable for them is the fairly evident détente reached in 1969 between the U.S.A. and the Soviet Union.

10. A note on Soviet imperialism

It was not Lenin but Rosa Luxemburg who saw Russia as an international revolutionary force. Lenin was quite prepared to make temporary accommodations with Russian peasant nationalism to advance the Russian revolution and defend its frontiers. Stalin built these accommodations into a permanent system. After Lenin's death Soviet pressure on neighbouring lands and Soviet influence on the world communist movement were less concerned with advancing the revolution than with defending the fatherland. This was particularly true under Stalin's régime, but there does not seem to have been much change in policy in this respect since his death.

The first revolution against capitalism did not come in a country where technological advances and an increasingly self-conscious and educated working class were pushing up against the frontiers of capitalist economic relations, as Marx had expected. It came where a backward capitalist state collapsed under the defeats of superior arms in total war. The revolutions in Eastern Europe (except in Yugoslavia) which followed the Second World War were less the result of internal communist development than of the force of the Red Army's tanks. With the exceptions of Czechoslovakia and East

Germany, communist regimes were established in economically backward countries. This was true also of the Chinese and Cuban revolutions. The result was that the Soviet Union tended to regard itself, and to be regarded (until the Chinese challenged such claims), as the champion of the peoples whose economies had been distorted by dependence on the advanced capitalist countries, rather than as champions of the proletariat in the advanced countries themselves. Soviet influence was greatest, therefore, in the countries lying along the Soviet frontiers and in the ex-colonial countries.

Neither of these explanations may seem entirely adequate to account for Russian rockets in Cuba and Russian tanks in Budapest, Prague or along the Chinese border, still less for the extent of the Soviet involvement in the space race. Two suggestions have been offered. It was the view of the late Isaac Deutscher that the Russians in 1917 lived through the last capitalist and the first proletarian revolution, both accomplished under Bolshevik leadership. In collectivising agriculture Stalin destroyed the capitalist revolution, at the expense, however, of creating a continuing conflict between town and country, which required the Stalinist apparatus and nationalist external policies to contain.[43] Others like E. H. Carr have argued that it was less a combination of capitalist and proletarian revolutions than of industrial and proletarian revolutions.[44] On this view, the communist party acted as 'caretaker' for the proletariat. In Eastern Europe the Red Army had this role; in China the Red Guards. The agenda in each case was a first stage industrial revolution to be carried through 'from above'. Oscar Lange has added that 'the assent of the population was obtained *ex post facto* through the propaganda and educational activities of the communist party'.[45]

What both Deutscher and Carr have in common is the view that Soviet rule, at least under Stalin, involved a tension between workers and peasantry that resulted from the process of accumulation of capital for industrialisation through the exploitation of the peasants. The dominant role of the Soviet military establishment arose directly from the need to contain this internal tension, as much as from the undoubted external pressures. Moreover the highly centralised form of economic planning that was required to carry through an industrial revolution 'from above' created a technocratic establishment side

43. Isaac Deutscher, 'The unfinished revolution, 1917–67', *New Left Review*, no. 43 (London, 1967).
44. E. H. Carr, 'Revolution from above', *New Left Review*, no. 46 (1968).
45. Quoted in Baran, *The Political Economy of Growth*, p. 278.

by side with the military. Stalin controlled them both through his own secret police. The technocrats have recently sought to challenge the dominant rǫle of the military, but the change does not seem greatly to have affected Soviet relations with the other communist countries or with the world outside.

Why the technocrats are just as anxious as the military to maintain control over the 'world socialist system' is not entirely explained by the Deutscher–Carr analysis. A number of Marxists would argue that socialist unity under central leadership is vital in a hostile world, but the Soviet occupation of Czechoslovakia and the fighting on the Chinese border have somewhat reduced this number. Marxists should not in fact be surprised if a social formation based on a fairly low level of technology turns out not to be a socialist one. Marx would not have expected it to. The correspondence within a social formation of the superstructure of political (and military) institutions to the mode of production, and, within the mode of production, of the economic structure (of property relations) to the technology (the forces of production), lay at the very heart of Marx's model of society. Nor would Marx have expected that ways of thought left over from earlier social formations would change very rapidly, even after changes had taken place to bring economic production relations into correspondence with technological forces. Is Soviet expansion just a hangover then of earlier phases of development?

The explanation given by a Czechoslovak 'reformer' like Professor Ota Sik for Soviet resistance to his economic reforms may provide the explanation we are looking for. The centralised form of Soviet planned economy has required complete control over the inputs and outputs of production units. As production processes have become more complex, the more advanced sectors and the largest plants have reached a dominating position in the plan. The gestation period of production has lengthened, and with it the importance of absolute control at every stage of production if targets are to be fulfilled. Sales to state organisations, including the military, are easier for planners and plant managers to control than sales to individual consumers whose tastes are fickle and cannot be manipulated by advertising. The technologically advanced sectors begin to dictate the growth path of the economy, as in capitalist countries. In so far as foreign trade is part of the plan, and the intratrade of the communist countries is certainly planned, this must also be subject to central control. Foreign sources both of raw materials or machinery and foreign markets must be dependable. It is not a long step before, as in the capitalist world system, they become dependent. Technological advances in industry demand much increased control in planning their use. Until forms of democratic control are developed, they move in the direction of least resistance, into military and paramilitary channels.

11. Capitalism and underdevelopment today

What has been suggested in this essay is that the central principle at work in the spread of capitalism has been the principle of cumulative causation. Although this fits naturally into Marx's model of polarisation, it was in fact first explicitly put forward by Myrdal.[46] In a competitive system the advantages for a capitalist—man or nation— of being the first in the field are overpowering. The more capital grows in one place the more it goes on growing. Wealth then attracts and poverty repels. 'Unto him that hath shall be given and from him that hath not etc. . . .' The most desperate measures of immunisation have to be taken by any nation to isolate itself from this polarising process once it has begun. Before the eighteenth century the standard of living of the present underdeveloped lands was almost certainly higher than that in Europe. It was certainly higher in Asia. But the tribute extracted by colonial plunder and, after Britain's industrial revolution, the destruction of native industries by imported manufactures reversed the situation. It did more than this; it led to an artificial world division of labour maintained by free trade, in which countries restricted to primary production became dependent upon those with diversified and mainly industrial output. On this view, maintaining the status-quo became an important object of policy for capitalist firms and governments in the industrial countries, since it held down the price of food and raw materials, and generated accumulation at the centres of capital.

This is a theory that fits well enough into Marx's model of capitalist economic relations, in which capital accumulation at one pole creates impoverishment at the other. It is a very different concept, however, from that of the Marxists, including Lenin, for whom the export of capital is from rich countries to poor, from places where capital is in surplus to those where labour is cheap. The reason that Lenin and others insisted on this theory of capital export is that they accepted Marx's determinist economic model, within his general theory, that

46. Gunnar Myrdal, *Economic Theory and Underdeveloped Regions* (London, Duckworth, 1957).

the structure of economic relations was essentially self-regulating and tended if not to inevitable breakdown (that was Rosa Luxemburg's 'mistake') at least to something near it. The theory is based on the argument that production for profit tends in a competitive situation to create accumulations of capital which cannot be profitably used because they are extracted from the very masses who have to provide the market for increased profitable production. These accumulations have then to be exported. There was an obvious contradiction in a theory based on capital exports to low wage countries because one would expect it to be still less possible to find profitable uses for capital in them after the initial investment was made, since the masses from whom super-profits were extracted would be still less able to buy the products of further investment. This is not to deny that there were rich fields for exploitation by capital in lands of cheap labour. The fact is, as we saw earlier, that most capital was exported to lands of labour shortage, where rates of profit were not markedly higher than at home.

The export of capital, in fact, did provide a counter to the polarising process, since it assisted real economic development in Europe and lands of European settlement, where independent governments were successful in breaking out of the polarising process by protection and subsidies for infant industries. Later still, governments countered the polarising process inside their own economies by welfare measures and Keynesian management of demand. The contradictions inside the economic structure of capitalism were partly solved, but only at the expense, first of all, of growing national economic rivalry and, then, of growing impoverishment and revolt among the remaining underdeveloped nations. On this view the poor nations take the place of Marx's proletarian masses.

The two key questions for the future are, first, whether these underdeveloped nations can break out of the artificial division of labour in which they are caught and, secondly, whether the advanced nations can unite to apply Keynesian measures on a world scale. The problem for the underdeveloped nations is that underdevelopment is not non-development but a distortion of development. Their economies are unbalanced both in the concentration upon production of one or two primary products for an export market and in the outward orientation of capital and enterprise. It is not necessary to give examples of the dominating position of two or three primary products both in the exports and in the whole national output of most underdeveloped economies. What is less widely understood is the effect this has on the

but wasn't British / Portuguese / Spanish / Dutch etc
capital "outward oriented" during the first phases
of those countries' imperialist expansion cum capitalist development?

direction of local capital and enterprise, and indeed on the whole social structure of underdeveloped societies. Money and power are to be sought more in the foreign trade sector than in domestic industrial development, which is limited to those products which do not have to compete with technically more advanced foreign products in free trade.

Paul Baran has analysed most clearly the whole 'morphology of backwardness', as he calls it, social, political and economic, in the underdeveloped lands.[47] Local capital and enterprise become what he calls 'comprador', taking the phrase from the Portuguese trade in China, that is to say, invested in foreign trade and often in foreign companies or in agencies of foreign companies. This makes it rather surprising that Baran assumes, as we saw in a quotation earlier in this essay, that a national bourgeoisie and proletariat will emerge to carry forward the 'historical movement in the backward echelons as in the forward'.[48] What in fact are the chances of this? With the outstanding exceptions of Japan and more recently of China, economic development has been limited to the lands of Europe and of European settlement (including Israel). We noted earlier that since natural resources are not limited in this way, and racial differences can be discounted, the explanation must have to do with the historical origins of the industrial revolution in Europe. Given these origins 'kith and kin' may well have found it easier to achieve a less dependent position in relation to the more advanced powers, to protect their infant industries by tariffs and to obtain capital for development on terms that were not prohibitive. This is as true of Israel as of the British dominions. The longer this independence was delayed the more difficult it has become of achievement. Moreover, the African continent, South and Central America and much of Asia have been divided up by colonial and imperial policies into a proliferation of states most of which are not economically viable. *meaning what? judged by which criteria?*

Detailed studies are now required of the way in which the rather limited economic development has been proceeding in the underdeveloped lands. Most have, in fact, begun to impose tariffs on foreign goods to protect their infant industries, but since these have usually been limited to luxury items the ironical situation has arisen that luxury industries have been the first to be established. Moreover, what has often happened is that even in these industries it is foreign firms that have established subsidiaries to produce inside the tariff walls.

47. *The Political Economy of Growth*, pp. 163ff.
48. *Ibid.*, p. 140.

Whenever a new market emerges the giant international company jumps in to extend its sales. Motor car assembly is now attaining major proportions in Argentina, Brazil, and Venezuela. The question remains whether a national capitalist class can emerge in such countries, determined to develop its own basic industries and to limit the outflow of capital; or alternatively an industrial proletariat, as in Russia, determined to do likewise. On the Chinese model there may be signs of peasant revolt against colonial rule, as in Guinea,[49] turning into revolutionary demands for economic development.

The revolts in what we call the Third World undoubtedly encompass the objectives of economic development. The advanced industrial countries have tended, however, to employ military means to put down such revolts, wherever they seemed to endanger their interests. Such military intervention is widely regarded as the most obvious example of imperialism today. We have still to determine whether these interests are fundamentally economic and whether they originate in capitalist expansion or in capitalist defence. It can well be argued that it would be in the interests of all the advanced industrial countries, and of the giant concentrations of capital inside them, if new and expanding markets emerged in the underdeveloped lands. There is no doubt about the rapid growth of the Soviet and East European market in the last twenty years. If others are prevented from following the communists' lead, the reason might be fear among the capitalists of the results for the general relationship of capital and labour in the advanced countries or the sheer difficulty of obtaining agreement between the advanced countries and their giant corporations on a common strategy.

The question that remains to be answered in assessing the value of the polarising theory in Marx's model, is whether capitalist governments are capable of uniting to control their economic rivalries and to apply welfare measures on a world scale. The answer that a Marxist would give is that they cannot do this because capital accumulation is still effected in individual profit-making and competing units, large as some of these may now be. Indeed, the very size of the modern giant international companies reduces the power of governments to manage their accumulations of capital. It is only confusing to refer to such companies as monopolies, when it is their competition that is the key to their operations. Control over sources of raw material, bases for their productive activities and markets for their products are sought

49. See Basil Davidson, *The Liberation of Guinea* (Harmondsworth, Penguin African Series; 1968).

or probably more ... than

just as competitively by the giant companies today as by the nation *Yes.*
states of Lenin's day. The fact that most of the giant companies are
American gives to the United States government a special role in
defending the general interests of capital. The other capitalist states
have an essentially client role, but the antagonisms are not easily
quieted; the chances of unity do not look good, in spite of general fear
and hatred of the Soviet Union. The fact is that few governments
deploy resources equal to those of the largest companies. Governments do the bidding of 'their' companies, in providing state support
for research and development at home and state protection for their
trade and investment overseas. Huge sums have been provided in aid
for underdeveloped lands; yet the evidence suggests that military
orders and military aid abroad are preferred to civil welfare and aid
at home. They can more easily be brought under central control;
they do not compete in the normal market of supply and demand;
obsolescence is built in. What is perhaps even more important in
answering our initial question is that, whereas national governments
can ensure that each firm pays its share of taxes to increase the total
size of the cake, there is no international government to ensure that
each international firm would do likewise. Nationalism remains a
powerful force.

12. Conclusion

The main feature of capitalist economic relations for Marx was the
accumulation of capital by a class of capitalists, not for hoarding, but
for the development under competitive pressure of new productive
forces to generate still more capital. This created great advances for
mankind; but the sheer pace of advance and the scale of capital
accumulation would, he believed, in time outgrow the framework of
private property relations. In particular Marx envisaged increasing
centralisation of capital as a polarising process leaving increasing
misery at the other extreme, from which the workers would revolt.

Centralisation of capital certainly took place inside the advanced
capitalist states, as Marx had expected, leading to the giant concentrations of capital inside the international firm of today. But in addition,
the spread of capitalism all over the world led to the development of
some countries and the underdevelopment of others. This also fitted
Marx's model of capitalist accumulation, although it was not clearly
foreseen by Marx. The result was not only to create a particular
structure of economic relations between states; with this unequal

development of countries emerged a strong national consciousness, first among the developed nations and then in response to this among the underdeveloped. And since it also happened, for very complex historical reasons, that capitalism appeared first in Europe and spread to lands of European settlement and little further, a strong racial consciousness arose, first among the Europeans and then, in response to it, among the non-Europeans. No theory of imperialism can possibly exclude this national and racial consciousness; but, unless one believes that there are adequate differences in endowment between nations and races, or between the territories they live in, to explain this unequal development, then some historical *economic* explanation must be sought as an explanation for differences in development.

What is left of Marxism in a possible theory of imperialism today seems to be Marx's central insistence on the conflict between the growth of technology under capitalism and the economic (or property) relations—that is of the production for capitalist profit of the separate capitals—appropriate to a lower level of technology. The increases in scale and complexity of production require longer and longer term planning of inputs and more and more control of the market for outputs. Competition makes this extraordinarily difficult to achieve. The larger firms use the state to provide them with privileged positions. So much is evident to an acute non-Marxist economist like J. K. Galbraith, who understands perfectly the importance of military spending (including that part involved in the space race) in both the U.S.A. and the U.S.S.R. as the most acceptable and manageable form of public spending.[50] What Galbraith appears to miss is the equal importance of overseas investment in the production of raw materials and, even more, in the production by subsidiaries of finished products for overseas markets.

Modern technology pushes firms far out beyond the frontiers of nations and even of national plans. The search for individual profit in a company, however big, creates anarchy in the world market when the state of technology demands planning. To replace the anarchy of the market by planning on a world scale requires a new concept of democratic social ownership of the means of production in place of the competition of private capitals. The Soviet concept was evidently effective in carrying through a first stage industrial revolution but it led to a system of bureaucratic nation-state control, not only of the Soviet economy but of its satellites. The giant Soviet department of

50. J. K. Galbraith, *The New Industrial State* (L   don, Hamish Hamilton, 1967).

state (no less than the giant American firm) demands control over its inputs and outputs because, in spite of state ownership, no system of social control of distribution has yet been brought to bear upon the plans of the technocrats. One may conclude that, only when the whole of society is involved in this control, will national antagonisms start to wither and imperialism come to an end.

DISCUSSION

International Keynesianism? A questioner asked whether it was possible for capitalist countries to cooperate together on a successful international programme designed to reverse the process of polarisation of income between rich and poor. Barratt Brown doubted if this could be done. 'The crucial point is that the accumulation of capital takes place in competitive industrial enterprises who are driven to invest by internicine competition.' As long as such enterprises remain competitive they will be driven to over-accumulate. This makes management of the international economy very difficult.

Another participant doubted whether it was even possible for capitalism to manage the economy well enough in the context of an individual third world country in order to ensure development. For example, it was obvious to any reasonable economist that the industrialisation of India was desirable to capitalism, but the objective conditions for it were just not there. 'India does not develop because it has a particular form of government.'

A contradiction between exploiting the third world and selling goods to it? A related question concerned Barratt Brown's assertion that there was a basic contradiction involved in Lenin's idea of imperialism as a system by which capitalism was able to obtain more markets for its products in the third world and his idea that imperialism was a system which permitted great exploitation. But was this so? If you looked at it in terms of individual capitalists you could see how both were possible. For instance, capitalists who invested in mining and agriculture in the third world were able to produce raw materials for other capitalists more cheaply than they had obtained them before. There was thus no contradiction for the investor, nor for the manufacturers since the latter were able to get raw materials at a cheaper price and to sell the finished products in another capitalist country. Barratt Brown disagreed. In his opinion the contradiction remained. If capitalist enterprises accumulated through profits, then there was no one to buy their goods.

The possibility of development in the third world. A number of points were made about the problem of third world economic development. In his answers Barratt Brown underlined the importance of the distorting effect of the international division of labour. This made development in the third world very difficult. Its national bourgeoisie, for instance, had become agents of foreign capital. Perhaps the only way ahead was for countries wishing to develop to isolate themselves completely from the international economy.

The state and the large international corporation.   Another group of questions concerned the relationship between the state and the large international corporations. It was pointed out that the latter often undertook their own foreign policy since they could not rely on any one state to defend them. At any moment it may not be politic for the United States or Britain to intervene on their behalf. Barratt Brown agreed. 'The important thing is that it is the giant companies and not the imperialist powers which are competing.' He also made the point that it was necessary to analyse the policy of the American state in an area like South-East Asia at two different levels. On one level the United States was trying to defend the whole capitalist system; on another the situation must be seen in terms of competition between large American firms, pushed on by technology, for a part of the most controllable domestic market: the military. 'Thus the whole question gets a second pressure from domestic factors.'

The reliability of statistics concerning capital exports and the rate of profit.   Lastly, various questions were asked about Barratt Brown's assertion that, the United States apart, and as far as he could tell, no countries which exported capital were getting a higher rate of profit abroad than at home. In particular it was argued that you could not draw any firm conclusions from the published figures because firms did not declare the real amounts involved; the use of transfer prices disguised the flow of capital and the real profit rates. (This is discussed again in the Conclusion, 4.)

III

Industrial growth and

Early German

imperialism

Hans-Ulrich Wehler

A second group of theories is concerned with the phenomenon of social imperialism. Like the Marxist theories they concentrate on developments inside advanced capitalist countries. But, unlike them, they have little to say about imperialism as a world system or about particular economic questions such as the investment of surplus capital. Rather they focus on the social problems produced by periods of rapid industrial development, notably the growth of class conflict; though at this point they have crucial links to the Marxist theory (see Conclusion, 4). In addition some writers on the subject have drawn attention to the strain imposed on the structure of the nation state by this same process of rapid development. For such theorists imperial expansion is seen primarily as a way of coping with potential domestic crises.

In the following paper Wehler seeks to apply some of these theories to Germany and, in particular, to the years between 1873 and 1896. Here was a state in which the first phase of its industrial revolution was followed, in the 1870s and 1880s, by a period of much more irregular economic growth and rising social tension. In these circumstances the leaders of the government began to worry about a possible threat to the position of the traditional social and political hierarchy while the leaders of business were anxious to return to an environment in which predictability and profit went hand in hand.

For both groups, as Wehler is concerned to demonstrate, the. only solution to their problem seemed to be further economic advance based on an expansion of overseas trade. This, for him, is the central explanation of Germany's bid for colonies in the 1880s. What his theory is not concerned with is the question of whether the policies pursued succeeded in the way in which they were supposed to do; or whether economic expansion was sufficient to produce both growth and an alleviation of social tension. His main preoccupation, like that of most historians, is with why things happened and when.

The historiography of imperialism urgently needs critical historical theories to provide illuminating analyses and explanations of the socio-economic and political processes which propelled western expansion. There is certainly no lack of theories of imperialism, but often they are either too general or too onesided. Moreover, in many cases they do not seem to satisfy certain minimal requirements for any social science theory, which has to combine a maximum of empirically obtained and verifiable information with as much explanatory power as possible, while covering a variety of similar phenomena; that is to say, it must enable the historian to compare the modern forms of imperialism.[1]

Herbert Lüthy's concept of colonisation, for example, seems to be much too general.[2] If one accepts it as a theory at all one would have to isolate a subsystem of his colonisation theory in order to gain a meaningful conceptualised framework for a discussion of modern imperialism.

David Landes has repeatedly argued for a theory of imperialism which proceeds from a general equilibrium theory and discusses imperial expansion as a consequence of power disparities.[3] This line of argument quickly leads to a discussion of uneven economic development and social change, and it seems to be more useful to discuss imperialism within that more specific framework. A general theory of social conflict, from the caveman to General LeMay, which is what Landes is aiming at in the long run, certainly needs more operational content if it is meant to explain a phenomenon like the new imperialism after the 1870s. This is not to deny the use of such general concepts, but rather to ask for the particular elements which are to be combined.

If one points to technological progress as the main factor of expansion, thereby defining imperialism as a sort of unavoidable 'natural' consequence of technological innovations, one is led astray too. There is no direct causal relationship between those innovations

---

1. The following discussion is partly based on H.-U. Wehler, ed., *Imperialismus* (Cologne 1970), pp. 11–36. Imperialism I would define as the formal-direct and informal-indirect rule of industrial countries over undeveloped regions.
2. H. Lüthy, 'Colonization and the making of mankind', *Journal of Economic History*, **21** (1961).
3. D. Landes, 'Some thoughts on the nature of economic imperialism', *Journal of Economic History*, **21** (1961).

and imperialism. One could argue more convincingly that imperialism is partly the result of the inability of ruling elites to cope with the economic and social results of technological change. Or one might maintain, on the other hand, that imperialism is partly a reaction to the lack of just those major technological innovations which supply some of the most important stimuli to modern industrial growth. That would seem to have a direct relevance for German and American expansion in the 1870s and 1880s.

The discussion of imperialism as extreme nationalism harks back to the arguments of Friedjung, one of the early continental historians of imperialism.[4] But Carlton Hayes and, recently, Wolfgang J. Mommsen have defended the same notion.[5] Extreme nationalism seems to be a highly complex variable, however, which should not be substituted for another complex variable called imperialism. Furthermore, if one uses figurative expressions like 'extreme nationalism' or 'fever of imperialism', one is actually talking about the symptoms of a sickness of society or the body politic. What one would have to do first would be to attempt a socio-economic and political analysis of that particular society before one could meaningfully define symptoms like 'fever'. This would entail the language of sociology and economics rather than the vocabulary of medical pathology. Lastly, it would be hard, indeed, to discover fever in the particular decision-making process in Washington D.C., Berlin or London. Responsible and professional politicians like Cleveland, McKinley and Taft, Bismarck, Witte and Salisbury were not directly affected by what some writers chose to call the fever of imperialism. As an explanatory model the theory of extreme nationalism is much too narrowly constructed.

Schumpeter's theory, which centres round the influence of atavistic, feudalistic mentalities and certain social structures on the development of imperialism, is highly arbitrary in its definitions, one of which excludes Great Britain as an imperialist power. Within its framework it is hardly possible to explain specific imperialism like the German, Japanese or American one. In many ways it overstresses the misleading idea of a superstructure. Politically speaking, however, it could be looked upon as a sort of anti-theory against the Neo-Marxist theories, even though it diverted historians into directing their

4. H. Friedjung, *Das Zeitalter des Imperialismus*, i (Berlin, 1919).
5. C. Hayes, *A Generation of Materialism*, (New York, Harper Row 1941, 1966), pp. 216–29; W. J. Mommsen, *Das Zeitalter des Imperialismus*, (Frankfurt, 1969; English translation forthcoming, Fischer-Weltgeschichte).

fire against precapitalist ideas and structures instead of helping them to begin the analysis of those sociopolitical systems which produced imperialism.

During the last decade the time-honoured cliché of the 'primacy of politics' has also been the subject of many attempts at reinvigoration. Like the bulk of German historiography since the last third of the nineteenth century some writers, like D. K. Fieldhouse, have made the 'Primat der Aussenpolitik' their central topic.[6] From the epistemological point of view their clearcut distinction between politics and economics is extremely unconvincing with respect to any period, and certainly with regard to the years following the industrial revolution. Secondly, it would be a difficult empirical task to find evidence which would allow one to explain American or German imperialism in terms of this particular political theory. As for the argument that there were no deep economic changes after 1870, this bizarre notion stems from a lack of knowledge of economic history. The various industrial revolutions—for example, in Germany, the United States, Belgium and France—certainly created a very specific set of factors conditioning later developments, not the least of which was the new quality of international competition. So much for some theories with obvious deficiencies.

Any theory of imperialism which promises empirical and explanatory success will, it seems to me, have to combine theories of economic growth, social change, and political power. It has to establish links between the problems of unsteady economic development in industrial countries and the changes in their social and political structure. I have tried elsewhere[7] to develop in detail such an eclectic, yet critical historical theory of imperialism, two elements of which call for discussion here since they are particularly important for this explanatory model.

1. The social consequences of unsteady economic growth

It is a dangerous legend that rapid economic growth promotes social and political stability, thereby inhibiting radical and irresponsible

6. D. K. Fieldhouse, 'Imperialism', *Economic History Review*, **14** (1961).
7. Cf. H.-U. Wehler, *Bismarck und der Imperialismus* (Cologne, 1970); also H.-U. Wehler, 'Bismarck's Imperialism 1862–90', *Past and Present*, **48**, Aug. 1970; parts of the following discussion are based on that article. I should like to thank the editors for their kind permission. Historical theory is being used here in the sense of J. S. Mill's 'principia media' or C. Wright Mill's notions of theory or J. Habermas's definition.

policies. Historical experience has shown quite the contrary, that rapid—and, economically speaking, successful—growth produces extremely acute socio-economic and political problems. Germany is an illuminating case. Here, after the breakthrough of the industrial revolution (1850–73)[8] industrialisation was linked to a large number of profound difficulties in Germany's internal development. More than half a century ago, Thorstein Veblen stated the basic problem: the absorption of the most advanced technology by a largely traditional society within a then unprecedentedly short time. And Alexander Gerschenkron had also the German experience in mind when he propounded his general theory that the faster and the more abrupt a country's industrial revolution, the more intractable and complex will be the problems associated with its industrialisation.[9] After the first stage of the German industrial revolution there followed a period of intensive industrialisation, punctuated by three industrial depressions (1873–79, 1882–86, 1890–95), while the structural crisis of agriculture from 1876 onwards increased the tensions of economic growth. To many contemporaries social change looked like upheaval or even social revolution. In other words, the problems of unsteady growth, together with all its social effects, were of immense importance in the new Reich. As a result, problems of social control of the growth process became particularly urgent. The system of organised capitalism, the 'corporation capitalism' of large scale enterprises, developed as one of the means to bring about stability of industrial development. Organised capitalism—as something qualitatively different from the early competitive capitalism of medium-scale units—grew up in the two decades before 1896, that 'watershed between two epochs in the social history of capitalism', as Schumpeter called it,[10] so that one can characterise the period from 1873 to 1896 as one of an extremely difficult structural crisis in the development of the modern industrial system.

In Germany the same period saw the beginnings of the modern interventionist state which sought to master the problems of unsteady industrial growth and the social changes it produced. Both the

8. Industrial revolution is defined here in a rather narrow economic sense (*per capita* income, growth rates of strategic industries, percentage of net investment); cf. H.-U. Wehler, 'Theorieprobleme der modernen deutschen Wirtschaftsgeschichte 1800–1945' in *Festschrift für H. Rosenberg* (Berlin, 1970).
9. A. Gerschenkron, *Economic Backwardness in Historical Perspective*, (Cambridge, Mass., Harvard Univ. Press) 1962.
10. J. A. Schumpeter, *The Theory of Economic Development*, (Cambridge, Mass., Harvard Univ. Press, 1961), p. 67.

interventionist state and organised capitalism, considered a pragmatic, anticyclical economic policy as an important means of stabilisation. Both, therefore, attached decisive importance to the promotion of an export offensive and to the winning of foreign markets, either through the methods of informal empire or through direct colonial rule. This was considered of decisive importance both for economic prosperity and for domestic, social and political stability, for the same reasons that make the law of the increasing importance of foreign trade during periods of economic depression still seem valid today.

It would be of no use to construct a depression imperialism before 1896 and a boom imperialism afterwards. The basic phenomenon between 1873 and 1914 was the inability of the business community to make rational calculations of economic opportunities in advance, because of the unsteadiness of growth. Therefore the welfare of the country was made dependent on the success of informal and formal expansions. If one accepts the premises of liberal–capitalism itself one may call this a pragmatic expansionism which adapted itself to the needs of a dynamic system which 'evidently' depended on the extension of the market beyond national boundaries.

2. The interventionist state and social imperialism

Since the preservation of the traditional social and political hierarchy was often the dominant motive behind expansion, one may also define this expansionism as a social imperialism. In its military stage Bismarck's greater Prussian Empire of 1871 was the product of the 'revolution from above'. The legitimacy of the young state had no generally accepted basis, nor was it founded on a generally accepted code of basic political convictions, as was to be immediately demonstrated in the years of crisis after 1873. Bismarck had to cover up the social and political differences in the tension ridden class society of his new Germany, and for this he relied on the technique of negative integration: his method was to inflame conflicts between those groups which were allegedly hostile to the Reich (*Reichsfeinde*), like the socialists and Catholics, left-wing Liberals and Jews on the one hand, and those groups which were allegedly loyal to the Reich (*Reichsfreunde*). Because of the permanent conflict between these in and out groups he was able to achieve majorities for his policies.

The Chancellor was also under constant pressure to provide rallying points for his Reichspolitik, and to legitimise his system, by periodically producing fresh political successes. Within a typology of contemporary power structures in the second half of the nineteenth century Bismarck's regime can be classified as a Bonapartist dictatorship, that is a traditional, unstable social and political structure which found itself threatened by strong forces of social and political change and which had to be defended and stabilised by diverting attention away from the question of emancipation at home towards compensatory successes abroad. In this way undisguised repression was blended with limited concessions while the neo-absolutist, pseudo-constitutional dictatorship of the Chancellor could be maintained even after the spell of his charismatic leadership had eroded under constant attacks. . By guaranteeing the bourgeoisie protection from the workers' demands for political and social emancipation in exchange for its own political abdication, by placating the land owning aristocracy suffering under the impact of the agrarian crisis and the industralists complaining about depressions and foreign competition with a fast increasing tariff, the executive gained a remarkable degree of political independence vis-à-vis the various social groups and economic interests. And just as overseas expansion, motivated by domestic and economic considerations, had become an element of the political style of French Bonapartism, so Bismarck, too, after a short period of consolidation in foreign affairs, saw the advantages of such expansion as a counter measure against recurring economic setbacks and the permanent direct or latent threat to the power structure he represented. Thus he became the German 'Caesarist statesman'.[11]

Early German imperialism can also be viewed as the initial phase of an apparently contemporary phenomenon. Habermas has demonstrated recently how, under the present western system of state regulated capitalism, political power is legitimised chiefly by a deliberate policy of state intervention which tries to correct the dysfunctions of the economy, in particular the disturbances of economic growth, in order to ensure the stability of the social system.[12] The demand for legitimation to which these societies are subject, leads to a situation in which a 'substitute programme' replaces the discredited ideology of the liberal–capitalist market economy. Ruling elites are thereby obliged to do two things if they wish to preserve the system and their own vested interests. First, they must ensure that favourable 'conditions for stability be maintained for the entire social system and that risks for economic growth be avoided'. Second, they must 'pursue a policy of avoiding conflict by granting compensations, in

11. H. Gollwitzer, 'Der Cäsarismus Napoleons III', *Historische Zeitschrift*, **173** (1952) p. 65.
12. J. Habermas, *Technik u. Wissenschaft als Ideologie*, (Frankfurt, 1969).

order to ensure the loyalty of the wage-earning masses'. Thus, technological progress and a steady rate of economic growth assume increasingly the function of 'legitimising political power'. These problems do not have an exclusively modern significance. Their historical genesis can be traced back to the last third of the nineteenth century, and in Germany back to the Bismarckian era.

It may be illuminating to view German imperialism since the 1870s, like many other actions of the growing interventionist state, as an attempt on the part of her ruling elites to create improved conditions for the stability of the social and economic system. Since traditional and charismatic authorities were losing their effectiveness, they thus hoped to take the heat out of internal disputes about the distribution of the national income and of political power, and at the same time to provide new foundations for the rule of an authoritarian leadership and of privileged social groups centering around the pre-industrial elites of the aristocracy. Bismarck's Bonapartist and dictatorial regime together with the social forces which supported it, like the later exponents of Wilhelminian 'Weltpolitik', expected that economic and social imperialism would legitimize their authority. Acute contemporary observers recognised this fact quite clearly.[13] *Mutatis mutandis* the same holds true for the effect of American overseas expansion on the political economy and the domestic power structure.[14]

From a consideration of these two theoretical questions the problem of unsteady economic growth and the need for an authoritarian system to legitimise itself when the emerging industrial society eroded its power base, there emerges one fundamental point: German imperialism is to be seen primarily as the result of endogenous socio-economic and political forces, and not as a reaction to exogenous pressures, nor as a means of defending traditional foreign interests.[15]

3. Commercial expansion and the acquisition of formal empire

In view of the long controversy over Bismarck's motives for entering the arena of *Weltpolitik* one important preliminary point must be

13. *Ibid.*, pp. 76ff; cf. Wehler, *Bismarck*, *passim*. Weber, Hilferding, Hobson, Bauer and Lenin saw, of course, this legitimizing effect of imperialism a long time ago.
14. Cf. W. A. Williams, *The Roots of the Modern American Empire*, (New York, Random House 1969); W. LaFeber, *The New Empire*, (Ithaca, Cornell Univ. Press, 1963); T. McCormick, *China Market*, (Chicago, Quadrangle, 1967).
15. Contra Gallagher and Robinson, cf. my arguments in *Past and Present*, 48.

emphasised: in Bismarck's overseas policies there is a striking continuity in both the ideas and the strategy of a free-trade commercial expansionism. He adhered to this particular policy from 1862 until 1898 because he clearly recognised the financial burdens, the political responsibilities, and the military risks that were involved in formal colonial rule. He was deeply influenced, too, by the enormous success of Britain's mid-Victorian informal empire. The years 1884–86 did not see a sudden revision of his basic ideas, or a sudden change of mind towards an enthusiasm for colonies. There were, however, some motives which induced Bismarck, for a time, to involve the state in the governance of Protectorates. It is indisputable that he would have preferred to hand these territories over to syndicates of private interest groups as trading colonies, with some form of loosely formalised imperial protection. The real problem, therefore, is not posed by the continuity of his intentions, but rather by the conditions for the formal empire strategy of the 1880s.

Bismarck pursued his overseas policies for motives which allow it to be designated in part as pragmatic expansionism. In contrast to the type of imperialism that was determined by ideas of prestige, of nationalistic self-assertion, and of a sense of mission, pragmatic expansionism resulted primarily from an assessment of economic and sociopolitical interests. Its ultimate aims were to assure a continuous economic growth and social stability by promoting expansion as a means of preserving the social hierarchy and the political power structure. At this point its affinity with social imperialism becomes evident. Bismarck's pragmatic expansionism corresponded perfectly with his attitudes concerning *Realpolitik*, which was well attuned, too, to the forces generated by a permanently expanding economy. Bismarck was under no illusion about the dynamics of modern growth in the 'age of material interests'. He had spoken in these terms since 1848, while, almost fifty years later, he explicitly recognised that it was a basic tendency of his times that the 'driving force' of 'economic affairs' was the 'principal agent' of modern development. His appointment as prime minister of Prussia coincided with the definitive breakthrough of the industrial revolution in Germany, and from the beginning of the 1860s onwards, he pursued an active overseas policy to promote foreign trade in industrial and agrarian products. His free trade policy was a reflection of the then dominant economic and political interests. In the Far East, for example, Bismarck pursued an 'open door' policy from 1862. If his intentions had been realised Prussia would have acquired a base there around 1870, her own Hong Kong; only his third war for hegemony in central Europe prevented that plan from being executed.

For more than fifteen years this commercial, free trade expansionism created no particular problems, but when the first of the three industrial depressions after 1873 hit the country, Bismarck eventually began to resort to protectionist measures. This trend was intensified after the impact of the agrarian crisis made itself felt at the end of the 1870s. His policy of a conservative alliance (*Sammlung*) between the large landowners and leading industrialists laid the basis for the protectionist system after 1879. The modern German interventionist state began its ascendancy during those years. Foreign trade was energetically supported and initiatives for its extension systematically coordinated. Bismarck defined his new economic policy as a pragmatic adaptation to changing developments, and his pragmatic expansionism was one aspect of the state's early anticyclical economic policy. That policy directly influenced his attitude towards formal empire.

Why did he decide in the mid-1880s that it was no longer possible merely to opt for free trade expansion? Why did he come round to the view, even if only hesitantly, that it was necessary to assume formal territorial control? He saw his own policies as a response to the exigencies of the economic, social, and political system. In Germany, as elsewhere, the new period of depression beginning in 1882 had a catalytic effect on imperialist policies. The protectionist measures which had been considered the most effective anticyclical device, proved to be of little use when the worldwide slump began. The agrarian crisis coincided with the new depression in industry: both the agrarian and the industrial elites were hard hit. Social tensions became more acute, fears of the 'red peril' spread in industrial areas. A feeling that the country was in a state of crisis became more and more widespread. Bismarck's Bonapartist regime and his conservative alliance were faced with a severe test. In the face of the economic, social and political effects of uneven economic growth the political elites in Berlin could not stand idly by: overseas expansion was one of the countermeasures aimed at easing this critical situation. 'Industrial development in Germany which has resulted in overproduction drives Germany to seek the acquisition of colonies'; this opinion of the French ambassador in Berlin was shared by numerous other observers, and the decision-makers too.[16]

16. *Documents Diplomatiques Français*, 1 ser. v, p. 427 (28 Sept. 1884).

While the representatives of the major economic interests were urgently calling for governmental support, Bismarck did initiate strong measures designed to help the export industries. A variety of measures was introduced: subsidies for steamship lines; the establishment of bank branches overseas; consular support for the export trade; special rates on railways and canals for export goods; preferential treatment under the tariff of 1879 for export industries. These measures must all be viewed together in order to recognise the way in which the interventionist state pushed its way forward. The policy which led to the acquisition of colonies in Africa and in the Pacific was only one of the methods whereby the state promoted foreign trade. Furthermore, the importance of the fact that national economic development no longer took place in relative isolation—as had been the case while the British were establishing their unique monopoly in the world markets—can hardly be overestimated. Now development was bound up with a bitter economic competition on a worldwide scale between a number of industrial states, each grappling with similar problems and effects of growth. David Landes has called this competitive struggle 'the most important single factor' among the pre-conditions for the 'new imperialism'. It looked futile to hope for success in this struggle unless the state gave energetic backing.[17]

There is little doubt that the 'open-door' policy remained Bismarck's ideal; he was still able to pursue it in China and in the Congo. If England and France had guaranteed free trade in Africa, unrestricted commercial expansion would have satisfied Bismarck's economic aims. But the crucial reasons which induced him from 1883–4 onwards to acquiesce in a gradual formalisation of imperial control were twofold: on the one hand the internal pressures resulting from the crisis were mounting and had to be reduced; on the other, the end of the free trade era overseas appeared imminent. In other words, the obvious disadvantages of the state playing a passive role were beginning to outweigh the equally obvious disadvantages of increased state activity. In West Africa it seemed that Germany was about to be completely dependent on other colonial powers with protective, even prohibitive tariffs. In South Africa, East Africa, and New Guinea, Great Britain and her colonies appeared to be on the verge of seizing further territory. It was believed in Berlin that unless the government acted, these rivals, with their 'preclusive' imperialism, would definitely gain ascendancy. There was an unmistakable fear of

17. D. S. Landes, *The Unbound Prometheus*, (Cambridge, Cambridge Univ. Press, 1969), p. 240.

being left out in the cold. Bülow's often quoted phrase of 'a place in the sun' or Rosebery's of 'pegging out claims for the future' also described an attitude that was influential during the preceding decade of the 1880s. So Bismarck gradually yielded to the pincer movement from without and within, to the threatening dangers of overseas competition and to the mounting desire to cope with the crisis caused by an explosive and unstable industrialisation. His expansionism sought to protect present advantages and potential opportunities from the claims of rival powers in such a way that he finally had to pay the price of formal colonial rule.

In many ways overseas expansion remained for Bismarck a question for which he did not have any rigid answer. He used both free trade and protectionist methods, state subsidies and direct intervention; he followed the trader and sometimes created for him areas where he could begin to operate. This wide variety of measures of assistance was directed towards one permanent objective—that of assuring, securing, and increasing economic advantages. Actual trading opportunities were to be defended, future possibilities kept open, and last, but not least, the business community was to be reassured of the state's readiness to assist it in overcoming the severe problems of the crisis. Expansion was a part of the anticyclical economic policy intended to counteract the pessimism of the depression years and to stimulate business. The intention always remained the same: to take pressure off the home market by extending foreign trade, to stimulate an economic revival and thereby to reduce the strain on the social and political system.

There is, of course, no empirical way of determining whether state support for foreign trade, state protection for foreign investment, or the formal acquisition of colonies did in fact ease the fluctuations of the German economy or even lead to the phase of recovery from 1886 onwards. On the other hand it is quite clear that, of the three important methods by which modern governments seek to control economic growth—monetary, financial, and foreign trade policies— the first two were unable to sustain Bismarck's economic policy during the period of extremely unsteady growth after 1873. Since the Reichsbank held to the gold standard, monetary policy could not supplement economic policy. Again, since there was no central, government-controlled institution, through which national financial policy could be made to influence the economy of the whole Reich, budgetary policy could also contribute little. Thus, according to the view then prevalent, the only remaining field of action where anti-

cyclical policies could operate was that of foreign trade. The government took exactly this course. First it experimented with the protection of the home market, then it concentrated increasingly on the
promotion of foreign trade by the state. 'If the German people as a
whole finds that its clothes are too tight-fitting at home', Bismarck
argued in 1884, then 'we are forced to grant protection to German
initiatives' abroad.[18]

The early Germany interventionist state did take the first important
steps towards subjecting the process of economic growth to social
control. The explosive forces released by unsteady economic growth
had shown themselves to be too dangerous to be left any longer to the
'invisible hand' described by Adam Smith. Henry A. Bueck, for three
decades chief executive of the Central Association of German Manufacturers and one of the leading champions of the conservative alliance,
was soon to express a view which had gained much ground. 'It is now
generally recognised that economic prosperity is the most important
task of modern civilised states', he said in 1906. 'The main task of
power politics (*Grosse Politik*) today is to ensure and promote this
prosperity under all circumstances.'[19]

4. Social imperialism and the defence of the *status quo*

Bueck's revealing statement leads on to our second problem. Not
only was the interventionist state compelled gradually to extend state
interference in order to guarantee material welfare and social stability,
but it also realised, at a time when old political traditions were
crumbling away and the charismatic authority of the Chancellor was
coming more and more under attack, that this wide field of socio-
economic policy provided new possibilities whereby traditional
authority could be legitimised. In the same way successful imperialist
policies promised to help to legitimise governmental authority
which more and more was being questioned. On the one hand
pragmatic expansionism followed the dynamics of irregular economic
growth and served as a means of providing an anticyclical therapy.
On the other, it took over special domestic functions of integrating
conflicting forces and of diverting attention from internal problems.
This way imperialism acted as a social safety-valve. It gave Bismarck

18. Bismarck to the Budget Committee of the Reichstag, 23 June 1884, *Akten des Reichstags*,
vol. 2621, 186, Deutsches Zentralarchiv I, Potsdam.
19. H. Kaelble, *Industrielle Interessenpolitik in der wilhelminischen Gesellschaft, 1894–1914*,
(Berlin, 1967), p. 149.

the chance of exploiting the colonial movement for domestic and electoral ends and of using the unifying effects of this propaganda to cover up the severe social and political tensions within the Reich. In this way too he strengthened his own political position as a Bonapartist dictator and revived the battered prestige of the government.

The unstable economic growth after 1873 subjected the socio-economic and political structure of the German empire to constant strains which intensified the pressure on the Chancellor to keep the elites and the people satisfied with his authoritarian leadership. From the end of the 1870s social imperialism became increasingly important for him as a tactic. This was so because of developments which were functionally and causally related to the basic socio-economic changes after 1873. Six years of the most severe economic depression were then followed in 1878–79 by the bitter quarrel about the protective tariffs, about the new conservative course of the Reich government, about the purge of the liberal bureaucracy and about the plans for state monopolies in industry. At the same time the National Liberal Party disintegrated, whereas the Social Democrats grew stronger each year.

Between 1873 and 1879 all the egalitarian aspects of modern nationalist ideology were revealed as illusions as the harsh reality of the class structure of an industrial society broke through to the surface of the new authoritarian state. Since Bismarck and the social forces supporting his policies had failed to institutionalise the possibility of that legitimate parliamentary opposition which is required by the constitutional structure of any modern industrial society attempting to be equal to the demands of constant social change, he had freed the political and social system of the Reich from legitimate pressures to bring about reform and modernisation. However, this increased the pressure to stabilise the traditional structures. Around 1880 Bismarck discovered the potential of overseas policy, both as a long-term integrating factor which helped to stabilise an anachronistic social and power structure, and as a tactical electoral gambit. He recognised that imperialism could provide 'a new objective for the Germans'; he hoped 'to steer the Germans towards new paths' abroad,[20] away from the numerous problems at home. Thus imperialism became an integrative force in a recently founded state which lacked stabilising historical traditions and which was unable to conceal its sharp class divisions.

When Bismarck recognised those domestic possibilities of imperi-

20. M. v. Hagen, 'Graf Wolff-Metternich über Haldane', *Deutsche Zukunft* **3** (1935), p. 5 (Metternich quoting Bismarck).

alism, he did not hesitate to exploit them. The ideological consensus that had grown up showed him that some of the necessary prerequisites were fulfilled; the enthusiasm for colonies was sufficiently widespread; its potential appeal was promising enough to act as a rallying point and electoral issue; it also gave sufficient scope to illusions and fears for a well-aimed propaganda which represented the colonial policy as a decision of fundamental importance for the material, social and political welfare of the Reich. The growing enthusiasm for colonial empire can surely be understood as a crisis ideology channelling the emotional tensions, the hysteria, and the growing frustration—which then, as later, accompanied periods of economic depressions—towards a vague external goal. In the terms of social psychology, the 'colonial fever' often worked as a form of escapism from the socio-economic and political problems resulting from Germany's transformation into an industrial society. The parallels with the political antisemitism of the 1870s, another form of the same escapism, are obvious.

Because of the colonial conflicts with Great Britain, Bismarck deliberately fostered anglophobic sentiments. This *Englandhass* was an especially appropriate instrument for diverting the pent-up pressures of internal problems towards the periphery and towards foreign opponents, because England, the powerful rival with an almost irretrievable lead in world markets, had increasingly come to be seen as a competitor against whom antipathies could easily be activated. Again, to some extent, German anglophobia was given the function of externalising anticapitalist sentiments by directing it against the capitalist state *par excellence*. Bismarck himself may have thought that he would be able to keep control of these currents, but the long-term effect of his crude anglophobic nationalism proved to be a severe burden for German policy in the 1890s and after.

Apart from following the expansive tendencies of an industrial state, German imperialism also served to assert the supremacy of the traditional ruling elites and to preserve the social hierarchy and authoritarian power structure. This social and domestic side of imperialism, this primacy of the internal political constellation should probably be considered the most important of Bismarck's (and, for that matter, of his successors') motives. Here was the juncture, as it were, where the tradition of the Prussian 'revolution from above', continued by Bonapartist methods, was transformed into the social imperialism of an advanced industrial state.

Thus all the policies of the 'conservative alliance' which had been pursued since the middle of the 1870s—the policy of protective tariffs, the 'purification' of the bureaucracy, the antisocialist laws and the new social policy, together with the tentative anticyclical policy and imperialism—belong to one and the same socio-economic and, above all, the same political context, as the government sought not only to restrain the dynamics of the industrial society, but also to exploit them as means of defending the *status quo* inside Germany.

In the event such a policy was not unlike labour of Sisyphus, involving as it did a never-ending attempt to shore up the politically and socially threatened position of the ruling classes, as well as Bismarck's own autocratic position at the peak of the pyramid of power. He himself was clearly aware of this aspect. Again and again he described the defensive functions of his measures. He remained aware of the fact that the Reich was a very precarious structure and he never lost his pessimism about whether it was possible to stabilise it at all. But he did continue to believe that the Reich could be permanently assured only if the traditional ruling classes were preserved, supported by a compliant conservative bureaucracy and a military machine independent of parliament and run on semi-absolutist lines. Secretly he felt that the situation may well have been hopeless. Nevertheless he thought defence worth while, regardless of the cost to society as a whole. Holstein, in spite of his increasing criticism of the Chancellor, admitted that only Bismarck could 'accomplish . . . the greatest of all tasks, that of holding back the revolution'.[21]

If one views imperialism as an integral part of Bismarck's struggle to defend his ideas of social order and his own power position, then one can understand his statement made to Ambassador Münster in London that 'for internal reasons the colonial question . . . is one of vital importance for us'. It is well known that Bismarck was very reticent in his use of terms like 'vital interest'. If he did decide to express the matter this way, then it was because he ascribed to imperialism such an important domestic function that he viewed 'the position of the government at home as being dependent on its success'. In 1886 Herbert v. Bismarck, at that time German Secretary of Foreign Affairs, declared on his father's instructions that it had 'been this concern for domestic politics' which had 'made it essential for us' to embark on formal colonial expansion, 'since all those elements loyal to the Reich have the keenest interest in the success of our colonising efforts'. This reveals the same social imperialist link

21. F. v. Holstein, *Die Geheimen Papiere*, (Göttingen, 1957), ii, p. 181.

with domestic policy that can be seen in President Cleveland's assessment of American expansion in Latin America, when he said that it was not a question of foreign policy, but 'the most distinct of home questions' upon the solution of which the 'welfare' of the United States depended.[22]

Thus Bismarck's overseas policy was also a component of his policy of preserving the *status quo* in state and society. Although he was familiar with the social Darwinism of his time and recognised that struggle was the essence of politics, he did have a vision of a state of ultimate social and political peace, free of permanent conflict. In spite of all his predilections for *Realpolitik* he pursued the illusory conservative utopia of a finally ordered and static community. There is, however, in the industrial world of permanent social change hardly any other utopia which is more dangerous and more certain to fail than this conservative endeavour to freeze the historically outdated structure of society. In historical perspective, therefore, the dilemma of Bismarck's policies, and thus also of his social imperialism, is to be found in the fact that his ideas of a conservative utopia induced him to react to a period of rapid development by repressive and divertionary measures, whereas a truly realistic *Realpolitik* should have tried to keep in step with the process of democratisation that accompanies —and partly is caused by—industrial growth. Like many others after him, Bismarck sought to slow down the irresistible process of modernisation.

This is not to say, however, there were not present in his Bonapartist system some prerequisites for a short-term success, among them a capable leadership, a strong bureaucratic machine, a relatively explicit independence of the Chancellor from society and from extreme influences from the right and left. Yet basically, in the long run, the regime's policies faced an insoluble problem. Modernisation seems to be impossible without a transformation of the social structure and of the power relationships existing within it; and similarly it is impossible without social and policital emancipation, if peace at home and abroad is to be preserved. The fatal effects of the government's policy, whereby the political control of the pre-industrial ruling classes was preserved during the period of intensive industrialisation, became absolutely clear between 1914 and 1929, when these old

22. *Große Politik der Europäisehen Kabinette*, iv. p. 96. H. v. Bismarck to Plessen, 14 Oct. 1886, Reichskolonialamt, vol. 603, p. 21–29, Deutsches Zentralarchiv I; K. v. Rantzau an Auswärtiges Amt, 29 Sept. 1886, *ibid*, 13; G. F. Parker, *Recollections of G. Cleveland*, (New York, 1909), p. 271.

structures crumbled. Until that time these policies had helped to create the dangerous conditions which allowed fascism in its most radical form to succeed in Germany.

5. Social imperialism after Bismarck

A glance at German policy after Bismarck's dismissal shows the continuity of strategy which he initiated. The basis of social-conservative and social-imperialist policy remained the conservative alliance between big business and the landowning classes which was one of the inheritances of the depression of 1873–79. Finance Minister v. Miquel, one of the powerful figures of the Wilhelminian administration, explained the programme of his cartel in 1897 by claiming that only imperialism was able to 'divert' the revolutionary elements and 'to put the nation's feelings . . . on a common footing'. Again Admiral v. Tirpitz produced a classical statement of social imperialist aims in the decades before 1914 when he argued that 'in this new and important national task' of imperialism and 'in the economic gains that will result from it, we have a powerful palliative against both educated and uneducated social democrats'. Wilhelminian *Weltpolitik* had its innermost origins in the internal class divisions which had to be covered by a vigorous social imperialism. Only this way—as Chancellor v. Bülow expounded most frankly—could the tensions between the authoritarian state, the landed nobility and the feudalised bourgeoisie on the one hand, and on the other, the advancing forces of parliamentarisation and democratisation be alleviated. 'Only a successful foreign policy can help, reconcile, conciliate, rally together, and unify' wrote Bülow, who went on to describe German imperialism as a policy that was intended to veil the internal divisions by diverting attention overseas. What else was Privy Councillor v. Holstein thinking of when, on account of the hopelessly confused domestic situation, he declared: 'Kaiser Wilhelm's government needs some tangible success abroad which will then have a beneficial effect at home. Such a success can be expected as a result of a European war, a risky policy on a world wide scale, or as the result of territorial acquisitions outside Europe.'[23]

---

23. Miquel, quoted by H. Böhme, *Deutschlands Weg zur Großmacht*, (Köln, 1966), p. 316; A. v. Tirpitz, *Erinnerungen*, (Leipzig, 1920), p. 52; Bülow, quoted by J. Röhl, *Deutschland ohne Bismarck*, (Tübingen, 1969), p. 229; cf. Bülow's *Imperial Germany*, (London, 1914) and the excellent discussion of it in Hugh Stretton's brilliant book: *The Political Sciences*, (London, Routledge, 1969), pp. 77–88; Holstein, quoted by Wehler, *Bismarck*, p. 499.

Just as in Bismarck's time the social imperialism of the Wilhelminian government fulfilled its most important function in slowing down the process of social and political emancipation. As a blueprint for political action it remains of fundamental importance to any consideration of continuity in modern German history. 'After the fall of Bismarck, there was a growing inclination to neutralize "the inherited" deep discrepancies between the social structure and the political system, which had barely taken into account the changed social situation brought about by industrialisation', Karl D. Bracher, the eminent historian of modern German history has declared. And this neutralization

> was achieved by diverting the pressure of interests towards objectives abroad—in the sense of social imperialism which helped conceal the need for the long overdue reform of the internal structure of Germany. Tirpitz in particular understood Germany's imperialism—together with its new instrument of power, the battle fleet—in this sense. He, too, was aiming for a conservative utopia, but one in which the place of the preindustrial elite was to be taken by the propertied and educated bourgeoisie. For him the reference group of social imperialism had changed, nevertheless this strategy still offered plenty of advantages to the old elites who for the time being profited more from it than the bourgeoisie. The motive forces continued to propel German policies on war aims and annexations during the First World War, for these policies also demonstrably aimed at postponing further the much delayed internal restructuring of Germany. Once more a successful expansionist foreign policy was supposed to be a substitute for a modern domestic policy.[24]

Even the debacle of 1918 did not finally destroy the seductive force of that social imperialism which delayed emancipation at home by means of expansion abroad. One last extreme effort was added, not many years later, to the fateful continuity of this policy pursued since the 1870s. If one pursues this specific line of development, the red thread of social imperialism, then one will be able to trace a line linking Bismarck, Miquel, Bülow and Tirpitz to the extreme social imperialism of the National Socialist variety, which once again sought to block domestic progress by breaking out first towards the *Ostland* and then overseas, thus diverting attention from the loss of all liberty at home; although the racist ideology of German fascism

24. K. D. Bracher, *Deutschland zwischen Demokratie und Diktatur*, (Munich, 1964), p. 155 and 'Imperialismus', in Bracher and E. Fraenkel, eds, *Internationale Beziehungen*, (Frankfurt, 1969), p. 123.

added a new element which in the long run was meant to restructure, biologically and qualitatively, the entire history of future mankind. The spell of the German conservative utopia remained dominant for about seventy years.

> However long and circuitous the path leading from Bismarck to Hitler may have been, the founder of the Reich appears to be the man responsible for a change of policy, at least for legitimising a policy, the ultimate and fatal consummation of which has, in our own time, become all too obvious.[25]

DISCUSSION

What type of theory is it? Wehler was asked a number of questions about the nature of his 'eclectic' theory. One concerned the status of the separate factors within it: economic, social and political. Did their importance vary according to particular circumstances? Or did the economic factor always predominate? In answer Wehler stated that in a social science theory it was not necessary to specify the weight of the different factors. What he had done was to combine them together in rather a loose way to produce a formula of general applicability. The weight of different factors was different at different times and could only be tested by empirical investigation. The problem of the motives for imperial expansion was too complex to be tackled by a narrow economic argument. It was necessary to study at various interrelated levels.

Wehler was always asked why he had not combined the four most important economic factors—the rapid growth from a backward position, unstable growth, the importance of foreign trade and the importance of growing international competition—into one general economic theory. He replied that the dominant feature of the period under discussion was one of unstable growth with many recessions. This was something about which the static models employed by economists had nothing to say. It was also something which had to be isolated for particular discussion.

How universal is the theory? Several questioners asked whether the theory could be applied to countries other than Germany. Wehler answered them by saying that, in his opinion, it certainly applied to the United States. America, like Germany, experienced two depressions in the 1880s. There was also another one between 1893 and 1896 which produced what the American historian Richard Hofstadter has called 'the psychic crisis of the 1890s'. A number of different phenomena—the appearance of 'armies' of unemployed, the rise of Populism, the near takeover of the American Federation of Labour by the Socialists in 1894—produced a general feeling of alarm based on the belief that the social forces operating in the American political system and determining American political culture were changing dangerously fast. The personal diaries of several cabinet ministers and

---

25. H. Rothfels, 'Probleme einer Bismarck-Biographie', *Deutsche Beiträge*, ii (Munich, 1948), 170.

other Presidential advisers reveal that this situation was taken very seriously in Washington. In the opinion of many, social revolution could only be averted by some form of external relief. This, in turn, led to a 'crisis policy' based on the extension of America's informal empire in the East.

Wehler also believed that a similar model could be used to explain French expansion under Napoleon III and Russian expansion towards the East in the 1880s.

Unstable growth, social tension and expansion. Wehler was asked to explain the links which existed between efforts to deal with certain pressing social problems at home and the argument that it was necessary to expand overseas. He replied by making a number of separate points. One concerned the United States where politicians were well aware that the right functioning of the political system depended on economic welfare. In their opinion, such welfare could only be obtained by an expansion of foreign trade. Again, in Germany, his own researches in the Bismarck archives had revealed that the Chancellor was very much better informed about economic matters than most people supposed. Over a long period of time he had received a fortnightly letter from his banker containing detailed information about the ups and downs of the economy. Lastly, there was great pressure for expansion from the business community, on which the depressions of the 1870s and 1880s had had a measurable effect. This pressure was particularly strong from those industries which had been the leaders in the first stage of industrialisation—cotton in America and Britain, iron and steel in America and Germany—but which now tended to lag behind. It was the American iron and steel interests, for example, which supported the drive into Latin America and northern China.

Gains from expansion: illusion or reality? Several questions were asked about the real nature of the gains made from trade expansion. To these Wehler replied that it was only possible to give an answer on an industry by industry basis. It was also necessary to look at the way particular industries were able to work to full capacity and thus to maintain their prices at home by sending only a small proportion of their products overseas. This was well illustrated by W. A. Williams's study of American agriculture at the end of the nineteenth century.

Nevertheless, it was also true that in some cases overseas expansion was based on the pursuit of an illusion. In the case of Germany, for example, there were exaggerated hopes of finding a huge African market, most of which were disappointed. Another, related, question concerned the extent to which statesmen like Bismarck shared this illusion or merely used it for their own ends. This was difficult to answer, said Wehler, but in his opinion Bismarck did not share it. Certainly there was evidence to show that he realised that the African market would take twenty or thirty years to exploit. It was also necessary to point out that Bismarck was very much influenced by the contemporary belief that it was vital to peg out claims for the future, that the great powers were engaged in some kind of race the outcome of which would determine their future for a long time to come. There were thus strong motives for what has been called 'preclusive' imperialism.

The success of social imperialism. Lastly, it was pointed out that a policy of social imperialism was often resorted to in the nineteenth century as a means of preventing working-class consciousness from developing into a revolutionary movement. There were many examples of this in Britain and elswhere. But could the success of this policy be explained only in terms of the creation of an ideological national feeling behind colonial drives? Or did the working class benefit objectively from such a policy? In reply Wehler asserted that, for whatever reason, the Bismarckian policy of seeking to contain the power of the Social Democrats by an emphasis on overseas expansion had been fatally successful. By the early 1900s most of the Social Democrats had come to accept the fact that Germany possessed colonies and that the working class derived some benefits from them. This left only a small group of radical dissenters like Rosa Luxemburg to continue to make a sustained protest against German colonial policy.

IV

Some African and third world theories of imperialism

Thomas Hodgkin

Almost all the works on the theory of imperialism available in the West are Eurocentric in two important ways: they are by Europeans and, very largely, they are about the economies, the societies, the political systems of European states. In the essay which follows Thomas Hodgkin tries to redress the balance by insisting on the contributions to theory made by non-European writers from the late nineteenth century onwards.

While the majority of those whose ideas he describes fall, very broadly, within the Marxist–Leninist tradition, they diverge from it in a number of important respects. One is their emphasis on cultural relativism—the impossibility of trying to rank societies on some scale of 'higher' or 'lower'; a second is the stress they place on the division created between Europeans and non-Europeans by the colonial experience itself, by the fact that one was the coloniser, the other the colonised.

But there are important implications for other types of theory as well. These writers are convinced that any general theory must assign a vital role to the effect of imperialism on non-European societies. Again, there is their insistence that the relationship between coloniser and colonised be defined not only in economic terms but also in respect to the socio-political and ideological attitudes and beliefs with which it is inevitably accompanied.

My purpose in this paper is to discuss a small sample of the theories of imperialism that have been developed by its consumers, or victims, in Africa primarily, but to some degree also in other regions of the third world. I want to consider particularly whether there are any continuing themes running through the writings of those late-nineteenth- and twentieth-century theorists who have been interested in the phenomenon of imperialism and have sought to explain it.

I also want to consider what is the importance of their ideas in any attempt to construct a general theory. I have chosen this topic partly because I believe that there is still a strong tendency among Westerners to ignore, or undervalue, or misunderstand non-Western contributions in this as in other fields of political and social thought.

1. The authors of the theories

First, let me say something about the people whose ideas I propose to discuss. Though my point of departure is African political thinking there is an obvious sense in which, culturally and intellectually, Africa forms a continuum with the West Indies and Black America in one direction and the wider Islamic world in the other. So it would seem reasonable, indeed essential, in a discussion of this kind also to take account of the theories of Edward Blyden and Marcus Garvey, Aimé Césaire and Frantz Fanon, Jamal al-din al-Afghani and Sultan Galiyev, among others. Historically these theorists can be thought of as belonging to three roughly distinguishable periods: the late nineteenth-century phase of imperial expansion; the 1900–45 phase of partially effective colonial domination; and the post-1945 phase of the rise of national movements and partial decolonisation. Though certain common themes do, I believe, recur in their writings, they were naturally much affected in their attitude to the phenomenon of imperialism and their mode of explaining it by the very different historical situations in which they severally found themselves. If I pay particular attention here to the ideas of a group of Paris-based West Africans of the interwar period—Tovalou Houénou, Lamine Senghor, Garan Kouyaté and Emile Faure—this is partly because I regard these ideas as of great intrinsic interest, partly because they have recently been the subject of an excellent and detailed study by Dr James Spiegler, to whom I am much indebted.[1]

I should perhaps add that, in speaking of 'theories' and 'theorists' of imperialism, I am not suggesting that those whose ideas I shall be discussing necessarily presented them in an organised and systematic way. In many cases their views were embedded in polemical and propaganda works, in newspaper articles, lectures, speeches and reports concerned with immediate contemporary problems. What marks them out, I think, is that they were sharply aware of modern Western imperialism as a relatively new, historically very important

1. J. S. Spiegler, 'Aspects of nationalist thought among French-speaking West Africans, 1921–1939' (Oxford Univ. D. Phil. thesis, 1968); hereafter cited as *Spiegler*.

global phenomenon, which needed to be understood—understood, that is, in order that it might be the more effectively resisted, modified, or transformed. In this they differed from those who continued to employ traditional categories of explanation, who, for example, saw the occupation of Sokoto by the Christians in 1903 as an historical event comparable with the sack of Mecca by the Qarmatians in 930 or the overthrow of the Abbasid caliphate and the sack of Baghdad by the Mongols in 1258.[2]

2. The scope of the theories

What specific contribution then have African and third-world theorists made to the effort to construct a general theory of imperialism? One way of approaching this problem is to consider what answers they have given to particular questions arising within this general field of enquiry. One such question—perhaps the most basic—is: What is a theory of imperialism meant to be about? What should it seek to explain? On this there seems to be a fairly clear consensus. A theory of imperialism should seek to explain, first: How did there come into being the particular kinds of relationship of domination and subjection between the industrially and technologically advanced, 'Western', and the industrially and technologically retarded, 'non-Western', societies that were established roughly by the turn of the nineteenth century? In what respects does modern Western imperialism differ from other empire-building processes in other kinds of historical situation? Second, what have been the main effects of Western imperialism, and the colonial and semi-colonial systems to which it gave rise, on the societies of the colonisers and the colonised, the dominant and the subject peoples, and on the overall world situation? Third, how can this entire system of relationships, and the attitudes arising therefrom, be abolished or transformed? What are the basic problems of liberation, or decolonisation, and how can these be resolved?

Three footnotes seem worth making at this stage. One, already touched on, is the necessary emphasis in most of these writers on the relationship between theory and practice. This is already evident in

2. These analogies were in fact drawn by Ahmad ibn Sad, the Alkalin Gwandu, and quoted by the Wazir of Sokoto, Muhammad al-Bukhari ibn Ahmad, in his 1903 *Risala*, justifying his collaboration with the British after the occupation. See R. A. Adeleye, 'The dilemma of the Wazir: the place of the *Risalat al-wazir ila ahl al-ilm wa'l-tadabbur* in the history of the conquest of the Sokoto Caliphate', *Journal of the Historical Society of Nigeria*, iv, 2 (June 1968), 297–8 and 308–9.

the approach of a nineteenth-century theorist like Afghani, who states his central problem very simply: 'What is the cause of the poverty, indigence, helplessness and distress of the Muslims, and is there a cure for this important phenomenon and great misfortune or not?'[3] (One exception to this generalisation is the later Blyden, who had come to accept a quasi-Hegelian belief in the cunning of historical reason which would ensure that, like the slave trade, Western imperialism would contribute to the eventual regeneration and renaissance of the African peoples and the Negro race.)[4] For thinkers of the period of maximum imperialism like Lamine Senghor and Kouyaté, and of course for the generality of post-1945 theorists, the purpose of understanding imperialism is conceived as being, essentially, to end it.

Second, it follows from this view of what a theory of imperialism is meant to be about that any theory which concerns itself only with some limited aspect of the questions I have referred to is necessarily inadequate. For example, theories which are exclusively concerned with the historical genesis of modern Western imperialism, or with mechanisms of control and the changing patterns of relationships between imperial rulers and indigenous collaborating groups, and which take no account of the social consequences of imperialism (both for the colonisers and the colonised) or of the problems of liberation and decolonisation, these (from the standpoint of most third-world theorists) are considered to be, at best, very partial and incomplete, at worst, modes of justifying the empire-building process and the colonial, or post-colonial, order. This is not to say, of course, that third-world theorists are uninterested in such limited questions— from Afghani on a fair amount has been written on the role of collaborating groups—only that their first requirement of a theory of imperialism is that it should be, in this sense, comprehensive.

A third point, somewhat connected with the foregoing, is that, understandably, third-world theorists have not in the main been deeply interested in that particular group of problems with which Western writers, both Marxist and anti-Marxist, have tended to be preoccupied: What (to put it crudely) was the nature of the drives, or contradictions, or structural changes in the advanced capitalist countries, or within the Western world in general, which generated,

3. Jamal al-din al-Afghani, 'The benefits of philosophy', in Nikki R. Keddie, *An Islamic Response to Imperialism* (Berkeley and Los Angeles, Univ. of California Press, 1968), p. 120.
4. See Hollis R. Lynch, *Edward Wilmot Blyden, Pan-Negro Patriot, 1832–1912* (London, Oxford Univ. Press, 1967), ch. particularly p. 197.

or helped to generate, modern Western imperialism? For the most part they have, I think, asserted or assumed that these drives arose directly out of the interests of the ruling classes in the advanced countries, whether these were interests in loot, or raw materials, or markets, or investment outlets, or job opportunites for the bourgeoisie, or military glory for the officer class, or varying combinations of these at different historical moments. There are some exceptions to this generalisation. Some, like the early Nkrumah, have adopted in essentials, a Leninist view.[5] Abdoulaye Ly, in his book *Les Masses africaines et l'actuelle condition humaine*, put forward an interesting analysis of the historical roots of imperialism on lines broadly similar to Rosa Luxemburg.[6] But in general these theorists have been much more concerned with Western imperialism as a phenomenon in African, or Islamic, or third-world, or indeed in world history, and particularly with the problem of explaining its overwhelming global success and the peculiar vulnerability of their own, non-Western, societies in the late-nineteenth-century historical context. At one level this can be explained, as Afghani constantly insisted, in terms of the correlation between political and military power and the mastery of modern science and technology:

> The Europeans have now [1882] put their hands on every part of the world. The English have reached Afghanistan; the French have seized Tunisia. In reality this usurpation, aggression and conquest has not come from the French or the English. Rather it is science that everywhere manifests its greatness and power. Ignorance had no alternative to prostrating itself humbly before science and acknowledging its submission.
>
> In reality, sovereignty has never left the abode of science. However, this true ruler, which is science, is continually changing capitals. Sometimes it has moved from East to West, and other times from West to East.[7]

But this merely pushes the problem of explanation a stage further back. How is one to account for the relative scientific and technological backwardness of the non-Western world in this historical situation? For Afghani a primary factor was the inadequacies of the intelligentsia (in Muslim society, the conservative *ulama*) and the traditional system

5. Kwame Nkrumah, *Towards Colonial Freedom* (1947; London, Heinemann, 1962).
6. Abdoulaye Ly, *Les Masses africaines et l'actuelle condition humaine* (Paris, 1956).
7. al-Afghani, 'Lecture on teaching and learning' in Keddie, *An Islamic Response to Imperialism*, pp. 102–3.

of education. 'Is it not a fault for a percipient sage . . . when the world has changed from one state to another and he does not raise his hand from the sleep of neglect?'[8] Others were interested in the internal contradictions within African—or third-world—societies at this period, and the extent to which these assisted the process of imperialist penetration, and thus began to explore questions to which the modern generation of historians has returned. Kouyaté, for example, stressed the importance of African internal political divisions in this context:

> Such disunity in face of the colonial solidarity of imperialist Europe in the nineteenth century brought Africa to her present state. . . . If Samory Touré, Behanzin, Rabat [Rábih], Albouri N'Diaye, Ahmadou Cheikhou, Babemba Traoré and other African kings fell in defence of their country, it was because they were disunited. Certain necessities of our national wars, encouraged and exploited by European slavers and imperialists, may sometimes have harmed them in the eyes of the masses.[9]

3. Characteristics of the epoch of imperialism

A second, related, question is whether there has ever in fact been an 'epoch of imperialism', an *ère coloniale*, in any intelligible sense of the term, and, if so, what have been its distinguishing characteristics. It seems to have become fashionable among some Western academics to regard it as an empty concept. The theorists of the consumers on the other hand, particularly those who lived through and experienced the phase of maximum imperialism, seem never to have seriously doubted the existence of a reality corresponding with the idea. Though the problem of distinguishing historical periods was not one of their main concerns, they were, I think, broadly agreed that certain fundamental changes in the relationships between Western societies and their own societies had taken place by the end of the nineteenth, or beginning of the twentieth, century, and that these changes possessed a certain coherence—indeed, as they understood them, were aspects of a general strategy of the imperial powers. The changes which they regarded as particularly significant were in the main the most obvious ones: the loss of sovereignty of existing states and stateless societies; the eventual defeat of movements of military and political resistance; the physical removal, by deportation, imprisonment, execution, etc., of resisting and non-collaborating rulers; the continu-

8. al-Afghani, 'The benefits of philosophy', in Keddie, *op. cit.*, p. 121.
9. Garan Kouyaté, 'Il y a 35 ans, le 12 mars 1894', in *Race Nègre* (1929), cited in *Spiegler*, p. 156.

ing process of 'pacification', i.e. of military operations against primary
resistance movements; the imposition by degrees of a colonial
administrative network, a hierarchy of salaried officials drawn from
the metropolitan bourgeoisie, enjoying a very wide spectrum of
powers in relation to the indigenous population; the development of
parallel systems of control over their commercial and cultural life,
through extraterritorial companies, missions, etc.; the construction
of a framework of institutions (e.g. the *Indigénat* in French territories)
designed to preserve European dominance for an indefinite period;
the organisation of a system of collaborating groups, drawn from
chiefs, marabouts, elements of the bourgeoisie and petty-bourgeoisie
(where these existed); the blocking, as far as practicable, of precolonial channels of communication across colonial frontiers; the
elaboration of an ideology of imperialism designed to explain and
justify the new structure of social and political relationships and the
new forms of European power, and the feeding back of this ideology,
and the racist attitudes associated with it, into the colonising society.

African theorists writing during the 'epoch of imperialism' and
able to take a retrospective view had in general no doubt that they
had moved into a new phase of history: that to live in the Anglo-
Egyptian Sudan was quite different from living in the Khalifa's
Sudan; to live in French Dahomey was quite different from living in
Behanzin's Dahomey; to live in Southern Rhodesia was quite
different from living in Lobengula's Ndbele state. Those living and
writing at a somewhat earlier period, in the late nineteenth century,
varied in the extent to which they grasped the nature of the changes
taking place. It is partly the relative clarity of his perceptions that
makes Afghani such an interesting writer. But as early as 1885, on the
conclusion of the Berlin Conference, the *Lagos Observer* described the
process of imperial partition in radical nationalist terms: 'The world
has perhaps never witnessed until now such high-handed robbery
on so large a scale. Africa is helpless to prevent it . . . It is on the cards
that this "Christian" business can only end, at no distant date, in the
annihilation of the natives.'[10]

These theorists were, however, perfectly well aware of the aspect
of continuity as well as change. They perceived, and indeed emphasised, the historical connections between the older forms of Western
dominance, ascendancy, influence, pressure, exploitation, etc., com-

10. *Lagos Observer*, 19 Feb. 1885, cited in J. F. A. Ajayi, 'Colonialism: an episode in African
history', in L. H. Gann and Peter Duignan, *Colonialism in Africa, 1870–1960; vol I, The History
and Politics of Colonialism, 1870–1914* (Cambridge, Cambridge Univ. Press, 1969), p. 507, n. 1.

bined with limited annexation, and the new model of imperialism, of which the typical expression, so far as Africa was concerned, was the establishment of organised colonial systems. The 'epoch of imperialism', they argued, must be understood as simply the most recent phase in the whole prolonged historical process by which the European nations used their superior technology and military power to enslave and subjugate non-European peoples for their own enrichment. They were particularly concerned to stress the resemblances between the underlying assumptions of modern imperialism and of the European slave trade, as a consequence of which:

> The development of African peoples was abruptly cut short and their civilization (which, in several places, had reached a highly advanced state) was most completely destroyed. These nations were later declared pagan and savage, an inferior race, destined by the Christian God to be slaves to superior Europeans.[11] . . . .

They were much interested too in the way in which the new model had developed out of the 'informal' European empires, which (so far as coastal West Africa was concerned) had been operating in one form or another since the end of the fifteenth century. Hence their interest in the alliance, or working partnership, as they saw it, between the European missionary, the trader, the politician-diplomat and the military man (or military adventurer)—which itself had ancient roots —and the part which this played in the establishment of colonial systems.[12] (Compare Charles Domingo's often quoted remark about the links between 'Christendom', 'Europeandom' and capitalism in the context of colonial Nyasaland.)[13]

Perhaps one should include another footnote at this point to make clear that the concept of an 'epoch of imperialism', as used or implied by African and third-world theorists, is entirely compatible with the notion of uneven development and overlapping phases (discussed by Barratt Brown, among others).[14] That is to say, there is nothing in

11. From the resolution on the Negro Question of the First International Congress of the League against Imperialism and Colonial Oppression, held in Brussels, 10–15 February, 1927, published in *Voix des Nègres*, March 1927, cited in *Spiegler*, p. 140, and also in *Das flammenz-eieven vam Palais Egmont* (Berlin, 1927). (Lamine Senghor presided over the Negro Commission which drafted this resolution.)
12. For an early example of the interdependence of arms supplies and missionary enterprise in Western diplomacy, see the 1514 letter from Manuel, king of Portugal, to the Oba of Benin, quoted in A. F. C. Ryder, *Benin and the Europeans, 1485–1897* (London, Longmans 1969), p. 47.
13. George Shepperson and Thomas Price, *Independent African* (Edinburgh Univ. Press 1958), pp. 163–4.
14. See ch. II above.

this conception that makes it odd or unexplainable that a rudimentary form of colonial system should have been established in coastal Algeria, for example, at a much earlier date than in Morocco; or that some states, such as Ethiopia, should have remained for the greater part of the 'epoch of imperialism' in a quasi-colonial relationship to a consortium of European powers and should only for a relatively brief period have been subjected to the formal colonial rule of a single power; or that there should have coexisted in the same geographical region at the same chronological time (e.g. north-west Africa in the early 1920s) continuing movements of resistance to colonial 'pacification', a partially fossilised precolonial monarchy embedded in a fairly typical colonial administrative apparatus, and a popular insurrectionary movement seeking to establish—and for a time in fact establishing—a modern independent republican state (the Republic of the Rif). There is indeed a sense in which one can say that decolonisation was already beginning before the imperial powers had succeeded in imposing their colonial systems. This does not, however, make the concept of an 'epoch of imperialism' otiose.

One quite serious question which arises in this connection is: Do these theorists have a clear, or agreed, view about the defining characteristics of imperialism, about what constitutes a 'colonial situation' or a 'colonial relationship'? Clearly every relationship of dominance and subjection between states, or societies, in the epoch of imperialism cannot be so described. Here there are, I think, different views. Fanon's position is interesting, partly because he develops ideas that are to be found in the writings of earlier generations of French-speaking third-world radicals. Fanon would seem to define the 'colonial situation' in terms of concepts such as violence—violence in constant and active use by the colonisers against the colonised and, potentially and in anticipation at least, by the colonised against the colonisers. With this is associated the idea of polarisation: 'The colonial world is a world cut in two, . . . a Manichaean world.' This fundamental dualism of the colonial world is expressed physically in the division between the *colons*' town, a town of well-fed whites, 'its belly always full of good things', and the native town, the medina, the reservation, a hungry town, 'a town of niggers and dirty Arabs'. 'At times this Manichaeism goes to its logical conclusion and dehumanises the native'; the European regards him as a kind of animal and refers to him in zoological terms.[15] This notion of the colonial

15. Frantz Fanon, *The Wretched of the Earth* (Harmondsworth, Penguin, 1967), pp. 29–33.

system as having as its necessary consequence the dehumanisation of
the colonised goes back at least to the early 1920s when it appears in
articles (probably by Ho Chi Minh) in the journal of the Union
Intercoloniale, *Le Paria*, which speaks of 'the abominable *indigénat*,
an institution which puts men on the same level as beasts and which
dishonours the so-called civilised world.'[16] From the standpoint of
the imperialists, 'the Algerians and Annamites are not men, but dirty
"nha que" and *"bicots"*'.[17] With this is linked the concept of the
emergence of a 'native intelligentsia', who have assimilated the oppressor's culture, been to the oppressor's universities, adopted his
forms of thought, so that 'deep down in his [the intellectual's] brain
you could always find a vigilant sentinel ready to defend the Graeco-
Latin pedestal'.[18] The existence of such an indigenous bourgeoisie—
indoctrinated with Western values, cut off from the mass of the
colonised, for whom the only values that matter are 'land, bread and
dignity' (which can only be achieved by the expulsion of the European
rulers)—as a mediating group is, for Fanon, and for representatives of
the radical tradition in general, another essential, or normal, characteristic of the colonial situation. (Note that Fanon and those who adopt
his general type of approach seem concerned to define a colonial
situation primarily in terms of its superstructure—that is, of the kind
of social–political relationships and attitudes and beliefs which it
generates, themselves capable of many variations and modifications,
based, it is assumed, on an essentially exploitative economic relationship between the colonial ruling class and the mass of the colonised.)

4. Critique of Western apologists of imperialism

Let me turn to a third question. Along what lines have these theorists
criticised the presuppositions of Western imperial historians and
apologists in general? They have made particular use of their own
form of dialectic, exposing the inadequacies of these presuppositions
(like Kant in the Antinomies of Pure Reason) by asserting their
contraries. For example, as against the classic Western (particularly
Western missionary) thesis that imperialism has meant the substitution
of 'civilised' for 'barbarous' systems of government, society, values,

16. Nguyen Ai Quôc, *Procès de la Colonisation Francaise* (Paris, 1925; Hanoi, 1946), p. 106, cited in *Spiegler*, p. 106.
17. *Ibid.*, p. 81.
18. Fanon, *The Wretched of the Earth*, p. 36.

etc.,[19] these theorists asserted the antithesis that imperialism has in fact meant the destruction of valid African, or non-Western, civilisations and the substitution of new forms of Western barbarism. In place of Africa's *anciens régimes* (whose oppressive aspects had been vastly exaggerated by colonial apologists) 'l'Europe a inauguré dans les colonies l'ère de la veritable barbarie et de la vraie sauvagerie; celle qui est faite avec science et préméditation, avec tout l'art et tout le raffinement de la civilisation', as Tovalou Houénou put it.[20]

It is worth while, perhaps, considering this particular counter-proposition, or counter-presupposition, which has played such an important part in third-world theories, in some detail, and asking: What exactly is it that is being asserted? It seems to me a somewhat complex kind of statement in which at least three distinct arguments tend to be combined, with varying degrees of emphasis on each. First, there is the proposition—self-evident so far as most third-world theorists have been concerned, but often denied or ignored by imperial historians—that the process of European penetration and conquest was itself a barbarous one: 'civilisation' had been imposed by the Europeans 'à coups des canons, à coups d'alcool et à coup de spirochète'.[21] (The continuing influence of imperialist apologetics on the treatment of this phase of history in the orthodox literature, even in the post-independence epoch, can be simply illustrated by the following sentence from a recent students' textbook on African history: 'The colonial system came into being because a number of people in Western Europe holding certain ideas in matters of religion, social policy, politics and economics came into contact with African peoples holding different ideas and living under a different system.'[22])

On this point—the essential barbarism of the 'civilising' hordes—there seems a clear consensus. Compare, for example, the West Indian, René Maran, in the preface to his famous novel, *Batouala*:

Civilisation, civilisation—the Europeans' pride and their charnelhouse of innocents. The Hindu poet, Rabindranath Tagore, one day in Tokyo,

19. For example, J. T. F. Halligay, chairman of the Methodist Mission in Yorubaland, 1886–90, cited in E. A. Ayandele, *The Missionary Impact on Modern Nigeria, 1842–1914*, (London, Longmans, 1966): 'The substitution of a civilised authority for the accursed despotism of Pagan and Mohammedan powers is a divine and gracious interposition.'

20. Tovalou Houénou, 'Le problème de la race noire', in *Action Coloniale*, (25 March 1924), cited in *Spiegler*, p. 66.

21. Houénou, in *Continents* (1 June 1924), cited in *Spiegler*, p. 62.

22. W. E. F. Ward, 'Colonial rule in West Africa', in Joseph C. Anene and Godfrey N. Brown, *Africa in the Nineteenth and Twentieth Centuries* (Ibadan, 1966), p. 308.

said what you are. You build your kingdom on corpses . . .[23]

with this more or less contemporary statement by the Tartar, Sultan Galiyev:

> It was necessary for tens of millions of natives of America and American Blacks to die and for the rich culture of the Incas to disappear completely in order that modern America, with its 'passion for peace', with its 'cosmopolitan' culture of 'progress and technology', should establish itself. The proud sky-scrapers of Chicago and New York and other towns of 'Europeanised' America were built on the bones of the 'red-skins' and of the Negroes murdered by inhuman planters, and on the smoking ruins of the Incas' cities.[24]

But it was not merely the process of European invasion and occupation that was presented as barbarous, but the colonial systems to which it gave rise, the new forms of government and administration, of economic organisation, of dominant ideology, which (as has been already suggested) involved essentially the dehumanisation of the mass of the indigenous population. To quote Tovalou Houénou again:

> Toute la fatalité qui pèse dans les tragédies éschyliennes n'approche pas la noirceur de la tragédie africaine. Sous couvert de civilisation on traque des hommes comme les fauves, on les pille, on les vole, on les tue, et ces horreurs sont presentées ensuite dans de beaux morceaux d'éloquence comme des bienfaits.[25]

Moreover, over and above the barbarism asociated with the normal working of the colonial system, Africans experienced the special barbarism of European 'wars for civilisation', particularly the 1914–18 war, in which 'the "refined" European bourgeoisie had terrified by its cruelty those whom it considered "savages"'.[26] The effect of this war on African—and third-world—political thinking and practice, the stimulus which it gave to the development of radical anticolonial movements, is of course itself a large and interesting theme. In this connection compare John Chilembwe's famous letter to the *Nyasaland Times* in December 1914, on the eve of the Nyasaland rising, quoted by George Shepperson:

23. René Maran, *Batouala* (Paris, 1948; first ed. 1921), p. 11, cited in *Spiegler*, p. 108; see also *Spiegler*, p. 103, n. 3.

24. M. Sultan Galiyev, 'La revolution sociale et l'Orient', *Zhizn National'nostey*, 42 (50), (2 Nov. 1919), cited in Alexandre Bennigsen and Chantal Quelquejay, *Les mouvements nationaux chez les Musulmans de Russie* (Paris and the Hague, 1960), p. 211.

25. Houénou, 'Le problème de la race noire', in *Spiegler*, p. 62.

26. Nguyen Ai Quôc, *Procès de la Colonisation Française*, cited in *Spiegler*, p. 107.

We understand that we have been invited to shed our innocent blood in this world's war which is now in progress throughout the wide world. On the commencement of the war we understood that it was said indirectly that Africa had nothing to do with the *civilised war*. But now we find that the poor African has already been plunged into the great war.[27]

A second element in this reinterpretation of the civilisation/ barbarism antithesis is the proposition that there is no necessary connection between the level of a people's technological development and the quality of its civilisation. This is, essentially, the cultural relativist view, which Blyden did much to foster, that terms such as 'higher' and 'lower' can be applied to levels of technological or economic development but not to civilisations; that no set of criteria exists on the basis of which one can rationally argue that the civilisation of the French bourgeoisie under the third republic was qualitatively superior to, say, the civilisation of the Segu empire under Ahmadu Shehu or the civilisation of the stateless Dogon—a proposition which has never been much favoured by the French, or for that matter the British, bourgeoisie. This view can be pushed further and developed into a Narodnik theory of the nastiness and undesirability of 'high' civilisations in general, as for example by Emile Faure in the 1930s:

> Because for centuries a few vicious rakes and whores succeeded in having palaces built for themselves at Versailles, and temples elsewhere, they're called 'civilised' . . . Peasant peoples, unambitious and hard-working, who till the land, tend their herds and venerate their ancestors, are despoiled and decimated by nations as industrious as they are inhuman.[28]

Hence Faure's particular emphasis on the brutality of 'Latin' civilisations, which acquired special importance during the Italian invasion of Ethiopia. But it was not necessary, or usual, for the thesis to be expressed in this Narodnik form. More fundamental was the assertion that, even assuming technological development was desirable for Africans, this did not at all imply the acquisition of European 'mentality' or culture: 'There's no relation between patent leather shoes, foxtrots or the Code Napoléon on the one hand and civilisation on the other. . . . It is not that Negroes can't modernise themselves within their own organisations, but Europeans stand in the way.'[29]

27. Shepperson and Price, *Independent African*, p. 234.
28. Emile Faure, 'Mon ami Indochinois', *Race Nègre* (Feb. 1932), cited in *Spiegler*, p. 233.
29. Faure, 'To be or not to be', *Race Nègre* (Feb. 1932), cited in *Spiegler*, p. 230.

The third element in this counter-presupposition is, crudely, that technological advance and social change, in a centralising, modernising direction, were in any case taking place in a number of African societies in the late eighteenth and nineteenth centuries, as a result both of internal forces and external stimuli. Note in this connection Kouyaté's very interesting assessment of Samory Turé:

> Samory's ambitions tended towards the political unification of West Africa. . . . One day history will say whether he was really a condottiere. Certainly the imperative necessity of national unity forced him to perpetrate, or to accept the perpetration of, abuses and a certain excessive rigour. A new social order is only born through the use of unflinching force against all resistance, a force just and salutary in reconstruction. Such, unfortunately, is human nature. Samory's mistake was to awaken too much fear in the Negro masses, and to have disaffected them, even though they loved him.[30]

This thesis—that Africa contained within itself the seeds of its own modernisation, and that the effect of European colonial systems was in general to retard rather than accelerate the processes of technical and social change that had been taking place during the previous century—though fairly widely accepted by contemporary African historians, was a bold generalisation when Kouyaté asserted it in 1930, challenging the imperial myth (or one version of it) that colonialism was the necessary precondition of 'the integration of Africa into the modern world'.[31]

These, I would suggest, are broadly the lines on which such theorists criticised the familiar Western 'imperialism equals civilisation' presupposition. Other similar antinomies are worth examining. For example, there is the thesis, which has played a prominent part in both ancient and modern colonial apologetics, of the 'reluctant imperialists'.[32] The imperial powers, it has been argued, particularly Britain, acquired their colonial possessions reluctantly, as a consequence of a series of historical accidents associated particularly with developments occurring in the non-Western· world—for example, the breakdown of collaborating mechanisms of an informal type, the growth of 'xenophobic populist reaction' to local Westernising

30. Kouyaté, 'Centenaire de la naissance de Samory Touré, 1830–1930', *Race Nègre* (July 1930), cited in *Spiegler*, p. 158.

31. For a critical discussion of this myth in the West African context, see Michael Crowder, *West Africa under Colonial Rule* (London, Hutchinson, 1968), particularly pp. 7–10.

32. See, for example, a recent book with this title, C. J. Lowe, *The Reluctant Imperialists*, vol. I, *British Foreign Policy, 1878–1902* (London, Routledge, 1967).

tendencies, the increasing 'fragility', 'instability', etc., of non-Western states, or even the rise of new non-Western imperialisms. Afghani mocked this general thesis as long ago as 1884 in a pleasantly ironical passage in an article in *al-Urwa al-Wuthqa*:

> The English entered India and toyed with the minds of her princes and kings in a way that makes intelligent men both laugh and cry. They penetrated deeply into India's interior and seized her lands piece by piece. Whenever they became lords of the land they took liberties with its inhabitants, and showed anger and contempt regarding their stay among them, saying that the English are occupied only with commercial affairs. As for tending to administration and politics, that is not their business. However, what calls them to bear the burdens of administration and politics is pity for the kings and the princes who are incapable of governing their dominions. When the kings or princes are able to control their land, no Englishmen will remain there, they said, because they have other important affairs that they have abandoned out of pure compassion. With this the English stole property from every owner on the pretext that work on property is oppressive to a person and fatiguing for mind and body. It is better for the owner of the property to relax and to die poor and humble, free of the pains of management. The English declare that when the opportunity presents itself, and the time comes when the affairs of this world and the hereafter will not influence bodies and thoughts, they are prepared to leave the country (on the Day of Resurrection). And today they are saying the very same words in Egypt.[33]

In other words what this antithesis essentially states is that to appear to acquire colonial territories reluctantly, to give an impression of reluctance to the colonised—and the colonising—society, even to seem to oneself to be reluctant, to write reluctant memoranda and dispatches, to produce evidence of reluctance to ease the work of future imperial historians, all this is one of the basic techniques of imperialism. It yet remains true that imperial expansion could not have occurred unless it had been willed by dominant interests within the ruling classes of the imperial powers. The significance of 'accidents' has to be understood within this wider historical context.

One might also consider the 'collaborators–resisters' antinomy which has become an interesting theme in recent historical controversy. According to the conventional imperialist thesis it was the collaborators with Western imperialism among the African political

---

33. al-Afghani, 'The materialists in India', *al-Urwa al-Wuthqa* (28 Aug. 1884), cited in Keddie, *An Islamic Response to Imperialism*, p. 175.

leaders of the late nineteenth century who were forward-looking and guided by rational considerations of national interest and 'good', the resisters who were backward-looking, misguided and 'bad'.[34] This thesis has been criticised, both by African theorists and by contemporary historians, along three main lines: (*a*) Resisters were also in many cases 'forward-looking' as regards their social and political objectives (cf. the Samory extract quoted above). (*b*) From the standpoint of national interest, collaboration was not necessarily more beneficial than resistance, even in the short-run colonial context. (Note in this connection Faure's article in *Race Nègre* early in 1936, contrasting the lives lost in the defence of Ethiopian independence with the much higher, and entirely futile, toll taken by forced labour in the construction of the Congo–Ocean railway a decade earlier, and pointing the moral: that submission to colonial rule turns out to be not only less honourable but even more dangerous than armed resistance.[35]) (*c*) From a longer-term point of view the resisters were in another important sense 'forward-looking', in that they were the historical ancestors of modern liberation movements.[36]

5. The relation of third-world to Marxist theory

The last question I would like to raise is: How far do the dominant ideas of these African and third-world theorists fit with the broad lines of Marxist, and more specifically Leninist, theory? Where do they essentially agree? Where do they supplement or modify? Where is there a clear divergence? This is obviously much too large and difficult a question to answer at all adequately here. I want in any case to consider mainly the position of those French-speaking African and West Indian theorists of the period since the Bolshevik Revolution and the end of the First World War, who have clearly been much influenced by Marxist–Leninist ideas on the one hand and by radical Pan-Negro and Pan-African theories on the other. But even here there are, of course, large divergencies between the positions of

34. For example, Roland Oliver and John D. Fage, *A Short History of Africa* (Harmondsworth, Penguin, 1962), p. 203, cited and discussed by T. O. Ranger, 'African reactions in East and Central Africa' in Gann and Duignan, *Colonialism in Africa, 1870–1960*, i, 302ff.
35. Faure, 'Ethiopie: leçons d'un drame, *Race Nègre* (Jan/Feb. 1936), referred to in *Spiegler*, p. 216, n. 4.
36. Ranger, *op. cit.*, pp. 317–21, and 'Connexions between "primary resistance" movements and modern mass nationalism in East and Central Africa'', *Journal of African History*, ix, 3/4 (1968).

different individuals, or of the same individual at different phases of his development.

Let me first briefly summarise what would seem to be some of the main points of agreement. These African theorists would seem in general agreement with Marxists on the question what a theory of imperialism is meant to be about, particularly as regards the total interdependence of theory and practice: that the primary purpose of seeking to understand imperialism is to end it. They seem also to agree that (to put it in its simplest terms) there is some kind of necessary connection between the development of advanced capitalist societies and the pursuit of active imperialist policies by their ruling classes. They agree on the destructive, distorting effects of imperialism on the economies, institutions and cultures of the colonised societies (in the 'epoch of imperialism' at any rate), and the dependence of the colonisers on the emergence within them of collaborating groups and interests, drawn usually both from the old precolonial ruling classes and from the new indigenous bourgeoisie. They are broadly in agreement about the corrupting effects of imperialism on the colonising society—as regards the strengthening of the political power of the most reactionary sections of the ruling class, the growth and diffusion of imperialist and racist ideologies, the increase of opportunism and chauvinism within the Labour movement, etc. They both, of course, regard the intensification of rivalries between the imperialist powers as a primary cause of international war. And both believe that the ending of imperialism requires as one of its essential preconditions the organisation of effective liberation movements within the colonised societies, including all sectors of the oppressed population (apart from small collaborating interests and groups)—peasants, nomads, working-class (or embryonic working-class), 'lumpen-proletariat',[37] petty-bourgeoisie and patriotic elements among the bourgeoisie—under a trained, disciplined, devoted, revolutionary leadership. As an early manifesto of the Union Intercoloniale put it: 'Que faut-il faire pour arriver à votre émancipation? Appliquant la formule de Karl Marx, nous vous disons que votre affranchissement ne peut venir que de vos propres efforts.'[38]

If one turns to points of disagreement one is confronted with a great diversity of positions, widely varying interpretations and emphases. Four themes, perhaps, deserve special attention. One is the importance

37. For a discussion of the concept of the 'Lumpen-proletariat' in an African context see C. H. Allen, 'Lumpen-proletariat' (unpublished mimeo, Oxford, 1969).
38. Quôc, *Procès de la colonisation française*, pp. 117–19, quoted in *Spiegler*, p. 103.

which, as I have already suggested, these theorists for the most part attach to the concept of cultural relativism; their emphasis on the communal, anti-capitalist (and not merely precapitalist), cooperative, democratic, fraternal values and institutions of African, or non-Western, precolonial societies, 'systematically destroyed by imperialism';[39] their rejection of theories which assert or imply the idea of unilinear progress from 'lower' to 'higher' stages of social organisation, and thus of those interpretations (or distortions or vulgarisations?) of Marxism which fall within this category. The following passage from Aimé Césaire's *Lettre à Maurice Thorez* makes this point very sharply, where he speaks of

> . . . quelques uns des défauts très apparents que nous constatons chez les membres du Parti Communiste Français: leur assimilationnisme invétéré; leur chauvinisme inconscient; leur conviction passablement primaire—qu'ils partagent avec les bourgeois européens—de la supériorité omnilatérale de l'Occident; leur croyance que l'évolution telle quelle s'est opérée en Europe est la seule possible; la seule désirable; qu'elle est celle par laquelle le monde entier devra passer; pour tout dire, leur croyance rarement avouée, mais réelle, à la civilisation avec un grand C; au progrès avec un grand P (Mémoin leur hostilité à ce qu'ils appellent avec dédain le 'relativisme culturel' . . .)[40]

This theme seems to me fundamental—underlying, to some degree, and sustaining the others, and deserving much fuller discussion than is possible here.

A second theme is the notion of the dehumanising effects of imperialism on the colonised societies and the reimportation of the ideas and attitudes and institutions and techniques which have been used by the bourgeoisie of the colonising countries to impose and maintain their domination over the colonised into the metropolitan societies for use against their own people. This idea, of the specially corrupting effects of imperialism on the social and political life of the imperialists, was of course present and important in Marx and his successors, Lenin in particular (and in the writings of liberal critics of imperialism like Hobson).[41] But for third-world theorists like

---

39. See, e.g., *Spiegler*, p. 229ff.
40. Aimé Césaire, *Lettre à Maurice Thorez* (Paris, 1956), p. 11.
41. See relevant passages in Marx and Engels, *On Colonialism* (Moscow and London, Lawrence & Wishart, 1960), including the well-known extract from Engels's letter to Kautsky quoted on pp. 306–7; passages from Lenin's *Imperialism, the Highest Stage of Capitalism* quoted in Hélène Carrère d'Encausse and Stuart R., Schram, *Marxism and Asia* (London, Allen Lane, 1969), pp. 140–2, and J. A. Hobson, *Imperialism* (London, Allen & Unwin, 1948), pt. ii, ch. i, 'The political significance of Imperialism'.

Césaire and Fanon the idea of the terrible feedback effects of imperialism has a new and pivotal significance. Fascism and Nazism are essentially imperialism turned inwards. The Western bourgeois liberal who permits non-Western people to be treated as non-human by 'his' imperialists is preparing the same eventual doom for himself:

> Il faudrait d'abord étudier comment la colonisation travaille à *déciviliser* le colonisateur, à l'*abrutir* au sens propre du mot, à le dégrader, à le réveiller aux instincts enfouis, à la convoitise, à la violence, à la haine raciale, au relativisme moral, et montrer que, chaque fois qu'il y a au Viet-Nam une tête coupée et un oeil crevé et qu'en France on accepte, une fillette violée et qu'en France on accepte, un Malgache supplicié et qu'en France on accepte . . . il y a le poison instillé dans les veines de l'Europe, et le progrès lent, mais sûr, de l'*ensauvagement* du continent . . .
>
> Oui, il vaudrait la peine d'étudier, cliniquement, dans le détail, les démarches d'Hitler et de l'hitlérisme et de révéler au très distingué, très humaniste, très chrétien bourgeois du XXᵉ siècle qu'il porte en lui un Hitler qui s'ignore, qu'Hitler l'*habite*, qu'Hitler est son *démon*, que s'il le vitupère, c'est par manque de logique, et qu'au fond ce qu'il ne pardonne pas à Hitler, ce n'est pas *le crime* en soi, *le crime contre l'homme*, ce n'est pas *l'humiliation de l'homme en soi*, c'est le crime contre l'homme blanc, c'est l'humiliation de l'homme blanc, et d'avoir appliqué à l'Europe des procédés colonialistes dont ne relevaient jusqu'ici que les Arabes d'Algérie, les coolies de l'Inde et les nègres d'Afrique.[42]

There is much here, clearly, that is common ground between Césaire and Western Marxists. Where tension or conflict is perhaps most liable to arise is over the total condemnation, on moral grounds, of Western imperialism in every possible kind of historical situation, so that all the familiar technological/sociological arguments for the 'ultimately' progressive or beneficial role of imperialism are excluded *a priori*.[43]

A third theme is the idea of a necessary, continuing, irreconcilable antagonism (in the context of a world in which imperialism remains a dominant force) between the interests of the advanced, Western, and predominantly 'white', colonising societies and the interests of the proletarian, non-Western, and predominantly 'non-white', colonial and semicolonial societies. In a sense this means taking the contradiction between the imperialist countries and the colonial peoples and

---

42. Aimé Césaire, *Discours sur le colonialisme* (Paris, 1955), pp. 12–13.
43. For example, Margery Perham, *The Colonial Reckoning* (London, Collins, 1961), ch. v, 'The colonial account'. For a discussion of somewhat comparable questions in the Soviet context see Bennigsen and Quelquejay, *Islam and the Soviet Union* (London, Pall Mall Press, 1967) ch. xv.

insisting that it has priority over all other contradictions, blurring (from a more 'orthodox' Marxist point of view) the internal contradictions within both colonising and colonised societies. Thus Sultan Galiyev argued that 'since almost all classes in Muslim society have been oppressed formerly by the colonialists, all are entitled to be called proletarian. . . . The Muslim peoples are proletarian peoples.'[44] It means asserting also that this basic contradiction is not simply a contradiction of economic aims and interests between oppressor and oppressed, exploiting and exploited, advanced and retarded, bourgeois and proletarian nations. It arises also out of profound differences between the Western and non-Western peoples as regards their histories and cultures, including differences arising out of the colonial experience itself (the experience of the agents of imperialism having been essentially different from the experience of its victims).[45] Hence, it is argued, this antagonism, or opposition, would not necessarily be eliminated by a transformation of existing economic relationships, or by social revolutions in the advanced countries, involving the substitution of proletarian for bourgeois regimes. Sultan Galiyev, writing in 1918, specifically discussed this point:

> Let us take the example of the British proletariat, the most developed of them all. If a revolution succeeds in England, the proletariat will go on oppressing the colonies and pursuing the policy of the existing bourgeois government, for it is interested in the exploitation of those colonies.[46]

Closely associated with this is the fourth theme, the Leninist conception of the essential interdependence of the interests of the working classes in the advanced capitalist countries and the exploited masses in the colonial and semicolonial countries, which must be expressed politically through an effective alliance between revolutionary proletarian parties in the former and national liberation movements under revolutionary leadership in the latter.[47] Towards this thesis these third-world theorists have tended to take up an attitude of methodical doubt, involving a whole range of attitudes from accep-

44. From an address by Sultan Galiyev to the Regional Congress of the Russian Communist Party at Kazan in March 1918, cited in Bennigsen and Quelquejay, *op. cit.*, p. 112.

45. There is not, or course, a clearcut opposition here: peoples, classes, groups, individuals, can be victims of imperialism in one context and agents of imperialism in another.

46. Bennigsen and Quelquejay, p. 114; see also their *Les mouvements nationaux chez les Musulmans de Russie*, p. 103, n. 2; and compare E. H. Carr, *A History of Soviet Russia, The Bolshevik Revolution, 1917–1923*, III, p. 256, n. 2.

47. Cf. Carr, iii, ch. xxvi, and d'Encausse and Schram, *Marxism and Asia*, Introduction, ch. ii.

tance with reservations to thoroughgoing rejection. This doubt, or scepticism, arises, I think, from a variety of factors, including considerations of both a practical and a theoretical kind. Among these are a questioning of the revolutionary potential of the proletariat in the advanced countries; and, perhaps even more, a fear of the subordination of the interests of the liberation movements in colonial countries to the interests, or the supposed interests, of the metropolitan working classes, or, quite simply, to the world strategies of metropolitan communist parties within the framework of an alliance dominated by ideas of what Césaire has called Western 'fraternalism'.[48] Linked with this has been a general revolt against Western habits of intellectual arrogance and dogmatism (characteristic of some Marxists, as well as of most liberals and all imperialists); a belief in the necessity for the colonial and former colonial peoples of the world to recover the historical initiative, and for the direction, character, pace and methods of change within the third world to be primarily their responsibility, not the responsibility of even the most radical or revolutionary sectors of the populations of the advanced countries; a new emphasis on the importance of the idea (asserted by Sultan Galiyev and others of his generation) of creating wider alliances among the peoples of the third world, which may be obstructed by excessive dependence on exclusive alliances with revolutionary, or supposedly revolutionary, metropolitan parties.[49] This last point has been particularly stressed by Césaire:

> Il n'y a pas d'alliés de droit divin. Il y a des alliés que nous impose le lieu, le moment et la nature des choses. Et, si l'alliance avec le prolétariat français est exclusive, si elle tend à nous faire oublier ou à contrarier d'autres alliances nécessaires et naturelles, légitimes et fécondantes, si le communisme saccage nos amitiés les plus vivifiantes, celle qui nous unit aux autres Antilles, celle qui nous unit à l'Afrique, alors je dis que le communisme nous a rendu un bien mauvais service en nous faisant troquer la fraternité vivante contre ce qui risque d'apparaître comme la plus froide des froides abstractions.[50]

48. Cesaire, *Lettre à Maurice Thorez*, p. 11.
49. For Sultan Galiyev's idea of a Colonial International see Bennigsen and Quelquejay, *Islam in the Soviet Union*, pp. 117–18. For a fuller discussion of his particular form of pan-Turan, pan-Islamic, pan-Asian, inter-colonial theory and strategy and its development see their *Les Mouvements nationaux chex les Muselmans de Russie*, particularly pp. 134–40 and 176–82, cf. d'Encausse and Schram *Marxism and Asia*, pp. 31–8, and Anouar Abdel-Malek, 'Marxisme et liberation nationale' *Le centennaire du 'Capital'* (Decades du Centre Culturel Internationale de Cerisy-la-Salle) The Hague, Paris.
50. Césaire, *Lettre à Maurice Thorez*, p. 15.

6. Conclusion

My main hope in writing this paper is that it will help the general effort to liberate ourselves from a continuing Eurocentric, or Western-centred, bias in regard to questions of theory. Theory is perhaps the last intellectual citadel of the imperialists. It has been conceded, however grudgingly and incompletely, that Africans have had their own histories, which are as interesting as the histories of other peoples and can be studied, essentially, by the same methods. But it has perhaps still to be recognised that Africans, and third-world peoples generally, have made their own contributions to the theories which we use to understand and interpret human history—including the history of Western imperialism, of which they have had their own special kind of experience—and that these theories are also intrinsically well worth studying.

DISCUSSION

How progressive were these ideas and movements?   A large part of the discussion concerned the doubts of many participants about the long-term progressiveness of anti-imperialist movements based on the ideas which Hodgkin had described. One questioner acknowledged the importance of Afghani who had introduced the idea of resisting European expansion in the eastern Mediterranean and who had used Islam as a way of reviving pride among the people; but he referred to the contrary arguments of Anouar Abdel-Malek in his book *Idéologie et renaissance nationale* (Paris, 1969). There he criticises Afghani, not for his undoubtedly important part in the 1882 revolution in Egypt, but because of his legacy. Afghani emphasised a kind of Islam which contains no cultural autonomy, leading to a fuzziness and woolly consensus which prevents people from thinking in class terms. The Afghani tradition was opposed by the liberal democrats and constitutionalists of the 1870s, from whose tradition the communists of the 1940s at length emerged.

Hodgkin agreed with much of this but thought that for Afghani Islam was an ideological convenience; his real concern was the anti-imperialist struggle. In any case it is important to judge ideas in their historical context and not in terms of what is made of them by later generations. Of course the weakness of ideologies of this kind was that they often passed into the keeping of reactionary groups; this does not mean that in his own particular context the originator of them does not contribute to a revolutionary way of thinking.

Sultan Galiyev, a Marxist, tried to see how Islam might be applied as a way of mobilising third world revolutionary potential, though this had brought him into conflict with the party.

Were they nativist or exclusivist?   One objection made to this was that such movements were in a sense reactionary because 'nativist'. They might ultimately not be anti-imperialist at all; often they were a boon to the imperial power when they emphasised the value of such institutions as chieftainship. Imperialism could tolerate such a group because it could 'encapsulate' it in a dependent relationship. The question of whether such groups could be progressive might depend on whether they arose before or after a dependent relationship was fully forged. If it was after, then they were objectively reactionary. Hodgkin rejected the description of 'nativist' for the movements he had discussed. Nor, for instance, were the ideas of Afghani about Islam always exclusivist, as his Indian writings show. Exclusive thinking—that it was only important to mobilise Muslims (or for other people, black Africans) —leads only to communalism, as in Pakistan. The idea of men like Césaire (or Sultan Galiyev) was one of concentric circles—an appeal first to the solidarity of local people, then to African and West Indian (or Islamic) people and then to the proletarian solidarity of the oppressed colonial and semicolonial people of the world.

Were they purely cultural?   Another participant argued that a purely cultural movement might be able to carry a struggle beyond narrow national-ism but it could not provide the solid basis for an anti-imperialist theory; for that some kind of economic analysis was needed. Once again Hodgkin denied that the movements were purely cultural. They tended to accept the economic analysis of post-Marxist thinking; where they added an original contribution to this was in seeing the colonial system from the standpoint of its political effects on the colonised and the colonisers.

Is racialism necessary to imperialism?   A suggestion was made that while Lenin had been concerned to define imperialism in economic terms, the third world theorists had defined it in political terms, especially in rela-tion to its ideological supports. With the insight of such theories it is easy to show, for instance, that racialism was an outcome of the imperialist epoch. Another contributor added that the attitude of the ruling class in the imperial-ist countries to its own working class may be a reflection of its attitude to the people of its colonies. But others doubted the extent to which these ideolo-gical features were necessary to the working of imperialism. Hodgkin argued that there cannot be a political system without the ideology appropriate to that system. Lenin, in any case, had not considered imperialism only from an economic standpoint but would have thought that an imperialist ideo-logy (including racialism) was inseparable from the economic and social relations generated by imperialism. The two were interdependent.

The lost history of colonial peoples.   Adding to the counter-proposi-tions against imperialism produced in the third world (see Hodgkin's paper, IV, 4), a participant mentioned a remark of Amilcar Cabral to the effect that with the arrival of the Portuguese the history of the people of Guinea stopped and only began again with the start of the armed struggle against the Portuguese. Hodgkin added that the recovery of historical initiative in the third world must mean the end of myths of a 'Trevor-Roperish' kind that African history was of only marginal interest. In general the effect of im-perialism on the teaching of history had been more recognised by third world than by metropolitan Marxists.

What are the economic assumptions?   The final part of the discussion concerned some of the economic assumptions about the third world which underlie theories of imperialism. It was suggested that those who have seen imperialism primarily in economic terms have not assigned much autonomy to revolution in the third world. They have either seen it as an adjunct to revolution in the advanced countries or they have argued that third-world countries have to pass through their bourgeois revolution and the economic stage associated with it. The opposition of the French Communist party to the establishment of Communist parties in Africa until development had generated a sufficiently strong proletariat is another instance of this. Another participant observed that this view must be based on the idea that colonialism arrested capitalist development which could then take place after national liberation. This was very different to the view which now prevails among Marxists, that independent capitalist development in the third world was no longer possible. (There is a fuller discussion of this in the paper by Sutcliffe, VII below.) It was different too from the Narodnik idea (now widespread in Africa) that, since the costs of capitalist development were so severe, a socialist development through traditional communal institutions should be attempted. In this context the view of Lenin and Trotsky on the progressiveness of capitalist development in Russia were perhaps a good starting point for thinking about the third world. Lenin was perfectly right, someone added, to see capitalism as historically progressive in Russia; what was different in the third world was that not only were the relations of production exploitative but political domination was also imposed; this changed the whole situation. Thomas Hodgkin remarked that, in the face of arguments that the impact of Tsarist expansion on the Tartars was progressive, or that South African blacks should be glad of having such an advanced industrial base, it was hard not to be forced back to the essentially moral attitude of Fanon and say that the whole process was bloody and should not have occurred.

V

Non-European foundations of European imperialism: sketch for a theory of collaboration

Ronald Robinson

Like the author of the previous paper, Robinson is also a critic of the Euro-centricity of the classical (he calls them 'the old') theories of imperialism; although for very different reasons. In his opinion any new theory must find room for an analysis of the most important mechanism of European man-agement of the non-European world: the use of local collaborating groups —whether ruling elites or landlords or merchants—as mediators between Europe and the indigenous political and economic system.

Using the definition (first put forward in his article, 'The imperialism of free trade') that imperialism is a political function of the process of integrat-ing some countries at some times into the international economy, he goes on to suggest that it was the character of the collaborative mechanism which determined whether a country was allowed to remain independent or whether it was incorporated into the formal or informal empire of one of the major European powers. The less 'European' the collaborators were in their social and political institutions, the less easy it was for their economies to be aligned with that of Europe without direct European intervention. There were also important changes through time so that, over the years, one collaborative system might no longer serve to maximise economic advan-tage and have to be replaced by another. Thus the form which imperial control took, as well as the particular point in history at which one form of control was transformed into another, is made dependent on a set of conditions which Robinson locates firmly in Afro-Asia, not in Europe.

The notion of a collaborative mechanism is also said to have two further advantages. It explains why Europe was able to rule large areas of the world so cheaply and with so few troops. It also provides an explanation of the process of decolonisation in terms of the growing ability of the indepen-dence movements in the colonies to disrupt the arrangements for collabora-tion or to use them for their own ends.

Fresh homage is paid elsewhere in this volume to the fearful symmetry of old theories of imperialism which confounded the politics of empire with the economics of capitalism. Since they were invented, nevertheless, perspective has lengthened and decolonisation has shattered many of their impenetrably Eurocentric assumptions. A more historical theory of the working of European imperialism in the nineteenth and twentieth centuries is badly needed.

The old notions for the most part were restricted to explaining the genesis of new colonial empires in terms of circumstances in Europe. The theory of the future will have to explain in addition, how a handful of European pro-consuls managed to manipulate the polymorphic societies of Africa and Asia, and how, eventually, comparatively small, nationalist elites persuaded them to leave.

There is however a more compelling reason to grope for a better synthesis than those of the old masters. Today their analyses, deduced more from·first principle than empirical observation, appear to be ideas about European society projected outward, rather than systematic theories about the imperial process as such. They were models in which empire-making was conceived simply as a function of European, industrial political economy. Constructed on the assumption that all active components were bound to be European ones, which excluded equally vital non-European elements by definition, the old theories were founded on a grand illusion.

Any new theory must recognise that imperialism was as much a function of its victims' collaboration or non-collaboration—of their indigenous politics, as it was of European expansion. The expansive forces generated in industrial Europe had to combine with elements within the agrarian societies of the outer world to make empire at all practicable.

To explore this more realistic first assumption as a basis for a fresh approach, is the object of this essay. It makes no pretension to accomplishing such a theory. It does suggest, however, that researches in the subject might take a new direction. The revised, theoretical model of imperialism has to be founded on studies of the nature and working of the various arrangements for mutual collaboration, through which the external European, and the internal non-European components cooperated at the point of imperial impact. Before reflecting on this idea, it is necessary to set it in a broader context.

1. A definition of modern imperialism

Imperialism in the industrial era is a process whereby agents of an expanding society gain inordinate influence or control over the vitals of weaker societies by 'dollar' and 'gun-boat' diplomacy, ideological suasion, conquest and rule, or by planting colonies of its own people abroad. The object is to shape or reshape them in its own interest and more or less in its own image. It implies the exertion of power and the transfer of economic resources; but no society, however dominant, can man-handle arcane, densely-peopled civilisations or white colonies in other continents simply by projecting its own main force upon them. Domination is only practicable in so far as alien power is translated into terms of indigenous political economy.

Historically European imperialism might be defined as a political reflex action between one non-European, and two European components. From Europe stemmed the economic drive to integrate newly colonised regions and ancient agrarian empires into the industrial economy, as markets and investments. From Europe also sprang the strategic imperative to secure them against rivals in world power politics. As the stock-in-trade of the old masters,[1] these may be taken for granted, although of course they were indispensible to the process.

Their role however has been exaggerated. They did not in themselves necessitate empire. If they had done, the territorial scrambles of the later nineteenth century would have taken place in the Americas, where Europe was investing the bulk of its exported economic and human resources, rather than in Africa and Asia. One country can trade with another and be interested strategically in it without intervening in its politics. There was nothing intrinsically imperialistic about foreign investment or great power rivalry. European capital and technology, for example, strengthened the independence of Japan and the Transvaal, at the same time as they undermined that of Egypt. The great power rivalry that carved up Africa also stopped the 'slicing of the Chinese melon' and delayed Ottoman partition. It ought to be commonplace therefore that from beginning to end imperialism was a product of interaction between European and extra-European politics. European economic and strategic expansion took imperial form when these two components operated at cross-purposes with the third and non-European component—that of indigenous collaboration and resistance.[2] The missing key to a more

1. These theories are well analysed in D. K. Fieldhouse, *The Theory of Capitalist Imperialism* (London, Weidenfeld & Nicolson 1967); cf. Tom Kemp, *Theories of Imperialism* (London, Dobson 1967).
2. Cf. the earlier formulation in J. Gallagher and R. Robinson, 'The imperialism of free trade', *Econ. Hist. Rev.* (March 1953), 5–6.

historical theory perhaps is to be found in this third element.

If this triple interaction in large measure made imperialism necessary and practicable, its controlling mechanism was made up of relationships between the agents of external expansion and their internal 'collaborators' in non-European political economies. Without the voluntary or enforced cooperation of their governing elites, economic resources could not be transferred, strategic interests protected or xenophobic reaction and traditional resistance to change contained. Nor without indigenous collaboration, when the time came for it, could Europeans have conquered and ruled their non-European empires. From the outset that rule was continuously resisted; just as continuously native mediation was needed to avert resistance or hold it down. Indian sepoys and Indian revenue, for example, conquered and kept for the Raj the brightest jewel in the imperial crown. China and Japan on the other hand provided no such collaborators as India and so, significantly, could not be brought under the yoke.

It is easy to mistake the source of the power upholding these African and Asian colonial empires. Their serried panoplies might indicate that it came from Europe. But had it come thence they would have remained paper tigers. Although potentially the power was there in Europe, in reality only a tiny fraction of it was ever committed to Africa or Asia. Europe's policy normally was that if empire could not be had on the cheap, it was not worth having at all. The financial sinew, the military and administrative muscle of imperialism was drawn through the mediation of indigenous elites from the invaded countries themselves.

Its central mechanism, therefore, may be found in the systems of collaboration set up in pre-industrial societies, which succeeded (or failed) in meshing the incoming processes of European expansion into indigenous social politics and in achieving some kind of evolving equilibrium between the two.

2. The idea of collaborating or mediating elites

As the agents of large-scale industrial civilisation invaded small-scale agrarian societies, the allure of what the big society had to offer in trade, capital, technology, military or diplomatic aid, or the fear of its vengeance, elicited indigenous political and economic 'collaborators'. It should be stressed that the term is used in no pejorative sense. From the standpoint of the collaborators or mediators the invaders imported an alternative source of wealth and power which, if it could not be excluded, had to be exploited in order to preserve or improve the standing of indigenous elites in the traditional order. As the cases of Japan from 1858 to 1867[3] and of Buganda from 1886 to 1900[4] among many other examples show, if the ruling elite chose resistance there was usually a counter-elite to opt for collaboration, or vice versa. At the same time the 'bargains' of collaboration were not, and could not be too one-sided or they ceased to be effective. Collaborators or not, the social elites of Africa and Asia who made up the great majority of imperialism's involuntary partners, had to mediate with the foreigner on behalf of their traditional institutions and constituents. Too drastic concessions in sensitive areas would undermine the basis of their authority and set their forced contracts with Europe at nought. The irony of collaborative systems lay in the fact that although the white invaders could exert leverage on ruling elites they could not do without their mediation. Even if the bargains were unequal they had to recognise mutual interests and inter-dependence if they were to be kept. When mediators were not given enough cards to play, their authority with their own people waned, crisis followed, and the expanding powers had to choose between scrapping their interests or intervening to promote them directly. Nor was it possible for them later as rulers to deal with subject societies as amorphous collections of individuals. Hence the terms on which collaboration took place were critical in determining not only the political and economic modes of European expansion but also its agents' chances of achieving influence, keeping control, promoting changes, and of containing xenophobic reaction.

Two interconnecting sets of linkages thus made up the collaborative mechanism: one consisting of arrangements between the agents of industrial society and the indigenous elites drawn into cooperation with them; and the other connecting these elites to the rigidities of local interests and institutions. Collaborators had to perform one set of functions in the external or 'modern sector' yet 'square' them with

3. See especially W. G. Beasley, *Great Britain and the Opening of Japan, 1834–1858* (London, Luzac, 1951), and *Select Documents on Japanese Foreign Policy, 1853–1868* (London, Oxford Univ. Press, 1955); A. M. Craig, *Chōshū in the Meiji Restoration* (Cambridge, Mass., Harvard Univ. Press, 1961); M. B. Jansen, *Sakamoto Ryōma and the Meiji Restoration* (Princeton Univ. Press, 1961).
4. D. A. Low, *Buganda in Modern History* (London, Weidenfeld & Nicolson, 1971), cap. 1; M. Twaddle, 'The Bakungu Chiefs of Buganda under British Colonial Rule, 1900–1930', *Journal of African History*, **10**, 2 (1969), and 'The Muslim revolution in Buganda', London Institute of Commonwealth Studies Seminar Paper (unpublished, 1971).

another and more crucial set in the indigenous society. The kind of arrangement possible in the one thus determined the kind of arrangement possible in the other. When collaborators succeeded in solving these complex politico-economic equations, as did the modernising samurai of Japan, progress was almost miraculous; when they failed to do so, as Chinese mandarins and Egyptian pashas found, the result sooner or later was catastrophe.

Although the mediators remained integrated in local society, in their dual role they rarely formed a united interest group or a unified modern sector within that society. Of necessity they played the part of collaborator more or less with reference to their roles in their own society. Their mutual rivalries within that society cut across their common interests as intermediaries. Hence collaborative systems tended to consist of collections of mediating functions isolated and dispersed through native society rather than of unified social groups within them. This differentiation between mediating roles and groups is plain, in that the same group at times allied itself to, but at other times opposed, the imperialists. The turnover of allies in a crisis was often remarkable.

The efficiency of this system was clearly proportionate to the amount of European wealth and power committed to it. This determined the weight of externally-oriented functions within indigenous society. Where the externalised activities were small by comparison with the traditional ones, collaborators naturally attached more importance to their traditional, than to their mediatory role. The greater the resources that came from Europe the less imperialism depended on indigenous mediation. In Algeria, Kenya and the Rhodesias up to the 1950s, for example, native politics were strangled by the presence of a minority of white colonists. Imperial control could thus dispense with native cooperation to a great extent; it could not, on the other hand, be upheld without the colonists' consent. Even in these special cases native mediators later became more necessary to colonial rule as African nationalist organisation grew. In west African dependencies where there were no white colonists, mediators were always vital to their rulers. The need for intermediaries varied again with the military force available and the rulers' willingness to use coercion as a substitute for collaboration. The military element in French imperialism in North and West Africa[5]

---

5. A. S. Kanya-Forstner, 'Myths and realities of African resistance', *Historical Papers 1969* (The Canadian Historical Association 1969), and *The Conquest of the Western Sudan, A Study in French Military Imperialism*, (Cambridge, Cambridge Univ. Press, 1969.)

in the period before the rise of African nationalism often made it less dependent on mediators than the British, a situation which reflected the different expansive resources of a continental country with a large conscript army and an island dependent for its European security on a large navy.

Throughout the imperial era, economic inputs into Africa and Asia with the exception of India remained small, barely scratching the social surface or interrupting the implacable continuities of indigenous history. Systems of cooperation there as a result remained comparatively ineffective and unstable. In white colonies, however, where European inputs were comparatively great, collaboration proved both stable and effective.[6] Accordingly colonial rule encroached on Afro-Asia more and more directly and extensively as it attempted to construct and uphold indigenous cooperation; while in the white dominions, the more reliable collaborative mechanisms became, the more colonial rule receded.

It might almost be said that the changing bargains of collaboration or mediation define the actual working of imperialism at the point of impact at a particular time. Hence the study of them appears to offer a more comprehensive view of the factors involved than does the one-eyed analysis of European forces.

Historical flesh for these abstract bones may be taken from the case of the lone London missionary to the Tswana tribes, illustrating the mechanism at its weakest, and from that of the nineteenth-century white colonist, showing it working at its strongest.

In Bechuanaland during the 1840s and 1850s the missionary was the sole agent of European expansion. Although his spiritual resources were great, it did not appear that he had either the great powers or the industrial economy at his back. His gospel moreover had no use or meaning for most Tswana chiefs and elders, who knew that it would subvert both their religion and authority. While permitting him to teach, therefore, they assigned to this one man 'modern sector' the roles of irrigation expert, chief of defence staff, gunsmith and commercial and diplomatic agent in dealings with the outside world. He had little reward in souls. By the 1870s he was calling up imperial power from the Cape to supplement the European side of the bargain with more material resources.

---

6. For an extreme example of what collaboration English capital could elicit outside formal empire, in Chilean politics from 1879 to 1883, without overt political intervention, see J. R. Brown 'The frustration of Chile's nitrate imperialism', *Journal of Pacific History* (Nov. 1963).

This simple episode,[7] which was repeated with variations wherever the missionary first went in black Africa, illustrates the tendency of collaboration, in the absence of sufficient input, to divert the agents of European expansion to the service of traditional society. On the one side the Tswana elite stretched the bargain to exploit the European for the purpose of strengthening their position in traditional politics; on the other, they neutralised his potentially disruptive effects and so largely frustrated the European objective. The missionary conceived of a European role. The role he actually played was assigned and defined in terms of Tswana society.

3. The white colonist: the ideal prefabricated collaborator

At the other extreme is the case of the white colonist with the power of an industrial economy behind him, transplanting European attitudes and institutions carried in his head. He was the ideal, prefabricated collaborator; but by what kind of mechanism did Britain project these profitable economic satellites, these congenial imperial dominions, onto continents thousands of miles away?

In Australia, New Zealand, and to a less extent elsewhere, although original cultural affiliation played its part, political collaboration stemmed largely from economic dependence. For the greater part of the century these colonies had no alternative to Britain as a source of capital, export markets, immigrants and protection. In the early stages of growth metropolitan investment largely pre-selected the colonial economy's immigrants and governed the direction and speed of its growth. The dominant export-import sector consequently shaped colonial politics in favour of commercial and political collaboration with London. Collaborative bargains proved easy to make and to keep when commercial partnership was mutually profitable and colonists were permitted to manage their own internal affairs. Their bread was buttered in the Mother Country. Exporter and importer, banker and docker, farmer, sheep drover and cattle herder in the colony voted for politicians who would respect the arrangements to keep export markets open and capital flowing in. Unemployment and defeat at the next election were the penalties for breaking them. Direct imperial control in such conditions was unnecessary. Indeed since it provoked violent nationalist reaction, it was

7. See A. Dachs, '*Missionary imperialism in Bechuanaland, 1826–1890*', Cambridge University Ph.D. thesis, 1968.

a positive disadvantage and rusted into disuse. Imperial cooperation was achieved mainly by economic attraction through the normal internal political processes of the colony itself. There were sufficient economic inputs to maintain political alliance.

This platonic construction of course is too good to be absolutely true historically, even in Australasia; but the higher the synthesis, the lower the detailed historical accuracy. The white colonial model had its snags and it could also break down. There are some awkward nuts and bolts to be added in the Canadian and South African cases which did not entirely square with the classic requirements of economic dependency. The Canadians had an alternative, external trading partner in the United States. Both the Canadian and the South African colonies up to the 1890s had a small export-import sector and a large subsistence sector. French Canadians, a large minority, and the large majority of Afrikaaners in South Africa of pre-industrial European stock had historic reasons for resenting British imperialism and no close commercial connections with it. Yet in Canada, curiously enough, after 1847, the French Canadians' fear of the 'yanquees' did most to anchor the Canadian colonies politically in the empire against the pull of the United States. Canadian nationalism and the counter attraction of British capital, markets and loyalties did the rest in generating collaboration between Britain and the Canadian colonies.

In the South African colonial mechanism during the first three-quarters of the nineteenth century, also commercial partnership with Britain seems to have attracted the Cape Dutch to cooperate economically, and so politically, with the English-speaking South Africans of the export-import sector and with the imperial connection. It was otherwise with their Afrikaaner cousins, the uncooperative republican *trekboers* in the introverted up-country economies of the Transvaal and northern Orange Free State. After 1887, a geological accident gave the Transvaalers political control of the export-import sector through that of the Witwatersrand mines; and its English politico-economic entrepreneurs, divided from their Cape Dutch collaborators, lost control over South Africa and evoked Nemesis in the Jameson Raid, the Boer War and the Afrikaaner nationalist reaction that followed.[8] It is clear from this case that greatly increased economic inputs, if they happen to hit on the weak points, can tear down, as well as build up a system of colonial collabora-

8. See R. Robinson, J. Gallagher and A. Denny, *Africa and the Victorians, the official mind of imperialism* (London, Macmillan, 1961), chs. 3, 7, 14.

tion. Other examples of this same type were the Argentine between 1828 and 1852[9] and Uruguay in the first half of the century. In both cases, the framework of political unification was too immature to contain the clash of politico-economic interests between the *portenos* of the export-import sector and the barons and *gauchos* of the subsistence backlands. Consequently, until the second half of the century, the *portenos* were unable to extend the political grip of the export-import sector inland quickly enough to induce the backlands to cooperate economically.

In spite of these difficulties with colonial nationalists, institutional gaps and temporary breakdowns, the collaborative mechanism of commercial partnership in white colonies converted external economic power into internal political cooperation. It worked constructively so that these colonies eventually 'took off'. Gradually as their economies diversified, local capital formation grew, the ties of political collaboration with Britain slackened and economic dependence diminished. In so far as their import-export sectors shrank in importance relative to their domestic economy, the collaborating elites associated with them lost influence to populist national movements in colonial politics. But by that time the collaborative system had done its work; for the white ex-colonies—the United States and Latin America, together with the British 'dominions'—had become expansive in their own right in pursuit of their own 'manifest destiny'.

4. Collaboration in Afro-Asia: the external or informal phase

A different mark of model altogether is required for Africa and Asia, although many Victorians believed at first that the white colonial model would do. Their expectations of free trade and Christianity turning Ottoman rayahs, Levantine traders, Chinese mandarins, Indian Brahmins and African chiefs into Europeanised collaborators, working to modernise their 'reactionary religions' and 'ramshackle' empires were to be disappointed.

From the 1820s to the 70s, in what might be called the external or informal stage of industrial imperialism, Europe attempted to lever

9. H. S. Ferns, *Britain and Argentina*, (London, Oxford Univ. Press, 1969); T. F. McGann, *Argentina, the United States, and the Inter-American System, 1880–1914* (Cambridge, Mass., Harvard Univ. Press, 1957); see also J. F. Rippy, 'The British investment "boom" of the 1880s in Latin America', *Hispanic American Historical Review*, (May 1949).

Afro-Asian regimes into collaboration from outside and to reshape their institutions through commerce. Naval and diplomatic power forced their rulers to abolish commercial monopolies, lower tariffs and open their doors to the 'Imperialism of Free Trade'.[10] Later, in return for loans, or under the muzzles of high velocity guns, they were bundled into liberalising their traditional political, legal and fiscal institutions to make elbowroom for their 'productive classes' in commercial collaboration with Europe, to take over power. But in fact these 'classes' really succeeded in doing so. Like contemporary development planners, classical económics overestimated the power of economic inputs to revolutionise Oriental society.

The result, sooner or later, was disaster everywhere except in Japan and India, already under the white Raj. In Japan after 1869 the western samurai overthrew the Shogunate, perilously modernised its quasi-feudal institutions and exploited neotraditionalist nationalism and carefully calculated bargains with the West to protect their independence on the basis of 'rich country, strong army'. By 1914 these Japanese collaborators had achieved what otherwise only white colonists seemed able to achieve. They succeeded in translating the forces of western expansion into terms of indigenous politics. By adapting European style techniques and institutions, they managed to control them so that they strengthened, instead of destroying, Japanese government, and worked not for imperialism, but for Japan.[11]

In contrast, the collaborative mechanism in China worked superficially. Admittedly the timing of the mid-nineteenth century European break-in was unfavourable, for China was then in the grip of a demographic crisis. The mandarin bureaucracy was challenged by widespread peasant revolt from the Tai-pings[12] and Muslims; and in suppressing them, the central government lost its power to provincial warlords and gentry. They used it to defend the traditional order against collaborators' efforts to reform Chinese institutions from above. Free trade imperialism enabled European merchants in the treaty ports, in partnership with Chinese merchants, to take over the

---

10. See Gallagher and Robinson, 'Imperialism of free trade' *op. cit.* 1953; B. Semmel, *The Rise of Free Trade Imperialism*, (Cambridge, Cambridge Univ. Press, 1970); A. G. L. Shaw, ed. *Great Britain and the Colonies, 1815–1865*, (London, Methuen, 1970); D. C. M. Platt, *Finance, Trade and Politics, British Foreign Policy 1815–1914*, (London, Oxford Univ. Press 1968) and 'The imperialism of free trade: some reservations', *Ec. Hist. Rev., xxi*, (1968).
11. See E. O. Reischauer, J. Fairbank, and A. M. Craig, *East Asia: The Modern Transformation*, (Cambridge, Mass., Harvard Univ. Press, 1965).
12. F. Michael, *The Taiping Rebellion*, (Seattle, University of Washington Press, 3 vols, 1966).

exposed riverine and maritime branches of Chinese domestic trade; but the Manchu regime rejected European capital and railways and so the export-import sector hardly dented the vast, introverted domestic economy. When K'ang Yu-wei in 1898 attempted to re-centralise Manchu government and to substitute western for confucian education in imitation of the Japanese, the traditionalist bureaucracy and gentry in effect vetoed all his decrees. And when rival European powers attempted to inject capital and railways forcibly into the society between 1895 and 1900, the dramatic xenophobic reaction of the Boxers drove them back, beleagured, into the legations of Pekin.[13]

From the conservative reform period of the sixties and seventies to the abortive military recentralization of Yuan Shi-k' ai in the 1900s the indigenous modernisers and collaborators within the Manchu regime, remained prisoners of the impenetrably confucian social units that connected lower bureaucracy with provincial gentry and peasantry.[14] This had once been an imperial system of peasant control. It had turned into a system of popular defiance, cancelling Pekin's collaborative bargains with the West. Modern ideas, military technique, capital and institutions, therefore, could by no means be translated into terms of indigenous political processes. The railways planned too late to reimpose the control of Pekin, the modern artillery, the battleships and the loans, provoked deeper provincial and populist resistance; so that the Manchu regime continued to crumble until it fell in the revolution of 1911.

In the Muslim societies of the Ottoman empire, Egypt and Tunis, however, collaborating regimes were at first more successful than in China. By the 1850s and 60s international free trade and capital investment had made a considerable impression on their economies through the enforced collaboration of traditional rulers and the commercial partnership of Levantine urban classes. Rulers tried strenuously to modernise their armies and navies and to exploit railways in order to strengthen their grip on rebellious provinces or conquer new ones. But the Ottoman regime consisted of a Muslim military autocracy and a Turkish heartland ruling over a multiracial empire disrupted by Slav nationalists, Armenian Christians and Arab

3. E. S. Wehrle, *Britain, China and the Antimissionary Riots: 1891–1900*, (Univ. of Minneapolis Press, 1966); Paul A. Cohen, *China and Christianity: The Missionary Movement and the Growth of Chinese Antiforeignism 1860–1870*, (Cambridge, Mass., Harvard Univ. Press, 1963).
14. See M. C. Wright, *The Last Strand of Chinese Conservatism: The T'ung-Chih Restoration, 1862–1874*, (New York, Stanford Univ. Press, 1966) *passim*.

dissidents. A handful of cosmopolitan Turks, the majority of them in the army—the main source of modernisers in Muslim states—tried to secularise the constitution and give non Muslims equal representation and equality of opportunity within the regime. The reforms decreed by Resid Pasha in 1839 and by Midhat and Huseyin Avni after the coup of 1876 at Constantinople however, like K'ang Yu-wei's in the China of 1898, were smothered at birth in xenophobic reactions from traditional elites.[15] The Tanzimat reformers attempted to do so much more than the Chinese. They ended up doing much worse. The Hamidian traditionalist reaction of pan-Islamism and pan-Turkism after 1876 was that much more passionate. If the Turkish collaborators were eventually ineffective, European statesmen and bankers who dealt them a bad hand to play in Ottoman politics were largely to blame.

5. The character of Afro-Asian collaboration

Some of the reasons why Afro-Asian collaborative mechanisms worked differently from white colonial systems are obvious from these examples. Afro-Asian economies, being largely undifferentiated from their socio-political institutions, were more or less invulnerable to the play of the international market. The institutional barriers to economic invasion proved intractable; economic reform was subject to the political veto of social conservatism; as a result the export-import sector normally remained a tiny accretion on traditional society, and this meant that commercial collaborators were few and unable to win power.

In white colonies the international economy worked through neo-European attitudes and institutions which enabled their export-import sectors to convert British economic power into colonial political collaboration with empire. In most Afro-Asian examples, institutional gaps kept industrial inputs too small to empower such a mechanism. Small as they were they had to be driven in by the hammer of European intervention. External political pressure had to supply the lack of economic leverage on the indigenous political economy before a measure of economic collaboration could be obtained. Consequently the main source of Afro-Asian collaborators was not in the export-import sector but among essentially non-

15. See R. H. Davison, *Reform in the Ottoman Empire, 1839–1876* (Princeton Univ. Press, 1963); W. R. Polk and R. L. Chambers, *Beginnings of Modernization in the Middle East, The Nineteenth Century* (University of Chicago Press, 1968).

commercial, ruling oligarchies and landholding elites. Again, the terms of the bargain under the imperialism of free trade permitted them to divert economic resources to the purpose of maintaining the *status quo*, in return for protecting European enterprise and a measure of political alliance.

Sooner or later consequently these collaborating Oriental regimes fell into the international bankruptcy court as did the Ottoman Sultan and Egyptian Khedive in 1876, the Bey of Tunis in 1867, and the Manchu empire in 1894. One by one they became bones of contention between European powers, subjected to increasing foreign interference to reform the management of their internal financial and political affairs. At this point Europe had forced its internal collaborators to play for high stakes with too few cards. Its demands were cutting off their régimes from the loyalty of the traditional elites which formerly upheld them—whether they were Turkish or Chinese landlords, Muslim or Confucian leaders—until eventually popular xenophobic, neotraditional uprisings confronted their impotence. The stress of free trade imperialism within and without cracked their hold on internal politics. At different times this kind of crisis wrecked collaborative systems of the informal type in most of Africa and Asia; and as they broke down European powers were compelled to change their mode of expansion from free trade imperialism into those of occupation and colonial rule. More often than not it was this non-European component of European expansion that necessitated the extension of colonial empires in the last two decades of the nineteenth century and the first decade of the twentieth.

6. The imperial take-over

Certainly a breakdown of this kind was the imperative behind the British occupation of Egypt in 1882 and therefore incidentally for much of the subsequent rivalry impelling the partition of Africa.[16] After the imposition of free trade in 1841 the Egyptian import-export sector based on cotton grew remarkably under the management of Levantine and European merchants.[17] Since these were extraneous to indigenous society, however, their commercial

16. *Africa and the Victorians*; R. Robinson and J. Gallagher, 'The African partition', *The New Cambridge Modern History*, xi, 1962; cf. C. W. Newbury, 'Victorians, republicans and the partition of West Africa', *Journal of African History*, 3, (1962); Newbury and Kanya-Forstner, 'French policy and the origins of the scramble for West Africa', Kanya-Forstner, *The Conquest of the Western Sudan*, E. Stokes, 'Late nineteenth-century expansion and the attack on the theory of economic imperialism, *Hist. Jnl.*, 12, 1969.

success enabled them to corrupt and exploit, but not to reform or direct, the political régime. The Khedivate overborrowed foreign capital for prestige projects, military and other non-productive purposes, and slid into bankruptcy in 1876. Europe then imposed drastic financial controls and constitutional reforms on the Khedive Ismail in return for further loans, which alienated him from the ruling elite. When he resisted the controls to regain his popularity, Britain and France had him deposed and set up Tewfik in his place. By 1881 as a result, the collaborating Khedivate had lost control of indigenous politics to a neo traditional reaction headed by Arabi and his colonels, Muslim religious leaders and landlords riding a wave of popular antiforeign feeling.[18] Confronted with the collapse, Britain and France had two choices: to scrap their commercial and strategic interest in the country, or to pick up the pieces and reconstruct the collaborative mechanism by throwing their own weight into Egypt's internal politics.[19]

Hence it was the crisis in Egyptian government provoked by heavier collaborative demands, rather than rivalry in Europe, which first set Britain and France competing for the advantage under the new arrangements; and the lack of reliable Egyptian collaborators, rather than fear of France or any increased interest in Egypt, which brought the redcoats onto the Suez Canal in 1882 and kept them there until 1956.

In the partition of China into European spheres of influence from 1895 to 1902, the breakdown of 'open door' collaboration based on an Oriental regime again played a major part. The forces which overthrew it—financial crisis, intensifying foreign intervention and anti-European reaction—looked remarkably similar to those that overthrew the Khedivate: but their Chinese sequence and combination were different. The Japanese victory over China and the war indemnity thus exacted in 1894 bankrupted the Manchu regime, making it for the first time dependent on European loans. An alteration in the eastern regional balance of power rather than European rivalry first precipitated the crisis. At bottom that alteration stemmed from the assault of Japan's revolutionary modernisation on China's reactionary

17. E. R. J. Owen, *Cotton and the Egyptian Economy, 1820–1914* (London, Oxford Univ. Press, 1969); G. Baer, *Land Reform in Modern Egypt, 1800–1950* (New York, 1962); P. M. Holt, *Political and Social Change in Modern Egypt*, (Oxford Univ. Press, 1968).
18. A. Hourani, *Arabic Thought in the Liberal Age*, (London, Oxford Univ. Press, 1962); S. G. Haim, *Arabic Nationalism* (Berkeley, Univ. of California Press, 1962).
19. See *Africa and the Victorians*, ch. 4.

resistance to modern reform. It was these essentially non-European factors which called for European imperialist action. The Japanese conquests threatened Russian strategic interests in north China. Manchu bankruptcy portended the collapse of the indigenous regime. Russia with France, her ally, felt the need, and took the opportunity, to take alternative measures for securing their stakes in the Celestial Empire. Having evicted the Japanese by diplomatic pressure, they extorted exclusive spheres of influence marked out with Chinese railway concessions from Pekin in return for foreign loans, and Britain and Germany necessarily joined in the partition to save their interests.

The antiforeign reaction to intensified imperialist intervention which had precipitated the British occupation of Egypt, helped to halt the occupation of China. The Boxer rebellion of 1900 provoked the Russians to occupy Manchuria in much the same way that Arabi's rebellion led to the British occupation of Egypt. Shortly, however, this Chinese popular resistance, together with the Anglo-Japanese Alliance of 1902 and Japan's defeat of Russia, restored the eastern power balance and halted the imperialist takeover of China. The original necessity for it having been removed, the Chinese partition was aborted. The wheel of collaboration had turned full circle— sufficiently at least to restore the international open door system, if not to save the Manchu regime from its own subjects.

To account for the imperial takeovers in Afro-Asia at the end of the last century exclusively in terms of European capitalism and strategy is to miss the point. The transition was not normally activated by these interests as such, but by the breakdown of collaborative mechanisms in extra-European politics which hitherto had provided them with adequate opportunity and protection.

7. Afro-Asian collaboration and non-collaboration under colonial rule

If Eurocentric theory misses the crucial role of collaborative systems in the transition from external imperialism to the takeover, it also exaggerates the break with previous collaborative processes that colonial rule involved. Admittedly the transition to formal empire looks dramatic in constitutional form and proconsular heroics, and the shooting was real enough. At first sight what seemed to have happened was that the colonial power had thrown its entire weight into indigenous politics, which it was now playing from inside. But this was not the way the proconsuls saw it. Even with colonies, European governments insisted on a policy of limited commitment in the use of metropolitan men and money. The amount of force at the disposal of colonial rulers locally seemed tiny in comparison with the possibility of disaffection and revolt. Reinforcement was usually sent with reluctance, the need for it regarded as a sign of administrative incompetence. Coercion was expensive and counterproductive except in emergency, and everyone knew that no amount of force could hold down indigenous politics for long.

Whether the official agents of imperialism were working from outside or inside Afro-Asian societies therefore, they still had to work through indigenous collaborators and political processes. Their own power was limited. It was enough to manipulate, but not to abolish them. The substance of ruling authority had to a great extent to be extracted from their subjects. Essentially, therefore, colonial rule represented a reconstruction of collaboration. This form of imperialism worked even more than in its earlier external manifestations, as a function of non-European politics.

Occupation of territory, however, made the old collaborative equations much easier to solve. With government patronage in their hands proconsuls could make better bargains with indigenous elites and enforce them. They were also able to manufacture a small modern elite of collaborators and set them in subordinate authority. The colonial regime altered the context in which indigenous political entities worked. However, because its power to maintain that context depended on their acquiescence, its ability to reform them remained slight.

Although good government and modern development were objectives of colonial rule, its first concern was to keep control. Incentives and rewards for its collaborators were partly commercial but mainly governmental—the perquisites of office, honours, contracts, social services and all the favours that could be given or taken away through its administrative land, fiscal and education policies. The rulers distributed them with the object of keeping the weightier part of the dependency's political elements on the government side. Their opponents' tactic, whether they came as at first, from traditional, or later, from modern elites, was to play on grievances and draw this same weightier part into non-cooperation or resistance against colonial rulers. There was never enough patronage to go round. Before the spread of national political organisations, however, rulers could make do with acquiescence if they could not obtain active cooperation. They were secure so long as traditional elites and the grass roots peasantry refused to be politicised by so-called 'agitators'. Hence the less proconsuls interfered with traditional authorities and institutions, the safer they were; and the more they attempted to alter them into modern secular shapes, the harder the collaborative equations became.

In India[20] and Africa up to 1947, there was an abundance of indigenous collaborators. They were of many kinds: some were active, but most were passive, some were modern, but most were traditional elites; some collaborated at central, others at provincial or local levels; some cooperated commercially, others administratively, ecclesiastically, or educationally. The secret of a successful system, from the European standpoint, lay in this variety of choice and combination. It is often said that this was a policy of divide and rule. More truly, rule was possible because its subjects were socially divided and could not unite. The European official bargained with traditional collaborators the more easily because their interests lay in regional politics and traditional activities, whereas he was concerned mainly with central politics and modern activities. Rulers had wide scope for action without clashing head on with the leaders of indigenous, social, religious and political establishments; and so many collaborative bargains took the form of tacit agreements for mutual non-interference and mutual support between colonial government and indigenous society. In India the indigenous political focus was provincial; in Africa, it was normally local or tribal. The miniscule nature of traditional units and their undifferentiated character usually made such bargains effective. Collaborators, on their side, were concerned to exploit the wealth, prestige and influence to be derived from association with colonial government, to increase their traditional followings or improve their modern opportunities. For these reasons collaboration, as colonial rulers well understood, could be a dangerous game. It involved dealing some of their best cards to potentially overmighty subjects. If one set of collaborators grew too powerful as a result, patronage had to be withdrawn and given to another.

20. For examples of Indian systems see A. Seal, *The Emergence of Indian Nationalism* (Cambridge Univ. Press, 1968); R. Frykenberg, *Guntur District, 1788–1848: a history of local influence and central authority in South India*, (London, Oxford Univ. Press, 1965); J. H. Broomfield, *Elite Conflict in a Plural Society, twentieth century Bengal*, (Berkeley, Univ. of California Press, 1968); G. Johnson, 'Indian politics 1895–1905' (Cambridge University Ph.D. thesis, 1969); for the micro-politics of breakdown see S. B. Chaudhuri, *Civil Rebellion in the Indian Mutinies*, and E. Stokes, 'Rural revolt in the Great Rebellion of 1857 in India', *Hist. Jnl. 12*, 4, (1969).

In these ways, European administrators were up to their eyes in the politics of their so-called subjects, even when they did not altogether understand them. They were in the indigenous business of faction and clientage-making with zamindars and talukdars, Hindu bhadralok and Muslim jihad leaders, African clan heads, paramount chiefs and kings. The permutations on which they rang the changes, the brinkmanship involved in pushing indigenous politics in desired modern directions, constituted the true genius of colonial administration.

Collaboration as the basis of colonial rule is richly exemplified in the working of the Indian Raj and African 'indirect rule'. There is space here for but one example: that of British administration in the Anglo-Egyptian Sudan.[21] After defeating its Mahdist rulers in 1898 with Egyptian troops and money, the British controlled this dependency up to 1924 through Egyptian and Sudanese subordinate officials in collaboration with anti-Mahdist 'Notables'. Kitchener's and Wingate's arrangements were designed primarily to forestall the political revival and rebellion of the Mahdist movement. They therefore allied their administration to the interests of the rival Khatmia Muslim order, the orthodox Muslim *ulama* and the anti-Mahdist sheikhs and chiefs of the rural areas. The Khatmia and Mahdist socio-religious organisations, from the British standpoint, were the keys to indigenous politics for only they had the organisation potentially to unite town and countryside, tribe with tribe into a widespread, popular uprising. Implicitly, therefore, the bargain was that the administration exercised its patronage in favour of the anti-Mahdist elements in return for their support; while their enhanced prestige, wealth and following strengthened mutual defence against a revival of Mahdist fanaticism.

After 1924 the rulers realigned their collaborative equations to meet the emergence, in the 'White Flag' mutiny, of a radical, pro-Egyptian minority in the tiny Sudanese modern elite. In the Sudan, as in India and elsewhere in black Africa, it was not the radical modern elite as such that colonial rulers feared. It was rather the combination of these urban malcontents with populist movements among rural peasantry and tribes through an alliance between modern urban, and rural traditional elites. To forestall this danger was the main objective of indirect rule systems of collaboration throughout the British

21. The example is taken from G. Bakheit: 'British administration and Sudanese nationalism', (unpublished Ph.D. Thesis, Cambridge University, 1966); see also M. Abd al-Rahim, *Imperialism and Nationalism in the Sudan* (London, Oxford Univ. Press, 1967).

empire between the two world wars.

Sir John Maffey's indirect rule policy in the Sudan from 1927 to 1933 bestowed official prestige, powers and patronage on the traditional chiefs and headmen of villages and tribes as 'local native authorities'. Its object was to strengthen both their loyalty to the colonial administration and their hold over local rural communities, thus cutting a firebreak to prevent urban radicals or neo-Mahdist agents from setting the grass roots of indigenous politics alight. The arrangements of indirect rule served three purposes: they strengthened local and ethnic compartmentalisation and so raised obstacles to anticolonial agitation on a national scale; they tightened the rural elite's grip on peasant and tribe against the possibility of radical efforts to loosen it; and they reduced contact between 'graduates' in the central administration and the provincial and local rural societies to a minimum.

In the modern elite politics of the three towns of Khartoum, Omdurman and El-Obeid, meanwhile, the colonial collaborative arrangements kept the majority of 'graduates' moderate and opposed to the radical minority. The term 'graduate' signified a man who had completed at least primary education in English. Almost all this modern elite in the Sudan were in the civil service. Their Union society and later national Congress of Graduates' clubs, like the earlier Indian Congress, were more interested consequently in better professional opportunity than mass organisation against colonial rule. The eviction of Egyptian officials and army officers after 1924 provided them with more and better jobs.

After 1933 the collaborative system had to be reoriented once again to meet the threat from neo-Mahdism. Not only was its rural organisation expanding, but its leader, Sir Abdel Rahman el Mahdi was outbidding the loyal Khatmia leadership for influence over the urban graduates. To forestall this conjunction of urban and agrarian discontents through the neo-Mahdist religious organisation, the new Governor, Sir George Symes, abandoned indirect rule to outbid the Mahdists for the support of the graduates. The new tactic offered them Sudanisation of the civil service, more higher education, consultation with the Graduates Congress on policy and, eventually, 'Sudan for the Sudanese'; and up to 1940 it succeeded in its purpose of keeping moderate graduates in control of congress, and of forestalling an alliance between the Congress and the neo-Mahdist politico-religious movement which could politicize the rural population.

After 1940, however, the pace of Sudanisation proved too slow. The Congress divided between neo-Mahdist and Khatmia religious alliances, was captured by the radical Graduates and demanded the right of self-determination for the Sudan after the war. In 1942, as a result, the colonial rulers switched to a rapprochement with the neo-Mahdists and moderate graduates, dividing the neo-Mahdists from their alliance with the radicals, but driving the Khatmia into opposition to the British and alliance with graduate extremists.

So out of the permutations of imperial collaboration emerged the two Sudanese nationalist parties which once they could agree on a united front of non-collaboration with colonial rule, were able to persuade the British to pack their traps and go in 1956. Each party combined elements of the tiny modern elite with a neotraditional Muslim religious organisation. By this means both eventually achieved that combination of modern elite grievances with popular rural discontents which the imperial system of overrule had striven so ingeniously to prevent. Independence became possible, colonial rule impossible, when nationalism had ceased to be merely a tiny elitist movement and succeeded in allying itself to the historic, popular religious forces of Sudanese history.

The conclusions to be drawn from the Sudanese example are more or less true of modern colonial rule in most Afro-Asian dependencies. Its organisation, policy and character were more or less determined by the need to elicit indigenous collaboration and split indigenous opposition. In that sense, imperialism in the form of colonial rule was a minor function of European society, but a major function of indigenous politics. The permutations of collaboration shifted whenever a collaborating element, whether of the modern or neo-traditional elite, grew too powerful or too dissatisfied, and above all, whenever a major element in colonial politics,[22] whether cooperating or in opposition, threatened to unite an urban elite with a mass, rural following.

22. See for African examples M. Perham, *Native Administration in Nigeria*, (Oxford Univ. Press, 1936), and *Lugard*, 2 vols (London, Collins, 1956, 1960); J. D. Hargreaves, '*West African States and the European Conquest*'; J. E. Flint, 'Nigeria: the colonial experience from 1880 to 1914', in *Colonialism in Africa 1870–1960*, ed. L. H. Gann and P. Duignan, i, (Cambridge Univ. Press, 1970); J. M. Lonsdale, 'Political associations in western Kenya' and other articles in *Protest and Power in Black Africa*, ed. R. I. Rotberg and A. A. Mazrui, (New York), (Oxford Univ. Press, 1970; Lonsdale, 'Some origins of African nationalism in East Africa', *Journal African History*, **9**, 1, (1968); T. Ranger, 'African reactions to the imposition of colonial rule in East and Central Africa', in *Colonialism in Africa, 1870–1960*, i; J. Iliffe, *Tanganyika under German Rule, 1905–1912* (Cambridge Univ. Press, 1969); M. Twaddle, '"Tribalism" in Eastern Uganda', in *Tradition and Transition in East Africa*, ed. P. H. Gulliver, (London, Routledge, 1968); M. Crowder, *West Africa under Colonial Rule*, (London, Hutchinson, 1968), and *West African Resistance* (London, Hutchinson, 1971); A. H. M. Kirk-Greene, ed., *The Principles of Native Administration in Nigeria. Selected Documents 1900–1947*, (Oxford Univ. Press, 1965); D. Austin, *Politics in Ghana, 1946–1960*, (Oxford Univ. Press, 1964); D. A. Low and R. Pratt, *Buganda and British Over-Rule*, (Oxford Univ. Press, 1960).

8. Non-collaboration and decolonisation

No less than colonial rule, the anticolonial nationalism of small modern elites had to be translated into broader terms of indigenous, neotraditional politics before it could challenge and overthrow the imperial collaborative system and set up a rival system of non-collaboration.[23] Nationalists had to contrive a situation in which their rulers ran out of collaborators. They had to realign against imperialism the same political elements which, hitherto, had been arrayed on the imperial side. Necessarily in pre-industrial societies, these were preponderantly neotraditionalist religious, social and ethnic units. In that sense all the national movements that won independence were more or less functions of neotraditional politics organised in the form of modern political parties. Each party was essentially a confederation of neotraditional local, ethnic, religious and status interests, managed by a small modern elite. The party, like the colonial regime before it, changed the context in which these social interests operated and integrated them with itself in new alignments. As the party became a function of them, they became to some extent a function of the party. So long as the national party was in opposition to a colonial regime, it was comparatively easy to reconcile these two roles. But when the party became the government of the nation its function as representative of neo-traditional interests conflicted increasingly with its role as development agent for the nation as a whole. The experience of the 1960s shows that the reconciliation of the two roles and the problem of neotraditionalist social collaboration involved, is not much easier for new nationalists than it was for old colonialists.

9. Conclusion

The theory of collaboration suggests that at every stage from external imperialism to decolonisation, the working of imperialism was determined by the indigenous collaborative systems connecting its European and Afro-Asian components. It was as much and often more

23. T. O. Ranger, 'Connections between "primary resistance" movements and modern mass nationalism in east and central Africa', *Journal of African History*, ix, 3 and 4, 1968; E. Stokes, 'European administration and African political systems, 1891–1897', Conference on Central African History, Lusaka, 1963; D. Ashford, 'The politics of rural mobilisation in North Africa', *Jnl. Mod. Afr. Studies*, 7, 2, (1969); J. M. Lonsdale, 'African politics in western Kenya': its leadership, scale and focus' (unpublished paper to Cambridge University Commonwealth History Seminar, 1967) and 'Decolonisation in East Africa', Cambridge University Commonwealth History Seminar, 1971.

a function of Afro-Asian politics than of European politics and economics.

At the outset it depended on the absence or presence of effective indigenous collaborators, and the character of indigenous society, whether imperialist invasions of Africa and Asia were practicable or not. Secondly, the transition from one phase of imperialism to the next was governed by the need to reconstruct and uphold a collaborative system that was breaking down. The breakdown of indigenous collaboration in many instances necessitated the deeper imperial intervention that led to imperial takeover. Thirdly, the choice of indigenous collaborators, more than anything else, determined the organisation and character of colonial rule; in other words, its administrative, constitutional, land and economic policies were largely institutionalisations of the indigenous, political alliances which upheld it. Fourthly, when the colonial rulers had run out of indigenous collaborators, they either chose to leave or were compelled to go. Their national opponents in the modern elite sooner or later succeeded in detaching the indigenous political elements from the colonial regime until they eventually formed a united front of non-collaboration against it. Hence the inversion of collaboration into non-cooperation largely determined the timing of decolonisation. Lastly, since anticolonial movements emerged as coalitions of non-collaboration out of the collaborative equations of colonial rule and the transfer of power, the elements and character of Afro-Asian national parties and governments in the first era of independence projected a kind of mirror image of collaboration under imperialism.

David Fieldhouse has labelled the general idea underlying this analysis the 'peripheral theory'.[24] More truly it is what might be called an 'excentric' approach to European imperialism. To borrow a figure from geometry, there was the Eurocentric circle of industrial strategy making varying intersections with circles centred in the implacable continuities of African and Asian history. Imperialism, especially in its time scale, was not precisely a true function of either circle. It was in many ways excentric to both. It should be emphasised that the Afro-Asian crises which evoked imperialism were often not essentially the products of European forces but of autonomous changes in African and Asian domestic politics. Changing over to a mechanical analogy, imperialism was in another sense the 'centre of mass' or resultant of both circles. Hence the motivation and modes of imperialism

24. Fieldhouse, *Theory of Capitalist Imperialism*, xv, 193–4.

were functions of collaboration, non-collaboration, mediation and resistance at varying intersections of the two circles. It is hardly surprising, therefore, that its European directors and agents, no less than its victims, looked on imperialism as an inevitable but random process receding out of control.

What is not evident yet is a firm answer to the critical question in assessing the third world's prospects in the 1970s and 80s. Their international frame has altered from imperialism to formal independence with foreign aid. However the importance of the external frame in deciding their fortunes is marginal. Their chances of stability indigenous politics and upon collaboration between modern and neo traditional elites. It is this factor that is likely to determine whether they become truly independent or remain victims of 'neocolonialism'. In over-throwing colonial regimes, how far did the nationalists of Africa and Asia merely realign the traditional and neo-traditional units of indigenous politics on a temporary basis? How far did they succeed, through national party organisation, in unifying and transforming them permanently? Nationalists are more 'representative' of the historic entities than colonial rulers ever were, and national leaders are able to play their politics more intimately and organise them better. It is precisely because nationalists are more 'representative' of neotraditional units that they may be in greater danger of becoming their political prisoners than their predecessors were. The experience of the 1960s suggests that the nationalists often realigned these units negatively rather than transforming them positively. That of the 1970s and 80s may prove otherwise.

DISCUSSION

The collaborative mechanism and wider theories of imperialism.
During the discussion a number of questions were raised about the relationship of the concept of 'collaboration' to a wider theory of imperialism. One concerned Robinson's assertion that imperialism was a function of the indigenous politics of the non-European world. By this did he mean to imply that countries were more or less subject to imperialism according to the nature of their political system, or that the way in which imperialism operated in individual countries depended on the nature of their political system? In reply Robinson said that in some sense he had meant to imply both. The first implication was a corollary of the definition he had already given of imperialism in which it was maintained that the capitalist system was not inherently imperialistic at all times but that it was imperialist in its relations with some countries at some times. However, he was also concerned to show that where such relations were imperialist the degree of imperialism

(by which he meant all forms of political influence as well as that economic influence which had a socio-political effect) was to a great extent a function of the political and social conditions in the satellite countries.

Another point which was raised in a number of questions related to the fact that the notion of collaboration, while throwing light on the nature of politics in a colonial situation, has nothing to say about how or why that situation came about or what political control was wanted for. For this it would be necessary to place the idea of a collaborative mechanism within a wider, more general, theory of imperialism. Robinson agreed; his use of the idea had to be seen in the context of an expanding Europe.

The economic aspect of collaboration.   Other questions concentrated more directly on the notion of collaboration itself. Was it not the case, for instance, that it was very difficult to translate the idea into economic terms? The way that it was used in the paper seemed to imply a bargain of some kind between groups of Europeans and non-Europeans, but it was difficult to see how whole economies could be said to strike bargains with one another. Robinson's answer was that he was not concerned with economies as such but only with the way in which they influenced, and in turn were influenced by, politics. To give one example, the Europeans used the collaborative mechanism to establish certain types of political arrangements in the non-European countries in order that the economies of the latter could develop in a certain way. Again, he was interested in the way in which certain types of economic activity, for instance the investment of large sums of money, produced certain political effects, for instance the emergence of new groups of potential collaborators.

Who were the collaborators?   A related question concerned the method by which collaborating groups were to be identified and defined. Was it not true that Robinson's paper gave little guidance? His nomenclature seemed to alter throughout the paper: sometimes he talked of classes, at others of groups or elites; sometimes he defined the collaborators in terms of a bargain with Europe, at others in terms of their local economic relationships. To this Robinson replied that his paper did not aim to provide a finished theory but only a programme for future study. There was much more work to be done before such questions could be answered properly. Nevertheless, he did think that it was possible to go some way towards discovering who the collaborators were. In a number of cases they were to be found not as groups but as collections of people of different kinds, at different levels, who had been drawn into collaboration as a result of the creation of European types of institutions within their societies. The most obvious example of this was the local people who worked for the colonial government. Another group could be defined in terms of the stage they had reached in the system of modern education, and so on. However, it was also important to bear in mind that there were few collaborators who collaborated 'straight across the board'. The majority of those in the modern sector also maintained their links with the traditional sector. In answer to a similar question about the fact that his theory had nothing to say about the way in which class structures had developed outside Europe as a result of contact with the world economy,

Robinson maintained that it was very difficult to know how to identify such classes in an area where societies tended to be fragmented and where economic interests were so closely related to religious and social custom.

PART TWO

Theoretical aspects of contemporary imperialism

VI

Imperialism without colonies

Harry Magdoff

The identification of imperialism with formal political control in the form of colonialism is one source of misunderstanding which plagues most discussions of imperialism, including the one in this book. (See Conclusion, 4.) It is a common feature of all Marxist approaches, as Magdoff argues here, that although the territorial division of the world was certainly a part of the 'new imperialism' of the later nineteenth century, imperialism has survived decolonisation intact.

One of the essential parts of this continuity is foreign investment on a large scale. Much of the paper is concerned with aspects of this capital export. First its causation: here Magdoff rejects explanations, like Hobson's, based on the existence of surplus capital (section 1) as well as those based on the falling rate of profit (section 2; compare Kemp above, 1. 2). Pointing out the fallacy of comparing average profit rates in an age of monopoly, rather than individual marginal rates on which decisions about capital movements are actually based, Magdoff finds the underlying cause of continuing capital export in the monopolistic structure of industry in the advanced capitalist countries.

Second, Magdoff's paper enlarges on the description of recent capital exports already partly outlined by Barratt Brown (II. 8b). He shows for example that U.S. capital controls more assets than its own; that only a small proportion of its foreign investment is financed by direct outflow of funds from the U.S., the rest being financed out of retained earnings or locally raised funds; and that the great majority of overseas American capital is in the hands of the largest corporations. All these features can be seen from another vantage point in the case study of imperialism in India by Patnaik, (sections 3 and 5 below).

After rejecting several misconceptions about imperialism and crisis and about the role of the state (sections 4 and 5) Magdoff outlines some of the characteristics and consequences of imperialism in the post-colonial age, finding it to be a method of perpetuating the existing international division of labour. This relates to Barratt Brown's view of cumulative causation (II. 12), and also to the discussion of industrialisation in the third world by Sutcliffe and Patnaik (VII and IX below).

The sudden upsurge during the late nineteenth century in the aggressive pursuit of colonies by almost all the great powers is, without doubt, a primary distinguishing trait of the 'new imperialism'. It is surely the dramatic hallmark of this historic process, and yet it is by no means the essence of the new imperialism. In fact, the customary identification of imperialism with colonialism is an obstacle to the proper study of the subject, since colonialism existed before the modern form of imperialism and the latter has outlived colonialism.

While colonialism itself has an ancient history, the colonialism of the last five centuries is closely associated with the birth and maturation of the capitalist socio-economic system. The pursuit and acquisition of colonies (including political and economic domination, short of colonial ownership) was a significant attribute of the commercial revolution which contributed to the disintegration of feudalism and the foundation of capitalism. The precapitalist regional trade patterns around the globe were not destroyed by the inexorable forces of the market. Instead, it was superior military power that laid the basis for transforming these traditional trade patterns into a world market centred on the needs and interests of Western Europe. The leap ahead in naval power—based on advances in artillery and in sailing vessels able to carry the artillery—created the bludgeoning force used to annex colonies, open trading ports, enforce new trading relations, and develop mines and plantations. Based on mastery of seapower, this colonialism was mainly confined to coastal areas, except for the Americas where the sparse population had a primitive technology and was highly susceptible to European infectious diseases.[1] Until the nineteenth century, economic relations with these colonies were, from the European standpoint, import-oriented: largely characterised by the desire of the metropolitan countries to obtain the esoteric goods and riches that could be found only in the colonies. For most of those years, in fact, the conquering Europeans had little to offer in exchange for the spices, and tropical agricultural products they craved as well as the precious metals from the Americas.

The metropolitan–colonial relation changed under the impact

1. Carlo M. Cipolla, *Guns, Sails and Empires: technological innovation and early phases of European expansion 1400–1700.* (New York, Pantheon, 1965), 'Epilogue'.

of the industrial revolution and the development of the steam railway. With these, the centre of interest shifted from imports to exports, resulting in the ruination of native industry, the penetration of large land areas, a new phase in international banking, and increasing opportunity for the export of capital. Still further changes were introduced with the development of large-scale industry based on new metallurgy, the industrial application of organic chemistry, new sources of power, and new means of communication and of ocean transport.

In the light of geographic and historical disparities among colonies and the different purposes they have served at different times, the conclusion can hardly be avoided that attempts such as have been made by some historians and economists to fit all colonialism into a single model are bound to be unsatisfactory. There is, to be sure, a common factor in the various colonial experiences; namely, the exploitation of the colonies for the benefit of the metropolitan centres.[2] Moreover, there is unity in the fact that the considerable changes in the colonial and semicolonial world that did occur were primarily in response to the changing needs of an expanding and technically advancing capitalism. Still, if we want to understand the economics and politics of the colonial world at some point in time, we have to recognise and distinguish the differences associated with the periods of mercantile capitalism, competitive industrial capitalism, and monopoly capitalism, just as we have to distinguish these stages of development in the metropolitan centres themselves if we want to understand the process of capital development.

The identification of imperialism with colonialism obfuscates not only historical variation in colonial–metropolitan relations, but makes it more difficult to evaluate the latest transformation of the capitalist world system, the imperialism of the period of monopoly capitalism. This obfuscation can often be traced to the practice of creating rigid, static and ahistoric conceptual models to cope with complex, dynamic phenomena. I propose to examine some of the more common misconceptions on which models of this kind are often based in the belief that it will help clarify the theme of imperial-

2. Obviously, the immediate objectives in the acquisition of colonies were not uniform; some colonies were pursued because of their strategic military value in building and maintaining an empire, others were pursued to prevent the enlargement of competitive empires, etc. The common factor referred to above is in the colonial experience itself. Regardless of the planned or accidental features of the acquisition process, the administration of the colonies (and the manipulation of the semicolonial areas) was aimed at, or led to, the adaptation of the periphery areas to serve the economic advantage of the metropolitan centres.

ism without colonies. Two such misconceptions are particularly common, both of which relate to the vital role played by the export of capital: those based on arguments concerning the export of surplus capital and the falling rate of profit in the advanced capitalist countries.

1. The pressure of surplus capital

A distinguishing feature of the new imperialism associated with the period of monopoly capitalism (that is, when the giant corporation is in the ascendancy and there is a high degree of economic concentration) is a sharp rise in the export of capital. The tie between the export of capital and imperialist expansion is the obvious need on the part of investors of capital for a safe and friendly environment.

But why the upsurge in the migration of capital during the last quarter of the nineteenth century and its continuation to this day? A frequently-met explanation is that the advanced capitalist nations began to be burdened by a superabundance of capital that could not find profitable investment opportunities at home and therefore sought foreign outlets. While a strong case can be made for the proposition that the growth of monopoly leads to increasing investment difficulties, it does not follow that the export of capital was stimulated primarily by the pressure of a surplus of capital.[3]

The key to answering the question lies, in my opinion, in understanding and viewing capitalism as a world system. The existence of strong nation states and the importance of nationalism tend to obscure the concept of a global capitalist system. Yet the nationalism of capitalist societies is the *alter ego* of the system's internationalism. Successful capitalist classes need the power of nation states not only

3. The analysis of the surplus question is well developed in Baran's and Sweezy's *Monopoly Capital* (New York, Monthly Review Press, 1966). A distinction needs to be made, however, between the question posed by Baran and Sweezy and the one we are examining here. In fact, they deal with the concept of 'economic surplus' and not 'surplus capital'. The term 'economic surplus' does not necessarily imply 'too-muchness' of capital. It is simply a surplus over necessary costs of production, and whether any of it is also surplus in the sense of the theories which relate surplus capital to capital export is a totally different and even unrelated question. Baran and Sweezy in *Monopoly Capital* deal with the basic dynamics of investment and employment in relation to the stagnation-inducing tendencies of monopoly. They argue that the export of capital does not offset the stagnation tendency since the income returning home is greater than the outflow of investment. Hence, the export of capital intensifies the surplus problem of investment outlets rather than alleviating it. It should be noted that Baran and Sweezy are dealing with the *effect* of capital export, not the *cause*. And, in dealing with the effect of this export, they do not attempt to analyse it in all its ramifications. They are concerned solely with its effect on the disposal of the economic surplus in the home country. This is quite a different question from the one we are posing: what is the cause of the rise in export of capital.

to develop inner markets and to build adequate infrastructures but also, and equally important, to secure and protect opportunities for foreign commerce and investment in a world of rival nation states. Each capitalist nation wants protection for itself, preferential trade channels, and freedom to operate internationally. Protectionism, a strong military posture, and the drive for external markets are all part of the same package.

The desire and need to operate on a world scale is built into the economics of capitalism. Competitive pressures, technical advances, and recurring imbalances between productive capacity and effective demand create continuous pressures for the expansion of markets. The risks and uncertainties of business, interrelated with the unlimited acquisitive drive for wealth, activate the entrepreneur to accumulate ever greater assets and in the process to scour every corner of the earth for new opportunities. What stand in the way, in addition to technical limits of transportation and communication, are the recalcitrance of natives and the rivalry of other capitalist nation states.

Viewed in this way, export of capital, like foreign trade, is a normal function of capitalist enterprise. Moreover, the expansion of capital export is closely associated with the geographic expansion of capitalism. Back in the earliest days of mercantile capitalism, capital began to reach out beyond its original borders to finance plantations and mines in the Americas and Asia. With this came the growth of overseas banking to finance trade with Europe as well as to help lubricate foreign investment operations. Even though domestic investment opportunities may have lagged in some places and at some times, the primary drive behind the export of capital was not the pressure of surplus capital but the utilisation of capital where profitable opportunities existed, constrained of course by the technology of the time, the economic and political conditions in the other countries, and the resources of the home country. For example, since military power was needed to force an entry into many of these profit-making opportunities, shortages of manpower and economic resources that could readily be devoted to such purposes also limited investment opportunities.

As mentioned above, a reversal in trade relations occurs under the impact of the industrial revolution and the upsurge of mass-produced manufactures. Capitalist enterprise desperately searches out export markets, while it is the overseas areas which suffer from a shortage of goods to offer in exchange. As a result, many of the countries which buy from industrialised countries fall into debt, since their imports tend to exceed their exports. Under such conditions opportunities and the need for loan capital from the metropolitan centres expand. Capital exports thus become an important prop to the export of goods. As is well known, the real upsurge in demand for British export capital came with the development of the railway. It was not only British industry that supplied the iron rails and railroad equipment over great stretches of the globe, but also British loan and equity capital, that made the financing of these exports possible. In addition, the financial institutions which evolved in the long history of international trade and capital export acquired vested interests in the pursuit of foreign business. Following their own growth imperatives, they sought new opportunities for the use of capital overseas, while energetically collecting and stimulating domestic capital for such investments.

The important point is that capital export has a long history. It is a product of (*a*) the worldwide operations of the advanced capitalist nations, and (*b*) the institutions and economic structure that evolved in the ripening of capitalism as a world system. It is not the product of surplus capital as such. This does not mean that there is never a 'surplus capital' problem (fed at times by the return flow of interest and profits from abroad), nor that at times capital will not move under the pressure of such surpluses. Once sophisticated international money markets exist, various uses will be made of them. Short-term funds, for instance, will move across borders in response to temporary tightness or ease of money in the several markets. Money will be loaned for more general political and economic purposes, for one country to gain influence and preferential treatment in another. But the main underpinning of the international financial markets is the international network of trade and investment that was generated by the advanced industrial nations in pursuit of their need to operate in world markets. Thus, while surplus domestic capital may at times be a contributing factor to capital movements abroad, the more relevant explanation, in our opinion, is to be found in the interrelations between the domestic economic situation of the advanced capitalist nations and that of their overseas markets.[4]

4. On the interrelation between British capital export and export of goods, see A. G. Ford, 'Overseas lending and internal fluctuations 1870–1914' and A. J. Brown, 'Britain in the world economy 1820–1914', both in the *Yorkshire Bulletin of Economic and Social Research*, May 1965. On the question of capital surplus and/or scarcity, note the interesting observation by A. J. Brown in the above article: '. . . Professor Tinbergen, in his remarkable econometric study of the United Kingdom in this period (*Business Cycles in the United Kingdom 1870–1914*, Amsterdam, 1951), finds a positive association between net capital exports and the short term interest rate, suggesting that money became scarce because it was lent abroad rather than that it was lent abroad because it was plentiful' (p. 51).

Why then the sudden upsurge of capital exports associated with modern imperialism? The answer, in my opinion, is consistent with the above analysis as well as with the nature of this later stage of capitalism. First, the onset of the new imperialism is marked by the arrival of several industrial states able to challenge Britain's hegemony over international trade and finance. These other nations expand their capital exports for the same purposes, increased foreign trade and preferential markets. Thus, instead of Britain being the dominant exporter of capital among very few others, a new crop of exporters come to the fore, with the result that the total flow of capital exports greatly expands. Second, associated with the intensified rivalry of advanced industrial nations is the growth of protective tariff walls: one means of jumping these tariff walls is foreign investment. Third, the new stage of capitalism is based on industries requiring vast new supplies of raw materials, such as oil and ferrous and non-ferrous metal ores. This requires not only large sums of capital for exploration and development of foreign sources, but also loan capital to enable foreign countries to construct the needed complementary transportation and public utility facilities. Fourth, the maturation of joint stock companies, the stock market and other financial institutions provided the means for mobilising capital more efficiently for use abroad as well as at home. Finally, the development of giant corporations hastened the growth of monopoly. The ability and desire of these corporations to control markets provided another major incentive for the expansion of capital abroad.

The facts on U.S. investment abroad in the present era are quite revealing on the issue of 'surplus' capital; they can help us to answer the historical questions as well. One would expect that if a major, if not *the* major, reason for the export of U.S. capital today were the pressure of a superabundance of domestic capital, then as much capital as could be profitably used abroad would be drawn from the United States. But that is not the case. We have the data on the capital structure of U.S. direct investments abroad in the year 1957. (This is the latest year for which such data are available. Another census of foreign investments was taken in 1966, but the results have not yet been published.) What we find is that 60 per cent of the direct investment assets of U.S.-based corporations are owned by U.S. residents and 40 per cent by non-U.S. residents, mainly local residents, but including overseas European and Canadian capital invested in Latin America, etc. (see Table I.B).

TABLE I.   U.S. direct–investment enterprise in other countries in 1957[1]: Assets owned by U.S. and local residents

A. *Percentage of total assets in equity and debt*

	TOTAL ASSETS		EQUITY ASSETS		DEBT ASSETS	
	$ BILLION	PER CENT	$ BILLION	PER CENT	$ BILLION	PER CENT
Owned by U.S. residents	$24·0	100·0	$19·7	82·3	$4·2	17·7
Owned by Local residents [2]	15·6	100·0	3·2	20·6	12·4	79·4
Total	$39·6	100·0	$22·9	58·0	$16·6	42·0

B. *Percentage distribution of assets by U.S. and local ownership*

	TOTAL ASSETS	EQUITY ASSETS	DEBT ASSETS
Owned by U.S. residents	60·5	86·0	25·4
Owned by Local residents[2]	39·5	14·0	74·6
Total	100·0	100·0	100·0

(Details may not add up to totals because of rounding off of decimals.)
1. Finance and insurance investments are excluded.
2. More accurately, non-U.S. residents. The owners are primarily residents of the areas in which U.S. enterprise is located, though there was probably a flow of funds from Europe and Canada to U.S.-owned enterprise in other areas.
Source: Calculated from *U.S. Business Investments in Foreign Countries*. (U.S. Department of Commerce, Washington, D.C. 1960), Table 20.

Now there is an interesting twist to these data. If we separate equity and debt assets, we discover that U.S. residents own 86 per cent of the equity and only 25 per cent of the debt. What this reflects is the practice employed by U.S. firms to assure control over their foreign assets and to capture most of the 'perpetual' flow of profits. As for the debt capital (long- and short-term), which in time will be repaid out of the profits of the enterprise, it is just as well to give the native rich a break. The supposedly pressing 'surplus' funds of the home country are very little tapped for the debt capital needs of foreign enterprise.

But we should also be aware that the 60–40 share of the capital assets, mentioned above, exaggerates the capital funds supplied from the United States. Here is how a businessman's publication, *Business Abroad*, describes the overseas investment practices of U.S. corporations:

> In calculating the value of capital investment, General Motors, for example, figures the intangibles such as trademarks, patents, and know-how equivalent to twice the actual invested capital. Some corporations calculate know-how, blueprints, and so on as one third of capital investment, and then supply one third in equity by providing machinery and equipment.[5]

Hence, a good share of the 60 per cent of the assets owned by U.S. firms does not represent cash investment but a valuation of their knowledge, trademarks, etc., and their own machinery valued at prices set by the home office.[6]

One may ask whether this phenomenon of using local capital is a feature predominantly of investment practices in wealthier foreign countries. The answer is no. It is true that the share supplied by local capital is larger in European countries (54 per cent) and lower in Latin American countries (31 per cent), but the practice of obtaining debt capital locally is characteristic of all regions in which U.S. capital is invested (see Table II).

The facts on the flow of funds to finance U.S. direct investments abroad are even more striking. We have data on the source of funds used to finance these enterprises for the period 1957 to 1965. While this information is for a limited period, other available evidence indicates that there is no reason to consider this period as atypical.[7]

These data reveal that during the period in question some $84 billion were used to finance the expansion and operations of direct

5. *Business Abroad*, 11 July, 1966, p. 31.
6. It is difficult to untangle all the factors to get a more realistic picture. First, not all the equity capital represents the original investment; some of it is reinvested surplus. The *Business Abroad* observation would apply only to the original investment. Also, there is a counter tendency which leads to an understatement of U.S. investment. In some industries, especially in the extractive ones, firms have written off assets which are still being productively used.
7. Note the more recent growth of U.S. direct investments abroad despite government restriction on the outflow of investment capital to reduce the balance of payments deficit. *Business Week* comments: 'More important, though, is the growing ease with which U.S. companies can borrow abroad. This year . . . companies will finance 91 per cent of their planned overseas spending from sources outside the U.S., up from 84 per cent last year. . . . Financing abroad has become so easy, in fact, that the federal controls on dollar movements from the U.S. have been only a minor obstacle to foreign spending plans' (9 August 1969, p. 38).

TABLE II. Percentage distribution of assets of U.S. direct-investment enterprises in other countries, by ownership and area (in 1957) [1]

OWNERSHIP	TOTAL ASSETS	EQUITY ASSETS	DEBT ASSETS
In Canada			
U.S. residents	62·0	78·5	37·2
Local residents [2]	38·0	21·5	62·8
Total	100·0	100·0	100·0
In Europe			
U.S. residents	46·2	83·9	11·1
Local residents [2]	53·8	16·1	88·9
Total	100·0	100·0	100·0
In Latin America			
U.S. residents	69·1	92·9	24·9
Local residents [2]	30·9	7·1	75·1
Total	100·0	100·0	100·0
In Africa			
U.S. residents	51·5	80·7	23·9
Local residents [2]	48·5	19·3	76·1
Total	100·0	100·0	100·0
In Asia			
U.S. residents	62·4	94·1	13·1
Local residents [2]	37·6	5·9	86·9
Total	100·0	100·0	100·0

Notes and source: as Table I.

foreign investments. Of this total, only a little more than 15 per cent came from the United States. The remaining 85 per cent was raised outside the United States: 20 per cent from locally raised funds and 65 per cent from the cash generated by the foreign enterprise operations themselves (see Table III.A).

TABLE III.   Sources of funds of U.S. direct-investment enterprises in other countries: 1957–1965

A. *Summary of all areas*

SOURCES OF FUNDS	FUNDS OBTAINED	
	$ BILLION	PER CENT OF TOTAL
From United States	$12·8	15·3
Obtained abroad	16·8	20·1
Obtained from operations of foreign enterprises	54·1	64·6
From net income	33·6	40·1
From depreciation and depletion	20·5	24·5
Total	$83·7	100·0

B. *Percentage distribution, by area*

AREA	PERCENTAGE OF FUNDS OBTAINED		
	FROM U.S.	FROM OUTSIDE U.S.[1]	TOTAL
Canada	15·7	84·3	100·0
Europe	20·2	79·8	100·0
Latin America	11·4	88·6	100·0
All other areas	13·6	86·4	100·0

1. Includes funds raised abroad from non-U.S. residents and from operations of foreign enterprises.
Source: 1957 data—same as Table 1; 1958–65 data from *Survey of Current Business*, September 1961; September 1962; November 1965; January 1967.

Here again the pattern is similar for rich countries and poor countries. If anything, the U.S. capital contribution is less in the poor countries than in the rich ones: the U.S. capital contribution is 16 per cent for enterprise in Canada, 20 per cent in Europe, 11 per cent in Latin America, and 14 per cent in all other areas. Too many inferences should not be drawn from these differentials; large funds came from the United States during these years to finance the rapid expansion of enterprises in Europe. However, it is proper to observe that only a small percentage of the supply of funds needed to finance its foreign investments is coming from the United States. And that is hardly what one would expect on the basis of a theory that the main reason for foreign investment is the pressure of a superabundance of capital at home.

2. The declining rate of profit

A second major ground often advanced for the rise in capital exports is the declining rate of profit. The reasoning behind this is that capital accumulation, accompanied by an ever-rising ratio of fixed capital to labour, produces a dominant tendency for the average rate of profit to decline. Such a decline induces domestic capitalists to invest abroad where labour costs are lower and profits higher.

We cannot now, and do not need to for this purpose, examine either the internal theoretical consistency of this theory, whether the facts bear it out, or, if it is true, how this tendency would work under monopoly conditions. This examination is not necessary, in my opinion, because in any case the declining rate of profit would not explain the pattern of international capital movements. In other words, it is not a necessary hypothesis in this connection, whether in itself it is true or not. This point can be substantiated in relation to two types of foreign investment, the purchase of foreign bonds and the development of oil wells and mines. However, before presenting my reasons for saying this, I would like to point out that there are two separate questions. We are concerned here with the *causes* of the export of capital in the period of imperialism. The *effect* of the export of capital on domestic profit rates is a different, though undoubtedly important, question.

To return to the pattern of international capital movements. First, the declining rate of profit hypothesis cannot apply to loan capital. Rates of interest on money lent abroad are generally attractive, but, for relatively safe loans, they are considerably below the industrial rate of profit. Thus, a purchase of foreign bonds by a corporation would not normally be an offsetting action against a declining rate of profit.

We also need to eliminate this hypothesis to explain the extensive direct investment in oil extraction and mining. Investments in these industries are not primarily motivated by comparative profit rates or falling rates of profit at home, but by the facts of geology. The decisive factors are where the minerals were placed by God, and the transportation problems of getting them to the consuming centres.

Profit rates are, of course, always involved, and they are usually very high. Also the investor will take advantage of as low wages as he can get away with. However, the profitability of these extractive industries is not based on low wages but on the abundance of the natural resources where they happen to be and on the monopolistic structures through which they are marketed.

It is true that comparative profit rates do enter the picture when, as in the case of iron mining in the United States, formerly rich iron ore reserves become depleted. A rush then ensues to develop iron reserves in Labrador, Venezuela, and Brazil. But here again the decisive factor is not a declining profit rate due to the process of capitalist accumulation: it is rather a declining profit rate due to the state of nature.

It is a third kind of investment, foreign direct investment in manufacturing, which provides the only real test of the thesis. Here, if anywhere, one might expect capital to flow in response to simple profit-rate differentials. What then about direct investments in manufacturing? It should go without saying that the profit rate dominates all investment decisions, and it should also be clear that capital will continuously seek the highest obtainable profit rate. Whether profit rates are rising or declining at home, we should expect capital to flow out as long as higher profit rates are obtainable abroad. But it is not necessary that profit rates obtainable abroad should be higher than average domestic profit rates to sustain this flow. What concerns the investor is a comparison of the profitability of additional (or marginal) investment in industry at home and industry abroad. Theoretically, the new investment abroad could have a lower return than the average rate of profit at home and still be attractive. For example, assume that a manufacturer of refrigerators is getting a return of 20 per cent on his domestic investment. He wants to make a new investment and finds that he will get only 15 per cent at home, but that he can get 18 per cent if he uses these funds to make refrigerators abroad. He will be prompted to go abroad, with the result that his foreign investments will yield less than his domestic investment. (This is one reason, by the way, why comparisons of data on average manufacturing profit rates at home and abroad are not really meaningful, aside from inadequacies of the statistics themselves.) So it is this gap in marginal profitability which produces the flow of foreign investment; it has no necessary connection with any fall in the average profitability of investment at home.

3. Monopoly and foreign investment

A much more useful hypothesis than the falling-rate-of-profit, I believe, is one that traces the main drive for direct investment of capital on a global scale to the imperatives of capital operating under monopoly conditions. Such an analytical framework embraces an explanation of (*a*) the main body of investment, in extractive as well as manufacturing industries; and (*b*) the step-up in capital exports during the period of imperialism. Its central purpose is to demonstrate the interrelation between the concomitant rise in capital exports and monopoly as the core of the new imperialism.

Business, in general, can best be understood as a system of power, to use a phrase of Robert Brady's. It is of the essence of business to try to control its own market and to operate, so far as possible, as if the entire globe were its preserve. This was true from the very outset of the capitalist era. As long, however, as there were many competitors in most industries, the opportunities for control were quite limited. With the development of monopoly conditions—i.e. when a handful of companies dominates each of the important markets—the exercise of controlling power becomes not only possible but increasingly essential for the security of the firm and its assets.

The emergence of a significant degree of concentration of power does not mean the end of competition. It does mean that competition has been raised to a new level: temporary arrangements among competitors about production, price, and sales policies are more feasible than before, and business decisions can be arrived at with reasonable anticipation of what the competitive response will be. Since capital operates on a world scale, the business arrangements to divide markets and/or the competitive struggle among the giants for markets stretch over large sections of the globe.

Furthermore, the competitive strategy changes from the period of competition. Price cutting is no longer the preferred method of acquiring a larger share of the market. Prices are kept high, and the expansion of production is restrained by the limitation of effective demand at high prices or the ability to win a larger share of the high-priced market from a competitor. Nevertheless, the necessity to grow persists and the capital available for growth mounts; hence the constant pressure for rivals to get a larger share of each others' markets wherever they may be. It should be noted that this struggle for larger markets will naturally take place in the more developed countries, where markets for sophisticated products already exist and where it is possible to take advantage of the privileged trade channels of each others' colonial or semicolonial empire. This struggle also takes place in the less developed countries, where new markets, however small, can be entered and where the first firms to get a foothold often have lasting advantage.

The impetus to invest abroad arises out of this competitive struggle among the giants. First, the ownership of raw material supplies is of strategic importance in the push for control over prices, to hold one's own against competitors who also control supplies, and to restrict the growth of competitors who do not have their own sources. Second, the need to control and expand markets is a major spur and incentive for capital export, especially where tariffs or other barriers to trade impede the expansion of commodity exports.

The correlation between monopolistic motives and the spread of foreign investment is supported not only by this analysis but by the actual pattern of investment, at least in the case of the largest foreign investor, the United States. The monopolistic aspects of U.S. (and other) investments in oil and metal ores are too well known to need dwelling on here. In manufacturing, it is clear, overseas investment is a game for the larger firms. Thus, in 1962, 94 per cent of the assets of U.S. foreign manufacturing corporations were controlled by firms with assets of $50 million or more.[8] Moreover, a study of the 1957 census of U.S. foreign investment showed that the bulk of manufacturing investments were made by oligopolistic firms in areas where the advantages of monopoly can be carried abroad: operations protected by patents, exclusive or advanced technical knowledge, and/or product differentiation through brand identification and similar techniques.[9]

This argument in no way denies the primacy of the profit motive. The whole purpose of monopoly control is to assure the existence and growth of profits. The profit motive and capitalism are, after all, one and the same. What needs explanation is why, with the profit motive always present, the export of capital in the form of direct investment accelerates with the onset of the imperialist stage. Here I suggest that tracing the answer to the nature and mushrooming of monopoly (or, more accurately, oligopoly) is a more meaningful explanation than that provided by the falling-rate-of-profit theory,

8. U.S. Treasury Department, *Foreign Income Taxes Reported on Corporation Income Tax Returns* (Washington D.C., 1969).
9. Stephen Hymer, 'The Theory of Direct Investment', Ph.D. dissertation, Massachusetts Institute of Technology 1960.

or, as discussed above, the pressure-of-surplus-capital theory.

Given a chance to make additional profit abroad at a higher marginal rate, the entrepreneur will grab at it, providing the politics of the foreign country is friendly to foreign investment and to the withdrawal of profits from that country. There are, however, many factors that influence the size of the profit margin. Low wages and cost of raw materials are only two of these elements; transportation expenses, productivity of labour, managerial ability, and overhead costs are also significant. And monopolistic or semimonopolistic influences which protect sales quotas at high prices carry enormous weight. In this context, it should be noted, that the investment decisions may be tempered by additional considerations. The fact that a major company has established a beachhead in foreign markets will spur competitors to follow suit: even when the immediate profit gain may not be clearly favourable the longer-run requirements of assuring one's share of the world market dictates such a strategy. And, as noted above, trade restrictions will motivate a firm to invest abroad to protect its market on the other side of the trade barrier. When the balance of ingredients is favourable to the profit and/or market strategy, the decision to invest abroad follows as a matter of course.

While on this subject it may be worth noting that one of the most common of the oversimplified explanations of the transnational movement of capital is that which assigns the decisive role to wage differentials between the capital-exporting and capital-importing countries. For the United States, where wages are relatively high, *any* export of capital could be interpreted this way. But one should not infer from this that the main current of foreign investment is to substitute foreign-made for domestic-made goods on the U.S. market. At best, one might argue that some of the overseas production takes the place of what would otherwise be exports from the United States. (In this fashion, wage differentials are eliminated as a competitive element in overseas markets.) The facts on the distribution of sales of U.S. manufacturing firms located abroad (from 1962 to 1965) show that, except for Canada, less than 2 per cent of U.S. production abroad is sent to the United States (see Table IV). The high percentage for Canada consists largely of manufactures based on Canadian resources (paper, for example).

Although complete data are not yet available, there seems to have been an increase since 1965 in U.S. firms manufacturing abroad parts and assemblies to be sold in U.S. domestic markets. Nevertheless, the

TABLE IV.   **Direction of sales of U.S. manufacturing affiliates located outside United States, 1962–65**

AREAS	TOTAL SALES	LOCAL SALES	EXPORTED TO U.S.	EXPORTED TO OTHER COUNTRIES
		PERCENTAGE DISTRIBUTION		
Total	100·0	82·3	4·1	13·6
Canada	100·0	81·1	10·8	8·1
Latin America	100·0	91·5	1·6	6·9
Europe	100·0	77·2	1·0	21·8
Other areas	100·0	93·9	1·4	4·7

Source: 1962—*Survey of Current Business*, November 1965, p. 19; 1963–5—*Ibid.*, November 1966, p.9.

relative importance of this activity does not yet support the argument that this is the major determinant of U.S. overseas investment. On the other hand, these low percentages do not mean that there is not a very real and severe impact on the U.S. working man of such shifts in production as do occur. The move to manufacture components and finished products in Japan, Italy, Korea, Hong Kong, etc., has surely been felt by certain sections of U.S. labour.

4. Imperialism and crisis

Before an account of how these economic relationships have persisted beyond the decline of colonialism there are two further areas of dispute about the new imperialism which have to be examined. These are the relation of imperialism to crisis and the role of the state.

We turn now to the first of these: imperialism as the capitalist way out of crisis. Whatever merit there may be to this approach, it can become confusing unless an attempt is made to sort out cause and effect. The depressions of the 1870s and 1880s, the agrarian disruptions as well as the industrial crises of those years, probably speeded up the birth of the new imperialism. But they themselves were not the cause of imperialism. If anything, both the severity of the economic disruptions and the imperialist policies are rooted in the same rapid transformations of the late nineteenth century.

The roots of imperialism go much deeper than any particular crisis or the reaction of any government to the crisis. They are to be found in the factors discussed above: the expansive drive of each advanced capitalist nation to operate on a world scale, the development of monopoly, and the national rivalries associated with the needs of advanced economies with monopolistic structures.

What economic crises frequently accomplish is to make ruling classes and governments acutely aware of the need for vigorous remedial action. They remind laggard governments of their 'duty' and prod them into action. Just as the reality of the contradictions of capitalism reveal themselves more frankly during periods of stress, so the reactions of governments become more overt under such pressure. But the policies and practices of economic and political imperialism are as much part of prosperity as of depression. More energetic and farsighted governments will act, or prepare to act, in periods of calm and prosperity. Timid and shortsighted governments will either wake up when the crisis hits them or be toppled by a tougher political group.

A corollary of the argument that imperialism was a way out of depression is the idea that capitalism will collapse as the area for imperialist expansion shrinks. This thesis is based on an unrealistic and rigid view of how capitalism works. Cutting off markets and sources of raw materials creates serious problems for capitalist enterprise but does not necessarily portend collapse.

It should hardly be necessary to point this out after the many years of experience during which sizeable sections of the globe have removed themselves from the imperialist orbit. Yet oversimplified, mechanistic formulations seem to have a life of their own. It is important to understand the degrees of flexibility that exist in capitalist society and which make the system more durable than its opponents have often supposed. Biological organisms show the same quality: the closure of one heart artery may be compensated by the enlargement of another artery to take over its function. To be sure, these organic adjustments are not eternal and they often lead to other and greater complications. But a significant lesson to be learned from the history of capitalism is that great troubles do not lead to automatic collapse.

The post-Second World War experience provides a good example of this flexibility. The enlargement of the U.S. military machine became a powerful support to the U.S. economy. In turn, the success achieved by the United States as the organiser of the world imperialist system on the verge of breaking down gave other advanced capitalisms an important boost, creating markets and enlarging international trade. This flexibility, however, is not limitless. Cracks in the most recent imperialist arrangements are clearly evident in the strains on the international money markets as well as in the mounting difficulties of the U.S. economy itself. Further shrinkage of imperialist territory will create more troubles: it might lead to a sharpening of the business cycle, prolonged depression, mass unemployment. Nevertheless, as we know from historical experience, these do not necessarily bring the downfall of the system. In the final analysis, the fate of capitalism will be settled only by vigorous classes within the society, and parties based on these classes, which have the will and ability to replace the existing system.

5. The role of the government

Another area of dispute over the meaning of imperialism concerns the role of government either as an initiator of imperialism or as a potential agent for the abolition of imperialism. Here there are two extremes: (*a*) those who see government as merely the direct servant of large corporations and banks, and (*b*) those who see government as an independent force that arbitrates conflicting interests and has wide freedom of choice in setting policy.

Neither of these views, in my opinion, is correct. The operations of government in a complex society result in the development of a political structure that takes on the character of a special division of society, with responsibilities and behaviour problems adapted to maintaining political power. As such, a government may be more or less responsive to the needs of particular firms or industries. Aside from differences over tactics, the actions of governing groups will be influenced by previous political experience and training, as well as by their own sense of what is best suited to keep themselves in power. Even a political régime responsive to the pressures of a particular industry or firm will, if it is competent and has integrity, withstand such pressure in the overall and long-term interest of the class, or classes, it relies on to remain in power.

On the other hand, the degrees of freedom enjoyed by ruling groups are much more limited than liberals are inclined to believe. To retain power, political régimes must have a successful economy. They therefore must work to improve the economic and financial structure at hand, and cannot pursue idle fancies of the 'what might be if' variety. The more farsighted and aggressive political régimes—those which understand the main dynamic levers of the economy—will foster the growth of the economic system: they will build roads, harbours, canals, railroads, merchant marine, acquire colonies for the stimulation of commerce, struggle for control of sea lanes to protect their commerce, and aggressively expand their territory (as in the United States in the eighteenth and nineteenth centuries). The incompetent régimes, especially those hampered by too much internal conflict among different wouldbe ruling groups, will rule over a limping economy. As pointed out above, a government often learns what is needed to sustain and advance the economic underpinning of its society the hard way; reminded and spurred by internal depression and/or the forward push of competing nations.

The limited alternatives open to political regimes have become increasingly clear during the history of imperialism. Here we must keep in mind the two strategically significant developments that mark the birth of, or prepared the way for, the new imperialism: (1) The internal conflicts among competing vested interest groups within the Great Powers become resolved in favour of the needs of large-scale industry and the financiers of these industries. Three such examples may be noted: (*a*) the compromise between the Northern industrialists and Southern bourbons in the United States after the Civil War; (*b*) the compromise between the landed aristocracy and large industrialists in Germany; and (*c*) the emphasis of the Meiji Restoration on creating the conditions for the rise of large-scale, heavy industry in Japan. (2) The successful development of large-scale industry is associated with increasing concentration of power.

Once the structure of each society had been successfully adapted to the needs of the major centres of industry, the path of future economic development became fairly narrowly defined. A later government, even one not a party to the previous resolution of conflict, has to pursue the same path: a comfortable environment for the leading industrialists and bankers, an environment that would stretch over as much of the world as these interest groups needed to operate in. The decisions on how best to create this environment, nationally and internationally, are arrived at by political and military officials, influenced by the latter's ambitions and ideologies. However, the ultimate test of government competence—its ability to achieve its political and military aims—is a successful economy: no welfare scheme can replace full and steady employment, operating factories, and smoothly-run finance. And that economic success, in turn, rests on the success of big business and big finance. The practices of the reform administration of Franklin Roosevelt offer a good illustration:

the stress on foreign trade expansion as the way out of the crisis, and the outright deal with the 'economic royalists' (the term used by President Roosevelt in his bitter diatribes against big business) when faced with the needs of war production. It is instructive also to learn from the practices of liberal and 'socialist' régimes in capitalist societies. Not having the kind of specific commitments and long-standing ties with particular business interests that conservative parties do, they are often *more* effective in making necessary repairs to the structure of monopoly business. What they do *not* do is undertake reforms which run counter to the basic interests of big business.

6. Imperialism without colonies

It would be wrong to say that modern imperialism would have been possible without colonialism. And yet the end of colonialism by no means signifies the end of imperialism. The explanation of this seeming paradox is that colonialism, considered as the direct application of military and political force, was essential to reshape the social and economic institutions of many of the dependent countries to the needs of the metropolitan centres. Once this reshaping had been accomplished economic forces—the international price, marketing, and financial systems—were by themselves sufficient to perpetuate and indeed intensify the relationship of dominance and exploitation between mother country and colony. In these circumstances, the colony could be granted formal political independence without changing anything essential, and without interfering too seriously with the interests which had originally led to the conquest of the colony.

This is not to say that colonialism was abolished gratuitously. Revolutions, mass rebellions, and the threat of revolution, the fear of further enlargement of the socialist world, and the manoeuvring of the United States to gain a presence in the colonial preserves of other empires, these all paved the way for the decline of colonialism after the Second World War. The important point, though, is that the requisite dissolution of the colonies was carried out in such a way as to preserve for the mother country as many of the advantages as possible, and to prevent social revolutions directed to real independence for the former colonies. As long as the socio-economic underpinning for the continuation of the metropolitan-colony relationship could be maintained, there was still a fighting chance that the interests that had benefited most from colonial control would not be endangered.

These observations do not apply to all the relationships of dominance and dependence which characterise modern imperialism. Some independent countries already possessing suitable social and economic institutions have fallen directly under the economic domination of one of the stronger powers and have thus become dependencies without ever going through a colonial phase. Some of these economic dependencies may even have colonies of their own. Thus Portugal was for a long time a dependency of Britain, and the Portuguese Empire was in a real sense an empire within an empire. It is not surprising therefore that the history of imperialism shows a wide variety of forms and degrees of political dependency. Nor is it difficult to understand why, on the whole, the major aspects of the imperialist design should exist in the era of declining overt colonialism just as they existed in the period of outright colonialism, since the primary determinants of imperialism remain: (*a*) the monopoly structure of big business in the metropolises, (*b*) the imperative for these economic centres to grow and to control materials sources and markets, (*c*) the continuation of an international division of labour which serves the needs of the metropolitan centres, (*d*) national rivalry among industrial powers for export and investment opportunities in each other's markets and over the rest of the world. To this has been added a new factor which generates fear in the advanced capitalist nations and makes the maintenance of the imperialist system more urgent than ever: the inroads made by the growth of socialist societies and the spread of national liberation movements which seek to remove their countries from the imperialist trade and investment network.

The decline of colonialism has of course presented real problems, some old and some new, for the imperialist centres:

1. How best to maintain the economic and financial dependence of subordinate nations, given the aroused expectations accompanying independence and the greater manoeuvrability available with political independence.
2. For the previous owners of colonies, how to maintain their preferred economic position and ward off the encroachment of rival powers.
3. For the United States, how to extend its influence and control over the privileged preserves of the former colonial powers.

The problem of maintaining economic dependency in the new environment since the Second World War has been complicated by the rivalry of the Soviet Union and by the straining at the leash by some of the new independent nations: the latter, in part due to the pressure of the masses and in part due to the new elite seeing an opportunity to get a bigger piece of the action. Despite these complications, which called for new tactics by the imperialist powers, the essential structure of economic dependency has persisted in the period of imperialism without colonies. It is not a simple matter to eradicate dependency relations that have ripened and become embedded over a long stretch of history, beginning with the days of mercantilism. In the several developmental stages of the trade and financial ties of the colonial and semicolonial economies, the economic structure of the latter became increasingly adapted to its role as an appendage of the metropolitan centre. The composition of prices, the income distribution, and the allocation of resources evolved, with the aid of military power as well as the blind forces of the market, in such a way as continuously to reproduce the dependency.

This point needs special emphasis since economists are inclined to think of the price-and-market system as an *impartial* regulator of the economy, one that allocates resources in such a fashion as to achieve the maximum efficiency in their use. This in turn, is based on the assumption that there is such a thing as an absolute, objective efficiency which is equally applicable to all places and at all times. In reality matters are very different. The allocation of resources is the result of many historic forces. To name only a few: wars; colonialism; the way states have exercised their fiscal and other powers; the manipulations (at different times) of influential merchants, industrialists, and financiers; the management of international financial arrangements. In due course, wages, prices, and trade relations become efficient tools for the *reproduction* of the *attained* allocation of economic resources. And in the case of the former colonial world, this means reproduction of the economic relations of dependency.

To become masters of their own destiny, these countries have to overhaul the existing international trade patterns and transform their industrial and financial structure. Short of such basic changes, the economic and financial framework remains, with or without colonies. Even vigorous protectionist policies, adopted by many of the semicolonies, have been unable to break the ties of dependency. True, to some extent, they did encourage development of domestic manufactures. But in many of the more profitable areas, foreign manufacturers opened up factories inside the tariff walls and thus actually expanded foreign economic influence.

The state of dependency is not supported and reproduced by the evolved market relations alone. It is also sustained by the dependent country's political and social power structure. In the most general terms, there are three constituents of the ruling class in these countries: large landowners, business groups whose affairs are interrelated with foreign business interests, and businessmen with few or no ties to the foreign business community.[10] While the nationalist spirit may pervade, more or less, all three of these groups, none of them has a strong motive to sponsor the kind of structural economic changes that would be required for an independent economy. The interests of the first two groups listed above would be severely impaired by decisive moves for independence. The one group that could visualize a gain from economic independence would be the native capitalists, that is, those whose prosperity does not depend on foreign ties and for whom new opportunities would open up as a result of independence. But this group is usually small and weak and to succeed, it would have to break the grip of the other two sectors and destroy the economic base of the latter's power. Success in such a struggle would require an ability to keep power throughout the disruptions involved in the transformation; and it would depend on mobilising the support of the workers and peasants, a hazardous undertaking in an era when the masses are seeking redress of their own grievances and when socialist revolution can quickly appear on the agenda.

Thus both the economic and political structures of the former colonies are well suited to the perpetuation of economic dependence along with political independence. And the needs of imperialism in the new situation could be met, except for one weakness: the instability of the power structure of the former colonies. This instability has its roots in the colonial system itself. In many colonies, the dominant power had in the past disrupted the traditional ruling groups and destroyed their political power. In addition, the mother countries created and sponsored elites which were psychologically and economically dependent on the foreign rulers. At the time, this was an effective and relatively inexpensive way to keep an annexed nation

---

10. This generalisation is obviously too broad to be useful in the analysis of any specific country. The class and social composition of a given country will be much more complex than indicated by the three large groupings indicated in the text; special country-by-country analysis is required if the dynamics of any particular area are to be understood. Thus, in some countries, attention must be paid to the role of small landowners, rich peasants, and rural moneylenders and traders. Urban business groups are also frequently more stratified than indicated in the text, with insignificant distinctions between commercial and industrial interest groups, and within each of these categories, different degrees of dependence on the industrial and financial affairs of the metropolitan centres.

within the empire. Its weakness was that it prevented the emergence of the self-reliance and strength needed by any one sector to take power in its own name and reshape the economy for its own purposes. On top of this, the alliances that did develop to take over internal political rule were temporary and necessarily unstable. Finally, the changeover to political independence, especially in those countries where the masses were involved in the independence struggle, led to greater expectations of improvement in the conditions of life than could be met by weak postcolonial régimes. The people of the colonies identified colonialism not only with foreign despotism but also with exploitation by those who had adapted themselves to, and cooperated with, the colonial powers.

The retention of influence and control by the metropolitan centres in the postcolonial period has therefore required special attention. The techniques stressed, some old and some new, fell into several categories:

(*a*) Where possible, formal economic and political arrangements to maintain former economic ties. These include preferential trade agreements and maintenance of currency blocs.

(*b*) Manipulation and support of the local ruling groups with a view to keeping the special influence of the metropolitan centres and to preventing internal social revolution. Included here, in addition to CIA-type operations, are military assistance, training the officer corps, and economic aid for roads, airports and the like needed by the local military.

(*c*) Establishing influence and control over the direction of economic development and, as much as possible, over government decisions affecting the allocation of resources. Under this heading fall bilateral economic aid arrangements and the policies and practices of the World Bank and the International Monetary Fund. These activities, in addition to influencing the direction of economic development, tend to intensify the financial dependence of aid recipients on the metropolitan money markets.

Central to the period of imperialism without colonies is the new role of the United States. The disruption of other imperialist centres following the Second World War and the concomitant growth of strong revolutionary movements generated both the urgency for the United States to re-establish the stability of the imperialist system and the opportunity to make inroads for its own advantage. Perhaps the greatest gain accruing to the United States as a result of the economic disruption of the war and early postwar years was the triumph of the U.S. dollar as the dominant international currency and the establishment of New York as the main international banking centre. Thus was created the financial mechanism for enlarging the economic base of U.S. business interests through expansion of exports and enlargement of capital investment and international banking both in the home bases of advanced capitalist nations and in the Third World.

In addition to using its new economic and financial strength, the United States stepped up its efforts to enter the preserves of the former colonial powers by (*a*) becoming the main provider of military and economic aid, and (*b*) constructing a global network of military bases and staging areas. The extensive system of military bases is designed to threaten the socialist countries and to prevent the breaking-off of components of the remaining imperialist system. By the same token, the U.S. global military presence (in conjunction with the military forces of its allies) and its predisposition to actively engage these forces (as in Vietnam) provides the substance of the political force which maintains the imperialist system in the absence of colonies.

DISCUSSION

Surplus capital.   Part of the discussion took up the points made in the paper against the ideas of surplus capital and the falling profit rate as an explanation of capital outflow. In the last years of the nineteenth century it was only in Britain, Magdoff argued, that there could be any question of the existence of surplus capital. But what is pointed to as evidence of this is in reality evidence of the entrenchment of British capitalism as a worldwide system. This was aided by the creation of a framework of financial institutions which facilitated a heavy flow of capital abroad. And while there is a major jump in capital exported during this period it is not capital export as such which defines the imperialist epoch. There had continuously been foreign investment, notably from colonial powers in an earlier epoch. At the same time he added to his remarks on the failing rate of profit theory. A falling rate of profit could be based only on a competitive economy with competing capitals able to be substituted for each other. Under monopoly, capitals are not substitutable and there are therefore discrete rates of profit.

Effects of capital export on domestic exploitation.   Magdoff was asked about the effect of capital export on the domestic rate of exploitation. He was not certain of the answer. On the one hand, the amount of manufacturing done abroad tended to depress wage rates in the United States, but the effect was marginal since few of these goods were re-imported into the United States, though some of them might otherwise have been produced with American labour and exported. On the other hand, in other ways the foreign investment programme had stimulated production for export from the United States.

Colonisation and imperialism: what difference?   There was some discussion of the distinction which Magdoff was making between colonialism and imperialism. One participant argued that while imperialism was an economic, political and ideological relationship, colonialism was merely a political form, sometimes necessary, within the overall framework of imperialism. Magdoff only partly agreed: he thought that colonialism could never be merely political; colonialism was a device, while imperialism, as he was using the term in its Leninist sense, was a stage of capitalism.

Continuity and change in imperialism.   In the course of discussion he enlarged on this in two ways. First, he argued that colonialism predated imperialism. It had existed since the beginning of capitalism; without certain features of it—the slave trade, for instance—capitalism could not have begun in the way that it did. Second, imperialism still existed after the end of colonialism. In some ways Lenin's analysis was outdated but in one way was not, since a crucial element of continuity in the imperialist system up to now was the monopolist structure of capitalism which Lenin had stressed. The features of imperialism which today had changed were caused by three things: the existence of the socialist countries, the nature of modern technology and the hegemony of the United States within the imperialist system.

Inter-capitalist contradictions?   There was some discussion of whether the third of these might soon change. In reply to a question about whether the Vietnam war is an imperialist war, Magdoff held that it is, but not because of a narrow and imediate economic interest in Vietnam itself. The war in Vietnam is one phase of the grand strategy of the United States in Asia. One of the components of this grand strategy is to assure control over raw materials, markets and investment opportunities in South East Asia as a whole. Another major consideration is the creation and extension of military power to secure what remains of the capitalist system in Asia, and if and when possible to facilitate the rollback of communist systems. The Vietnamese national liberation movement threatened to narrow down the capitalist system. This the system could not permit and the weakest links had to be protected. On this basic need to keep the system intact there was no conflict between the capitalist powers. Nevertheless the present conflict between French and American capitalism was more than the minor contradiction which one speaker claimed it to be. Any implicit agreement between the U.S.A. and the U.S.S.R. might have an effect on national rivalries in Western Europe; and Japan might soon require a strong military arm to protect its overseas economic strength. Magdoff suggested that a common purpose among capitalist countries under accepted United States leadership could not be assumed for the future.

VII

Imperialism and industrialisation in the third world

Bob Sutcliffe

To many Marxist and other left-wing writers imperialism is regarded as the same as or at least an integral part of the capitalist system at an advanced stage of its development. It is held that imperialism in this sense perpetuates an unbalanced international division of labour. (This is argued in the papers by Barratt Brown, II, and Magdoff, VI.) In particular imperialism is thought to prevent, arrest or distort the industrialisation of underdeveloped countries. In this paper Sutcliffe examines the economic aspects of this question and surveys recent Marxist writing on the subject, relating it to earlier Marxist views about capitalism and economic backwardness. Within these he finds an implicit theory of the nature of imperialism in backward areas which, he argues, should be integrated into the more explicit part of the Marxist theory of imperialism. Recent industrial growth in underdeveloped countries is examined in relation to the theoretical considerations. The paper is mostly concerned with the question of why capitalist development in underdeveloped countries no longer appears to take the form of independent industrialisation. The same question is tackled in a more concrete form in the paper by Patnaik, IX, in which the nature of capitalist development in India is examined.

1. Problems of definition, coverage and periodisation

Imperialism, as defined by Lenin, is a certain stage of development of the capitalist system—in brief, the monopoly stage of capitalism, characterised as a result of monopoly by intercapitalist rivalries, and also by the export of capital on a large scale; in addition it is a period in which finance capital acquires great importance in comparison with industrial capital. While this definition served Lenin well in the political purposes for which he wrote *Imperialism*, it is perhaps not so useful when the problem is not to explain the genesis of imperialist war (the First World War) but to observe the status of the under-developed countries within the world capitalist/imperialist system, in particular their prospects of industrialising within it (the subject of this paper) and ultimately (but not in this paper) the status of and prospects for its revolutionary movements—in other words the laws of motion of modern imperialism as they affect the third world.

But there is an overwhelmingly important characteristic of Lenin's definition of imperialism which must in no way be discarded—namely its breadth: it sees imperialism as a totality embracing all the salient characteristics of the stage of capitalism, rather than applying narrowly to the relationship between the state in advanced capitalist countries and the colonies. Non-Marxist writers tend to use the word imperialism in such a narrow sense; hence it is not surprising that they seem unable to comprehend Marxist propositions on the subject.

Of course the problem of definition is closely allied to that of historical timing or periodisation, which is used by attackers of Marxism as a method of refutation. Some of these argue that imperialism always existed; others claim that nothing fundamentally changed in the objectives and methods of imperialism between the eighteenth century and the First World War; in either case, the argument goes, Lenin and the Marxists were wrong to point to some major change late in the nineteenth century.

Now within Marxist writing on the subject there are, I think, three quite distinct phases (defined logically rather than temporally) in the relations between capitalism and the peripheral countries and areas of the world. One (prominent in Marx's and Engels's writings) involves plunder (of wealth or slaves) and exports of capitalist manufactures to the peripheral countries. The second (uppermost in Lenin's writing) involves the export of capital, competition for supplies of raw materials and the growth of monopoly. The third involves a more complex, post-colonial dependency of the peripheral countries, in which foreign capital (international corporations), profit repatriation, adverse changes in the terms of trade (unequal exchange) all play a role in confining, distorting or halting economic development and industrialisation.

In each of these phases of the imperialist relationship the peripheral areas furnish the needs of a capitalism whose home is in the advanced countries. In the first they assist primary accumulation and allow it to carve out its essential initial markets. In the second, they play a role in the partial escape of a more mature capitalism from the consequences of its contradictions. And in the third advanced mature capitalism secures itself against the emergence of competition which might threaten its stability, organisation and growth. But it is this third phase (the main topic of this paper) which is the least well defined.

Not that the others are free of problems. For one thing, general historical timing is very difficult. Primary accumulation for capitalist industrialisation took place, of course, at very different dates in the case of different European countries. So a mature British capitalism may have needed the peripheral areas for the export of surplus capital at the same time as a nascent Russian or Japanese industrial capitalism required them for primary accumulation or (more likely by the late nineteenth century) to carve out an initial market for factory products. More generally, if the different phases of the imperialist relationship are systematically related to capitalist development, then it makes sense to compare imperialism not only in different epochs but between different countries in the same epoch, since the stages reached by capitalism were different in different countries at the same time.

Of course, it is not enough to think in terms of national capitalisms, since capitalism does move, though very unevenly, towards becoming a world system. This probably means that in the third phase in particular any idea of a *national* capitalist imperialism needs to be modified greatly. Moreover, historically some countries may have moved from a position where they were predominantly subject to imperialism to another position in which they became imperialist countries; or features of both statuses may have been present simultaneously. Russia before 1917 and Japan were certainly examples of this.

So we return to the need for the breadth of Lenin's definition of imperialism. But it is better, I believe, not to be closely bound by its explicit form, for the reasons stated above and because all which Lenin (and his contemporaries) had to say on the subject of imperialism is not to be found in his explicit discussion of it.

Lenin's theory of imperialism is nowadays often criticised on the grounds of its Eurocentricity: in stressing the impulses to imperialism in the advanced capitalist countries it is claimed that he said too little about the changes wrought by imperialism in peripheral economies and societies. But this is not an entirely fair accusation. The ambiguous position of late-Tsarist Russia as both subject and object of an imperialist relationship has already been mentioned. And Lenin certainly analysed late nineteenth- and early twentieth-century Russia in a way which is relevant to an understanding of the impact of imperialism, even though he did not do so as part of an explicit counterpart to his theory of the origins and drives of imperialism. This implicit view, together with the ideas of the Narodniks with whom he came into conflict, and the more explicit and detailed analysis of Trotsky, provide a profoundly important contribution to understanding the question of whether the evolution of the imperialist economy ends the possibility of further independent capitalist industrialisation in the third world.

In answer to this question it is held as almost an axiom of Marxist (and much other left-wing) thinking that no third world country can now expect to break out of a state of economic dependency and to advance to an economic position beside the major capitalist industrial powers. This is a very important proposition since it not only establishes the extent to which capitalism remains historically progressive in the modern world but also thereby defines the economic background to political action. Yet too often the question is ill-defined; it is not self-evident; its intellectual origins are a little obscure; and its actual foundations both debateable and in need of a fuller analysis.

2. The conditions of independent industrialisation

Industrialisation involves both a quantitative increase in industrial production and a qualitative change in the nature of society, with the growth of new social classes and new styles of work and living. The notion of independent industrialisation involves something more than this. It does not mean autarky but carries with it the idea that industrialisation is not merely 'derived' from the industrialisation of another economy like that of small European principalities was derived from, and was no more than a part of, the industrialisation of their larger neighbours.[1] So the idea of the independence of an industrialisation is partly one of its origins and driving forces. An independent industrialisation should originate with and be maintained by social and economic forces within the industrialising country.

An important part of this notion concerns markets. While export markets may have some importance (as they did in the industrialisation of Britain and Japan), the domestic market is paramount. Hence

---

1. Alexander Gerschenkron outlined the idea of derived as opposed to autochthonous industrialisation in 'The typology of industrial development as a tool of historical analysis', in *Continuity in History and Other Essays*, (Cambridge, Mass., Harvard Univ. Press, 1968).

the importance of the existence of a home market for Russian capitalism in the late nineteenth century, which Lenin insisted on in argument with his Narodnik opponents.[2]

Independence of industrialisation has salient features other than markets. One concerns the structure of industrial production. An industrialisation could not be considered wholly independent unless the country concerned contained within its borders a wide range of industries, including economically strategic capital goods industries.

A further characteristic of independence concerns the source of finance for industrialisation. Foreign industrial capital can normally be expected to undermine independence, though essentially what is important is control rather than the source of funds as such. Foreign capital, while important in the nineteenth century industrialisation of the United States, for instance, did not apparently jeopardise its independence. That is because the users of the capital were not its providers and were not very subject to their control. There is a major distinction here between direct and indirect investment. Bondholders or holders of portfolios (i.e. indirect investors) never have more than loose control over the uses of their capital, unless a government intervenes in a country on their behalf, through the establishment of colonial government or some other form of occupation or control. In that way, through the intermediary of the state, indirect investors may exercise some control over the use of their capital; at least they can expect that it will be protected from expropriation. Direct investors by co ιtrast almost always have fairly complete control over the use of their capital; normally it is exported only for some specific use; and they can protect it from expropriation by many means such as monopolisation of markets, maintaining technical secrets, refusing to train local skilled workers and so on.[3] In addition they may exercise much more control than their ownership suggests.[4]

The final element in the notion of economic independence relates to technology. Technology is a rather abstract concept; it is therefore

---

2. V. I. Lenin, *The Development of Capitalism in Russia*, (Moscow, 1956).
3. This suggests one of the reasons why decolonisation since World War II has been such a smooth process and it gives a clue to the nature of neocolonialism. Modern foreign investment is mostly direct and thus, in the absence of formal colonialism, guarantees to its owners some control (except in crises) over taxation, nationalisation etc. By contrast foreign investment before World War I was almost exclusively indirect and if control was to be exercised at all this required more formal arrangements. For more discussion of this point see the papers by Barratt Brown (II) and Magdoff (VI); both discuss the changing nature of capital exports during the imperialist epoch.
4. On this point see the papers by Magdoff, VI and by Patnaik, IX.

hard to say in a concrete or precise way what constitutes technological independence. No country has in modern times been technologically isolated. And yet clearly independent technological progress has been one of the cornerstones of all the successful industrialisations since the English industrial revolution. The ability and opportunity to copy, develop and adapt, or at least to choose, a technology suitable to a country's resources has been a condition of industrialisation. Technological independence/choice/progressiveness has been a frame which has held together a nascent industrial system and has finally bound it into an integrated structure capable of independent, though not wholly autarkic or isolated, development.

This question of technological independence is related, both causally and consequentially, to the other aspects of economic independence. For instance, a growing industrial sector cannot always supply the home market unless it can develop a new, or at least adapted, technology capable of producing products to the specification demanded by that market. The alternative is for the nature of tastes in the home market to be changed so that they coincide with what the available, unadapted, foreign technology is capable of producing. At the same time if a country's industry is to manufacture primarily for the foreign market it is in nearly all cases forced to use the foreign technique. Again, the breadth of the industrial structure also has important links with the possibility of technological independence: an independent technology requires a fairly broad structure with links between final demand industries and producers' goods industries.

Furthermore since foreign techniques tend to be highly capital-intensive, the income they produce is concentrated in a few hands, thus reinforcing the tendency for the tastes of the minority, alone able to consume significant quantities of goods, to duplicate the tastes of more advanced capitalist countries. Whether such socially determined tastes can be prevented from arising depends on the policy and autonomy of the government.

No single exact definition of economic independence can be given, but the notion is clearly composed of these elements: location of markets (exports or home market), nature of the market (tastes), source of investment capital and completeness of industrial structure, and technology, all of which are interrelated in a complex and as yet not fully understood way.

These are economic factors which have their social and political counterparts. Economic development only happens when the surplus gets into the hands of those who will use it productively, that is, to finance industrial investment. This partly implies the need for an industrial bourgeoisie supported by a state which is capable of defending its interests. And historically it has been shown conclusively that a nascent bourgeoisie in an industrialising country requires increasingly the powers of the state to support and defend it; when industrialisation starts from extreme levels of backwardness, the role of the bourgeoisie may predominantly have to be performed through the state.[5] The state must be largely independent both of those local social interests opposed to industrialisation and also of foreign interests—capitalists or other states. It is as a result of this that some success in promoting industrialisation has sometimes been expected from governments in the third world which were opposed to traditional agrarian interests and were at the same time aggressively nationalistic.

3. Recent Marxist views on the possibility of industrialisation in the age of imperialism

Quite frequently, however, the view is expressed that further capitalist industrialisation is no longer either possible or desirable. One indirect support of such an idea derives from the achievement in the U.S.S.R. (and the obvious potentiality in China, North Korea and at length North Vietnam) of successful industrialisation under socialism. In principle too the existence of wealthy socialist industrialised countries should lessen the burden of primary accumulation in other socialist third world countries setting out to industrialise. In practice there are obvious reservations to this; and in any case it is hard to see how the experience of Stalinist industrialisation can have directly persuaded anybody that less burdensome forms of development had become possible. Moreover, Lenin for one would probably have argued that since the Soviet revolution was the outcome of Russia's incomplete capitalist industrialisation, then the more complete post-revolutionary industrialisation offers no model for another underdeveloped country with a lower development of the proletariat than Russia in 1917. Presumably a Maoist would disagree.

The view that imperialism is an insuperable obstacle to further capitalist industrialisations, though quite contrary to that at times

---

5. On this subject see A. Gerschenkron, *Economic Backwardness in Historical Perspective*, (Cambridge, Mass., Harvard Univ. Press, 1962), chs 1, 2 and 3 and postscript; and David Landes, *The Unbound Prometheus* (Cambridge, Cambridge Univ. Press, 1969).

178   *Bob Sutcliffe*

propounded by the Comintern in the Stalinist era, is now fairly widespread. In spite of this it is hard to find a good account of it in the literature. The clearest statement is that of Mandel who has a section of *Marxist Economic Theory* headed 'Imperialism as obstacle to the industrialisation of underdeveloped countries'. According to Mandel there are four reasons for this—political control against industrialisation by the imperial countries, the weak competitive position of potential third world industrial capitalists against more efficient producers in the imperialist countries, declining terms of trade and the repatriation of profits by foreign-owned corporations.[6] But Mandel's view is not made entirely clear since he claims that 'all the colonial and semicolonial countries which have won political freedom, or have been governed by representatives of the industrial bourgeoisie, have undertaken a vigorous effort at industrialisation which sharply contrasts with the attitudes of the governments under imperialist control. The examples of the Argentine under Peron and Egypt under Nasser are typical, likewise the Indian Five Year Plans.'[7] It is doubtful if these countries are to be counted as exceptional to the pattern elsewhere in the third world; though this raises the question of what we are to take industrialisation to mean.

Baran's view on this subject is even less clear. In one place he certainly seems to contemplate capitalist industrialisation. For as he argues:

Under conditions of capitalism, if it is to be successful in contributing to overall economic development and not to bog down in the propagation and multiplication of rural slums, agrarian reform must not only go together with accumulation of capital, but must be accompanied by a rapid advance to industrial capitalism.[8]

Obviously Baran does foresee capitalism leading only to 'rural slums'. But later on he remarks more unequivocally that:

whatever market for manufactured goods emerged in the colonial and dependent countries did not become the 'internal market' of these countries . . . While significantly stimulating industrial growth in the West, this turn of events extinguished the igniting spark without which there could be no industrial expansion in the new underdeveloped countries.[9]

6. E. Mandel, *Marxist Economic Theory*, (London, Merlin Press, 2 vols, 1968), ii, 476–9.
7. *Ibid*, p. 476.
8. P. Baran, *The Political Economy of Growth*, (New York, Monthly Review Press, 1962), p. 169.
9. *Ibid*, p. 174.

Baran, along with Barratt Brown in *After Imperialism*[10] and very many Indian anti-imperialist historians[11], and indeed Marx, holds that British imperial policy in India was responsible for arresting its industrial growth.[12] And Baran, like Mandel, cites Japan as an example of a country whose industrialisation succeeded because of its isolation from the rest of the capitalist world.[13] Yet on a more abstract level Baran's position has much in common with that of Andre Gunder Frank when he says: 'The rule of monopoly capitalism and imperialism in the advanced countries and social and economic backwardness in the underdeveloped countries are intimately related, represent[ing] merely different aspects of what is in reality a global problem.'[14]

Frank notes that quite rapid bursts of independent capitalist industrialisation took place in periods when relative isolation from the world market was possible—in the slump of the 1930s and during the Second World War. But recent developments have more deeply integrated the Latin American economies into the 'metropolis-satellite structure of the world capitalist system';[15] and now, in the case of Brazil for instance, 'it would be much more difficult or even impossible for Brazil to react with a similar active capitalist involution and another push towards industrialisation. Even Brazil's industry will have become too dependent on the metropolis to permit it such independent capitalist development.'[16] Frank implies that the same is equally true *a fortiori* of other Latin American countries with even weaker industrial sectors than Brazil. And in more recent writing he has come down quite explicitly for the view that the 'historical and continuing process of underdevelopment cannot be reversed and turned into economic and social development for the majority of the American people until they destroy the capitalist economic and class structure through revolution and replace it by socialist development'.[17]

10. M. Barratt Brown, *After Imperialism* (London, Heinemann, 1963), pp. 174–6.
11. For a recent discussion on these lines see Bipan Chandra, 'Reinterpretation of Indian nineteenth-century economic history', *Indian Economic and Social History Review* (March, 1968).
12. Baran, *op. cit.*, pp. 144–50.
13. *Ibid.*, p. 160; Mandel, *op. cit.*, p. 476 and D. Horowitz, *Imperialism and Revolution* (London, Allen Lane, 1969), p. 125.
14. Baran, *op. cit.*, p. 250.
15. A. G. Frank, *Capitalism and Underdevelopment in Latin America: Historical Studies of Chile and Brazil*, (New York, Monthly Review Press, 1969), p. 213.
16. *Ibid.*, p. 214.
17. A. G. Frank, 'Economic dependence, social structure and underdevelopment in Latin America', (typescript 1969), p. 1.

Some writers now seem to maintain that, in view of the continued development of technology towards larger and larger scale operations, and given the structure of the world economy, no significant progress towards industrialisation is any longer possible even after a socialist revolution in a third world country. On this view all significant progress in this direction is now held up pending socialist revolution in the advanced countries.[18]

4. Earlier Marxist views

There is no doubt that on the face of it the idea that further capitalist industrialisation is impossible goes against the spirit and often the letter of a good deal of historical Marxist thinking. This of course does not prove it wrong; but it is worth counterposing the idea to earlier views in order to examine whether the difference is one of circumstance or diagnosis.

To begin with Marx himself, in one later letter he emphasises that the economic laws of motion described in *Capital* were devised for the case of Western Europe only;[19] and the drafts of the controversial letter to Vera Zasulich suggest that he may have come to believe that for Russia (and hence also presumably for yet more backward countries) the price of capitalist development in terms of human misery was too heavy for it to be counted as a progressive development.[20] But for all this it is quite clear that for most of the time Marx believed that capitalism would industrialise the world. In the famous phrase, which presumably he did not put lightly into the preface to the first edition of *Capital*, 'the country that is more developed industrially only shows to the less developed the image of its own future'.[21] 'So far as can be seen', V. G. Kiernan states, 'what he had in mind was not a further spread of Western imperialism but a proliferation of autonomous capitalism, such as he expected in India and did witness in North America'.[22] At the same time Marx's writing on India does emphasise, aside from imperial policy, a feature of capitalist penetration which must be a major feature of any explanation of the inhibit-

18. See M. Kidron, 'Memories of development', *New Society*, 4 March, 1971.

19. Marx and Engels, *Correspondence, 1846–1895*, pp. 354–5.

20. E. J. Hobsbawm, Introduction to Marx's *Pre-capitalist Economic Formations*, (London, Lawrence & Wishart), p. 50.

21. Karl Marx, *Capital*, (Moscow, 1961), i, 8–9.

22. V. G. Kiernan, 'Marx on India', *Socialist Register 1967*, p. 183.

ing aspects of imperialism on industrialisation: that is the effect of imports of English factory textiles, and other manufactured goods, on traditional Indian (and Chinese) industry. From England's standpoint the Indian market allowed the textile industry to grow far ahead of the growth of English demand and it grew in a pre-existing market where its only competition was the produce of a much inferior technology. From the Indian point of view, however, this had several consequences which Marx never spelled out. First, it led to the destruction of capital stock which could otherwise have provided future income out of which accumulation could take place. Second, it took over a market which was thereby less easily assailable by an indigenous Indian factory textile industry, now needing to compete against technologically superior rather than inferior products. Third, it did something to break the vital link between a producer good industry in India (with growing yarn production) and the consumer good textile industry which used its products.

Altogether, corresponding to the decline of a large traditional industry, there took place the rapid expansion of a modern industry; but not only did the expansion take place in England, but also, by this fact, it became less possible in the future in India. Marx explained the importance of this process for the carving out of the early English industrial market, though he did not explicitly say that it was to hamper future industrialisation. In addition, the importance which Marx attached to plunder, slavery and unequal exchange in financing English primitive accumulation carries a similar implication—that once these things have occurred they are not available for any future industrialising country which must therefore look to other methods to finance its primary accumulation from domestic sources.

It appears that Lenin's views as well are utterly at odds with the contemporary idea of the role of capitalism: 'The progressive historical role of capitalism may be summed up in two brief propositions: increase in the productive forces of social labour, and the socialisation of that labour. But both these facts manifest themselves in extremely diverse processes in different branches of the national economy'.[23] The purpose of Lenin's *The Development of Capitalism in Russia* was primarily a political one; it was a weapon in his struggle with the Narodniks who favoured political alliances with the bourgeois liberalism rather than a party of the working class. The Narodnik economists provided the theoretical underpinnings for this political

23. Lenin, *The Development of Capitalism in Russia*, p. 595.

strategy by arguing that Russia was not, nor could it become, a capitalist country, since the obstacles to capitalist development were too great; any capitalist development which occurred could not be held to be historically progressive.

Aside from its political aspects, the economic dimension of the debate has to some extent a life of its own, and considerable contemporary relevance. Indeed it is in the Narodnik writings that the first expressions of the view of the impossibility of capitalist industrialisation seems to be stated. According to Vorontsov 'the more belated is the process of industrialisation, the more difficult it is to carry it on along the capitalist lines'.[24] At the same time backwardness provided an advantage in that the technological benefits of modern capitalism could be used while its structure was rejected, Russia, the Narodniks insisted, could omit the capitalist stage of development and move straight to socialism through the agency of a somewhat restructured traditional rural commune. At one point it looked as if Marx was himself almost persuaded of this point of view; but Engels later came out decisively against it.

But the decisive attack was from Lenin. Capitalism in Russia, he argued, though its effects were dreadful was historically progressive because it had already (by 1899) led to the differentiation of the peasantry into a rural petty bourgeoisie and a growing class of landless rural proletarians; at the same time the growth of industry fostered the growth of the proletariat. The Narodniks were quite simply wrong on their facts: 'Commodity circulation and, hence, commodity production are firmly implanted in Russia. Russia is a capitalist country. On the other hand . . . Russia is still very backward, as compared with other capitalist countries, in her economic development'.[25] In observing that capitalism led in Russia to unemployment and underemployment on a massive scale, the Narodniks, according to Lenin, 'have transformed one of the basic conditions for the development of capitalism into proof that capitalism is impossible'.[26]

From all this controversy there emerges, I think, some sort of implicit theory of the effects of the imperialist expansion of the capitalist system into and in Russia. Lenin, for instance, notes the fact that traditional industries had been ousted in Russia partly by the products of Western European industry but partly too by the products

24. V. Vorontsov, quoted in A. Walicki, *The Controversy over Capitalism*, (London, Oxford Univ. Press, 1969), p. 121.
25. Lenin, *op. cit.*, p. 503.
26. *Ibid.*, pp. 582–3.

of the new Russian industry. Marx said in the preface to *Capital* that we 'suffer not only from capitalist development, but also from the incompleteness of that development'.[27] This was especially true in Russia as Lenin implicitly admits. But the incompleteness, partly the result of the imperialist relationship, was not so great that capitalism was not historically progressive. This view was later made more explicit by Trotsky who stressed two features of Russian capitalism. The first was the great significance of foreign (Western European) capital in its development, a fact which led to Russia's possessing only a small, weak and dependent bourgeois class of its own.[28] The second feature was the fact that the industrial proletariat, though small as a proportion of the population, was, as a result of the introduction of the latest products and productive techniques of capitalism, much more concentrated into large factories (more socialised) than at an equivalent stage in the development of capitalist industrialisation in Western Europe. The outcome of this was the vital independent political role of a quantitatively not very large industrial proletariat.

To a degree Russia was the first country to experience modern capitalist underdevelopment. It began to industrialise 'late', with foreign capital and techniques playing a leading role. The emergence of social classes was different from, perhaps more complex than, in Western Europe: the bourgeoisie comparatively weak and dependent, the proletariat small but powerful and the 'subproletariat'—the unemployed and very underemployed for whom capitalism had no use—comparatively large. Whether this model fitted the more backward regions of the world has since then been an underlying question of debate among Marxists.

The question of the possibility of capitalist industrialisation in colonial countries played an important, if not a central role in debates and policy changes in the Comintern in the 1920s and 1930s, and in determining the foreign policy of the U.S.S.R. then and since. Lenin's famous theses on the colonial question adopted at the second Congress of the International, advocating limited and conditional alliance with bourgeois democratic national liberation movements, while maintaining Communist Party organisation intact, were at least partly based on the assumption that colonialism constituted a significant obstacle to the full development of a national bourgeoisie in the colonies, though they implied little about what sort of economic

27. *Capital*, i, 9.
28. L. Trotsky, *History of The Russian Revolution* trans. M. Eastman (London, Gollancz, 1934), vol. i, chs 1, 3.

advance that bourgeoisie would be capable of achieving after the victory of colonial revolution. Lenin's adversary at this and later Congresses, however, the Indian Communist M.N. Roy believed that the crucial contradiction was already that between proletariat and bourgeoisie in the colony, rather than between the whole population of the colony and imperialism. And he based this idea on his view that 'capitalism, far from wishing to hinder industrial development in the colonies, was bent on speeding it up in order to create new markets in the overseas countries. This being the case the national bourgeoisie of the colonies was naturally inclined to seek an understanding with the imperialist powers, whose policy was favourable to its interests, and thus found itself radically opposed both to the urban proletariat and to the peasantry.'[29]

The sixth Comintern Congress in 1928 changed tactics and rejected any policy of alliance with the bourgeoisie. This policy seems to have been based not so much on any change in assumption about the role of capitalism in the colonies as on the idea that capitalism in the advanced countries had entered a new phase in which it had increased its hostility to the Soviet Union.[30]

A number of further changes of policy followed this until at the Twentieth Soviet Party Congress in 1956 a major revision was made. The theses accepted were in fact similar to those advocated in the early days of the Comintern by the Muslim communists, namely 'that the contradictions between the national bourgeoisie of the newly independent countries and imperialism were infinitely more profound than the contradictions between the national bourgeoisie and the proletariat within a given country'.[31] To some extent of course this attitude was based on the view that 'the imperialists fear the industrial development of the colonies and ex-colonies like the plague'.[32] At the same time it appears contradictory, since if imperialist hostility towards industrialisation in the colonies was so firm it was hard to see that the bourgeoisie had any very progressive role to play. And yet the theses were seen as the basis for enduring alliances with the bourgeoisie.[33]

29. H. Carrière d'Encausse and S. R. Schram, *Marxism in Asia*, (London, Allen Lane, 1969), pp. 42–3 and see p. 57; also see Franz Borkenau, *World Communism*, (Ann Arbor, Univ. of Michigan Press, 1962), p. 292.
30. d'Encausse and Schram, pp. 38–9.
31. *Ibid.*, p. 71.
32. Zhukov, quoted in d'Encausse and Schram, *op. cit.*, p. 291.
33. *Ibid.*, pp. 70–1.

5. A characterisation of industrialisation in the third world

The parallels between Russia and the third world are fairly obvious. Two questions, however, are raised here. The first is whether capitalism anywhere in the third world could lead to full independent industrialisation on the model of Japan (this is at one point the question implied by Andre Gunder Frank). The Russian experience raises the second: whether capitalism can still be seen as historically progressive because it may, while unable to produce a complete industrialisation, go far enough to create progressive socio-political forces.

Any answer to these questions requires some information about current third world industrial growth. In the first place the last twenty years have in some capitalist underdeveloped countries seen the very rapid rate of industrial growth. Between 1950/54 and 1960/64 the average annual growth rate of manufacturing output was 6·9 per cent in underdeveloped countries, compared with 5·2 per cent in 'developed market economies' and 10·4 per cent growth in industrial output as a whole in 'centrally planned economies'. This rate is quite a lot higher than the rate achieved by most industrialised countries in the nineteenth century; but now population growth is more than twice as high as then, so the rates per head may well be lower. In a number of countries the growth was very rapid indeed—for example, Brazil, Venezuela, the United Arab Republic, Formosa, South Korea, Israel, Pakistan, Puerto Rico and Hong Kong.[34]

The character of industrial growth in these countries requires much more analysis than it has yet had. But there are certain obvious qualifications to the figures. The statistical rates of growth may be inflated due to monopoly pricing; in Pakistan they partly reflect the fact that after partition the country had less than its 'natural' level of industrial production; small islands are obviously atypical and anyway get political privileges from the imperialists; because they began from such a low base the figures may anyway be misleadingly high; and since profit repatriation by foreign industrial capitalists may be high, then the rate of growth of industrial production will overstate (sometimes grossly) the growth of national *income* derived from industry.

These points certainly do not invalidate all examples of sustained industrial growth in capitalist third world countries. But there are

34. See United Nations Industrial Development Organisation, *Industrial Development Survey* (1969), vol. i.

further reservations. First there is the fact that in most instances rapid industrial growth has been based on import substitution where at some stage opportunities for further growth diminish. Industrialisation is based on the production by foreign capital and techniques of goods identical to those previously imported. The demand for these, usually, luxury consumer goods reflects income distribution which in turn reflects social structure. The production of such goods, inevitably by capital-intensive methods, reinforces that income distribution and social structure.

A second major feature of recent third world industrial growth is its failure to create industrial employment. There are many countries where total industrial employment has fallen in recent years in spite of sometimes quite rapid growth of industrial output. And over a longer time period the structure of the labour force has not changed greatly. In 1960 a lower proportion of the labour force in South Asia (including India) was estimated to be employed in industry than in 1900.

It is, therefore, an exaggeration, but not too great a distortion, to say that this industrial growth has often been characterised by the absence of a bourgeoisie and the absence of a proletariat. At least the situation appears to be qualitatively different from the one in Western Europe which led Marx to remark that 'capitalism is the growth of the proletariat', or in Russia of which Lenin said 'the industrial (i.e. non-agricultural) population grows faster than the agricultural and diverts an ever-growing part of the population from agriculture to manufacturing industry'.[35] Such trends are much less evident in the contemporary third world.

It seems more likely in fact that even in countries where growth has been comparatively fast a process of polarisation is taking place with the great majority of the population being either unaffected, or more likely, finding their position significantly deteriorating as a result of the type of growth which takes place.[36] Sweezy's description of this process remains true:

At the same time, however, the development of colonial economy is not well balanced. Under the domination of imperialism, industrialisation advances very slowly, too slowly to absorb the steady flow of handicraft producers who are ruined by the competition of machine-made products from the factories of the advanced regions. The consequence is the swelling of the ranks of the peasantry, increased pressure on the land and the deterioration of the productivity and living standards

35. Lenin, p. 67.
36. Frank, *Capitalism and Underdevelopment in Latin America*, p. 206.

of the agricultural masses who constitute by far the largest section of the colonial populations. Imperialism thus creates economic problems in the colonies which it is unable to solve.[37]

6. Economic obstacles to capitalist industrialisation

Many of the obstacles which exist to further capitalist industrialisation have already been implied in the definition of independent industrialisation. But it is worth while to set them out more explicitly, in order to see their relation to the Marxist views, recent and classic, which have been described.

The first respect in which industrialisation is hampered in comparison with Western Europe is through the preemption of sources of primary accumulation. Here Europe, through its plunder of the underdeveloped parts of the world, removed potential capital and set it to work in financing European industrialisation. At the same time markets were preempted: the widespread existence of hand production of various consumers' goods was a major advantage to early factory capitalism; a market already existed for the kinds of goods which mechanised production could produce cheaper. But European capitalism had taken advantage of this not only in its own countries but in the underdeveloped countries too.

For underdeveloped countries the situation has been reversed. New industrial capital has to compete for markets not with traditional and inefficient handicraft production which can easily be overcome but with the products of the most advanced industrial enterprises of the advanced countries of the capitalist system. Entry to the home market is difficult enough and is only possible with considerable protection; entry to foreign markets, especially those of the developed capitalist countries themselves, is even more difficult, since naturally their tariff structures discriminate in favour of their own capitalists. So the problem of carving out an initial market for industrial products combines with a comparative absence of opportunities for primary accumulation to explain why the construction of an independent capitalist industry is so difficult.

After these initial relative disadvantages the next group of obstacles are more permanent. These are unequal exchange and the role of foreign ownership in alienating some of the surplus. Unequal exchange is a feature of the world market resulting from the fact that

37. P. M. Sweezy, *The Theory of Capitalist Development*, (New York, Monthly Review Press, 1956), p. 326.

the exporters of industrialised countries possess more monopoly power than the exporters of underdeveloped countries. This largely reflects the fact that markets for industrial products are less competitive than most markets for raw materials. The result of unequal exchange is that the value of total production in the underdeveloped economy is smaller than it would otherwise be; hence the available surplus to finance further capital accumulation is smaller accordingly.[38]

But much of the trade of underdeveloped countries is not subject to unequal exchange since it represents transfers of goods between vertically integrated branches of international firms and is thus a transaction internal to the firms. This trade, however, also allows the potential surplus of the underdeveloped country to be reduced since the trade takes place at 'transfer prices' which need bear no relation to market prices for the products concerned. They allow the firm to locate its profit wherever it wishes; and on occasion (usually of course to avoid taxation) it will declare low profits in underdeveloped countries regardless of the scale of its activities.[39]

Where this device is not open then of course profits made by international firms in underdeveloped countries are repatriated; the potential surplus is drained out of the country. While this drain may be the condition of further inflows of foreign capital, such foreign capital cannot be the agent of an independent industrialisation.[40] In principle nationalisation would appear to be a way of both halting the drain and promoting a national industrialisation simultaneously. In practice it usually does neither, both because of the high rate of compensation which are given and because of difficulties of selling the products of nationalised enterprise on the world market. Where the foreign capital is producing for a home market in the underdeveloped country this, as often as not, is a high income consumer market. Hence, if the nationalised capital is to be profitable, the existing unequal distribution of income must be maintained so that the market for its output remains. That in turn implies that the taxation of the rich to finance industrialisation is inconsistent with the realisation of profits on

38. The literature on unequal exchange is not satisfactory. The idea originates with Marx and has been recently much elaborated from an international standpoint by A. Emmanuel in *L'Echange inegal*, (Paris, 1969).
39. Some discussion of the significance of these transfer prices is in E. T. Penrose, *The Large International Firm in Developing Countries*, (London, Allen & Unwin, 1968).
40. The idea of foreign investment as a pump by means of which the surplus is removed from a country is now very widespread. See, for instance, Paul M. Sweezy, 'Obstacles to economic development' in C. H. Feinstein, ed. *Socialism, Capitalism and Economic Growth, Essays presented to Maurice Dobb*, (Cambridge, Cambridge University Press, 1967). The idea is further discussed in the Conclusion to this book.

nationalised industry. So previously exported profits in that case can only be obtained by forfeiting the possibility of mobilising another part of the potential surplus.

There are a number of features of their historical situation from which underdeveloped countries are suffering:

(*a*) the lateness in time at which they approach the problem of industrialisation: this means they have lost potential advantages and face a more complex and large scale technology than earlier industrialisers;

(*b*) their economic backwardness: a poor community with few skills under any social system obviously cannot easily finance a large programme of capital formation;

(*c*) their relative backwardness in comparison with that of European countries on the eve of their industrialisation;

(*d*) the present coexistence of underdeveloped countries with the developed countries in the world markets;

(*e*) the contact between them which facilitates the drain of the surplus and distorts tastes and the pattern of production;

(*f*) colonial or neo-colonial policy—deliberate policies pursued by capital or the state in developed countries to prevent industrialisation in the underdeveloped countries.

Of these categories of obstacle the first four are irrevocably unavoidable. Only the last two are in principle subject to some redress.

7. Monopoly, protection and uneven development

Monopoly is a central element in Lenin's theory about the drive behind European imperialism in the late nineteenth century. It is also central to the explanation of why the capitalist system so operates as to allow only some of its component countries to become fully industrialised; others are prevented from following the same path. One of the defining characteristics of a monopolistic situation is that monopoly restricts freedom of entry. On the other hand, as we have seen, industrial growth has occurred in some underdeveloped countries, sometimes at a faster rate than in any European countries in the nineteenth century. The monopoly, therefore, is not absolute; its nature must be evolving.

And on this point Andre Gunder Frank has made an important suggestion, worth quoting at some length:

Technology intercedes in the metropolis-satellite relationship and serves to generate still deeper satellite underdevelopment. It is technology which is rapidly and increasingly becoming the new basis of metropolitan monopoly over the satellites. . . .

During the mercantilist era, the metropolitan monopoly lay in commercial monopoly; in the era of liberalism, the metropolitan monopoly came to be industry; in the first half of the twentieth century the metropolitan monopoly switched increasingly to capital goods industry. It then became more possible for the satellites to produce light industrial consumer goods at home. In the second half of the twentieth century, the basis of metropolitan monopoly seems to be switching increasingly to technology. Now the satellites can even have heavy industry at home. Such heave industry might, 100 or even 50 years ago, have freed a satellite from dependence on the metropolis; it would have converted the satellite into still another part of the metropolis and would have made it an imperialist power. But no satellite was then able to break through the metropolitan monopoly of heavy industry. Only the U.S.S.R. did so by abandoning the imperialist and capitalist system altogether and going over to socialism.

In our time, however, heavy industry no longer is enough to break out of this metropolitan monopolist domination, for the domination has come to have a new base, technology.[41]

This interesting observation is still not a complete answer to the problem. It does not say for instance whether this is an ultimate stage of the monopoly or whether it too in its turn will be replaced. It is hard to envisage by what. And that difficulty points to an unsatisfactory aspect of Frank's idea. Technology is a different type of thing from capital goods industries or consumer goods industries. Technology is not disembodied but is embodied in certain capital goods. In a sense therefore technology has always been the basis of the metropolitan monopoly. The underdeveloped areas have been unable to establish a complete industrial structure because they have been unable to establish the industries possessing at the time the most complex and advanced technology. In that case the basis of technology today has shifted not to a new category, technology, but to a new more restricted group of capital goods industries.

A partial counterpart to the idea that it is monopoly which prevents the possibility of independent industrialisation is the notion that protection (of capital by the state) is essential to promote it. It is quite clear that all capitalist industrialisations after (or perhaps

41. Frank, *Capitalism and Underdevelopment in Latin America,* p. 211.

even including)[42] the British were successful because they were protected by comparatively high tariffs as in the United States, Germany and Italy, or supported by the state as in prerevolutionary Russia or Japan, or both. Hence if any further independent capitalist industrialisation at all is contemplated it must be in conditions of high protection and state intervention along the lines of, say, Mexico or India. A careful assessment of such countries from this point of view is a pressing necessity.[43] So on a more general plane is an analysis of whether, given the extent of exisiting capitalist penetration into the third world, the protective weapons are any longer strong enough to defend a nascent third world capitalism. In many Latin American countries in spite of very high tariff levels they still seem to have been too weak.

It may still be wondered whether a socialist protection would have any greater power. The two are not strictly comparable since socialist protection would be in the context of planned production and its weapons would be planned trade rather than tariffs. As Preobrahzensky argues, socialist protection has a different nature and objective:

> If there is sometimes a protectionist tariff policy in countries with weakly developed industry, aimed at protecting a particular industry from the competition of a capitalistically more developed country, this has nothing in common, beyond external forms, with socialist protectionism. In the one case it is a matter of protecting one industry from another *belonging to the same economic system*. In the other we have the protection of one mode of production, which is in a state of infantile weakness, from another economic system mortally hostile to it which even in the period of its senile decrepitude will inevitably be stronger, economically and technically, than the new economy. Only with utter carelessness in theoretical matters can one see in socialist protectionism a complete analogy to capitalist protectionism.[44]

In conclusion, industrialisation, economic independence or monopoly are all concepts in terms of which only relative rather than absolute statements are possible. What we can say about countries or groups of countries in terms of these concepts at present is not true for all conditions, past or future. In the past there have been periods during which a number of underdeveloped countries appeared to be moving in the direction of an independent capitalist industrialisation,

42. See F. Engels, 'Protection and free trade', in *Marx and Engels on Colonialism*, (Moscow, undated), p. 233.
43. For such an analysis of India see the paper by P. Patnaik (IX below).
44. E. Preobrahzensky, *The New Economics*, (London, Oxford Univ. Press, 1965), p. 121.

even though the movement was later halted. These mainly occurred during times either of war between capitalist countries or in times of acute capitalist crises, such as the 1930s, when the basis of the superior competitive position of enterprises in the advanced countries was undermined and monopoly strength partially collapsed. In recent decades while rapid industrial growth seems to have taken place only, or at least mainly, in those capitalist countries most obviously satellised by the advanced countries, this is not necessarily a permanent situation. Capitalism has not freed itself from crisis; and we cannot be sure that the renewed intensive competition within the capitalist system between the United States and the rejuvenated European capitalism and the restrengthened Japanese capitalism will not at some point erupt into war. On these grounds it is not impossible that, as a result of changes in the structure of imperialism, we shall see further attempts at independent capitalist industrialisation. On the other hand, if the present crisis of capitalism marks its end then this prospect will cease to have even the limited relevance it still possesses today.

PART THREE

Case studies in the

working of imperialism

The final section of the book is concerned with the relation between theoretical and factual questions. It is wrong, of course, to think too much in terms of a clear dichotomy between theory and fact. The facts in any situation do not just present themselves *in toto* for inspection. They emerge from historical investigations, and they then have to be selected, ordered and presented in a certain way. Neither the search for the facts, nor their selection and presentation, are independent of a theory, even though it may be only an implicit one. To use historical 'facts', therefore, as a test of a theory or hypothesis is a hazardous business, since the facts may contain in them an implicit theory which is the same as, or inconsistent with, the one which is being tested.

The six case studies which follow are all about regions or countries in the third world. Four of them are predominantly concerned with the nineteenth century; those on India and Guinea, however, both extend their analysis to more recent times. All the case studies are about how imperialism operated or took root in the underdeveloped areas; but Stengers, Kanya Forstner and Platt focus attention on the activities motives and policies of the advanced imperialist countries; while the other three papers are much more concerned with how the experience of imperialism affected the underdeveloped areas themselves.

Together the case studies provide some illustration of the range of ways in which theory can be related to concrete historical situations. In general there are two ways in which theory is being related to the events. In the first place theory is seen as suggesting a pattern which events in any area are expected more or less to follow. It provides in other words a paradigm train of events and motives against which an actual situation can be matched. Here, therefore, the concern is with the consistency of the actual set of events and motives with those implied in the paradigm. In the second place, a theory of imperialism provides a way of organising what factual historical material is available; and in this way it gives a pattern to the events. So there are two approaches: on the one hand, facts are being used to test the theory; on the other hand, the theory is being used to organise the facts.

In the first two case studies—Owen on Egypt in the nineteenth century and Patnaik on India, largely in the twentieth century—the second approach is uppermost. Both of them find that the Marxist theory, or aspects of it, provide a more or less satisfactory basis for making the events coherent. For Egypt, Owen argues that there are a few important areas, including the role of the state, where existing theory is inadequate; for India, Patnaik finds it necessary to add more analysis of the Indian bourgeoisie and of the state than the theory directly provides. In the case of Guinea, Johnson is combining the two approaches: on the one hand, he tries to fit Guinea into the pattern of world capitalist expansion; and on the other, he compares what happened in Guinea to an implied paradigm of events; Guinea appears not to be very close to this paradigm; but the history of its involvement in imperialism is in no way inconsistent with the Marxist theory.

In the other three papers the first approach is uppermost. The Marxist theory or an implied version of it is not being used, but is in a sense being tested. In the Congo, Stengers argues that the facts and Leopold's motives do not fit the pattern implied by the theory; but that this is no reason to think that the theory does not work better elsewhere. The Congo is an exception: it does not prove the rule, but nor does it disprove it. French motives in Africa were also, according to Kanya Forstner, a long way from those implied in the theory; and he concludes that theory is more or less irrelevant to the events he describes. British motives in South America were economic enough; but, Platt argues, the political behaviour of the British was quite different to what the theory would lead us to expect. In this case he believes the facts to be inconsistent with the theory; it should be regarded therefore as an exception which does something to disprove the rule.

VIII

Egypt and Europe: from French expedition to British occupation

Roger Owen

The absorption of a country as a dependent state within the imperialist system was more protracted than dramatic occupations, like that of Egypt in 1882, might suggest. In Egypt it involved a long term transformation of the economy. Efforts to use the state to promote independent industrialisation failed as the economy was dragged into the international division of labour; and, as in India, the state lost its autonomy in relation to outside powers (see Patnaik, IX).

Owen argues that much of what happened in Egypt in the nineteenth century is well accounted for in the theories of Marx, Hobson, Luxemburg, Hilferding and Baran. But there remain three areas where the theories do not provide an adequate framework: the role of the metropolitan states in relation to their capitalists, the nature of the Egyptian state and the changes in the Egyptian social structure which imperial penetration produced.

The bombardment of Alexandria and the invasion of Egypt by British troops in 1882 roused something of the same passions that were later to be let loose by the Anglo-French attack on Suez in 1956. Government policy was bitterly attacked in Parliament by Radical and Irish M.P.s. It was also the subject of hostile comment in a series of books and pamphlets such as J. S. Keay's *Spoiling the Egyptians*. A minister, John Bright, resigned from the cabinet in protest.

Among the opponents of the attack on Egypt a single theme predominated: the assertion that it was undertaken to insure that the Egyptian government continued to pay the interest on the country's large external debt. 'It is a stock-jobbers' war', wrote one of John

Bright's friends, 'we shall very likely have more of this sort of thing.'[1] For the first time in Britain's history it was the financial community rather than the soldiers or colonial officials who were held to be chiefly responsible for an act of imperial expansion. This point of view was soon to become the stimulus to a new and more radical critique of empire which paid increasing attention to the notion that colonies were obtained because they were a source of profit to certain groups of businessmen and financiers, one which found its most vigorous exponent in J. A. Hobson, whose *Imperialism: a study* appeared in 1902. The invasion of Egypt thus occupies a central role in the genesis of theories of capitalist imperialism.

It was for reasons of this same type that the invasion continued to be seen not merely as just another example of European expansion but as one of its classic cases. As such it has an important place in the books of early writers on capitalist imperialism like Hobson[2] as well as those who have continued to write in the same tradition, such as John Strachey.[3] It follows that the invasion also occupies a central position in the works of writers like Robinson and Gallagher[4] and D. C. M. Platt[5] who are concerned to demonstrate that Egypt was taken for strategic rather than economic motives. Once the British occupation was presented as one of the prime exhibits of nineteenth-century imperialism it was inevitable that it should become a battleground for rival theories.

Whether this is a particularly fruitful way of looking either at the phenonemon of imperialism or at Egyptian history is another matter: my belief is that it is not. It is a major argument of the present case study that the British occupation cannot be studied in isolation, that it can only be understood in terms of an important series of developments which had been taking place since 1798, most of which were related to the transformation of the economy as a result of the policies of the Egyptian state and of its incorporation, as a producer of raw materials, within the European economic system. Seen in these terms an analysis of the relations between Egypt and Europe in the nineteenth century becomes a very different type of case study from these which concentrate simply on the events leading up to the British occupation. It is concerned with changes in the character of European

1. G. M. Trevelyan, *The Life of John Bright*, 2nd edn, (London, Constable, 1925), p. 434.
2. Hobson, *Imperialism: a study* (London, Nisbet, 1902), p. 54–5, 108, 199.
3. *The End of Empire* (London, Gollancz, 1959), pp. 97, 118.
4. *Africa and the Victorians* (London, Macmillan, 1961), ch iv.
5. *Finance, Trade, and Politics*, (London, Oxford Univ. Press, 1968), pt iii, ch vii.

economic expansion over many decades and with the impact of these changes on all sections of Egyptian society. Again, it involves a study of the crisis of the years between bankruptcy in 1875 and occupation in 1882, not so much in its own terms but rather as one of those periods in which, under the pressure of events, basic processes of economic and social change are laid bare for our examination.

An approach of this type has a number of advantages. It allows us to focus attention on one of the special characteristics of nineteenth-century imperialism: the way in which, in many cases, the colonisation of an African or Asian territory was preceded by a breakdown of local political and social institutions resulting from a period of enforced contact with the European economy. Again, it enables us to take a new look at major works on the theory of imperialism to discover which of them provide useful guidance not simply about the occupation of Egypt but also about the whole character of European expansion and its effect on non-European societies. In addition, such a study is made more interesting by two other considerations. First, Egypt contained what was certainly one of the most varied societies which Europe encountered in Africa. This was partly a function of the fact that there had been settled life in the Nile valley for so many thousands of years. Furthermore, Egypt had always stood across important routes of international trade. It had been occupied many times and incorporated in a series of world empires. In the early Middle Ages it was Egyptian merchants who had introduced such vital commercial techniques as the bill of exchange to Europe. Even in 1798, when little of its former political or economic importance remained, when Napoleon is credited with having reintroduced the wheeled carriage to Egypt, its long history continued to be reflected in the fact that it contained one of the oldest universities in the world, a complicated system of municipal organisation, a high degree of commercial consciousness and an agricultural population, many of whom were well used to growing cash crops for export or for sale in numerous market towns. Second, more information exists about nineteenth century Egypt than about almost any other African or Asian country. From the *Description de l'Egypte* produced by the scholars of Napoleon's expedition and the works of the great Egyptian historian al-Jabarti to Ali Mubarak's voluminous encyclopaedia, *al-Khitat al-Taufiqiya al-Jadida* and the works of contemporary Egyptian writers like Anouar Abdel-Malek, there are a vast number of books by authors anxious to trace the impact of Europe on Egyptian society. In addition, there is a wealth of material in the Egyptian,

Turkish and other government archives.

What follows is a brief analysis of the major economic and social developments in Egypt between 1798 and 1882. It will begin with a description of the transformation of the economy. There will then be an account of changes in the position of certain important social groups inside Egypt. Finally, it will conclude with a schematic account of the prolonged crisis of the years 1875 to 1882.

1. The transformation of the economy[6]

Egypt in 1798 was a country of some 2,500,000 to 3,000,000 people, of whom perhaps a tenth lived in Cairo, far and away the largest city. The great bulk of the population worked in agriculture. In Upper Egypt peasants concentrated on the cultivation of winter cereals watered by the annual Nile flood. But in Lower Egypt (the Delta) one-eighth or so of the cultivated area was devoted to the production of high value crops like flax and short-staple cotton which required larger amounts of capital and a more complex system of irrigation to provide them with water through the summer months when the river was at its lowest. Another difference between Upper and Lower Egypt lay in the fact that in the Delta taxes often seem to have been collected in cash rather than kind with the result that cultivators were forced to sell a portion of their harvest in the nearest market. For this and other reasons most peasants in the Delta had some experience of operating on the fringes of a money economy, while in a number of areas cash seems to have been as important as custom or tradition as a basis for rural relations.

Meanwhile, the towns served as markets for rural products as well as centres for the production of those manufactured articles, notably linen and silk, which required greater skill, capital and organization than could be provided at village level. Some of the larger ones were also important centres of consumption of the luxury goods which made up the greater part of the merchandise which then entered international trade.

By the end of the eighteenth century the power of the government was weak. Not only was the central administration unable to maintain

6. cf. G. Baer, *A History of Landownership in Modern Egypt 1800–1950* (London, Oxford Univ. Press, 1962); A. E. Crouchley, *The Economic Development of Modern Egypt* (London, Longmans, 1938); A-M. Hamza, *The Public Debt of Egypt 1854–1876* (Cairo, 1944); E. R. J. Owen, *Cotton and the Egyptian Economy 1820–1914* (London, Oxford Univ. Press, 1969); and S. J. Shaw, *Ottoman Egypt in the Age of the French Revolution* (Cambridge, Mass., Harvard Univ. Press, 1964).

security in country areas or to supervise the upkeep of the major canals but it had also virtually lost control over the system of rural administration and tax collection. As a result the bulk of the agricultural surplus did not reach the government treasury but remained in the hands of a caste of hereditary tax-farmers who used it largely to provide themselves with the private armies they required in their endless struggles with one another for wealth and power.[7]

In the early years of the nineteenth century this predominantly agricultural economy was acted on by two new sets of forces. One was the efforts of a series of rulers—Muhammad Ali (1805–49), Said (1854–62), and Ismail (1863–79)—to modernise the army and the bureaucracy or, as they saw it, to lay the foundations of a modern state. The other was the impact of the expanding European economy, first through increasing trade, then through the export of European capital. Let us take them in order.

Muhammad Ali.   Once he had seized power in 1805 Muhammad Ali's basic aim was to preserve his own rule by building up a large army and navy. During the first years of his regime he relied almost exclusively on foreign mercenaries. But during the 1820s he began to recruit native Egyptians and by the early 1830s he may have had as many as 100,000 men under arms. Such an army obviously required large sums of money and he was quick to see that the key to this was to increase the amount obtained from the land tax by replacing the tax-farmers with a system of direct collection by government agents. This had the further advantage of destroying alternative centres of political power and allowing the government to put an end to the anarchic conditions in the countryside. In addition, further sums were raised by an extension of the state monopolies to cover almost every type of agricultural produce. Crops were taken from the peasants in lieu of taxes and sold abroad on government account, leaving the cultivator little more than enough for bare existence. Finally, a labour tax, the corvée, was imposed on every adult male. In this way Muhammad Ali sought to perfect a system by which the government was able to appropriate the greater part of the rural surplus, using it either for military purposes or for an ambitious attempt to develop the country's resources. Unlike his predecessors Egypt's new ruler

---

7. cf. S. J. Shaw, *The Financial and Administrative Organisation and Development of Ottoman Egypt 1715–1798* (Princeton Univ. Press, 1958), pp. 62–3, 95 and A. Raymond, 'Essai de géographie des quartiers de residence aristocratique au Caire au XVIIIème siècle', *Journal of the Economic and Social History of the Orient*, 6 (1963), p. 84–5, 95.

seems to have been fully aware of the fact that a continuous increase in government revenues was impossible without a continuous expansion of economic activity. It was for this reason that he was so anxious to encourage the introduction of new crops like long-staple cotton which had a growing market in Europe, to build new canals, and to improve communications. Later, in an effort to reduce imports, Egyptian textile workers were taken from their workshops and placed in government factories producing cotton cloth (much of it for army uniforms) with European machinery. Meanwhile an increasing number of young Egyptians were sent abroad to learn the most modern industrial techniques.

However, Muhammad Ali's attempt to set the state at the centre of the development of the Egyptian economy soon proved too much for the country's rudimentary system of administration and from the late 1830s onwards factories began to be closed or handed over to private individuals and much of the land assigned to senior officials and members of the royal family who themselves were made responsible for supervising agricultural production and collecting taxes. This process was hastened by the Anglo-Turkish Commercial Convention of 1838 which outlawed state monopolies and established a low external tariff of 8 per cent. Three years later the size of the Egyptian army was reduced, by order of the Ottoman government, to 18,000 thus depriving Muhammad Ali of a protected market for the products of his factories. As a result further industrialisation was made very much more difficult while, once Egypt's ruler was finally forced to abandon his monopolies in the mid-1840s, the government lost the considerable sums it had derived from its control over agricultural exports.

European commercial expansion.   Muhammad Ali's attempts to develop the economy required European assistance and European markets, but he was anxious to reduce the impact of Europe to a minimum. European merchants were confined to Alexandria and forbidden to make contact with the peasants in the interior. Professional schools were established and young Egyptians sent abroad in order to reduce the need for European technical expertise. Strenuous efforts were made to replace European imports with locally manufactured goods. This policy came to an end in the 1840s, however. As a result of European political pressure, first at Istanbul, then on Egypt itself, the country was rapidly opened up to foreign trade, a process which was undoubtedly assisted by Egypt's own large landed proprietors who were anxious to end the monopoly system so that they could sell their produce direct to European merchants rather than to the government. The export of cotton increased by 300 per cent between 1840 and 1860 as moneylenders established themselves throughout the Delta to provide the credit previously supplied by the government, as steam gins were introduced, and as the first railway was built linking Cairo with Alexandria. This paved the way for the rapid expansion of production during the American Civil War (1861–65) when the area placed under cotton increased five times and the size of the harvest by four. Meanwhile, the growing importance of the close ties which were being developed with the British economy can be seen from the fact that between 1848 ánd 1860 Egypt rose from twenty-sixth to twelfth place as a market for British exports while between 1854 and 1860 it moved from being the tenth most important supplier of British imports to the sixth.

European financial expansion.   Increasing trade with Europe was followed by a rapid growth in the import of capital. During the 1850s the first European banks were established in Alexandria. At the same time the construction of more public works, further modernisation of the army and of the bureaucracy, and, above all, the need to finance the great part of de Lesseps's Suez Canal project meant that government expenditure rapidly began to outstrip current receipts. Said began to borrow heavily from local bankers and merchants, then (perhaps at de Lesseps's suggestion) to issue treasury bonds. Finally, in 1862, he obtained his first foreign loan. This was followed by many others until by 1875 Egypt had borrowed a nominal sum of nearly £100 million from Europe, of which the Treasury had actually obtained no more than £68 million.

David Landes has described this process from the European side: how the end of the railway boom in the 1840s was followed by the development of new financial institutions, notably the finance company, which were able to obtain large sums of money from new groups of investors; how the particular character of these institutions drove them to seek speculative outlets for their capital abroad; how European money was drawn to the Middle East by the lure of the fabulous rates of interest which, it was supposed, could be obtained from lending money to merchants and agriculturalists.[8] Other writers, notably J. Bouvier, have described the way in which in the

8. D. Landes, *Bankers and Pashas* (London, Heinemann Education, 1958), pp. 47–68.

early 1870s, a number of French finance companies became heavily dependent on lending money to the Egyptian government.[9]

But how was the money borrowed from Europe used? In brief, Ismail had the same general aims as his grandfather, Muhammad Ali. These were: to build up a modern state, to assert Egypt's independence against both Turkey and Europe, and to diversify the economy. Unfortunately they proved to be mutually contradictory. All his efforts to use European capital to build up a state and an economy strong enough to withstand European pressures only led to increasing dependence on Europe. This can be seen clearly in his efforts to develop the economy. Here three factors were important. First, in so far as the money borrowed from Europe was put to good use and not just wasted it was employed in infrastructural investment of a type which could only benefit government revenue in the medium to long term. Meanwhile government efforts to raise more money from the land tax were thwarted by an inefficient system of collection and the fact that the bulk of the land was passing into the hands of powerful officials. In these circumstances, failure to meet interest payments on the foreign loans was inevitable. Second, efforts to diversify the economy were inhibited by the growing strength and importance of the cotton sector. As an ever-increasing proportion of Egypt's resources were being devoted to the production and export of this one crop it became more and more difficult to develop alternative forms of economic activity. The rich landed proprietors who grew to cotton, the merchants who sold it, were all united in their efforts to defend their particular interests and to make sure that they were the first to benefit from expenditure of government money, changes in the legal system or any other aspect of state activity. Third, unlike the rulers of Japan after 1868 Ismail was unable to place any barriers between the Egyptian economy and that of Europe. His attempts to create a sugar industry, for example, were hindered by the fact that he was unable to prevent the import of cheap government-subsidised sugar from Russia and Germany. The result of all these three factors was Egypt's incorporation, as a producer of cotton and a market for manufactured goods, within the European economic system. However hard he may have striven for independence Ismail was destined to end up by serving the purposes of Europe.

9. 'Les intérêts financiers et la question d'Egypt (1875–76)', *Revue Historique*, **224**, July–Sept., 1960.

2. Changes in the position of important social groups[10]

The transformation of the Egyptian economy during the nineteenth century led to significant changes in the position of a number of social groups. Four are of particular importance.

The foreign community. The number of Europeans in Egypt rose from approximately 8,000 to 10,000 in 1838 to over 90,000 in 1881. The majority were concerned with the production and export of cotton or with banking and finance. But there were a growing number who were employed by the government itself, either as officials or experts. By the end of the 1860s, for example, there were over a hundred Europeans in the police.[11] Later, as a result of the report of the Commission of Inquiry in 1878 over 1,300 foreign officials were brought into the administration.[12] The European community occupied a privileged position as a result of the Capitulations, the treaties governing the status of foreigners within the Ottoman Empire. Europeans were virtually beyond the scope of the Egyptian law until the introduction of the Mixed Courts in 1876. They imported goods at their own valuation. They could only be taxed with the greatest difficulty. In addition, with the support of their consuls, they became an increasingly powerful pressure group, committed to defending their own interests as bankers and exporters as well as, by virtue of their extensive holdings of Egyptian bonds, to ensuring that the government maintain payment of interest on the various loans.

Egyptian landed proprietors. The growth of a class of Egyptian landed proprietors came about in three ways. First, in the late 1830s and early 1840s much of the best land in Egypt was parcelled out in estates and placed under the control of members of the royal family and senior officials. Although some of these estates were taken back from their owners during the rule of Abbas (1849–54) a large number remained in private hands. At the same time many local notables, particularly the village shaikhs, were able to take advantage of their position as agents of the central government to obtain land for themselves. There was every incentive to do this, of course, once the production of cotton

10. cf. A. Abdel-Malek *Idéologie et Renaissance Nationale: L'Egypt Moderne* (Paris, 1969); I. Abu-Lughod 'The transformation of the Egyptian elite: prelude to the Urabi revolt', *Middle East Journal,* **21,** (Summer, 1967); G. Baer *Studies in the Social History of Modern Egypt* (Univ. of Chicago Press, 1969); S. Nour Ed-Dine 'Conditions des fellahs en Egypte', *Revue d'Islam* (1898).
11. Stanton, 7 Oct. 1869: FO 78/2093 (Public Record Office, London).
12. Malet, 18 May 1882: FO 78/3436.

and other crops became increasingly profitable. Finally, during Ismail's reign palace favourites, army officers, bureaucrats and others were given land either as a gift or in lieu of a pension. Meanwhile, the ruler himself added extensively to the lands owned by the royal family until, at the end of his reign, he controlled something like a fifth of the whole cultivated area.

As yet no historian has been able to make a satisfactory distinction between landed proprietors of various types, but there is no doubt that, as a group, they occupied a particularly favourable position, often working their estates with corvées of local labour, diverting water from the canals to their own fields whenever they needed it, and paying lower taxes than their peasant neighbours. In addition, it was the landed proprietors who were the major beneficiaries of all the public money spent on digging new canals and building the railway system. It was they, as much as the European consuls, who were responsible for the abolition of Muhammad Ali's agricultural monopolies; they too who may well have put pressure on successive Egyptian governments to pass the laws necessary to create a system of private property in land.

For the most part the large and medium-sized estates created between 1840 and 1880 came from land formerly worked by peasants on their own account. The majority of these peasants remained as agricultural labourers in their villages, or were grouped together on the new estates in hamlets known as *ezbas*. Cotton production is particularly labour-intensive and the landed proprietors seem to have been concerned to maintain the old labour force more or less intact. These labourers were either paid in kind or, more usually, by being allowed to cultivate a tiny plot of land.

The bureaucrats. Efforts to create a modern state required an increasing number of civil servants. These were found at most levels, from among the graduates of Muhammad Ali's and Ismail's schools and from the many young Egyptians sent to Europe to study. As time went on the bureaucracy was subject to a process of rationalisation. Separate ministries were formed; jobs were made more specific; pensions were introduced. As a result there developed something which Abdel-Malek is certainly right to characterise as a special bureaucratic interest.[13] Civil servants tended to share common ideas about the role of the state. Further, in the 1870s, they were more or less united in their

13. Abdel-Malek, pp. 420–3.

desire to prevent any increase in the numbers and the privileges of Europeans within the government service. On the other hand, it is often difficult to make a clear distinction between the bureaucrats as a group and the landowners, once the former began to be given estates of their own.

The Turco-Circassian ruling class. During the eighteenth century almost all the senior posts in government and in the army were held by a Turkish-speaking minority, the descendants of Mamluk slaves or of officials sent from Istanbul. Later, during the early nineteenth century many of them were replaced by Ottoman soldiers of fortune who had served in Muhammad Ali's army. In the course of time their importance as a separate group began to diminish, particularly once the administration became more 'Egyptianised' as a result of the increasing employment of native Egyptians and the regulations providing for the use of Arabic in the government service. Meanwhile, for their part, more and more of the Turco-Circassians married Egyptian wives, took up posts in the district administration or in other ways became more closely incorporated within Egyptian society. Nevertheless, their power and prestige was still resented particularly in the army where, in the 1870s they held every position above that of colonel.

3. Bankruptcy and occupation 1875–1882[14]

Egypt's bankruptcy in 1875 marked the beginning of a seven-year period of rapidly accelerating change in many areas of Egyptian government and society. A series of financial arrangements designed to ensure that the country paid its debts paved the way for increasing European control over the administration. This, in turn, provoked a strong Egyptian response, led first by Ismail, for which he was deposed in 1879, and then by a growing number of soldiers and officials. Finally, the emergence of a popular, national movement in 1881 and 1882 seemed sufficiently threatening to European interests to call for the occupation of Egypt by British troops.

Efforts to explain these developments generally concentrate, on the one hand, on tracing the genesis of the national movement; on the other, on seeking to discover what were the motives for increasing European intervention. This method has two major drawbacks.

14. cf. Abdel-Malek, ch 12, Bouvier, *op. cit.*; P. J. Vatikiotis, *The Modern History of Egypt*, (London, Weidenfeld & Nicolson, 1969), ch 6 and 7.

First, it encourages writers to ignore the socio-economic context in which these developments were taking place. Second, most accounts of the crisis, by concentrating either on the Egyptian or on the European side of the story, tend to underestimate the importance of the constant interaction between these two elements. What follows is an attempt to make a few brief points about the crisis in the light of these two considerations.

(*a*) The Egyptian national movement is best seen as a coalition of different groups all of which were, in some way, affected by the financial regime imposed on Egypt by its European creditors after the declaration of bankruptcy. These included the landowners (who were anxious to block the attempts being made by Egypt's European financial controllers to raise more revenue by increasing their taxes), the bureaucrats (disturbed by the numbers of Europeans being employed in the civil service), the Egyptian army officers (many of whom were threatened with premature retirement as a result of plans to economise on military expenditure), and the *ulama* or religious notables.

(*b*) In the late 1870s the fears of members of these four groups were encouraged by the Khedive Ismail for his own purposes but, just before his deposition in 1879, they began to cooperate more closely on the basis of a programme aimed at limiting the powers of the ruler by the introduction of a liberal constitution. This movement continued under Ismail's successor, Taufiq, even though it remained largely ineffectual until the summer of 1881. It was only when the civilian constitutionalists began to ally themselves more closely with the nationalist army officers led by Colonel Arabi that they obtained sufficient power to force a change of regime.

(*c*) The coalition of different interests which went to make up the Egyptian national movement was at its most cohesive in the last months of 1881 and the early part of 1882 when its strength was constantly being revived by the efforts of the British and French government to maintain Taufiq's failing authority. It also gained strength from a constant appeal to social groups which had previously had no part to play in the country's politics, notably the small land-owners who were worried about the amount of land which was being seized for non-payment of debt following the introduction of a European type of mortgage law in 1876. Later, however, as the threat of European intervention became more real and as the leaders of the national movement became more successful in obtaining widespread popular support, many of those with important economic interests to defend left the movement and went over to the side of the Khedive and the Europeans.

(*d*) From a European point of view a distinction must be made between the interests and activities of the British and French bondholders and the British and French governments. In the first few months after the announcement of Egypt's bankruptcy it was the bondholders, not their governments, who managed to patch up their differences sufficiently to obtain a financial settlement which would protect all their interests. This was the so-called Goschen-Joubart arrangement of 1877. It was only when this arrangement threatened to break down that the British and French governments intervened more directly, first by instituting a Commission of Enquiry into Egypt's financial situation, then by forcing Ismail to accept a cabinet containing two European ministers to implement the recommendation of the report. The next year they intervened again when it seemed that he was about to alter the existing arrangements.

(*e*) Anglo-French cooperation hid important differences of aim. On the whole the French were more anxious to protect the interests of their bondholders, the British to prevent the situation deteriorating to such an extent that another power might intervene in Egypt and thus stand across the route to India. Nevertheless, both governments were able to act in concert, first in support of a programme of upholding whatever financial arrangement had been made on the bondholder's behalf, then in 1882, in seeking to strengthen the authority of Egypt's ruler against the national movement. It was this last policy which led directly to the British occupation.

(*f*) Finally, the events of the years 1875 to 1882, cutting as they do across a period of rapid economic and social change, help to expose the essential nature of the transformation then taking place. The nature of the links which bound the Egyptian economy to that of Europe are clear; so too is the way in which they were reinforced by the presence of powerful groups within Egypt. Again, the composition of the national movement shows the extent of hostility to European encroachment present in almost all sections of Egyptian society, just as it also reveals something of the division between those who were prepared to resist further foreign intervention by force if necessary and those who were not.

4. Conclusion

What I have been trying to describe in this case study is a process

208   *Roger Owen*

analysed in part by a number of theorists. Marx and Hobson have provided an account of the way in which Europe entered the non-European world by means of trade and the export of capital,[15] while Rosa Luxemburg has written of the economic and social dislocation which this caused.[16] Baran and others have described the process by which a country's enforced incorporation within the European economic system imposes a straightjacket on further development by forcing it to concentrate all its effort and resources on the export of primary produce.[17] Hobson and Hilferding pointed to the way in which the expansion of Europe led, inevitably, to the creation of movements of national liberation.[18]

But I have also been trying to suggest, if only by implication, that a study of relations between Egypt and Europe in the nineteenth century reveals a number of areas in which existing theories give little guidance. Three of these are of more than usual importance. The first concerns the role of the European state and, in particular, its relations with its own business community. To take only one example, in the period after 1815 Britain, and, to a lesser extent, France, consciously used state power to open up the Eastern Mediterranean to their own trade. This process was marked, among other things, by the Anglo-Turkish Commercial Convention of 1838, which established what was virtually free trade for British and French goods in the area. Again, each state was willing to use its local representation to intervene on behalf of its own nationals in their pursuit of profit. One way of characterising these efforts might be to say that a primary aim of the capitalist state in the nineteenth century was to extend its own economic system—its own laws, its own commercial practices, its own pattern of relations between government and merchants and industrialists—out beyond its own borders. But too little work has been done on the relationship between economic and political power to be dogmatic. (See, however, Platt's 'Economic imperialism and the businessman: Britain and Latin America before 1914' ch. XIII below.)

A second area in which there is little theoretical guidance concerns the nature of the Egyptian state. Rosa Luxemburg's characterisation of it as an 'oriental despotism'[19] is certainly misleading. For one thing

15. Marx, *Capital*, vol. i, pt viii, chs xxi and xxiii; Hobson, pp. 76–79.
16. Luxemburg, *The Accumulation of Capital* (London, Routledge, 1963), ch 29.
17. P. A. Baran, *The Political Economy of Growth* (New York, Monthly Review Press, 1962 edn) pp. 163 ff.
18. Hobson, p. 11; R. Hilferding *Das Finanzcapital* (Vienna, 1923), pp. 384–9.
19. Luxemburg, p. 358.

there is the fact that, throughout the nineteenth century, Egypt's rulers made continuous efforts to organise the machinery of government along more rational lines and to provide it with the expertise to carry out an increasing number of ever more complicated tasks. Again, in the sphere of ideology, there was the introduction into Egypt of the new and increasingly powerful European notions that growth was natural to an economy and that this growth could be encouraged by judicious state action. But did this also mean that Egypt was necessarily committed to a 'European' pattern of development along capitalist lines? The question remains an open one.

Finally, there are the problems posed by the attempt to analyse the changes produced in Egyptian society by the country's incorporation within a world economic system. How far, for instance, is it possible to talk about the creation of classes in Egypt before 1882? To some extent this is part of the general difficulty surrounding the use of such terms when talking about a pre-industrial society. It also stems from a situation peculiar to Egypt in which there was no definite category of 'landowner' and in which many of those who held agricultural estates were also merchants or bureaucrats or army officers or religious notables. In these circumstances it may be better to look at nineteenth-century Egyptian social development less in terms of classes, strictly defined, more in terms of the creation of a number of overlapping interest groups the members of which 'form a class only in so far as they have to carry on a common battle against another class'.[20]

Nevertheless, these problems aside, the broad lines of the developing relationship between Egypt and Europe in the nineteenth century are clear. Once Muhammad Ali's attempts at economic autarchy had been brought to an end, the international division of labour rapidly asserted itself and Egypt was drawn into the world capitalist system as a producer of industrial raw materials, as a market for manufactured goods, and as a field for the investment of European capital. This, in turn, had a profound effect on the structure of Egyptian society and led, among other things, to the emergence of a movement of national protest and then to foreign occupation. The pattern is simple: the loss of economic independence not only preceded the loss of political independence, it also prepared the way for it.

20. Marx. *Pre-capitalist Economic Formations*, with an introduction by E. Hobsbawn, (London, Lawrence and Wishart, 1964), p. 132.

IX

Imperialism and the growth of Indian capitalism
Prabhat Patnaik

The possibility of an independent capitalist industrialisation in an under-developed country within the imperialist system depends on whether the local bourgeoisie, and a state to back it, can acquire enough power, indepen-dence and incentive to carry out the tasks involved. In this context Patnaik examines the development of the Indian bourgeoisie in the colonial and postcolonial ages. He finds that, in spite of some progress towards an independent industrialisation after independence, when Indian capital was growing and the state had some autonomy in relation to the imperialist countries, a new phase began in the early 1960s. This was a phase of greater dependence in which both the state and the Indian capitalist class were weakened in relation to both the governments and capitalists of the imperialist countries.

A fundamental proposition underlying much Marxist thinking on the third world countries is that capitalist development is not possible for them today, that their productive forces cannot be adequately develop-ed under capitalist relations.[1] The proposition must be interpreted carefully. First it is not an abstract economic proposition. Since spontaneous breakdowns of the economic system do not occur, some sort of growth will continue to take place; and given time the pro-ductive forces can always develop sufficiently. To believe, as many left-wing groups do, that any serious challenge to capitalism must wait till some form of an automatic breakdown has proved tht the system

1. P. A. Baran, *The Political Economy of Growth* (New York, Monthly Review Press, 1957).

has exhausted its potential, is to court passivity. Such a failure to expose the contradictions of capitalism allows it to become relatively stronger and therefore renders the passivity self-justifying and self-perpetuating. What needs to be looked at is the totality of the situation, that is, the interaction between all the elements, including the element of conscious action.

Secondly, there is no simple criterion for assessing whether capitalist relations are a 'fetter' on development or not. 'It would be a mistake to believe that . . . tendency to decay precludes the rapid growth of capitalism'.[2] Equally wrong is the Narodnik-type argument that the unevenness of growth as such is equivalent to no growth at all. In reality, to assess the achievements and prospects of capitalism, we have to go behind the growth process to look at its nature—its structural implications, its ability to generate its own momentum, and of course its ability to meet people's aspirations, themselves changing through greater consciousness. By and large, studies on this theme have focused their attention on the role of imperialist penetration in third world countries. An aspect of the question that has not received much attention, however, is the interrelation between the domestic bourgeoisie of the third world countries and international capital. Even perceptive writers have tended to treat the domestic bourgeoisie either as a hindrance to development as is foreign capital,[3] or as a genuinely progressive force thwarted by foreign capital.[4] In either case, the domestic and the imperial bourgeoisie are looked at separately and their interconnection is lost. I shall in this essay sketch some aspects of this interconnection, taking India as my specific example.

1. Colonialism and the evolution of the Indian bourgeoisie

India is a specially interesting case, because the bourgeoisie there was more developed and mature compared to many other third world countries and there was only a small strictly comprador element (i.e. those involved only in foreign trade or serving foreign capital in other ways, for example as local agents). Of course, like other national bourgeoisies, it developed in a colonial environment and

2. V. I. Lenin, *Imperialism, the Highest Stage of Capitalism*, in *Collected Works* (Moscow, 1964), xxii 300.
3. P. M. Sweezy 'Obstacles to Economic development' in C. H. Feinstein, ed. *Socialism, Capitalism and Economic Growth*, (Cambridge, Cambridge Univ. Press, 1967).
4. The latter view in particular characterises much ECLA thinking on the subject.

therefore shared certain common characteristics, but there was a difference of degree partly reflecting the significant economic development which had taken place in pre-British India. The pre-British structure was extremely complex with a hierarchy of land rights and also, at least to some extent, identifiable class relationships. There was considerable monetisation and commodity production with the consequent tendency towards differentiation among the peasantry and the emergence of trade as a twoway process between country and town.[5] Manufacturing was quite developed—non-mechanised but catering for an international market.[6] The system, whether or not we choose to characterise it as a feudal one,[7] was in a state of decomposition, and the possibility of a Japan type development could not have been ruled out.[8] Merchant capital was significant and though the later bourgeoisie was not the literal descendant of the earlier one, there was some continuity. Domestic capital persisted in internal trade and a large section of the modern industrial bourgeoisie has come from a mercantile background.

Colonial rule destroyed this precapitalist economy in two phases: first through the so-called 'drain of wealth' which, one can argue, continued throughout the colonial period but which was particularly important in the late eighteenth century. Private loot and the East India Company's treatment of the administration as a profitable business resulted in a shortage of specie, leading to recession in agriculture and dislocation of trade and industry.[9] The second phase, starting after the Napoleonic wars, involved the decline of handicrafts through factory competition. Urban handloom industry was more or less totally destroyed. The destruction spread to rural weavers as well, but many lingered on—partly through market imperfections and partly by cutting into subsistence—only to fall victims of the famines. The exhaustion of land, the increase in rents and the fall in the wages

5. For a brief discussion see Irfan Habib 'Distribution of landed property in pre-British India', *Enquiry* (Delhi, Winter, 1965); see also B. N. Ganguli, ed., *Readings in Indian Economic History* (London, Asia Publishing House, 1964), pp. 80–1.

6. H. R. Ghoshal 'Industrial Production in Bengal in Early Nineteenth-Century' in Ganguli.

7. D. D. Kosambi *An Introduction to the Study of Indian History* (Bombay, 1956) calls the structure a 'feudal' one. For a contrary view see D. Thorner 'Feudalism in India' in R. Coulburn, ed., *Feudalism in History* (Princeton Univ. Press, 1956).

8. T. Raychaudhury 'A reinterpretation of nineteenth-century Indian economic history?' in *Indian Econ. Soc. Hist. Review (Delhi)*, **5**, no. 1 (March, 1968).

9. For a summary of recent research on the subject, T. Raychaudhury 'Recent Writings in British Indian Economic History' in *Contributions to Indian Economic History*, vol. i (Calcutta, 1960) edited by him.

of rural labourers, suggest a large population being thrown out of employment, but how long and with what severity this process continued is still a matter for debate.[10]

It is hardly surprising in these conditions that Indian industrial capital did not grow. Being pre-empted from its potential markets, facing a state which followed a policy of 'discriminatory interventionism'[11] in the interests of British capital and being excluded from the British dominated old-boy network which controlled much of the banking and external trade,[12] it hardly had a chance. The Parsi businessmen with an entry to the exclusive club naturally did somewhat better. It is more difficult to explain the reluctance of foreign capital to start manufacturing on any large scale. Even Marx's prediction that the railways would herald the growth of metal and engineering industries, remained largely unfulfilled.[13] Climate is a possible explanation.[14] It ruled out immigration from Britain, restricting the flow of skills and giving British capital only a transitory interest in India.[15] A more powerful factor perhaps was the very fact of British political control. Capital tends to be regionally concentrated. It creates an environment which draws other capital to it and this process is cumulative. The restriction of Indian capital broke this process. As the linkage effects were not spread through the economy, each act of investment became an isolated episode, no more than a shift of some processes in the manufacturing chain from England to India, and this further restricted capital inflow. Besides, since the market was carefully preserved, there was little need for industry to be established on the spot. Moreover political pressures sabotaged the growth of the potentially important locomotive industry.[16] For a long time, of course, no other industrial power was anywhere near providing effective competition to Britain.

The situation began to change around the turn of the century.

10. See Bipan Chandra's controversy with M. D. Morris on 'Reinterpretation of nineteenth-century Indian economic history' in *Ind. Econ. Soc. Hist. Rev.* (March 1968).
11. The phrase was coined by S. Bhattacharya 'Laissez-faire in India' *Ind. Econ. Soc. Hist. Rev.,* **2**, no. 1 (Jan. 1965).
12. A. K. Bagchi, 'European and Indian entrepreneurship in India 1900–30', in E. Leach and S. N. Mukherji, ed, *Elites in South Asia* (Cambridge, Cambridge Univ. Press, 1970).
13. A. K. Bagchi, *Private investment in India 1900–1939*, (Cambridge, Cambridge Univ. Press, 1972). Ch. x discusses the development of the engineering industry.
14. Baran, *The Political Economy of Growth*, ch. v.
15. Complementarity between capital and skills inflow is emphasised in R. Nurkse, 'The problem of international investment today in the light of nineteenth-century experience', *Economic Journal* (1954).
16. F. Lehman, 'Great Britain and the supply of railway locomotives to India', *Ind. Econ. Soc. Hist. Rev.* **2**, no. 4 (1965).

214   *Prabhat Patnaik*

Germany and America challenged Britain's lead and started penetrating the Indian market. In India a political movement led by the bourgeoisie took shape.

Periods of crisis for British imperialism, like the two world wars, were of benefit to both major challengers—Indian industrialists and the Americans.[17] Fighting to keep its international rivals out, Britain made concessions to Indian capital. The government's contract to buy steel helped the Tatas to set up India's first steel plant.[18] The introduction of protection on the 'infant' industry criterion led to notable industrial expansion. At the same time, the system of imperial preferences, the dollar pool and the attempted freezing of dollar reserves were attempts to bind India closer to Britain. Despite all this, at independance the United States was India's major trading partner. This trade reached a peak during the Korean War when, apart from jute goods, India exported large amounts of strategic materials such as monazite, mica, manganese ore and others, in which American interest had been aroused for some time.[19]

But if the Americans had hoped to take over Britain's hegemonic role in India, the Indian bourgeosie was not going to concede it. It sought to strengthen its own position with the help of the Indian state. This period of economic nationalism was characterised by the fight against foreign capital and the growth of state capitalism. Much of the old foreign capital had been closely connected with the empire. It was in the form of branch investment and was in such areas as trading, insurance, banking, tea, jute and mines. With the passing of the empire, its decline was inevitable. The nationalisation of the Imperial Bank removed British capital from a commanding position. Indian big business took over a number of foreign enterprises, for example in jute, tea and trading. Some leading agency houses changed hands, for example Forbes & Campbell;[20] in others substantial minority holdings were offered to Indian houses, for example Macneil and Barry. Where no changes in ownership were effected, there has been relative stagnation as in the case of Andrew Yule and Bird Heilger.[21] Little

17. The nature of Indian gains is clear. Disruption of imports meant larger markets and profits. For American gains of markets, see L. Natarajan, *American Shadow Over India* (Delhi, P.P.H., 1954), ch ii.
18. S. K. Sen, *Economic Policy and Development of India* (Calcutta 1966), ch iv.
19. Natarajan, ch ii.
20. Between 1947 and 1952, 66 concerns of which 64 were British were bought over by Indians, K. M. Kurian, *Impact of Foreign Capital on the Indian Economy* (Delhi, 1966), p. 71.
21. R. K. Hazari, *The Structure of the Corporate Private Sector* (London, Asia Publishing House, 1966), ch 7.

new foreign capital came in during this period. The increase in foreign assets in the early 1950s was largely due to the ploughback of profits or to asset revaluation.[22] It is true that India's industrialisation had not begun and foreign capital was not yet interested, but mutual hostility was undeniable. With Russian backing, the government had denied the Germans substantial equity participation in the Rourkela Steel Plant. Government policy was at least partly the reason why America's imports of strategic materials from India declined and why she turned elsewhere to develop captive sources of supply. Manganese mines in Gabon and Brazil were developed by U.S. Steel and in Ghana and Guyana by Union Carbide.[23] Finally this hostility took the form of open war between the government and the oil companies.[24]

2. The nature of state capitalism in India

The need for state capitalism was recognised early by the bourgeoisie,[25] but its precise form was a result of the class nature of the state. The colonial structure having left no single strong class, state power continues to be based on a coalition between the bourgeoisie and large landowners. More specifically, the coalition has three elements: the monopoly bourgeoisie whose members control business empires spread across a number of spheres and a number of states; the small urban bourgeoisie consisting of businessmen confined to single industries or states and professional groups who are not direct exploiters but integrated into the system of exploitation, like lawyers, managers and upper bureaucracy; and finally the class of landlords and rich peasants, who live mainly by exploitation, either through rent or through wage labour or both. This last may appear too heterogeneous, but post-independence land reforms have caused its constituents to coalesce into a more or less single category, so it is better treated as such. Bourgeois democracy and a federal political structure create the environment for this coalition to work. If state capitalism was considered a permanent phenomenon and the state did not contemplate handing over factories to private entrepreneurs as in Pakistan or Japan, it was because such a step would damage the alliance. It would necessarily benefit the monopoly houses; and the smaller bourgeoisie

22. Kurian, ch 3.
23. G. R. Sheshadri's report on India in *Mining Annual Review* (June, 1969), p. 369.
24. M. Kidron, *Foreign Investments in India* (London, Oxford Univ. Press, 1965) pp. 166–75.
25. P. Chattopadhyaya 'State Capitalism in India', *Monthly Review* (March, 1970).

supported by the petty bourgeois class would oppose it.

The weakness of state capitalism lay in the fact that the nature of the state, while apparently giving it enormous strength, made it fundamentally weak. While on the one hand it had to maintain the balance of the class coalition (by effectively curbing any constituent group that became too strong), and to make periodic concessions to the exploited, on the other it could not change the position of any constituent group too strongly, for that would affect the collective strength of the coalition. Thus, although the state appeared independent, placed high above all classes, in reality it had to conform closely to the rules of the game. The limits to state action were sharply drawn and any radical structural reform was ruled out. The precise location of this weakness we shall discuss later.

During the First Plan, state activity was largely confined to the construction of overhead capital. Serious industrialisation only began with the Second Plan, which provided for a large outlay by the state sector, much of it for building up heavy industries.[26]

But this was the period of John Foster Dulles, and if the policy of non-alignment met with American hostility, so too did the economic policy, which was after all a similar move in the direction of relative independence. The industrialisation programme was attacked—implicitly by a Ford Foundation team[27] and explicitly by a World Bank mission—as being 'over-ambitious'. A simultaneous attack was made against the state sector. The World Bank demonstrated its willingness to finance private sector expansion by providing aid for the two private steel plants.

Of course, India's independence must not be exaggerated. In August 1956 the government agreed to buy surplus American wheat—which India did not need at that stage—at inflated prices, against rupee payments which gave the Americans potentially extensive powers over the Indian economy.[28] Again, although the Americans did provide large amounts of aid, most of it was either for food imports or for infrastructural investment. Aid for developing the industrial base was limited. American private capital was as yet hardly interested in India. Britain and West Germany by contrast showed greater willingness to come to terms with Indian policy and

26. For a summary of India's planning experience see Charles Bettelheim, *India Independent* (London, MacGibbon & Kee, 1968), ch vii.
27. A critique of the team's report, 'Ploughing the plan under' is contained in D. Thorner and A. Thorner, *Land and Labour in India* (London, Asia Publishing House, 1964).
28. V. I. Pavlov, *India: Economic Freedom Versus Imperialism* (Delhi, 1963), p. 120.

make the most of it. Suggestions of collaboration between the government and private German capital began as early as 1953 over the Rourkela steel plant. After the deal was completed in 1956, Britain followed up with a similar arrangement at Durgapur. Great eagerness was also shown to collaborate with Indian private capital. The Soviet Union and the Eastern European countries provided more enthusiastic support for state capitalism. Beginning with cooperation in oil exploration and the setting up of refineries in the state sector, the Eastern Bloc gave strategic aid for building a heavy industrial base. The actual viability of state capitalism was thus closely linked with the Soviet Union.

American attitudes changed noticeably in the late 1950s. Politically, Soviet influence could be counteracted only by greater participation in the development effort, while the economic benefits of such participation did not go unnoticed. With state capitalism expanding the Indian market, exports, especially of machinery and sophisticated manufactures, could be pushed up through development assistance (and here by her earlier reticence America had lost out even to Britain and Germany). Not only did America increase her aid, but she also insisted on tying it to prevent its being spent on cheaper European goods. This was an important change: as late as mid-1958 of the 5,000 million rupees India owed to the U.S.A. 3079·5 million was on account of food; only at the end of 1957 $225 million was promised to India for buying equipment. This change did not mean a letting up of political pressures and constant threats to postpone aid hung over India; rather India flaunted Soviet aid to keep political strings to the minimum.[29] Thus Indian state capitalism survived without making too many compromises, partly because of the specific nature of the international situation.

3. The 'new' foreign investment

Meanwhile, a new kind of private foreign capital was flowing into the country. The foreign exchange crisis of 1957–58 had led to drastic import controls, including quantitative restrictions. The resulting protection, combined with large government expenditure, created extremely profitable markets in India for a whole range of commodities. To exploit this market Indian capital had necessarily to turn abroad for technology. Foreign capital was attracted both by the

29. Pavlov, pp. 120, 126.

expanding market and by the need to jump tariff (and later quota) barriers. In the new circumstances it was necessary and useful to have an Indian ally, and the 'joint-venture' emerged as a marriage of convenience.

This new foreign capital differed from the old in three main respects. First, it was interested in the modern, technologically advanced sectors of industry which were the most dynamic areas of the economy. Between 1948 and 1955 only 284 collaboration agreements were approved by the government, but in 1956 there were 82, 81 in 1957, 103 in 1958, 150 in 1959 and 380 in 1960. Since then there have been around 300 to 400 a year. Of a total of 1,051 such agreements studied by the Reserve Bank, manufacturing accounted for 1,006: 115 were for transport equipment, 250 for machinery and machine tools, 107 for metals, 162 for electrical goods and 177 for chemicals. Secondly, foreign capital began to rely more on the participation of Indian capital. The form of investment was no longer in branches of a European company, but in local subsidiaries or more frequently in ventures involving a minority participation. Even in subsidiaries there was a fall in the parent company's share.[31] At the other end of the scale, pure technical collaboration agreements, though more numerous, either were of no financial importance (involving transfers of trade marks etc.) or more recently involved payment being made in shares. Out of 2,000 approvals before 1963, 1,750 were purely technical agreements. But in 1967, out of 341 of these agreements, 211 involved financial participation.[34] This suited the government as well as the foreign partner, which got a foothold in the Indian market. Lastly, the foreign partner, significantly, was normally a large international corporation interested exclusively in the Indian market. This was in direct contrast to the old foreign capital. In its total operations, the Indian partner was extremely small by comparison, particularly since it was the smaller monopoly houses which displayed the greatest enthusiasm for teaming up. Their gains were obvious. The Mafatlal group increased its total assets by 176 per cent between 1963–64 and 1966–67 largely by expanding its interests in chemicals with foreign collaboration.[35] If Indian capital was not to be swamped, it needed state backing and in the first phase of develop-

31. Reserve Bank of India, *Foreign Collaboration in Indian Industry, Survey Report* (Bombay, 1968), pp. 4, 102, 14

34. R. K. Hazari ed. *Foreign Collaboration*, (Bombay, 1968), p. 140.

35. Government of India, Department of Company Affairs, *Company News and Notes* (Delhi, 1 Jan., 1969).

ment, the state retained a certain autonomy in relation to foreign capital and foreign states.

4. The contradictions of Indian state capitalism in the first phase of development

The situation however, contained a number of contradictions. The weakness inherent in the nature of Indian state capitalism was expressed in its inability to mobilise adequate resources for economic growth. Given the level of productivity the possible rate of accumulation is determined by two factors—first, the growth-rate of agriculture, which provides the bulk of the necessities and second, the strength of the various classes, which determines the extent to which mass consumption or luxury consumption can be restricted. In essence, therefore, the resource problem is how to increase accumulation by acting on these factors.

The chief barrier to agricultural growth has been the structure of agrarian relations. Extreme inequality of ownership and operation generally leaves the bulk of the farmers with neither the means nor the incentive to invest. Meanwhile, for those who get the surplus, conspicuous consumption and gold hoarding, the purchase of land for leasing out or cultivating with labourers and money lending, all compete with productive investment in land. With production largely dependent on rainfall, the risks of productive investment are large, so the amount invested is relatively small. The coexistence of capitalist and precapitalist modes (i.e. tenancy and small farming) implies a choice for the landowner between *expansion* of rent or wage exploitation by obtaining more land and an *intensification* of wage exploitation by increasing the productivity of his existing land. The relative attractiveness of the former constricts the latter. Reform of this structure has been a minimum requirement for rapid agricultural growth. And yet agrarian reforms, while eliminating some excesses like the very large absentee landlords who often controlled dozens of villages, left the old structure essentially intact.[36] Thus, although a relatively more homogeneous landowning class was created, strengthening the ruling class-coalition, the barriers to growth remained. Agricultural output, virtually stagnant over the half-century before independence, increased in the 1950s at a rate of 3·5 per cent a year, the increase being almost equally attributable to increases

36. D. Thorner and A. Thorner, 'Agrarian problem in India today', in *Land and Labour in India*.

in area and yield (45 per cent each),[37] resulting largely from the extension of irrigation.[38] There were limits to this process, however.[39] Poor rainfall disastrously affected output in the early 1960s accentuating the resource problem.

The barriers to restrictions on consumption were equally strong. Mass consumption was squeezed through inflation, real wages in 1964 being not much higher than the 1951 level.[40] But despite its weak organisation the working class was able to impose limits to this process. On the other hand, with savings and investment decisions still in private hands, and the state so closely associated with many vested interests, luxury consumption was not adequately restricted. After an initial increase the savings rate remained steady at around 10 per cent for over a decade.[41] Hence any attempt to raise the investment rate meant an exchange deficit which could be financed only through aid. Moreover, construction of an industrial base by means of import substitution requires, as its financial counterpart, an increase in the marginal savings ratio. The available resources are then concentrated on strategic sectors and not frittered away through unplanned shifts to other parts of the economy. Though statistical evidence suggests a high *realised* marginal savings rate, this could be due to lags in consumption,[42] and it is doubtful if the ex-ante rate increased very much. In this situation a policy of import substitution merely shifted a range of manufacturing processes to India from abroad while maintaining Indian dependence on imports required for previous stages of production, such as machinery and maintenance. Other factors like a more liberal machinery import policy and the difficulties of finding Western collaborators for plant-making also played a role, but 'import-dependent import substitution' with its continuous dependence on aid to finance an exchange deficit underlined state capitalism's failure to mobilise enough resources for the required growth.

The possibility of import substitution in knowhow was equally

37. B. S. Minhas and A. Vaidyanathan, 'Growth of crop output in India—1951–4 to 1958–61: analysis by component elements', *Journal of the Indian Society of Agricultural Statistics* (Dec. 1965).
38. K. N. Raj 'Some questions concerning growth, transformation and planning in agriculture in developing countries', United Nations, *Journal of Development Planning* no. 1 (1969), pp. 26–34.
39. Raj, p. 34.
40. Government of India, *Pocket Book of Economic Information 1969*, Compare tables 2.5 and 11.1.
41. *Reserve Bank of India Bulletin March, 1965*; 'Estimates of savings and investments in India', and P. D. Ojha, 'Mobilisation of savings', *Econ. and Pol. Weekly (Bombay) Annual Number* 1969.
42. K. N. Raj, 'The marginal rate of saving in the Indian economy', *Oxf. Econ. Pap.* **14**, no. 1 (Feb. 1962).

limited. As most of the information based on research within giant corporations was of a private character, India's technological dependence could be reduced only if research was undertaken within the country itself. Yet virtually no Indian enterprise has any research department. Foreign collaborators, far from stimulating research, tended to hinder it. Control over technology was an effective tool in the hands of foreign firms while for many the sale of knowhow was a lucrative business. Thus some agreements explicitly put limits on the research and development of new products by the Indian partner.[43] Foreign collaborators possessed both a valid economic argument for centralised research and a superior bargaining power which enabled them even to withold vital technical information and to keep strict control over the activities of their top technological personnel. In addition, the free import of knowhow reduced the need for import substitution in it. Thus for large sectors of industry technological parasitism was inherent in the situation.[44]

Finally, economic nationalism was possible because of the specific nature of the internal political situation. There was no serious revolutionary challenge to the hegemony of the ruling classes. They had emerged strong from the independence movement and the early challenge of the Telengana peasant revolt had been dealt with successfully. As a result, the political situation in the 1950s was tranquil. The bourgeoisie had felt secure enough at home to stake its claim vis à vis foreign capital. If the circumstances had been different, it might have had to turn abroad for help.

5. A new phase of development

The heightening of some of these contradictions coincided with a shift in the international situation. After the 1962 clash with China, India became militarily and politically more dependent on America. The large defence budget put an additional strain on resources, making the state even more vulnerable. Meanwhile, the Soviet Union began looking for a thaw in the cold war. Its aid, never large, became less reliable. India's new, and current, phase of development had begun.

If in the earlier phase state policy had been relatively autonomous, now there was greater subordination to imperialism. The net external liability of the official sector increased from Rs 10,734 million in

43. Kidron, *Foreign Investments*, pp. 287–96.
44. A. V. Desai 'Potentialities of collaboration and their utilisation', in Hazari, ed. *Foreign Collaboration*.

December 1961 to Rs 23,416 million in March 1965.[45] Amortisation of debt alone absorbed about 11 per cent of exports in 1966—and 27 per cent if payments on investment income account are included.[46] Whereas in March 1967 total money supply with the public was Rs 50,030 million United States government-owned deposits (the result of American Public Law 480 food sales) were Rs 20,700 million giving America extensive powers over the Indian economy.[47] Foreign and local pressures on state policy have led to a shift away from controls towards greater freedom for capital. Three specific aspects of this change deserve attention. First, at donor countries' insistence, the attitude towards foreign capital has softened. If in 1948–49, the government while promising 'fair' treatment had talked of 'carefully regulating' foreign capital and ensuring effective Indian control, in 1963 the Finance Minister thought 'we would be justified in opening the doors even wider to private foreign investment'.[48] Again, before 1962, the issue of shares to non-residents for considerations other than cash were disapproved of, but now share issues in return for plant and machinery or technical assistance were common. The trend is clear and foreign capital has considerably expanded its operations in India. Some indication of its importance even as early as 1963–64 is given by a comparison of the total capital employed in all public limited companies with foreign financial collaboration (that is, subsidiaries and minority ventures) with total capital employed in a selected group of 1,333 public limited companies for which figures are available. This latter group includes some, though not all, companies belonging to the former group. It is not too inappropriate for comparison because it represents a very large segment of the Indian corporate sector: the companies which are included account for about 70 per cent of paid up capital of all non-financial and non-government public limited companies, and roughly the same proportion of paid-up capital in most individual industries.

Of course we have included minority ventures but 92 per cent of capital employed in this group was in companies employing Rs 10 million or more, and the foreign share in such large companies is often substantial. Between 1956 and 1963, for example, of all the initial issues with foreign participation which were approved, forty-eight

45. 'India's international investment position in 1963–4 and 1964–5', *Reserve Bank of India Bulletin*, Jan. 1967.
46. H. Magdoff, *The Age of Imperialism* (New York, Monthly Review Press, 1969), p. 155.
47. '*Satyakam*', 'P.L. 480 and India's Freedom', *Liberation* 2, no. 5, Calcutta (March 1969).
48. Quoted in Hazari, ed., *Foreign Collaboration*, p. 6.

TABLE I. Ratio between (1) total capital employed in public limited companies with foreign financial collaboration in an industry and (2) total capital employed in companies belonging to the same industry in the sample of 1333 companies (percentages).

INDUSTRY	CAPITAL EMPLOYED IN		
	SUBSIDIARIES	MINORITY VENTURES	TOTAL
Plantations and mining	0·3	28·3	28·6
Petroleum	48·0	51·3	99·3
Food, beverages, tobacco	19·7	10·0	29·7
Textile products	—	7·1	7·1
Transport equipment	14·5	56·1	70·6
Machinery and machine tools	8·1	33·0	41·1
Metals and metal products	13·3	13·9	27·2
(excluding iron and steel)	29·43	30·96	60·39
Electrical goods and machinery	27·9	52·9	80·8
Chemicals and allied products	49·3	46·7	96·0
(of which medicines and			
pharmaceuticals)	58·4	45·1	103·5
Rubber goods	82·5	—	82·5
Miscellaneous	3·4	23·6	27·0
Services	5·7	25·3	31·0
TOTAL	13·1	24·1	37·2

Source: Compiled from Reserve Bank Survey tables, 'Finances of Indian Joint-stock companies, 1965–66', *Reserve Bank of India Bulletin*, Dec. 1967, pp.22, 51.

were minority ventures with an equity of above Rs 10 million; and of these, twenty-eight involved foreign participation of above 25 per cent, often more than enough to ensure control. We can safely say, therefore, that foreign capital has a significant position in petroleum, engineering, chemicals and rubber. Moreover, the Reserve Bank's study of what it calls 'foreign-controlled rupee companies', both public and private (limited), shows these to be growing much faster than Indian companies. For example in 1965–66 the gross capital stock of 320 foreign companies increased by 13·9 per cent as against the 9·6 per cent increase of 1,944 Indian private and public companies.[50] Whatever the criterion, foreign companies are more profitable than the Indian companies in the corporate sector. All

50. 'Finances of branches of foreign companies and foreign-controlled rupee companies', *Reserve Bank of Indian Bulletin* (June 1968).

available studies show that they are also more profitable than their parent companies. Thus foreign capital, collaborating with and often dominating Indian capital, seems to have acquired a strategic hold over the most profitable and dynamic sector of the economy.

Though British investment continues to lead that of other countries, American capital has also begun to play an important role. To take agreements involving financial collaboration, the distribution in the period 1956 to 1960 was: U.K. 94, West Germany 36, and U.S.A. 18. During the following four years, 1961–65, on the other hand, the figures had changed to 120, 38 and 77 respectively.[51] This growth does not mean that capital has been flowing into India in large quantities. Even giant companies in India account for a very small share of the parent companies' operations. Besides, this growth itself has taken place while there has actually been a substantial outflow of surplus from India. For example between 1956 and 1961 the net outflow (i.e. the excess of investment income and royalty transfers over net capital inflow) on account of foreign private enterprise was Rs 672 million.[52]

A second aspect of the change is the tendency towards the removal of trade restrictions. Caught in the contradictions of half-hearted import substitution, the government, on World Bank advice, decided to devalue in 1966 as well as to liberalise imports of some essential commodities. This was to be financed by aid organised by the World Bank. Whatever changes are made now, the old policy of controls certainly belongs to the past. Freer trade, however, is not always in the interests of metropolitan capital. If one metropolitan capital dominates an economy, protection is after all protection of that capital. However, in India the control by foreign capital, let alone a single country's capital, is far from complete. Freer trade thus enhances the freedom of investment and is particularly to the advantage of American capital so long as it remains in second place.

Finally, the state's role as the controller of private capital is being directly undermined while its role as an investor is being undermined indirectly. Even though state initiative is necessary for private capital, state ownership implies so much area of activity out of bounds to private investors. For this reason sporadic attempts have been made to use aid as a means of restricting the state sector. More important, the persistent demand that aid be replaced where possible by foreign

51. Reserve Bank *Survey* tables on p. 25 and p. 53.
52. S. Kumarasundaram, 'Foreign collaborations and Indian balance of payments' in Hazari, ed, *Foreign Collaboration*, p. 207

private capital represents a systematic attempt in the same direction. In any case 'Where [foreign equity participation] does not exceed 50 per cent of total equity, approval of such foreign investment seldom encounters any difficulty'.[53] Furthermore, with the recent liberalisation of licensing procedure[54] private, including foreign, capital is being allowed to operate freely over a large segment of the economy.

6. Contradictions of the new phase

These changes appear minor and have the support of many economists on the grounds of efficiency. What is relevant for us, however, is not an abstract comparison between two sets of policies to determine which is more efficient, but a concrete analysis of the contradictions of the new situation. If the contradictions of the phase of economic nationalism have led directly to the new situation, where may the new contradictions lead? Greater freedom of capital and a reliance on market forces will certainly result in India's closer integration into the imperialist orbit. In addition, virtually *all* the old contradictions still remain. Of course with a liberal import policy the utilisation of equipment will improve, but so will India's indebtedness. Again, the increase in output will only allow a net improvement in the resource position if consumption is adequately restricted. Given a large pent-up domestic demand, one cannot be sure of this restriction happening automatically; indeed in some countries there is evidence of an actual fall in savings efforts as aid increases. Moreover, an increase in imports may adversely affect the present programme of import substitution.[55] Already in some cases it has forced Indian producers 'to reduce production (alloy steel) or prices (polythene), close factories (superphosphates) and even to export (aluminium).'[56]

The least we can say therefore, is that the resource problem is not substantially modified. The result is that contrary to the tenets of orthodox economics, a *continued* foreign dependence is necessary to maintain growth. Furthermore, this dependence is increased by those additional contradictions which arise when centralised international capital faces a nation-state.

53. Hazari, *ibid.*, p. 7.
54. A very brief report on the latest position on licensing is in *The Financial Times*, London, 29 Sept. 1970.
55. For a discussion of the case of Pakistan, see K. N. Raj, *India, Pakistan and China* (Allied Publishers, Bombay, 1967), pp. 13–16.
56. '*Arthagnani*', 'Profligate ignorance', *Econ. and Pol. Weekly (Bombay)* 8 Feb., 1969.

Because of its greater foresight and preference for safety monopoly capital constantly needs external stimuli to sustain a rapid expansion;[57] and the large state outlays which have enormously expanded the Indian market have played this role. But state and private capital compete for the same resources and the greater the freedom of the latter, the more restricted is the state. Reliance on aid enables it to maintain the momentum but only at the expense of further limiting its ability to encroach upon private capital, particularly foreign capital which enjoys the protection of a more powerful state. There are three formal possibilities here. First, the maldistribution of resources may not show itself in any immediate way through a large surplus outflow, for instance, if the state sector continues growing; but this needs a continuous increase in aid. Second, state investment may actually shrink, markets grow less fast and foreign capital look elsewhere. As a result the actual outflow of surplus increases, as does domestic luxury consumption; and long-run industrial expansion slows down. Third, the same rate of growth may be maintained for some time by means not of state investment but of providing large incentives to private capital, including concessions to foreign capital. Thus, the maintenance of growth requires *either* greater aid *or* more concessions, both leading to the progressive weakening of the state and the strengthening of foreign capital.

But a weaker state means a weaker domestic capital as well, so that the latter tends to get swallowed by foreign capital and, as in Brazil, sections of the bourgeoisie are reduced to rentier status.[58] Moreover, once the hegemony of the state is undermined, *internal* contradictions also help foreign capital. In India, the nationalisation of domestically owned banks, a move forced by the smaller bourgeoisie against the growing strength of the monopoly houses, if it *succeeds* in restricting credit to big business and diffusing it wider, would indirectly strengthen foreign capital.

This is a point which is often overlooked. For example, some have argued that the Indian monopoly bourgeoisie, or a section of it, joins forces with foreign capital at the risk of being dominated, to weaken the state. Thus a distinction is drawn between two groups among the bourgeoisie: one, consisting of the big bourgeoisie, is an ally of imperialism while the other is 'progressive' and anti-imperialist. The distinction is unreal and misleading: it is unreal because with the

57. P. A. Baran and P. M. Sweezy, *Monopoly Capital* (New York, Monthly Review Press, 1966).
58. 'Denationalisation of Brazilian industry', *Monthly Review*, November, 1969.

American-backed 'green revolution' the landowner class (which is becoming a rural bourgeoisie) has emerged as a potential political ally of imperialism and one at least as important as the big bourgeoisie; it is misleading because it approaches the problem in an oversimplified manner. Where state power is based on a class coalition, contradictions exist among the ruling classes and between each class and the state. Therefore, each class or group manoeuvres to promote its own interest; for example, the smaller bourgeoisie demands bank nationalisation, while the monopoly bourgeoisie demands the restriction of the state sector. As long as the state preserves a certain relative autonomy vis-à-vis foreign capital, the latter is kept at bay and cannot profit from these manoeuvres; but when this autonomy is undermined, foreign capital can profit, as it has, for instance, from the bank nationalisation move. Therefore, it is not the manoeuvres themselves which are pro- or anti-imperialist; their effect on the interests of metropolitan capital depends on the objective conditions, that is on how strong the state is against foreign pressures. The strength of the state, which must not be confused with the extent of the state sector, depends ultimately on its ability to raise resources domestically. It was argued above that short of drastic changes, which would hit at the ruling classes, including the bourgeoisie as a whole, the Indian state cannot raise sufficient resources internally.

Thus the position of the bourgeoisie is paradoxical—it wishes to introduce independent national development yet it cannot do so without relying on metropolitan countries. It is nationalist yet it must collaborate with imperialism. The failure to appreciate this paradox leads to the identification of one group of the bourgeoisie as nationalist, the other as collaborators. A contradiction which underlies the position of the bourgeoisie as a whole is identified as existing between sections of the bourgeoisie. Clearly, however, it is not the anti-nationalism of any particular group, but the nature of the situation which favours foreign capital. The weakening of the state and the bourgeoisie proceed apace and the movement away from economic nationalism leads cumulatively to the imperialist camp. There is no half-way equilibrium.

An additional factor strengthens this tendency. So far we have concentrated on the resource question as a whole, taking the exchange deficit as a mere reflection of it. This need not always be the case and an exchange deficit may arise from independent structural reasons, when, for example, foreign capital which is exclusively interested in the host country's market imposes export restrictions.

Of 1,051 agreements surveyed for India, 455 involved export restrictive clauses; 52 per cent of these set out the countries (often India's neighbours) to which exports were permissible, 33 per cent required the foreign collaborator's permission and 8 per cent imposed a total ban. Agreements with restrictions made up 44 per cent of the total for subsidiaries, 57 per cent for minority companies and 40 per cent for companies with technical collaboration only. Since restrictions need not be explicit in the first group, nor important in the last group, the effective degree of restriction is probably greater. Moreover, restrictions were high in transport equipment (62 per cent of the total in this sector), machinery and tools (50 cer cent), electricals (50 per cent) and medicines and pharmaceuticals (50 per cent), relatively low in metals and metal products (39 per cent), basic industrial chemicals and very minor in food and textiles.[59] This means that as imports grow and the economy is at the same time deprived of potential exports from its most dynamic sectors, the resulting deficit requires further reliance on aid and foreign capital.

Of course, absorption into the imperialist orbit would not preclude growth. Such growth, however, would be jerky and would lead to greater indebtedness. It would also leave the bulk of social labour at a low level of productivity. After all between 1951 and 1961, the proportion of the working force employed in manufacturing remained relatively unchanged. In this context, one must also consider recent attempts to find a technological solution to India's agricultural problem through the so-called 'green revolution'. But its likely impact is debatable.[60] If it raises the agricultural growth rate, it can certainly ease the resource position. But the existing contradictions and their economic results would be far from eliminated. As the pillar of this 'revolution' is the landowning class, its economic and political bargaining power in the ruling class coalition increases, so that land reform or the restriction of rural luxury consumption become even more impossible. At the same time, increasing differentiation among the peasantry, with growing economic inequalities, adds to the political challenge to the ruling classes. In these circumstances, there will inevitably be a growing political reliance on imperialism.

No doubt, if the internal and international circumstances become favourable once again, a reversal to nationalist policy is always possible. Even then, however, the tendency towards subordination

59. Reserve Bank, *Survey* pp. 106–8.
60. K. N. Raj, 'Some questions . . .' *Jour. Dev. Plann.* (1969), pp. 34–8.

would assert itself once again. Total freedom from imperialism demands, as a necessary condition, the removal of internal obstacles to growth, i.e. a transformation of the social structure. In the classical era of capitalism, the bourgeoisie, having established its own state, demolished feudalism and went on to defeat the challenge of the embryonic proletariat in a process which Gramsci calls the 'permanent revolution'.[61] In France the aristocracy was destroyed while in England it was absorbed into the bourgeoisie. In a later period in Japan the bourgeois revolution was carried through, without first demolishing feudalism altogether, by a fascist state which had its own colonies. Today in India or other third world countries, the bourgeoisie, arriving too late on the scene, is forced to ally itself with remnants of feudalism; and, having no colonies and being threatened by the increasing political consciousness of the people, it is reintegrated into the imperial structure. Compromising with feudalism, it is forced to compromise with imperialism. The fact that the Indian bourgeoisie sought its independence testifies to its relative strength: the fact that it failed testifies to the objective limits to bourgeois revolution today.

---

61. A. Gramsci, *The Modern Prince and Other Writings*, (New York, 1968, paperback edn) p. 167.

X

French imperialism
in Guinea
R. W. Johnson

Did colonies pay? This is a question which continues to be the subject of heated debate among historians of imperialism. In the case of French Guinea—the subject of the following paper—there can be no doubt. Whether we look at the budgets of the colonial state or at the profits obtained, first from the collection of wild rubber, then from plantations and mines, the colony always yielded a good return.

The paper is also concerned with the methods by which these profits were obtained, and like the previous two papers, with the impact of imperialism on the indigenous society which it encountered. In particular it focuses attention on the way the machinery of colonial government was used to supplement the activities of trader and colonist. When the main export was wild rubber the institution of a poll tax insured that the Africans were forced to collect it for delivery to merchant or tax official; then, with the establishment of large plantations after the First World War workers were pushed into the capitalist sector of the economy by the introduction of a system of forced labour. In each case the effect was to continue the disruption of the traditional organisation of local society.

> To Messur Noel, named the neat
> By those who love him, I bequeath
> A helmless ship, a houseless street
> A wordless book, a swordless sheath
> A bell sans tongue, a saw sans teeth,
> A bed sans sheet, a board sans meat,
> To make his nothingness complete.
>
> *The Testament of Francois Villon*

The territory of what is today the Republic of Guinea fell within the ambit of French colonial control in the last two decades of the last century and escaped from French political control in 1958. This paper sets out to examine and characterise imperial economic activity in Guinea in this period. While it is not possible to draw general conclusions about any theory of imperialism from the study of any single country or area, it is certainly arguable that much of what is said in this paper could be paralleled fairly closely by the imperial–colonial experience of a number of other African countries. Inasmuch as discussions of imperialism involve us in considerations of the manner and nature of the imperial exploitation of colonies, Guinea is a good test case for it had so much to offer an imperial power: gold, diamonds, ivory, rubber, high-quality coffee and tea, wood, livestock, rice, leather, and a tremendous range of agricultural products and byproducts, most notably bananas, pineapples and oranges. Moreover, the territory possesses some of the world's largest known deposits of high-grade iron ore and bauxite. The list is far from complete even today because of inadequate surveying and prospecting but it now seems likely that there are also significant amounts of nickel, cobalt, manganese, copper and other semi-rare metals to be mined. Guinea is perhaps the best endowed country in West Africa, particularly when one considers that a large proportion of its natural riches are to be found near the coast, close to major rivers and good natural ports, and that the country has the means to provide cheap and superabundant hydroelectric power. In a word, the scope for imperial economic activity was very large.

The general questions with which this paper is concerned relate to the changing nature of the imperial economic implantation in Guinea, the nature of the economic changes it brought about, and the implications of these changes for the indigenous social structure. In order to focus more sharply on the major characteristics of change this paper sets out to order the material we have to hand[1] into a rough pattern by which the colonial period is subdivided into three epochs according to the type and extent (or lack) of imperial investment: (1) The period to 1920: (2) the 1920–1945 period; (3) the period since 1945. While the author is conscious that in historical fact there was considerable

1. This paper relies heavily on information gathered in the course of a research visit to West Africa in 1968 generously financed by the British Social Science Research Council, and on the writings on Guinea of the distinguished French Africanist, Jean Suret-Canale, in particular his article 'La Guinée dans le système colonial', *Présence Africaine*, **29**, Dec. 1959–Jan. 1960; the sections dealing with Guinea in his book, *L'Afrique Noire—l'Ere Coloniale* (Paris, 1964); and his book, *La République de Guinée* (Paris, 1970).

overlap between these epochs in terms of investment and economic activity, and is only too aware of the dangers of erecting schema, some such device is at least heuristically desirable.

1. The period to 1920—the economics of pillage

Conquest. From the sixteenth century onwards[2] the Guinea coast was fairly systematically slaved by all the major European powers, particularly the Portuguese. Exactly how great was the haemorrhage of human resources suffered in this period is impossible to estimate, but it is likely to have been enormous. The most thorough and demanding of the slavers were the Portuguese, and Bissau was the central entrepot of their trade. Portuguese influence stretched deep into Senegal, Guinea and the Gambia and slaves were drawn from all these countries. James Duffy records that

> by 1700 Brazil was demanding 10,000 slaves a year, a quota which could not always be met by Angola. . . . In the middle of the eighteenth century the powerful Grão-Pará and Maranhão Company, in which the Portuguese dictator Pombal held interest, was formed to finance the rebuilding of Bissau into an important slave centre. During part of the period Guinea actually surpassed Angola in the number of slaves sent to Brazil. By the end of the century, however, Guinea was virtually slaved out.[3]

During the nineteenth century a number of European trading houses were established on the Guinea coast, dealing in a variety of goods— gold, diamonds, ivory, rubber and agricultural produce. Although the majority of these concerns were French, the British, Germans and Americans were also represented. Between 1865 and 1890 the whole coastal strip was brought under French colonial control, consolidating the position of the French trading houses, and by 1896 this control had been extended to cover the Fouta Djalon in the interior. In 1899 the vast savannah hinterland of the southern Soudan was added to Guinea and the forest area bordering on Liberia was forcibly annexed, the entire colony comprising an area slightly larger than the modern United Kingdom.

The motivation for this headlong expansion of imperial control

---

2. The author does not wish to imply, in starting with this date, that Guinea had no economic history before then. In omitting discussion of this history and of the 'traditional' economic system(s) of Guinea this paper follows the dictates of length rather than those of historical interest.

3. J. Duffy, *Portugal in Africa* (Harmondsworth, Penguin African Series, 1962), pp. 36–7.

appears to have been roughly three parts commercial and one part military—if one allows the perhaps dubious concession that there can ever be a *purely* military reason for doing anything:

(a) The Marseilles-based trading houses established in Guinea were intent on carving out a commercial hinterland independent of the Bordeaux-based houses established in Senegal. It was to their advantage that the Fouta trade should be routed through Conakry, Benty, Boffa, and Boké instead of Dakar and St Louis.

(b) The French sought to pre-empt the British who were believed to entertain imperial and commercial designs on the same territory. In particular the French were unwilling to see the mainly Manchester and Liverpool-based companies in Sierra Leone build up trading links with the hinterland.[4]

(c) Many African chiefs in the interior continually pillaged caravan trains bound for the coast; only conquest and colonial control would ensure 'freedom of commerce'. On the other hand the same chiefs showed a predeliction for routing much of this traffic towards Freetown, so the same means were required to restrict *their* freedom of commerce.

(d) Where African leaders—Samory in the Soudan, numerous chiefs in the forest area—resisted the French by force of arms, the military were given their head and allowed to conduct a fight to the finish. The entire credibility of the imperial enterprise demanded the destruction of such leaders, more or less regardless of commercial considerations.[5]

4. In March 1892 the Lieut.-Governor of Guinea received an intelligence report from Sierra Leone furnished by the Compagnie Française de l'Afrique Occidentale (C.F.A.O.) which nicely illustrated the difficulties of separating military and commercial motives. A Mr Williams, an envoy of the Liverpool Chamber of Commerce and of the (Liverpool-based) Sierra Leone Cooling Company, was reported to have set off to make contact with Samory in the Soudan at the same time that the Company's Director, a Mr Jones, was reported to have been lobbying the Under-Secretary of State for the Colonies in London for the establishment of a British protectorate over the area. The Company's main business seems to have lain in selling arms to Samory. *Politique Générale. Rapports sur la Situation politique (et agricole) des Rivières du Sud et de la Guinée Française. 21 avril 1890–30 septembre 1895. Rapport de fevrier 20—mars 7, 1892. Archives Fédérales de Dakar. 7 G 53.*

5. It is difficult to argue that even such 'purely military' operations were devoid of commerical considerations. In winning commercially pointless victories in the Soudan the French were demonstrating (as also were the British in the Sudan) that resistance to imperialism did not pay. To put it bluntly, they were helping to create a world safe for colonial exploitation. Even if such aims are regarded as unrealistically remote, it must be remembered that in Guinea not only did the military plunder all they could for their own gain, but that without their intimidating presence the French would have been unable to collect taxes, conscript labour, or enforce trade on unfavourable terms.

Exploitation. The main pickings up to the end of World War I came in the form of rubber. Rubber plants grew wild and uncultivated in many parts of Guinea and there was a tremendous world demand for this commodity from the late 1880s on. The result was that until the bottom fell out of the market in 1911 (though it picked up again till 1918–19 with the war), large profits were made by the trading companies from the rubber obtained from Africans. This, then, was the major feature of the private sector's development up until 1920. The other major aspect of economic activity—the public, French administrative side, lay in two main areas: (*a*) the provision of a basic infrastructure—roads, the port of Conakry and above all the Conakry–Kankan railroad (crucial because the rubber was mainly found in the savannah region and the Fouta); at this stage the French clearly anticipated a boom period of large-scale evacuation of Guinean rubber and other resources; (*b*) the imposition of a uniform poll tax on every African aged eight and upwards. The 'official mind' laid great stress on the necessity of the Administration balancing its books and getting away from the substantial deficit of the early years. Of course, imposing and collecting this tax required considerable (and expensive) military force for a number of years (and the Forest Region remained under military rule until 1931) but even by 1905 the Administration was running into a sustained and substantial surplus. The poll tax alone accounted for over 90 per cent of all income from taxation.[6] Even a Gallagher and Robinson accounting system[7] would find that the French made money out of Guinea, though of course the crucial fact here is not the Administration's budgetary surpluses but the huge profits the private trading companies were making out of rubber.

To sum up then, this initial period constitutes a single epoch by virtue of the fact that essentially the same type of economic activity continued unbrokenly from the sixteenth century on: that is, pillage. By this I mean the evacuation of resources pure and simple, with the absolute minimum outlay of capital investment within the colony, in order to satisfy in an extremely mechanistic manner the crude and short-term demands of French imperial economic interests. This was as true of the rubber boom as it was of slavery. There was no attempt whatsoever to cultivate rubber plants or invest in plantations. Instead

6. In 1905 the poll tax accounted for 93·8 per cent of total budget receipts; in 1915 the proportion was 89·9 per cent; in 1925 81·9 per cent; in 1935 55·4 per cent. Figures based on author's calculations from statistics provided by the annual *Budget Générale de la Guinée Française.*
7. See J. Gallagher and R. Robinson, *Africa and the Victorians* (London, Macmillan, 1961), ch. xv.

Africans were encouraged and indeed coerced simply to pull up the plants whole and transport them down to the trading houses at the coast. It is only when we examine the nature of rubber pillage that we understand how the diverse strands of this period come together, and it is only in this way we can see how—despite superficial tensions between the two groups—the Administration worked systematically to increase the commercial advantages and profit margins of the trading companies. There was, indeed, a happy coincidence of interest between the Administration and the companies. The companies wanted the largest possible amounts of rubber obtained at the lowest possible price from an unresponsive African population. Had the companies relied on the price mechanism alone to stimulate the African population deep in the interior to pick, collect and transport to the coast the quantities of rubber they demanded, they would have had to raise their offered purchase price very considerably and per- haps even cut their profit margins as a result. This unpleasant alter- native was avoided by means of the Administration's fiscal policy. A considerable poll tax was imposed on a population which had little or no contact with a cash economy and thus quite literally had no money to pay with. So Africans were forced to gather rubber to sell at derisory prices to the companies in order to get the money with which to pay the tax. Indeed, in the early days the tax was itself pay- able in rubber. The Fouta and savannah areas were systematically defoliated of rubber plants as every year the African peasants moved out in ever wider circles from their villages to gather rubber. Thus, the Administration's fiscal policy was aimed at coercing Africans into the cash economy for the greater profit of the trading companies, and coincidentally to help balance the Administration's budgetary books.

2. The period of plantation: 1920–1945

Settlers. The development of the Malayan rubber industry (based on the cultivation of rubber trees which were hugely more productive than the rubber plants found in Guinea) had brought the Guinean rubber boom to a complete halt in 1911. Although during the war rubber production was resumed, it was obvious by 1919–20 that the boom was over for ever.[8] The war period had been a dreadful one in Guinea. Thousands of Africans were conscripted for the French

8. Suret-Canale records that in 1910 Far East (tree) rubber accounted for 12 per cent of the world rubber market; in 1913 the figure was over 50 per cent. At Conakry the offered price per kilo of rubber fell from 15–20 Fr. in 1909–10 to 2·50 Fr. in 1915. *La République de Guinée*, p. 102.

Army, the majority never to return. Given the increased demands made by France on her colonies during the war for produce of all kinds, conscription greatly exacerbated an already acute shortage of labour with which to meet these demands. The *corvée* and other forced labour practices had been introduced and were now systematically exploited for the first time in order to circumvent this shortage.

After the war a small but important number[9] of French settlers migrated to Guinea and extended this fitful exploitation into a more permanent pattern of economic activity. Particularly in the coastal region, but also in the Forest, a significant plantation sector was created, producing mainly bananas, pineapples and a variety of other fruits for export to the metropolitan market. Whereas rubber had been sold on the world market, the settlers were relatively secure under the umbrella of imperial preference which gave them protected markets in France and the rest of the French Empire, a fact which contributed greatly to the process of the integration of the Guinean economy into the greater imperial economy. Banana exports went from 7 tons in 1903 to 260 tons in 1920, 26,000 tons in 1934 and 52,000 tons in 1938— over 80 per cent of the entire AOF (Federation of French West Africa) figure. From about 1930 on coffee began to be produced for export too—11 tons were exported in 1932 and 1,000 tons in 1940.[10] The creation of several hundred large and thriving plantations marked a new stage in the territory's economic development. While actual investment involved in these ventures was small, this was no longer pillage so much as rational exploitation.

The whole of the interwar period saw very little new investment, in fact. The railway, originally intended to link up with the Dakar–Bamako–Niamey line, stopped at Kankan. Port facilities at Conakry were somewhat improved and several new roads cut, but that was all. The trading companies continued their activities, expanding out of rubber into a much wider range of commodities and several thousand Lebanese and Syrian traders moved in to fill the interstices of the economic system. The several thousand white settlers and the Lebanese represented a new economic interest in the Guinean situation, but not one which clashed fundamentally with that of the big

9. There were 1,600 whites in Guinea in 1910; 2,262 in 1926; 4,135 in 1945; 7,052 in 1951: Maurice Houis, *Guinée Française* (Paris, 1953), p. 51.
10. Suret-Canale, *La République de Guinée*, pp. 115–18. Banana production reached a record of 98,000 tons in 1955, coffee a record in 1956 at 12,000 tons.
11. Most notably, the Compagnie Française de l'Afrique Occidentale, the Société Commerciale de l'Ouest Africain, and the Compagnie du Niger Français—despite its name, a United Africa Company (i.e. Unilever) subsidiary.

established trading companies.[11] The major demand of the settlers, and particularly the planters, was for a large reservoir of cheap African labour. The companies' main demand remained fundamentally the same as before the war, except that there was now a pressing need for a variety of other products to replace rubber. The Administration maintained its policy of fiscal equilibrium and it too exhibited a large and growing appetite for cheap African labour. To some extent this was for purely Parkinson's law reasons, including the large personal appetites of administrators for numerous servants and large houses; but it was also because the Administration was committed to building and maintaining at least a rudimentary communications infrastructure. Combined with the balanced budget policy this meant that all public works projects mainly used cheap local labour, so as to minimise the horrors of capital outlay.[12] Since the infrastructure, once built, facilitated political control and commercial profit, what this involved in fact was taxing the Africans in order to pay the overhead costs for their own exploitation and subordination.

For the fact was that the Africans still bore virtually the whole burden of taxation and the settlers were only indirectly taxed and the trading companies were exempt altogether. (They paid some customs duties but no company tax.) The poll tax was doubled, redoubled and doubled again, and continued to constitute a major proportion of total government revenue right up to 1945.[13] Africans were also subject to a regional tax, tribute and levies in kind paid to the chiefs (and often informally to administrators as well), a tax on animals, income tax, and of course bore the overwhelming weight of indirect taxation as well. This might appear to have been quite inevitable since they constituted 99 per cent of the population; but in fact the Lebanese, the trading companies and the settlers were so much better off than the Africans that they did represent a not inconsiderable potential tax base.

The mobilisation of labour. The main point of the tax system, however, lay—as before—not so much in budget balancing but in its use as a lever with which to force large numbers of Africans into the cash economy. In order to pay the tax Africans simply had to produce

12. In 1935, for example, 2,705,000 man-days of forced labour and 50,700 man-days of requisitioned labour were worked. Gouvernement General de l'A.O.F., *Annuaire Statistique de l'A.O.F., 1936–1937–1938* (Paris, 1939), p. 123.
13. In 1938 direct personal tax receipts made up 57 per cent of total budget revenue; in 1943 60 per cent; in 1944 54 per cent. Author's calculations based on the annual *Budget Générale de la Guinée Française*.

cash crop surpluses or to offer their labour power to whites, or both. The surplus produce was routed to the market through the specially created Sociétés Indigènes de Prévoyance (SIPs), set up by the Administration for this purpose. They worked as authoritarian co-ops in which, as no less a person than the Minister of Colonies was to admit in 1947, the population was systematically coerced by administrators and chiefs to produce surpluses which were often almost entirely misappropriated from them by these two groups and sold to the trading companies at bargain prices. In essence, of course, this was merely the rubber story retold. What was new and different about the interwar period was the way in which the same fiscal weapons were used to produce a flood of cheap labour to fill the needs of the Administration and the planters. It also produced considerable labour migration; this is the first period which sees significant urban growth and also the beginning of the annual mass migrations to Senegal to gain seasonal employment in order to pay the tax. These migrations wrought havoc in the traditional social structure of many areas and ethnic groups.

The major feature of the economic history of the interwar period, then, was the creation of a pool of African labour. As we have seen, this was achieved basically in the interests of the planters and the Administration. Potential conflicts of interest between these two groups and the trading companies were limited to mere bickering because all their economic demands were simply heaped cumulatively on the backs of the African population.

The administration's attempt to create this pool of labour brought about a crucial confrontation between the 'traditional' and the elementary 'modern' economy. Put another way, it was a set-piece battle between imperial economic and social demands on the one hand, and the existing African socio-economic structure on the other; a battle which the former was always certain to win. It was a particularly crucial confrontation for the great Peul chiefs of the Fouta whose power and wealth rested not on the ownership of capital or land but in their ownership of and rights in people, the serfs and slaves of the Fouta. If these were to be lost, all was ultimately lost. But the foot-dragging resistance of the chiefs was only one reason why it took time and trouble to create a reservoir of labour. The general harshness of colonial rule, the cumulative pressures on African income and food production and the large and continuing drain on human resources represented by military conscription resulted in a long period of demographic stagnation.[14]

This in turn created a labour shortage within the 'traditional' subsistence economy, and made it doubly difficult to recruit labour for the 'modern' sector. Faced with the demands for tax payments Africans sought other means to satisfy it, using income sources within the 'traditional' commercial circuit—the fruit of labours in the gold-diggings or from itinerant trading (the dioula trade). Many more simply attempted to evade payment in every way possible. Some hid from tax-collecting chiefs and administrators, while others emigrated from the territory altogether on a temporary or permanent basis. (Such migration, of course, often resulted in a hidden subsidy flowing back to the rural economy in the shape of repatriated earnings from Senegal. But overall migration represented a net resource loss to the 'traditional' rural economy and increased the squeeze on it even more.) The fact was, finally, that Africans did not stream readily to work for the French planters and administrative officials because they were often afraid of them. Working conditions on the plantations were notorious. Wages were extremely low—indeed, were often 'forgotten' altogether, hours were long, discipline tough and sickness endemic. Stories of awful brutality and deprivation were common and were matched only by similar tales of the horrors of railroad construction labour conditions before the first War.

The solution to all this was fairly obvious and straightforward: forced labour. The Administration had had recourse to this expedient since 1910 but after 1920 a systematic effort to extract forced labour on a permanent basis was made. Every African male was liable to seven days of unpaid forced labour every year. In fact this law was 'liberally' interpreted by administrators and planters alike to the effect that they could call on as many Africans as they wished to peform unpaid labour services for as long as they liked. These levies in turn produced fresh population movements out of the range of the administration's labour overseers. Nevertheless, by the 1930s the system was sufficiently well established for the Administration to find that they simply could not use the millions of days of unpaid labour 'owed' to them by the African population.[15] So the system was modified to allow the more fortunate to buy themselves out of the

14. Throughout the colonial period to the 1950s the African population was estimated at around 2 million. The end of conscription and forced labour after 1945 coincided with a steep population rise to 2·8 million in 1958 and to 4 million in 1970.
15. To take the 1935 figures already cited (n. 13), 4,769,000 man-days of forced labour were 'owed' and only 2,705,000 of them were actually worked. Gouvernement Général de l'A.O.F., *Annuaire Statistique de l'A.O.F. 1936–1937–1938*, p. 123.

system on an annual basis, thus creating a valuable extra source of revenue.

By this stage, however, a crucial watershed had been reached. As labour was torn away from the 'traditional' economy to the benefit of the 'modern' economy, or simply drifted away in emigration, so naturally the position within the rural subsistence sector deteriorated. And as conditions got worse so a relatively unforced flow of labour in the 'modern' sector commenced, largely because conditions were so bad in the countryside. New social patterns were established and Africans began to settle permanently in and around the growing urban centres. Naturally enough this occasioned a further crisis for the heavily indebted rural economy. The Fouta suffered the worst drain of labour and this was the major factor behind the great famine there from 1931–36. This in turn produced a further haemorrhage of resources and increased impoverishment. Gilbert Vieillard recorded the scene there in 1936:

> The chiefs' young men sent out to gather the tax had still not returned. The taxpayers who had left, hidden or fled and the deaths registered in the census returns all greatly increased the burden to be borne by those who remained. Worse still, they had to find money (with which to pay); accordingly they were reduced to selling not only things which are customarily bought and sold, but also things which are not normally thought of as saleable commodities. . . . but no-one would dare to complain too much. First they sold their animals, their cows, sheep and chickens; then their grain, their cooking implements and their Korans—everything that *could* be sold. Prices were very low, for the chief's men and the Syrians were fishing in troubled waters. The taxpayer seldom mentioned the difference between the sale-price and the increasing of the tax owed. When there was nothing left they would put in pawn their standing crops and their children.[16]

World War II was an even more horrendous period. Once again large numbers of Africans were conscripted: first for the Allied cause in 1939–40; then by Vichy, though relatively few of them owing to Vichy racialist doctrine; then a vast number more by the Free French from 1942 on. Indeed, there is little doubt that life became significantly harder under the Free French. Again there was a tremendous demand for produce of all sorts for the beleaguered home market. Above all this was true of rubber, after twenty years when none at all had been produced. When Guinea came under Vichy rule in 1940 it

16. G. Vieillard, 'Notes sur les peuls du Fouta-Djalon', *Bulletin de l'I.F.A.N.*, Jan.–Feb. 1940, no. 1, p. 171.

was again operating in a market where Malayan competition did not exist. The Germans could not obtain rubber from Allied-held Malaya and this was a vital raw material. So the Guinean puppet economy was jerked into life again and all the horrors of the earlier rubber boom reborn. In 1942, just as Guinea fell back into the Allied camp, so the Japanese took Malaya and deprived the Allies of their principal rubber source.[17] Allied demand was even more urgent and forced labour reached new heights of intensity.

Long before World War II, however, the battle over labour resources had been fought and won and lost. The existing social structure of African rural society—particularly in the Fouta—had been deeply mined. As Guinea experienced the full blast of the postwar world the fissures were widened. What had been a steady demographic trickle from the Fouta became a swollen stream and then a flood. Over time the Administration's use of the chiefs as intermediaries had gradually subverted their traditional status and authority in all parts of Guinea. In the Fouta, however, the institutions of chieftancy were exceptionally strong, oppressive and authoritarian. As the Fouta (the home of some 40 per cent of Guinea's entire population) suffered an increasing drain of human resources (particularly young active males), so the same or even increased amounts of chiefly tribute were extracted from a numerically diminishing and anyway impoverished social base of serfs and freemen. Thus the final result of the victory of the 'modern' economy was to produce a rising rate of exploitation in the 'traditional' rural economy. These developments were to reach an entirely new level of intensity in the post–1945 period. It is in them—and in the response they elicited—that one finds the basic explanation for the revolutionary nature of the peasant struggle against the chiefs in the 1940s and the 1950s. And it was this struggle which provided the basic dynamic on which the radical *Parti Democratique de Guinée* (PGD) rode to power in this period. By then, however, a new set of considerations had entered the 'official mind'.

3. The 1945–1958 period

The emergence of the mining interest. The 1945–58 period was chiefly

---

17. The A.O.F. Governor-General, Boisson, declared for Vichy in May 1940, after which the federation theoretically became neutral territory until Boisson declared the Free French in the week following the Allied landings in North Africa on 21 November 1942. Meanwhile Malaya had fallen to the Japanese in late 1941, Singapore falling on 15 February, 1942.

characterised in the economic sphere by the appearance in Guinea of the sort of large-scale investment which, on strictly Leninist assumptions, one might have expected to occur much sooner. The presence of iron ore and chrome had been discovered in 1902 and of bauxite in 1920, but no very determined efforts were made either to exploit this wealth or to discover its full extent. Several small companies existed to buy gold and diamonds from African prospectors, but otherwise the only activity in the mining field was the granting of a number of concessions for mineral rights to companies who did nothing with them. Or not quite nothing. They wished at all costs to refrain from capital investment and seem generally to have had the normal attitudes of the *immobiliste* entrepreneurs of the interwar Third Republic. But at no capital cost they floated their shares on the Paris stock exchange and large amounts were made in speculation on the basis of fine-sounding company prospectuses.

It was only in 1948 that the first mineral exports were made by mining firms established right on the coast. Both the iron and bauxite operations were conducted by international consortia with predominant French interests. The siting of operations again evidenced a desire to keep infrastructural investment down to a minimum. In 1953 an international consortium was formed to exploit the enormous bauxite reserves at Fria, though it was not until 1957 that the plant was completed and the first exports made.

In a few years these developments had entirely changed the economic face of Guinea. The mineral ventures involved investment on a time and financial scale quite different from anything that had gone before. A new phase of the territory's economic history had begun: that of capital-intensive, technologically advanced and scientific exploitation of natural resources.

Given that this phase had been delayed for so surprisingly long, one might well ask why it *did* finally occur. In fact it is difficult to be certain as to the exact nature of the motivation for this rush of mining enterprise, but it is safe to say that the following considerations were all important: (*a*) the general French hunger for raw materials in the post-war period of reconstruction; (*b*) a conscious decision in Paris that the colonies must be developed more than they had hitherto been; a very deliberate *mise en valeur* policy was evident in all the French African colonies, administered by a number of exceptionally tough Governors—in the Ivory Coast, Péchoux, in Guinea, Roland Pré; (*c*) strategic mineral considerations stemming from the Marshall Plan and the Korean War mineral boom; (*d*) a consciousness that the iron might not remain hot for striking (in 1949 Pré was already speaking of the need to develop Guinea given the impending loss of Indo-China to the Empire), or that someone else might strike first (in 1947 an American company had begun exploitation of Conakry's iron ore).

The emergence of a powerful mining interest then, may well have stemmed originally from largely political and strategic considerations.[18] Certainly the new phase had a political dimension within Guinea itself. It is this which we must now consider: that is, to reverse the title of Berg's well-known article,[19] the political basis of economic choice.

The political dimension. The end of the war had ushered in a new political era in Guinea, together with the rest of French Africa, and 1945 brought the beginnings of African representation, of opportunities for Africans in the middle ranks of the Administration and of hope of better things yet to come. Most important, 1946 saw the abolition of forced labour, formally anyway, though administrators and planters both were slow to forget the bad old ways and quick to learn bad new ones of achieving not dissimilar results. But in any case there was a steady, plentiful and unforced flow of African labour into the modern economy and it was simply no longer necessary to have recourse to forced labour on the massive scale of prewar days. More important, the concession, however reluctant, of the right to engage in politics and to form trade unions, meant that economic decisions now had to be taken with an eye to their probable political effects. Such considerations did not greatly concern the planters, who were mostly diehard reactionaries, nor the men who manned the trading companies; both groups tended to display a shortsighted concern with their immediate economic advantages without weighing the possible political disadvantages subsequent upon such acts as trying to break the African trade union movement or playing an active and conservative role in local politics. But the Administration, though it tended to take

18. Roland Pré, in the foreword to his book, *L'Avenir de la Guinée française* (Conakry, 1949), quotes the Head of the Division of Strategic Minerals in Washington: 'With regard to the O.E.E.C. and the Fourth Truman Point of January 1949, we know that the greatest possibilities of mineral wealth—and the best extraction opportunities—are to be found in French Africa.' See also J. Chardonnet, *Une Oeuvre nécessaire: l'industrialisation de l'Afrique* (Paris, 1956) esp. p. 54 where it is argued that the future Soviet occupation of Western Europe will necessitate retreat to an African redoubt which, suitably industrialised, will serve as the base for 'offensives of reconquest and liberation'.
19. Elliot Berg, 'The economic basis of political choice in French West Africa', *American Political Science Review* (June 1960).

the side of such groups, had necessarily to concern itself with what economic decisions were politically productive and counter-productive.

By 1953 the importance of the mining interest—and the certainty of its increasing future importance—meant that such considerations were becoming increasingly relevant. The mining companies, with their large and irretrievable capital stake, and their much longer business time horizon, clearly had an interest in a much more flexible and liberal set of policies towards Africans than the simple gut-reactions of the RPF-voting planters. Above all they required long-term political and social stability and whatever immediate measures which this might require.[20] They neither needed nor wanted un-skilled forced labour—they could afford to pay, they wanted a stable labour force, they wanted skilled and semi-skilled labour, and they were conscious that attempts of the planters to perpetuate the forced labour system were richly productive of African political radicalism.

From about 1950 on the Administration began to take the same sort of view, a fact which entailed a movement away from its old position of straightforward support of the economic interests of the planters and trading companies. Thus in 1952–53 the Administration finally gave way to African agitation for the long-promised Labour Code which these interests had fought so long and bitterly. Even more dramatically, it became clear that attempts to raise the poll tax—or even collect the existing poll tax—were highly counterproductive politically. For anti-poll-tax agitation was one of the great enduring themes of the PDG which was growing so alarmingly fast. Given the enormous strength of peasant feeling against the tax, it became clear to those with a long-term stake—the mining companies and the Administration—that some change here was absolutely necessary. Officially, of course, the time-honoured justification for the hated tax was that it was the only way that Guinea could balance the budgetary books. In fact, as we have seen, its real economic justifica-tion had been to divert labour resources and services in a different direction. Now that this had been achieved; indeed, now that there was growing urban unemployment, only the 'official mind's' stress on fiscal probity stood in the way of change. And the 'official mind' chang-ed quickly enough once the long-term priorities of major vested

20. Sekou Touré alleges that in 1952 the (American-owned) *Compagnie Minière de Conakry* bribed the then Secretary-General of the PDG and its only deputy, to resign from the Party. A. S. Touré, *Le Pouvoir Populaire* (vol. xvi of Touré's *Works*), (Conakry, 1968), pp. 37–8.

interests became clear. Despite the Administration's strictures, repeated for half a century, that the budget must always balance, from the early 1950s on less and less serious attempts were made to collect the tax and Guinea was allowed to run into a heavy and continuous budgetary deficit. Despite all the dire warnings of earlier days, the deficit was simply met by subventions from public funds.

Thus the 1950s saw the triumph in the political sphere for the enlightened liberal capitalism of the big new mining interests, partially at the expense of the older-established interests. The apotheosis of this process was apparently reached in 1957 with the climax of the PDG's sweep to power. The first economic measures of the new African administration were to cut back the poll tax and impose a series of taxes which shattered the previously (virtually immune) tax position of the *colons*, notably a tax on all alcoholic beverages. Since (in theory) only bad Muslims drink, this mainly affected whites, and a tremendous furore resulted. But there were no proposals for new or increased taxes on the mining companies—a much wealthier and more obvious target. Indeed, by 1957 the triumph of liberal enlightenment appeared to be complete, for now that the once alarmingly radical PDG was in power, it turned out that it and its leader, Sekou Touré, were by no means as unfriendly to private capital as had been feared. Touré vied with the Governor in his praises of the mining sector's contribution to the country's economy and appealed for much more private foreign investment of the same sort.[21]

The uniquely political crisis of 1958 and the sudden and unexpected acquisition of independence has naturally complicated this picture very considerably. It is now extremely difficult to characterise Guinean economic development with the same broad strokes I have employed above. Nevertheless, there is no doubt that despite the socialist rhetoric and, more ambiguously, the socialist behaviour of the regime, the heritage of this last period is still very much with us. But the planters are gone and so are the trading companies—bought out and chased out and taken over. The mines are now the only really dynamic sector of the economy and provide over 80 per cent of all Guinea's exports and hard foreign currency. They continue to enjoy a highly privileged position.

The mines apart, however, one's overwhelming impression in

21. On Touré's rapprochement with the Administration in this period see R. W. Johnson, 'The P.D.G. and the Mamou "deviation"', in C. H. Allen and R. W. Johnson, eds, *African Perspectives*, (Cambridge, Cambridge Univ. Press, 1970) and also R. W. Johnson, 'Sekou Touré and the Guinean revolution', *African Affairs*, **69**, no. 277 (Oct. 1970).

Guinea today is really how very little the French developed this potentially very rich country. In very many ways Guinea is still right at the beginning in most matters economic. The pillage and exploitation of fifty years produced little that has endured. The railway never got further than Kankan, though it might with Chinese help later on. The hospital the French built in Conakry in 1902, remained the only one in Guinea until 1955. The roads are still extremely rudimentary or even fictional for the most part, the sort of roads that interest cartographers but terrify travellers. And, of course, much of what the French did install in Guinea they destroyed or removed in the dreadful wrecking operation of 1958.

4. Conclusions

It has long been common for apologists of imperialism to offer concluding justifications for imperialism by appealing for a rudimentary cost-benefit analysis ('Colonialism may have been unpleasant for the colonised but they would still be in the Dark Ages without it'). The present writer has nothing to add to this pointless and ahistorical debate except the suggestion that it ought to be phrased not in terms of cost and benefits but of investments and exploitation.

We have seen that in Guinea there were three distinct phases of imperial investment, increasing in magnitude and sophistication over time. The exploitation (of men and materials) to which this investment directly and indirectly gave rise in each phase shaped the nature of the response from the traditional social structure for each successive phase. That is to say, there was a crucial timelag between cause, effect and indirect effect, which meant that the purely political remedial measures of the postwar period could never be wholly effective. To put it bluntly, the Administration's grudging tolerance of African trade union and political organisations in the post-1945 (third phase) period did it little good because the African social structure was still responding to the effects of prewar (second phase) exploitation. On the other hand, had the first phase of conquest and pillage been followed immediately by the large-scale mineral investment of the third phase, it seems unlikely that the French would have had to countenance such a coherent and radical response from the African population.

None of these remarks, it must be noted, sheds any great light on theories seeking to explain the reasons for the original thrust of imperialism and the conquest of colonies. On the evidence provided by the Guinean case alone one must argue that conquest was essentially a pre-emptive exercise whereby France reserved to herself the possibilities for future investment and exploitation which the colony offered. That this exploitation was so intense, but that investment was so fitful and late, simply points the need for a second sort of theory altogether, a theory to explain not how an imperial power came to colonise other territories, but to explain how this process of colonisation (and eventually decolonisation) actually worked.

XI

King Leopold's
imperialism

J. Stengers

One of the strangest chapters in the history of nineteenth century imperialism concerns the activities of Leopold II, of the Belgians. Here was a king, a constitutional monarch, who was determined to give his people the advantage of overseas possessions whether they wanted it or not. To this end as Stengers describes, he tried to obtain territories to exploit in almost every part of the world, and by almost any method. Those he could not hope simply to occupy he proposed to buy, or to lease. No scheme was either too big or too small for him to contemplate and in the end he was able to obtain a huge slice of Africa, the Congo, as what was virtually his own personal fief.

In this essay Stengers is concerned to try and demonstrate that the activities of this eccentric but singleminded monarch are an exception to 'economic theories' of imperialism. His reasons for this are twofold. First, they were the deeds of an individual who had no support whatsoever from the leading capitalists or capitalist institutions within his own society. Second, their aim was simply 'pillage' of the most old-fashioned kind and had nothing to do with the more sophisticated economic relationships developed by late nineteenth-century capitalism. This is the argument which was challenged, in another African context, by Johnson's essay on Guinea (X above).

King Leopold is best known as the founder and sovereign of the Congo Free State. The particular brand of imperialism he displayed in Africa could only be described as voracious. Stanley himself wrote that Leopold displayed 'enormous voracity'—meaning sheer territorial greed—in establishing his domain.[1]

1. Stanley to Sanford, 4 March, 1885, in François Bontinck, *Aux origines de l'Etat Indépendant du Congo* (Louvain–Paris, 1966), p. 300.

1. Leopold's territorial voracity

The story of Leopold's territorial expansion in the heart of Africa is quite amazing. Between 1880 and 1884 the king sent out expeditions, led mainly by Stanley, which established a fairly loose occupation of territory in the Congo by means of outposts. Most of these stations were in the lower Congo, between Leopoldville (now Kinshasa) and the sea. Even by 1884 his occupation beyond Leopoldville was limited to a few stations along the river, sometimes hundreds of kilometres apart, the most distant being Stanley Falls. Yet when Leopold turned to Bismarck in an attempt to obtain Germany's recognition of his Association Internationale du Congo, he unashamedly demanded the greater part of the Congo basin. In August 1884 he sketched in on the map of Africa the frontiers he wanted, and extraordinary boundaries they were. In some cases they stretched as much as 1,000 or 1,500 kilometres beyond the Association's outposts. To the north, the boundary followed the fourth parallel; to the east, it reached Lake Tanganyika, and it extended downwards to the sixth parallel south of the Equator. This represents roughly two-thirds of the present Congo.

Looking at Leopold's map Bismarck was at first alarmed; but in October 1884, towards the end of their negotiations, he decided, apparently on impulse, to give the king what he wanted. He presumably reasoned that there was nothing against giving a little elbowroom to a philanthropic sovereign ready to sacrifice his personal fortune in order to open up Africa.

Leopold was not content with this success for more than a few weeks. In January 1885, during similar negotiations with France for French recognition of his rights in the Congo, representatives of Leopold's Association produced a new map. The northern and eastern boundaries were those which had already been recognised by Germany, but to the south they had been pushed down as far as the watershed between the Congo and the Zambezi. In relation to the frontiers approved by Bismarck this represented a southward increase of over four degrees latitude, and it was by no means because in the interim the Association's agents had pushed their occupation further down. The fact was that Leopold's greed was showing. He must have reasoned that since under the terms of a treaty with the Association France had a right of preemption over its territory, the French would not object to his rapacity.

Hence the Congo State, which was set up in 1885 with its frontiers thus defined, turned out to be a territory monstrously disproportionate to the resources at its disposal. Its slender finances did not at first allow the establishment of more than a rudimentary government. In vast areas—the 'Arab' zone to the east and the Katanga to the south—the influence of the state remained negligible. The King, although unable effectively to occupy more than a fraction of his territory, remained faithful to his motto of expansion and went on trying to extend his frontiers in all directions.

In 1888–89 he had his eyes on distant goals: the Upper Zambezi, Lake Nyasa, Lake Victoria and the Upper Nile. Expeditions were planned. Time was pressing, Leopold explained to his most intimate collaborator, for 'after next year there will be nothing more to acquire in Africa'.[2] His basic idea was clear: the more the better. Most of his efforts to push beyond the agreed frontiers of the state proved fruitless; but in the direction of the Nile they persisted until the moment the Free State ended. This particular campaign alone constituted a long chapter in the history of Leopold's imperialism in Africa.

Leopold's grandiose designs on Black Africa should not obscure his more general imperialism, for throughout his life his imperialistic efforts literally spanned the globe. Even when he had his hands full with the Congo he never overlooked the rest of the world. On the contrary, as soon as the Congo changed from being a liability to a financial asset on account of the rubber revenues Leopold's schemes outside the Congo became grander than ever before.

2. 1898

By way of example it is worth looking at Leopold's activities in a single year, 1898.

(*a*) Leopold was still possessed by his great dream of extending his sovereignty over the Upper Nile. His forces had reached the Nile near Lado and had established themselves. So far, however, they lacked the strength to push northwards into an area where the Dervishes had a firm grip. There was also a diplomatic obstacle to that move in the shape of the treaty with France of 14 August, 1894. After Great Britain had leased to him (12 May, 1894) that part of the Nile basin south of the tenth parallel (the same latitude as Fashoda), Leopold had yielded to overwhelming French pressure to renounce most of the advantages of this agreement with Britain. He had, in fact, undertaken to refrain from any political occupation of most of the territory leased to him.

2. Brussels, Archives of the Ministry of Foreign Affairs, Strauch Papers.

Consequently, he gave orders to reinforce his Nile contingents so as to make the push northwards possible. The orders date from September 1897; the Congo authorities must

> tout faire pour qu'il y ait à la fin de l'année une bonne force, de l'artillerie, des armes, des munitions, des embarcations, des marchandises à Redjaf afin que Chaltin [the commanding officer] soit outillé de façon à pouvoir exécuter . . . nos plans, c'est-à-dire de descendre le Nil en reconnaissance en évitant de fonder des postes . . . en amont de Sennaar, et s'il ne rencontre pas d'obstacle à cette hauteur, de fonder un établissement sans drapeau à Sennaar ou aux environs de cette ville et un autre plus solide dans la partie de l'ancien territoire italien, de celui qui leur fut reconnu par le protocole anglo-italien de 1892, le plus rapproché de la ville de Sennaar.[3]

The plan, as renewed here (it was already two years old), was thus to cross the country forbidden to Leopold by his treaty with France and to establish his Congolese forces much further to the north in the Sennaar region. This was obviously the prelude to a diplomatic gamble whereby Leopold would try to get recognition of his control over that area and also over the intermediate territory between the Sennaar and the Congo State. However, in early 1898 this plan became impossible to implement owing to the persistent military weakness of the Nile forces, which had to face a counteroffensive launched by the Dervishes. Realising that he could expect no military results in the near future, the king tried rather to succeed by diplomacy. His aim was to induce England to give him the territory on the Upper Nile which he already leased from her (since 1894) and possibly another slice as well. That way he could avoid the impending difficulties between France and England. Accordingly, diplomatic contacts were made at the highest level.

On 6 April, 1898 King Leopold met Lord Salisbury in the South of France. He reported as follows of the interview:

> J'ai fait remarquer qu'il y aurait peut-être un moyen d'aplanir les difficultés internationales en se servant du bail. Lord Salisbury a paru abonder dans cet ordre d'idées, a dit que c'était une question qu'il aurait à examiner avec nous, que peut-être ce bail aurait à être très étendu, que les pays au nord de Khartoum coûteraient très cher à l'Egypte à administrer, coûteraient sans doute moins à l'Etat du Congo. Vous êtes libre-échangiste, m'a dit Lord Salisbury; j'ai dit: absolument. Et cela nous va,

---

3. King Leopold to Liebrechts, 2 Sept. 1897; Brussels, Archives Générales du Royaume, Van Eetvelde Papers, 106.

a repris Sa Seigneurie. Les Français sont protectionnistes, et nous redoutons cette tendance. J'ai fait alors remarquer que lorsque l'on en serait à traiter les questions d'amour-propre international, il serait peut-être plus facile d'employer un petit qu'un grand.[4]

Lord Salisbury's own report of the meeting is rather different; he describes himself as having remained throughout noncommittal about the King's suggestions.[5]

On 13 April, 1898 the king met Hanotaux, the French foreign minister. Leopold told him that 'le moment approchait où il lui serait loisible de servir sa politique en reconnaissant le bail qu'il avait combattu jadis'. Hanotaux, Leopold added, 'se réserve d'y réfléchir et croit aussi qu'il y a là peut-être un élément de conciliation'.[6]

Later that year a renewed effort was made in the press to popularise the idea that Leopold's effective occupation of the Upper Nile could allow a 'conciliation' between France and England. Several articles appeared in newspapers and periodicals both in Britain and Belgium, all of which bore the mark of Leopold's paid propaganda. They achieved little.

(*b*) If Leopold was so anxious to get to the Sennaar it was because he had a finger in another pie: Eritrea. Seeing that since Aduwa the majority of Italians appeared disgusted with Eritrea, Leopold hoped to have Italy lease him the territory. The plan was put to the Italian Government in December 1896, and quite serious negotiations were begun in the following year. The Italian prime minister and foreign secretary both seemed to be fairly responsive to Leopold's idea. An Italian negotiator, General Dal Verme, twice came to Brussels to meet the king in March and July 1897. The lease was to be given to a Congolese company—a kind of 'Chartered'—controlled by the king himself.

There were two main obstacles to be overcome. First, Italian public opinion had to be placated, for an outcry against Italy's humiliation in the transaction was almost certain. Second, England had to agree. In fact, a double British agreement was essential, to sanction both the lease itself (which could not survive British opposition) and also Leopold's dèmands. The king considered that the lease of Eritrea by Italy should be concurrent with the lease of the Sennaar by Britain so as to establish a link, further down, with the Congo Free State. This

4. Van Eetvelde Papers, 122.
5. F.O. 10/710.
6. Van Eetvelde Papers, 122.

was the only way in which he could achieve his vision of one huge possession stretching from the Atlantic to the Red Sea. It was for this reason that Leopold asked Italy to intervene in his favour over the Sennaar lease.

British reactions turned out to be negative. In November 1897 the Italian foreign minister, while saying nothing whatever about the Eritrea lease, sent a memorandum to the British ambassador explaining Leopold's wishes as regards Sennaar:

Memorandum.

Le Roi des Belges comme Souverain de l'Etat du Congo désire ouvrir à son domaine africain un débouché sur la Mer Rouge.

Son projet est d'établir à cet effet entre le Congo et Massowah une série d'étapes commerciales.

Pour ce qui concerne l'Angleterre, le Roi Léopold lui demanderait:
1. le simple libre transit à travers les pays compris dans sa zone d'influence depuis la frontière congolaise jusqu'au Sennaar.
2. le bail de cette dernière province.

Si l'Angleterre adhère à cette double demande, le Roi Léopold se propose de demander également à l'Italie le libre transit à travers l'Erythrée.

Le Roi attacherait un prix tout spécial à connaître, en principe, les dispositions du Cabinet de Londres envers ses projets pour autant que ceux-ci touchent aux droits et aux intérêts de l'Empire britannique.[7]

The Foreign Office seem not to have taken this plan very seriously, and decided to leave the memorandum unanswered.

In Rome in 1898 the king was continuing to insist on a speedy end to the negotiations on the Eritrean lease. In case the terms of the lease were objected to, he added, an alternative might be that the Congolese Company should become responsible for administering Eritrea for a *per contract* (*à forfait*) fee. 'Le Gouvernement italien paierait à la société une somme annuelle de x à débattre et la société administrerait la colonie, en solderait les dépenses et dès qu'il y aura un boni de recettes, en remettra les trois quarts au Gouvernement italien' (January 1898).[8]

In July 1898 this plan was firmly vetoed by Rome; fear of public opinion must have been the decisive factor. 'On dirait dans le pays et ailleurs,' pointed out the Minister of Foreign Affairs, 'que nous sommes

7. Sir Clare Ford to Salisbury, 22 Nov. 1897; F.O. 45/768.
8. Count de Borchgrave to Van Loo, 9 January 1898; Brussels, Royal Archives, Van Loo Papers.

incapables d'administrer. . . . Le Gouvernement ferait un aveu d'incapacité'.[9]

(c) Simultaneously, Leopold was playing what he hoped would be a winning game in Abyssinia. In December 1897 he had given an audience in Brussels to the celebrated Russian adventurer Leontiev. Leontiev boasted of having been granted a concession which included governorship of the 'Equatorial Provinces of Abyssinia' (a rather ill-defined territory where the Negus's authority was still tenuous). He was trying to raise money to exploit his territory for, he believed, there were gold mines in it near Lake Rudolph.

Leopold was interested. 'Leontieff fait l'effet d'un condottiere', he wrote. 'Il peut réussir'.[10] He drafted the basis of an agreement between Leontiev and potential investors in his venture. 'La concession des mines d'or si on en trouve en Abyssinie avec partage par moitié des bénéfices au-dessus de la rémunération des capitaux d'exploitation'.[11] However, as this required the creation of a commercial company the king was unable to act in his own capacity. He would have to be content with encouraging the setting up of such a company along the lines discussed with Leontiev.

Private capital, mainly Belgian, was mobilised by the Belgian financier Colonel Thys. This led to the founding of the Société anonyme belge pour le développement de l'Industrie et du Commerce dans les Provinces équatoriales d'Abyssinie (May 1898). But Thys acted only under the direct guidance of the King, with whom he was in close contact; this was the King's private venture proceeding with the King's full support.

This kind of royal patronage did not necessarily preclude disaster, though. Leontiev turned out to be a crook as well as an adventurer; all the Belgian and foreign investments in the Société anonyme belge—a total of nearly two million francs—were lost.

(d) During the Spanish-American War, King Leopold once more turned his attention to a territory which he had tried very hard to get a quarter of a century earlier: the Philippines. Here again the idea was that of a lease, as in the case of Eritrea; it seemed to be a favourite ploy of the king's. The Philippines would be leased to the same Congolese company as had been proposed for Eritrea: the Société Générale Africaine. This company was, needless to say, the King's

9. Van Loo to Borchgrave, 21 July 1898; Van Loo Papers.
10. King Leopold to Van Eetvelde, Dec. 1897; Van Eetvelde Papers, 33.
11. Brussels, African Archives of the Ministry of Foreign Affairs, series 'Archives de l'Institut Royal Colonial Belge'.

tool. He explained in a letter that it had been set up to fulfil 'les fonctions administratives dans de vastes territoires que lui confieraient soit une charte soit un bail'.

Il y a maints grands propriétaires qui afferment leurs terres, ne voulant pas eux-mêmes s'en occuper, ou chargent un intendant de la gestion de leurs biens. La Société Générale Africaine est un instrument analogue qui s'offre non pas aux particuliers mais aux Etats qui voudraient ne pas gérer par eux-mêmes des territoires leur appartenant.[12]

In July 1898 the king made two proposals. In Madrid he told the Spanish Government that the Société Générale Africaine was ready to lease the Philippines from Spain. Then one of the Société's directors told the American Minister in Brussels that his Company was quite willing to serve the United States. For a start, it was ready to send black troops to help in the pacification of the Islands. 'Ma compagnie', remarked the man disarmingly, 'ne recherche aucune souveraineté et se bornerait à servir d'instrument de pacification et de civilisation, au nom du Pouvoir supérieur quel qu'il soit'.[13] This way the king had two irons in the fire.

But when a little later peace negotiations started between Spain and the United States, the king was obliged to propose the same formula to both parties—namely, the lease of the Philippines by Spain. This was considered as a kind of compromise between Spain and America. It seems as though in November 1898 the Spanish Government fully agreed with the idea as being the only way of maintaining Spanish sovereignty over the Philippines. However, they would not bring the matter up with the Americans themselves since this would have weakened their position in the peace negotiations; instead, they asked the king if he would broach the subject on their behalf. On the American side, too, Leopold's suggestion aroused initial interest; in the case of the American minister in Brussels this was quite marked. Accordingly the king sent an agent to Paris to contact the American plenipotentiaries at the peace talks, but suddenly everything fell through when the Americans decided to keep the Philippines for themselves.

As in the case of the Upper Nile, the king had hoped that the antagonists would seize the chance he was offering of a 'neutral

12. King Leopold to Verhaeghe de Naeyer, 16 July 1898; Brussels, Royal Archives, Congo 365.
13. Memo of Sam Wiener, 2 Aug. 1898; Brussels, Royal Archives, series 'Cabinet Léopold II'.

solution'. But in both cases the stronger party—England in the Upper Nile, the United States in the Philippines—was too imperialistic itself to accept any solution other than its own.

(*e*) Still later in 1898 when Leopold heard that Spain would perhaps be willing to sell the Caroline and Mariana Islands, he told the Belgian Minister in Madrid to ascertain the price immediately.[14] King Leopold was in the market again. But this time Germany was on the alert and refused to tolerate a competitor in a sale where she was already a buyer. Germany entered a protest in Brussels and the king withdrew.

(*f*) Leopold also made another tentative approach to Madrid at the same time as the preceding one (November 1898). Would Spain perhaps be ready to sell the Canary Islands and Fernando Po? And if so, at what price? These questions met with an immediate rebuff. The Canary Islands were part of the national territory, the Belgian Minister in Madrid was told; and as for Fernando Po, that was being exploited by Spanish companies.

(*g*) Meanwhile, in still another part of the world, Leopold was hard at work on one of his major schemes. In the summer of 1898 a Belgian company was granted a contract for the construction and exploitation of the Peking–Hankow railway—a 1,200 km line in the heart of China. This achievement was due in large measure to Leopold's own strenuous efforts. For him it was just a beginning. He followed it up with a special mission to China, and in a letter to the Belgian Minister in Peking dated December 9, 1898, he explained what he was after.

> Je voudrais pour les Belges un quartier à Hankow avec municipalité belge.
> La concession des mines du Kansu.
> La concession du chemin de fer Hankow-Foutcheou et Amoy et futurs embranchements.
> La concession des mines dans les provinces traversées par cette ligne, concession indépendante de celle du chemin de fer.[15]

Leopold reasoned that the concessions for mines and railways would serve as a stepping-stone to territorial control. One man in the king's confidence was Emile Francqui, the Belgian Consul in Hankow who was later to become the greatest Belgian financier of the twentieth century. He, at least, was in no doubt of Leopold's intentions:

---

14. King Leopold to Borchgrave, 28 Nov. 1898; Brussels, Royal Archives, Congo 365.
15. King Leopold to Baron de Vinck, 9 Dec. 1898; Brussels, Royal Archives, series 'Cabinet Léopold II'.

Dans l'esprit du Souverain, la ligne de Peking-Hankow doit servir de base à toute une série d'affaires belges dont la plus importante est la mainmise sur deux provinces (Hupeh et Honan) en obtenant le monopole des concessions minières dans ces deux provinces. Sa Majesté veut se réserver ces deux provinces pour le jour où les Puissances se partageront la Chine.[16]

In the years to follow, China was to usurp the place of the Upper Nile and all other parts of the world in the King's preoccupations and activities.

3. Leopold's methods

All these schemes date from the single year 1898. Even though it was a particularly busy year, it was quite characteristic of the general scope of the king's activities. He had, after all, been looking for opportunities throughout his life. This was not apparent to his contemporaries, though, and it is still partly ignored by historians; the reason is the extreme secrecy which surrounded most of the King's efforts. Here again, 1898 can provide examples.

Although Leopold's Nile policy gave rise to great suspicion, his instructions to the Nile forces to try and reach the Sennaar were never discovered. The Eritrea negotiations, too, were top secret. On the Belgian side, only the king's *chef de cabinet* and the Belgian minister in Rome were in the know. The head of the Congo State administration remained in ignorance; so did secretary of state van Eetvelde, although he was a close collaborator of the king's in African affairs. Similarly, when Leopold was dealing with the Italians the secret was closely guarded. When the Italian negotiator General Dal Verme came to Brussels the Italian Minister there asked his British colleague if he had any idea what the visit was about.[17] The French Minister admitted that he had 'surveillé les faits et les gestes' of Dal Verme, but suspected nothing.[18] Yet again, when the Belgian Minister in Madrid spoke to the Spanish about the possible sale of the Caroline and Mariana Islands, he did so on the king's orders but without the knowledge of the Belgian government. When it came, the German protest took them completely by surprise and the Belgian minister of foreign affairs in turn protested to the king. The

16. Jean Jadot's memo of an interview with Emile Francqui, 4 Jan. 1899; Brussels, Jadot Papers.
17. Plunkett to Salisbury, 1 Aug. 1897; F.O. 10/687.
18. Montholon to Hanotaux, 25 Oct. 1897; Paris, Quai d'Orsay, Correspondance politique Afrique, Ethiopie, 7.

tentative sounding-out over the Canary Islands and Fernando Po
was apparently not suspected by anybody; while as to the king's
ultimate designs in China, it is doubtful if more than five or six people
had any idea of them.

The extraordinary variety of the king's projects was not at all the
result of insane megalomania, however. On the contrary, it was the
direct consequence of a firm and reasoned conviction that one had to
do whatever necessary to reap the maximum profit. 'La richesse et la
prospérité des peuples ne tiennent pas à une seule entreprise, et ne
sauraient venir d'une seule contrée. Il faut travailler partout, ne
négliger aucune chance, aucune veine', he wrote in 1886 (and this at
the time of his worst financial difficulties in the Congo).[19] Or, as he
observed in more homely vein: 'Il faut déposer des oeufs de tous
côtés, en cent endroits différents, il y en a toujours plusieurs qui
finalement viendront à éclore.'[20] Since his earliest days Leopold had
been 'à l'affût' or on the watch for any bargain worth snapping up.
This phrase occurs frequently in his letters; he remained 'à l'affût'
until the day of his death.

The years 1888–94 will furnish a few examples of what Leopold's
watchfulness meant in practical terms. He thought, for instance, of
sending a German explorer to somewhere in Oceania: Je reste à la
recherche d'un voyageur, de préférence Allemand, pour une mission
très délicate en Océanie. Il s'agirait à la fois d'y amener un sultan à
nous céder son état et de ne pass laisser deviner la chose aux Anglais
(23 February 1888).[21]

At the moment when England appeared to recoil at the prospect of
taking responsibility for Uganda, Leopold offered to take it himself. A
lease of Uganda, he wrote obligingly to Gladstone on 29 September
1892, would suit him perfectly . . .[22] Two years later, he made a
discreet inquiry via the Belgian chargé d'affaires in Athens as to
whether 'les Grecs seraient disposés à vendre Corfou pour remettre
leurs finances'.[23] Finally in November 1894 he asked the Portuguese
Government whether they would consider conceding their colony of
Macao to a company.[24]

19. In Jean Stengers, 'Rapport sur les dossiers "Reprise du Congo par la Belgique" et "Dossier
économique" ', *Institut Royal Colonial Belge. Bulletin des Séances*, **24**, 1953, p. 1225.
20. Baron van der Elst, 'Souvenirs sur Léopold II', *Revue Générale*, 15 Mar. 1923, p. 268.
21. Brussels, Musée de la Dynastie, Strauch Papers.
22. British Museum, Add. MSS 44.516 (Gladstone Papers).
23. Count van den Steen de Jehay to King Leopold, 24 Sept. 1894; Brussels, van den Steen de
Jehay Papers.
24. Verhaeghe de Naeyer to King Leopold, 28 Nov. 1894; Brussels, Archives of the Ministry
of Foreign Affairs, Lambermont Papers.

A new colony was what counted, no matter where it was. He urged van Eetvelde in 1897 that they should be ready to 'entreprendre l'une ou l'autre affaire coloniale.' For instance, one could 'reprendre la gestion de la North Borneo Company si celle-ci se décourageait'.[25] And three years later he again stressed to another of his advisers the importance of being 'à l'affût': 'L'intérêt des Belges, c'est d'obtenir là ou l'on peut coloniser des concessions territoriales sans en avoir l'air; nous devrions tâcher de nous renseigner sur tout ce que nous pourrions entreprendre dans cet ordre d'idées'.[26]

Leopold never missed a chance. To understand him it is necessary to take into account his notion of 'opportunity', something which was clearly very important to him. The king was never a gambler in the casino sense, but he was in many respects a political gambler; by taking chances he courted success. In September 1897 he ordered his Nile forces to reach the Sennaar, a thousand kilometres away from where they were, and was respectfully reminded by a high Congo official that this would be extremely difficult. 'Il m'a nettement dit', this official wrote, 'qu'il ne croyait pas au succès, mais qu'il fallait cependant le risquer, que le sort pourrait être très favorable'.[27] On the same subject the king wrote to another official: 'Ne pas faire actuellement des efforts pour être puissant sur le Nil serait s'exposer à manquer des chances. . . . Je préfère de beaucoup des embarras financiers momentanés à l'abandon d'aucune chance. Les uns se réparent et les autres ne se retrouvent jamais'.[28]

This, then, was the rabid imperialism of a man whose policy was to take his chance whenever possible. The question of his motivation remains.

4. Leopold's motives

There is one motive which several of his contemporaries would readily have ascribed to him, and that is personal greed. At least, that is what was openly rumoured towards the end of his life. Leopold's image, in fact, underwent the most extraordinary transformation in his contemporaries' eyes. From being a noble philanthropist he sank to the level of an international pariah.

As a master of political propaganda Leopold did for a long time

25. King Leopold to Van Eetvelde, 9 Aug. 1897; Van Eetvelde Papers, 106.
26. King Leopold to Sam Wiener, 18 Jan. 1900; Brussels, Sam Wiener Papers.
27. Liebrechts to Van Eetvelde, 4 Sept. 1897; Van Eetvelde Papers, 45.
28. King Leopold to Van Eetvelde, 31 Aug. 1897; Van Eetvelde Papers, 33.

succeed in making his African activities look like philanthropy. In 1876 he had founded the Association Internationale Africaine, a truly scientific and independent organisation. This gave him a wonderful aura which he succeeded in keeping for years, long after the ideals of the Association had been abandoned. His explanation of his own aims, and those of his newly founded International Congo Association, at a time when he was actually striving for political control of the Congo, was a masterpiece of subtle ambiguity and deception. 'The International Congo Association', he announced boldly in March 1883, 'as it does not seek to gain money, and does not beg for aid of any State, resembles in a measure, by its organisation, the Society of the Red Cross; it has been formed by means of large voluntary contributions, and with the noble aim of rendering lasting and disinterested services to the cause of progress'.[29] The king's admirers responded wholeheartedly to his propaganda. Jacob Bright wrote in 1883 to a Belgian friend: 'The generosity and public spirit of your King are admirable. It is a rare thing for a person in his position to make such sacrifices for the benefit of humanity'.[30] The American Sanford in May 1884 saluted the king's enterprise in Africa as 'the most beneficient work of the century'.[31] In 1885 Mackinnon spoke of the 'noblest and most self-sacrificing scheme for Africa's development that has ever been or ever will be attempted'.[32]

All this goes to explain why certain eminent Englishmen, Lord Wolseley among them, thought in early 1884 of giving Leopold the nominal sovereignty of the Sudan, with Gordon to serve under him. In this way, the Congo and the Sudan would both have been gathered under the aegis of a single philanthropic organisation.

For the general public as well, the king's image remained for years one of noble altruism. 'When has the world witnessed, in recent years, the devotion of a king to a more kingly task, with truer philanthropy, with so utter a lack of self-interest, with such royal liberality?' asked an American scholar in 1887. 'Such an enterprise is, indeed, enough to make a reign illustrious. It is enough to make an American believe in kings forever'.[33]

Twenty years later, however, after the world had heard the Congo atrocities denounced, the language was quite different. When in 1908

29. *The Times*, 28 Mar. 1883, article 'from a Belgian correspondent'; the article was from the King's pen.
30. Jacob Bright to Emile de Laveleye, 15 Mar. 1883; Brussels, Royal Archives, Congo 1.
31. Brussels, Royal Archives, Congo 98.
32. Bontinck, *Aux origines de l'Etat Indépendant du Congo*, p. 276.
33. William T. Hornaday, *Free Rum on the Congo* (Chicago, 1887), pp. 44–5.

the Belgian Chamber of Deputies discussed the terms of the Congo's annexation, which provided for a financial 'témoignage de gratitude' to the king, the members remained silent when a veteran Liberal statesman thundered: 'Un témoignage de gratitude? Jamais. L'amnistie, peut-être.' Outside Belgium, even amnesty was refused.

So Leopold came to be described as a man driven by insatiable greed. Everyone believed he had made huge personal profits in the Congo. This was certainly Sir Edward Grey's firm conviction when he spoke in 1908 of 'taking the Congo out of the hands of the King'. This could be done, he said, without any indemnity 'for it would leave him still with all the gains he has made by his monstrous system'.[34] Some people, therefore, have tried to explain away Leopold's imperialism as simply a search for personal profit. But this would certainly be wrong in the case of the Congo, as witness Leopold's own admission in 1906, that 'financially speaking I am a poorer man, not a richer, because of the Congo',[35] a statement which nobody believed at the time but which is now proved from documents to have been perfectly true. In point of fact the King Leopold we know from presentday sources is a long way from being what is generally considered as greedy. He undoubtedly did not despise the benefits of wealth (his generosity to his mistress at the end of his life is only a single instance); but when he used money as a political instrument he usually did it for his country rather than for himself. He did make money out of the Congo, but he used it almost exclusively to enrich the Belgian national heritage by acquiring property, building monuments and developing towns. His own fortune did not obsess him; Belgium's wealth and greatness did.

Nearly every time Leopold spoke intimately about his imperialism he did so in a fervently patriotic way. There is no reason to doubt the sincerity of ardent references to his 'patrie passionnément aimée'. There is every reason to believe—as all who knew him best did believe—that they are the key to the special form of imperialism of a king serving his country. This must be carefully qualified, however. Patriotic imperialism is often more or less synonymous with painting the map red. Leopold's 'enormous voracity' might seem to indicate this interpretation, but it would be no more accurate than the hypothesis of personal greed. The colour of the map was a matter of complete indifference to the king; if one of the numerous territories he tried to lease had remained under its nominal local sovereign it

34. G. M. Trevelyan, *Grey of Fallodon* (London, Longmans, 1937), p. 200.
35. Interview of King Leopold, published in the *New York American* of 10 Dec. 1906.

would not have worried him. What he was after was not political grandeur but economic advantage. Belgium, having gained its political independence in 1830, had to be economically 'completed' by overseas possessions. This, and nothing else, was Leopold's mission.

A third interpretation which has to be completely dismissed is that his patriotic imperialism was a direct response to his country's wishes and aspirations. At the time when he began his colonial activities the Belgian Government, the upper classes and opinion in general were united in thinking that overseas ventures would be both burdensome and dangerous for the country. It is impossible to point to any group or even to a single influential individual who would have thought otherwise and encouraged the king. 'Le gouvernement ni les Chambres ne veulent de colonies, on leur offrirait demain les Philippines gratis qu'elles seraient refusées', wrote Leopold in 1873.[36] The feelings of the Belgian public, said one of his advisers a year later, 'sont encore si confuses qu'il regarderait aujourd'hui l'acquisition d'une possession coloniale comme un malheur'.[37] Such attitudes explain why the king had to act alone. At first he had hoped to induce the country as a whole to think colonially, but when he found the task impossible he took colonial action himself. As the years passed, he did succeed in rallying the support of an increasing number of his countrymen, especially for his work in the Congo; and in some cases this support even became tinged with enthusiasm. But support and enthusiasm always came *after* the king had taken the initiative. In none of his many ventures throughout the world is there any sign that he was ever given the least encouragement or inspiration.

The mainspring of imperialism in this case was entirely the obstinacy of a single man. His contemporaries' economic doctrines certainly provided him with no incentive; his first push for colonies came at a time when practically all economies were hostile to them. Even when later economic thinking by men like Leroy-Beaulieu turned out to be favourable to colonialism, it certainly pleased the king, but did not particularly impress him. The argument in favour of colonies among economists of the new school—and still more among those who took their cue from them—consisted of stressing the overriding importance of colonial markets. To the king, however, the question of markets was not a prominent one. He spoke of them from time to

36. Léopold Greindl, *A la recherche d'un Etat Indépendant: Léopold II et les Philippines, 1869–1875* (Brussels, 1962), p. 266.
37. A. Roeykens, *Le Dessein africain de Léopold II* (Brussels, 1956), p. 24.

time, and even with eloquence; but this was more to conform to his audience's views. He himself was concerned with something he thought much more vital than markets: the spoils of efficient exploitation.

Throughout his life the core of his imperialism was the belief that the outside world offered golden opportunities to Europe. He was particularly sanguine about the prospects of a colony, or domain as he sometimes called it. This belief in the great advantages of colonial exploitation did not derive from any economic theory; it seemed rather to be a theory of his own which he had formed when young and never seen fit to revise. One example, above all, had made an impression on him and helped to shape all his thinking, and that was the Dutch colonial empire. In his youth Leopold was a passionate admirer of the Dutch colonial system which, as it was functioning in the middle of the nineteenth century, produced huge profits for the Dutch treasury from the East Indies and especially from Java. Some of the Spanish overseas territories seem also to have been similarly profitable, although the exact figures were not so clear. In any case, Leopold got the idea that the well-planned exploitation of an overseas possession could directly enrich the colonial power, and this idea never left him.

The king's early letters and notes dating from 1860–65 clearly show the genesis of this concept. With youthful exuberance they display a mass of arguments in favour of colonies. Colonies would offer new careers to the citizens of the motherland.

> L'armée des Indes néerlandaises, la marine des Indes, l'administration des Indes [sont] trois immenses carrières ouvertes à l'activité de la jeunesse néerlandaise. [They were also a source of personal fortunes which would benefit the parent country.] Dans l'Inde, toutes les familles anglaises ont un ou deux de leurs enfants qui y vivent, y cherchent et y font fortune. Ces fortunes se rapportent à Londres et cette capitale, semblable à une ruche d'abeilles où ces insectes, après avoir sucé les meilleurs fleurs, viennent déposer leur miel, est une des plus riches villes du monde.

In colonies one could invest capital at a much higher rate than in Europe ('Dans l'Inde, le capital anglais se place à 20, 30 et 40 pour cent'); they were also good markets for the parent country's products (l'Angleterre a avec l'Inde un commerce immense, elle règle les douanes de ce vaste empire qui constitue un débouché sans pareil pour tous ses fabricants'), and hence would stimulate its commercial activities ('Que ne deviendrait pas Anvers, ville de commerce et port de guerre, si nous avions une province en Chine?'). Leopold does not overlook a single argument in favour of colonies, but above all there is the most striking and decisive one: colonies can provide a huge revenue. The Dutch East Indies are quoted again and again for 'l'immense revenu que ces îles donnent à la mère-patrie'.[38]

A few months before he came to the throne in 1865 Leopold produced a 'Note sur l'utilité et l'importance pour les Etats de posséder des domaines et provinces en dehors de leurs frontières européennes'. We are proud of our national possessions, he says, and cites the railways which are largely State owned and which were lucrative. But what about colonies?

> Si l'on étudie les budgets des divers états, on constatera que Java, les Philippines, Cuba sont les plus riches domaines nationaux qui existent et que leur rendement annuel au profit de la Hollande et de l'Espagne dépasse de beaucoup celui de notre chemin de fer.
>
> La Hollande et l'Espagne, après avoir fait payer par leurs possessions extérieures tous les frais de la conquête et de son maintien, se procurent encore là-bas des ressources indépendantes de l'impôt levé en Europe.
>
> Si la Belgique, qui a déjà son railway, pouvait y ajouter quelque nouveau Java, on pourrait espérer la réduction de l'impôt du sel, la suppression des douanes, etc., etc., tout cela sans amener la moindre diminution de nos ressources ou de nos dépenses actuelles.
>
> Les douanes tomberont le jour où des revenus transatlantiques viendront fournir à la mère patrie une dotation égale au produit des droits de douane.
>
> Java donne annuellement 75 millions de francs, les Philippines et Cuba peut-être de 15 à 20 millions.[39]

If they were well managed, colonies were a good thing from a financial as well as from an economic point of view. This was a conviction of Leopold's which nothing could shake. For this reason he never stopped looking for them wherever he might be successful, and when he did find one he tried to make it as large as possible. Hence even when his Congo State appeared to be on the verge of collapse he never lost faith. Foreign observers analysing the Congo's gloomy prospects after 1885 were amazed by the king's 'robust faith in the future of the country'. It was his unshakeable belief in colonialism:

38. Léon Le Febve de Vivy, *Documents d'histoire précoloniale belge, 1861–1865. Les idées coloniales de Léopold, duc de Brabant* (Brussels, 1955), pp. 18–24.
39. *Ibid.*, pp. 30–6.

being a colony, the Congo must in time inevitably produce good results.

5. Leopold's patriotic vision

But Leopold's faith would never have led to action had it not been combined with extraordinary dynamism and, even more importantly, unusual imagination. As he believed in colonies, so he dreamed of them; and his dreams at the age of fifty-seven were every bit as grandiose as they had been at twenty-four.

He was twenty-four in November 1859 when he wrote to a Belgian minister about China, where he hoped to send Belgian troops to accompany the Franco-British expedition. He sketched his plans as follows:

> On prétend que la Chine proprement dite n'offrira que peu de chances de satisfaction à l'avidité européenne. C'est tout autour de la Chine, dans l'Archipel Indien, dans l'Amérique centrale, vers Guatemala, que se trouvent les îles ou territoires que nous devons chercher à posséder. Cette prétendue pauvreté du Céleste Empire n'est pas une objection, la Chine sera il est vrai notre première étape, le but avoué de nos efforts, la raison de nous faire transporter par une grande puissance, mais qui nous empêcherait, la besogne faite et dans le cas où les avantages récoltés ne seraient pas assez considérables, de nous lancer de suite à la poursuite d'un meilleur lot? Si nous parvenons à envoyer 4.500 Belges à Pékin, il faudrait être bien maladroit pour ne pas profiter d'un tel pivôt stratégique, et avec l'aide de nos alliés ne pas rayonner fructueusement dans toutes les directions.[40]

The same global ambitiousness appears in 1892 when Leopold, then fifty-seven, remarked during a conversation:

> Pour moi, je voudrais faire de notre petite Belgique avec ses six millions d'habitants la capitale d'un immense empire; et cette pensée, il y a moyen de la réaliser. Nous avons le Congo; la Chine en est à la période de décomposition; les Pays-Bas, l'Espagne, le Portugal sont en décadence; leurs colonies seront un jour au plus offrant . . .[41]

Leopold's imagination offered permanent nourishment to his energy. But such an imagination was not always a help; more than once it led him to dream up the most unlikely schemes. As long as the king relied on the sound advice of those around him his wilder notions

40. Brussels, Musée Royal de l'Armée, Chazal Papers.
41. A. Roeykens, *Le Baron Léon de Béthune au service de Léopold II* (Brussels, 1964), p. 56.

could be kept under some sort of control. But at the end of his life, when he had shaken off most of his old advisers and had become almost entirely wilful, he occasionally staggered those who heard his latest plans. In 1896, for instance, in the presence of a polite but bewildered Lord Salisbury, he outlined a scheme by which, under a lease from the Khedive—in fact, of course, from Britain—he would acquire that part of the Nile valley still in the hands of the Mahdists. Salisbury later wrote:

> He dwelt with great fervour on their [the Mahdists'] excellent military qualities and on the profit we could draw from them if we had them in our service. This result was to be brought about by our lessee (himself) and he seemed to recognise no difficulty in the task he was undertaking. When he had subdued them, and made them pliant instruments of England's will, they would be at our disposal for any work we wanted done. . . . We could use them for the purpose of invading and occupying Armenia, and so putting a stop to the massacres which were moving Europe so deeply.[42]

The 'idea of an English General at the head of an army of Dervishes marching from Khartoum to Lake Van in order to prevent Moham-medans from maltreating Christians' struck Salisbury as really very 'quaint'. It also elicited from Queen Victoria, as she read his report, some sorrowful comments: 'The Queen really thinks her good cousin King Leopold must have wished good-bye to his reason in speaking . . . in such an extraordinary way. . . . He is clever and the Queen is really quite distressed at his suggesting such things.' His parentage, she went on, would not have made one suppose such queerness. 'His Father, the Queen's beloved Uncle, was one of the wisest and most prudent of men, and his mother was very clever and an angel of goodness. His brother the Count of Flanders is quite different, very nimble, clever and prudent—but unfortunately stonedeaf.'[43]

Contrary to Victoria's interpretation Leopold had not 'wished good-bye to his reason'; his intelligence was as alert as ever but his imagination was no longer being restrained.

The following year, in another flight of fancy at the height of the Cretan crisis, Leopold came up with a plan by which the island would be given a German governor who would then call in Congolese

42. *The Letters of Queen Victoria*, 3rd series, vol. iii, ed. by G. E. Buckle (London, Murray, 1932), pp. 24–5.
43. Oxford, Salisbury Papers.

troops to establish law and order. By using Congolese forces the king hoped to earn good money, and he put forward this suggestion both in St Petersburg and Berlin.

But whatever his schemes, Leopold never stopped thinking of Belgium. In whatever part of the world he was engaged, he worked for Belgium. His efforts had to benefit his country so, inevitably, they would; and that was all there was to it. His heart was never in the Congo (he never wanted to visit it), nor was it in China; it was firmly in Belgium. At a period when he was trying to do as much as possible in Africa he wrote to one of his best men: 'Voyez comment nous pourrions faire et encore en ce 19e siècle de Bruxelles la vraie capitale de l'Afrique centrale' (3 January, 1891).[44] The eternal flame at Leopold's core was patriotism.

6. Leopold's patterns of action

Taken as a whole, Leopold's imperialistic ideas and efforts ranged from the Canary Islands and Africa to the Pacific. Even the European approaches received his attention, as in the case of Corfu. But Leopold could not adopt identical methods uniformly over this huge area; he had to adapt them to suit circumstances. Outside Black Africa, however, his work could be said to have followed two main patterns. The first may be called the 'Java pattern' and the second the 'Egypt pattern'.

The Java pattern was the king's favourite. It meant establishing control over a territory where the native population would be methodically set to productive work so as to reward its European masters by financial and economic benefits. It meant, in short, obtaining a profitable colony.

Within this general pattern various formulas could be adopted. One was the use of military force. Leopold conceived this at a time when he still hoped he could push Belgium itself into action and could therefore use the Belgian military. His plan around 1860–65 was to compel China by force to cede one of her provinces; in particular, his hopes centred on Formosa. Another formula was that of peaceful occupation, which he thought suitable for the Pacific Islands. A third approach consisted in trying to buy or lease from a colonial power one of its existing possessions. With this in mind Leopold contacted or negotiated with Spain, Portugal and Holland, although it was really in the Philippines that he hoped for success.

44. Tervuren, Musée de l'Afrique Centrale, Thys Papers.

Trying to find another Java occupied Leopold from the outset. He subjected the Far East and the Pacific Islands to particularly close scrutiny. The island of Borneo illustrates particularly well the scope and obstinacy of his efforts. For Leopold, the most promising part of Borneo was naturally Sarawak, which was in the hands of the famous 'White Rajah', Rajah Brooke. Brooke might perhaps be induced to sell, so in the summer of 1861 Leopold made overtures to him. Negotiations continued in strict secrecy following the return of the Rajah to England at the end of the year. Certain sums were even discussed; Sir James Brooke remained hesitant. But at the end of 1862 his nephew, who was in charge of the Sarawak Government in his absence, sent a definite 'no'—much to his uncle's annoyance. This ended the negotiations but not Leopold's hopes. As late as 1874 he wrote to one of his associates: 'Si nous nous entendions un jour avec Sarawak, il faudra lever quelques hommes pour nous y défendre et nous y étendre. . . . Nous y étendre.'[45] The Rajah's possessions looked pretty small to the king.

Another part of the island which tempted him—the largest part— was under Dutch sovereignty. In February 1862 Leopold sounded out the Dutch minister in Brussels about the possibility of Holland ceding part of her Borneo possessions to Belgium. When this produced no reply and he deduced that the idea of a formal cession was unacceptable, Leopold tried another way. Shortly after he came to the throne he made fresh overtures through England. At Leopold's request Lord Clarendon communicated to the Hague the King of the Belgians' 'extreme desire that the relations between Belgium and Holland should not only be friendly but cordial'.[46] 'His great wish is that the two countries should be bound together by commercial ties and that in some way or other the capital of Belgium should be utilised in the Dutch colonies.' Leopold also suggested the founding of a 'Dutch–Belgian company for the further exploration and cultivation' of part of the Dutch possessions; at the top of the list in April 1866 came Borneo. The Dutch reactions were icy. The Minister of Foreign Affairs told the British Minister in the Hague 'that he did not see how the suggestion about the exploration and cultivation of the Island of Borneo by a Dutch–Belgian Company could be carried out'.[47] Matters went no further, but the appeal to England to intercede shows how much the project meant to Leopold.

45. Greindl, *A la recherche d'un Etat Indépendant,* p. 330.
46. Oxford, Bodleian Library, Clarendon Papers.
47. *Ibid.*

A third possibility in Borneo was to establish a brand new colony, and Leopold toyed with this idea in 1876. In a note to Queen Victoria dated June that year he wrote:

> Borneo est une si grande île qu'à côté des Hollandais il y a place pour d'autres nations. En s'inspirant de l'exemple de Sir James Brooke, on pourrait créer un établissement près de Sarawak. Il paraît que le Rajah de Sarawak serait disposé à favoriser un pareil plan qui est tout dans son intérêt puisqu'il aurait ainsi près de lui un voisin civilisé et ami.[48]

Before he started, the king wanted to know whether there would be any objection to the plan by the British Government. Owing to a misunderstanding there seemed at first as if there might be, causing the Queen to express herself in what should rank as a memorable dictum: 'The Queen must say she cannot think it right that we always object to any other nation but ourselves having colonies.'[49] However, after considering the matter the Colonial Secretary could see no reason why Britain should object. He nevertheless wished to warn the king. 'Lord Caernarvon thought it right to add', the Queen's Secretary wrote to Brussels,

> that he would suggest to the King to consider this question very carefully before embarking on what appears to him a most hazardous venture. . . . The experience of Labuan is not encouraging, the colony there has had a miserable and precarious existence even with all the help that our Eastern Trade and our Colonial system could afford. A climate in which Europeans cannot work, wars with savage tribes, an enormous expenditure and political complications are all against the success of an undertaking which might prove to be but a bottomless quicksand for men and money.[50]

This warning must have cooled the king considerably, and he dropped the project. The area of Borneo he had had in mind was shortly afterwards taken into the control of the North Borneo Company. As already mentioned, however, even as late as 1897 Leopold had ideas of taking over that Company's possessions.

This brief mention of the plans Leopold had for only one part of the Far East show the nature of his efforts: they were often tentative, but he repeated them over and over again.

The other shape Leopold's activities took, the so-called 'Egypt

---

48. Windsor, Royal Archives. By courtesy of Her Majesty the Queen.
49. *Ibid.*
50. *Ibid.*

pattern', was of a different kind. It was a kind of imperialism applied to countries where the existing political power could not—at least, in the short term—be dislodged. In these cases the idea was to extract assorted privileges, grants and concessions from that power. The first place where Leopold tried this system was Egypt hence the name. It was in 1855, when Leopold was not yet twenty. The following extracts from his letters will speak for themselves:

> *27 January 1855, from Trieste* [Leopold was leaving for Egypt, where he would meet Said Pacha]: Il y aura peut-être moyen d'extorquer de ce Prince des avantages commerciaux. Il est bien disposé pour les Européens, vient d'abolir l'esclavage, a accordé à une compagnie française la concession du canal de Suez ... Pour profiter de ces tendances il faut que je sois armé en conséquence et puisse m'emparer de ses bonnes grâces par le côté faible. Je suis le premier Prince qu'il reçoit. Je crois qu'il se mettra en quatre pour me plaire.

> *3 February 1855, from Alexandria:* Il y a des affaires d'or à conclure ici ... J'espère pouvoir arranger les choses de manière que mon voyage profite non seulement à ma santé mais aussi à mon pays.

> *15 March 1855, from Cairo:* Il y a beaucoup de terrains vagues en Egypte. Le Vice-Roi n'est pas éloigné de les faire coloniser. Je tiendrai surtout à obtenir pour une société belge le dessèchement des trois lacs Mareotis, Bourlos et Manzaleh. J'ai offert à Saïd Pacha de m'en charger.... L'Egypte est une mine d'or, mais pour l'exploiter il ne faut pas s'épargner de peine. L'affaire des lacs serait d'un rapport annuel d'au moins 5 millions de francs.

> *20 March 1855:* J'ai revu le Vice-Roi. . . . J'ai parlé de m'affermer des terrains vagues qu'il suffit d'arroser pour pouvoir cultiver. L'hectare rapporterait de 5 à 6 livres sterling. Il y en a plusieurs centaines de mille. Son Altesse a promis d'examiner la chose . . . J'ai vu M. de Lesseps. C'est une canaille [Leopold was to become later a great admirer and friend of de Lesseps.] Je pense que lui usé, nous parviendrons à obtenir sa succession. [And by way of conclusion to the same letter:] Ne perdons pas une minute, pas la plus petite occasion de nous developper.[51]

After Egypt many other countries gave Leopold the opportunity of acting in similar vein during the following fifty years. Among these were Morocco, Ethiopia, China and various countries in Asia Minor. On such occasions the king's vocabulary, although becoming a little

51. E. Vandewoude, 'Brieven van de Hertog van Brabant aan Conway in verband met Egypte, 1855', *Académie Royale des Sciences d'Outre-Mer. Bulletin*, 1964, p. 872–6.

less flamboyant as time passed, remained strikingly consistent; so did his schemes. The 1855 sentence, 'Il y a des affaires d'or à conclure ici', is for instance echoed in 1899 in some lines about China: 'Il y a intérêt national à ce que les Belges tirent parti des plus belles affaires de Chine. . . . La ligne Pékin-Hankow, si on pouvait y ajouter Hankow–Canton, serait la colonne vertébrale de tout le mouvement intérieur commercial et industriel de la Chine, l'affaire la plus importante et la plus productive du monde.'[52]

Two things must be said about the 'Egypt pattern'. First, if it were successful it would necessarily lead to a commercial or industrial concession, or at least to a concession with lucrative possibilities. But as the king could not himself engage in commerce or industry he would be personally unable to accept such a concession and it would have to be given to a company. The companies Leopold tried to establish were by no means always purely Belgian; in this respect the king was not narrowly nationalistic. In fact he rather favoured the association of Belgian with foreign capital because, he considered, such an arrangement was often a guarantee of strength and success, the only requirement was that such companies had to be of use to Belgium. On the other hand the king did not inevitably invest his own money in his ventures; when he did so there is every indication that his main concern was with helping the companies he wished to promote rather than with making money. 'Vous savez que mon devoir et mon métier m'obligent à chercher activement à servir sans cesse les intérêts belges', he wrote in 1899.[53] He cared much more for that 'métier' than for money.

Secondly, whatever he undertook by employing the 'Egypt pattern', Leopold never lost sight of the 'Java pattern', which he regarded as ideal. While promoting several enterprises in China at the end of the nineteenth century, he never stopped thinking about the possible partition of the country. Railways and mines would eventually lead to provinces, which were much more to the point. As early as 1860–65 Leopold had aspired to a Chinese province; it was still his goal thirty-five years later.

One question remains. When the king turned his gaze on Central Africa in 1875–76, having hitherto devoted most of his energies to the Far East, which of his patterns did he decide to adopt? The simple and amazing answer is: neither. For Leopold had no model for the exploitation of such vast, mostly unknown, regions which he was

52. King Leopold to Borchgrave, 14 Feb. 1899; Brussels, Royal Archives, Congo 340.
53. King Leopold to Thys, 28 May 1899; Thys Papers.

unable to conquer by force because he had no forces at his disposal. But what he lacked in plans he made up for in resolve, being at all costs determined to have a slice of whatever was going—or, as he put it in 1877, 'nous procurer une part de ce magnifique gâteau africain'. The question was, how? Having no precise solution to a problem which was quite new to him, he kept switching from one plan to another. The story of his first years in Africa is one of constant evolution.

He first thought of establishing a group of trading stations somewhere in Africa, possibly in the Cameroons, to monopolise the commerce of the more promising regions. Then, as he sent Stanley to the Congo, he had a vision of an enormous trading company whose activities would stretch from one ocean to the other by means of an uninterrupted chain of stations stretching from the mouth of the Congo to Zanzibar. Later, he realised that such trading stations ran the risk of being captured by foreign powers like France, so for the time being he abandoned all his efforts at commerce and opted instead for the political formula of 'free stations'—sovereign stations dotted around Central Africa. Subsequently, in order to provide some defence against foreign attack, he tried to extend the sovereignty of these stations to include the local chiefs and tribes. The easy success of this policy, which was simply that of treaty-making, not only gave him 'free stations', but also 'free territories'. Finally, noticing that these 'free territories' (which he chose, after a while, to call 'free states') sometimes became oddly contiguous as they grew larger, he felt that the idea of a single state would be a lot easier to grasp, and the Congo Free State was born.

It was largely a story of trial and error. As long as he was aiming at a commercial company, Leopold concentrated on acquiring commercial privileges and monopolies. Once he had opted for a political formula, he also opted—and this was a total change of policy—for a regime of free trade which would be of maximum popularity with all foreign countries. From being at first the prospective founder of a big privileged commercial concern he finally turned into that of an 'Etat sans douanes'.

7. The results of Leopold's imperialism

Having examined the king's efforts, it is time to draw up some sort of a balance-sheet to see what they achieved.

Where he adopted the 'Java pattern' technique, all Leopold's exertions came to nothing despite being many, varied and persistent. He failed to induce Belgium to conquer any overseas territory at all, and when he turned his ideas from conquest to lease or purchase he never found a foreign country willing to let or sell. Here the verdict must be one of total failure.

The 'Egypt pattern', on the other hand, gave some results although they were hardly commensurate with his efforts. The best results were those he obtained in China at the turn of the century. By and large, though, one could describe Leopold as having been only half successful in this ploy.

In fact, the king was only fully rewarded on the occasion when he improvised: in the Congo. This is not hard to explain. By trying to gain a colony or a concession, Leopold was joining in a game where there were many other players who knew the rules: winning was very hard indeed with such stiff competition. In the Congo, however, he practically invented a new game. In his 'state without customs' he was offering the world something unique and unheard-of. The state he was establishing in the centre of Africa, he promised, would not levy any import duties: it would be open to the commerce of the whole world as a paradise of free trade. It was this wonderful promise which alone won him recognition for his state.

It should cause little surprise that he was the only person to be making such a promise; it was, in fact, an extraordinarily foolish scheme. At the time, all the economists considered that during the first phase of a newly opened country's existence its most lucrative resources were in its import duties, and the economists were right. Depriving the Congo State of all import duties meant depriving it of an essential source of revenue. Leopold's position only seemed less bizarre to his contemporaries because they attributed it mainly to philanthropy (proving yet again how important his reputation of an altruist was); they were convinced he was ready to go to enormous expense for the sake of civilisation and free trade in Central Africa. But those who knew the king better and were aware that he had not the slightest intention of squandering his fortune for philanthropic purposes gloomily considered that he was heading for ruin. Certainly that was the opinion of several intelligent Belgian statesmen. The Congo State, they pointed out, had been called to life but had deprived itself of its livelihood. They feared the worst for the future.

They, too, were right. From a logical point of view, once the king had stopped pouring his money into the Congo State (and his purse was not bottomless), it was doomed. At first it seemed as though logic would prevail, for the financial difficulties of the state seemed insuperable and its downfall appeared imminent.

On the verge of collapse, it was saved by two things—the king's ingenuity and sheer luck. By what his honest advisers considered as a breach of faith, but by what he himself regarded as a smart piece of legal reasoning, Leopold succeeded after some years in almost completely evading the strict legal commitments he had undertaken when founding the state. Instead of free trade, he introduced what really amounted to a system of state monopolies. Most of the wild rubber and ivory of the Congo were decreed to be products of the state's domain and were to be collected by the state alone. Since there was little else to trade in, this, as some critics remarked, was tantamount to saying that commerce was absolutely free except that there was nothing to buy or sell.

At about this time fate also took a hand by revealing a source of wealth which nobody had so far suspected. It just happened to be the one thing over which the State had asserted its almost exclusive rights: wild rubber. When this was discovered, production soared within a very short period. In 1890 the Congo exported a mere hundred metric tons of rubber; in 1901 exports reached 6,000 metric tons. This meant salvation and then prosperity.

By all logic, Leopold should have lost in the Congo. He took his chances and won. It was a gambler's success.

8. Conclusion

Leopold's imperialism was economic imperialism in its purest form— the pursuit of profit. Yet it does not fit into any of the existing economic theories of imperialism. All these theories are based on the needs of, and trends within, industrial societies from whose economic situation imperialism itself is said to have sprung. Leopold's imperialism was a product solely of his own beliefs; it reflected nothing other than his own mind. It might of course be objected that the passage from industrial capitalism to imperialism, as described in the economic theories of imperialism, is a phenomenon which can influence individuals as well as societies and shape the psychology of a man. But it certainly did not shape Leopold's. His ideas and ideals were those of profit in its most old-fashioned form. 'Le monde a été déjà fortement pillé', he wrote in 1865, but there were still good prospects for fruitful exploitation.[54] He would have said the same thing just before

54. de Vivy, *Documents d'histoire précoloniale*, pp. 33–4.

his death. This has little to do with industrial capitalism.

If Leopold's own imperialism is to be looked on as an exception to the rule, then, considering the Congo's place in the history of imperialism, it is no small one.

DISCUSSION

Leopold's imperialism—and economic theories of imperialism. A number of questions were asked concerning Stengers' assertion that King Leopold's imperialism does not fit into 'any of the existing economic theories of imperialism'. The point was made that Belgium itself could not be considered an exception to the Marxist theory which stresses the importance of commercial expansion and the export of capital by mature capitalist countries; nor was the role of the Congo different from that of any of the other African colonies in their relations with European capitalism at the end of the nineteenth century. Others doubted whether it was right to try to separate the policies of the king of a capitalist country from the policies of that country itself. Others again put forward the view that Stengers' assertion about Leopold's imperialism not fitting with existing theories was based on the false assumption that the king himself could be equated with a part of the capitalist system. No one man can behave 'like a model of world capitalism'. Finally, it was argued that you could not ask for a theory which would explain the actions of every individual imperialist.

In his reply Stengers was concerned to stress the fact that Leopold was always forced to act on his own and that Belgian capitalists were singularly unimpressed by his various schemes. As an example he cited the case of Belgium's leading financial institution, the Société Générale, which could not be persuaded to support his activities in any part of the world. 'Leopold was the king of a capitalist country, yes. But the main capitalist enterprise remained indifferent to his efforts.' As for theory in his opinion, it must offer a general explanation of all phenomena connected with imperialism.

The importance of the context. Much the same kind of question was asked with reference to the world context in which Leopold had to operate. Was it not true that all his efforts to obtain overseas possessions only made sense in terms of a general context of world capitalist expansion? Would he have been able to act at all if it had not been for a situation in which some, at least, of his 'weird' ideas were taken seriously? Stengers agreed that the king had only been able to gain entry into the Congo because he was hailed by all European capitalists as a champion of free trade. But this was not the same as to say that Leopold went into Africa specifically in order to benefit from such a policy. What he (Stengers) was trying to do was to draw attention to the fact that Leopold's 'inspiration' did not come from the economic reasons which are suggested by the economic theories of imperialism.

The question of context also involved a number of interventions about Leopold's supposed internationalism and humanitarianism. For example, did not his success in the Congo depend largely on the fact that he was able to make good use of the fact that many Europeans were beginning to think in terms of international cooperation rather than national rivalry? Stengers' view was that this was true in part. But it also had to be remembered that Leopold often suffered from the fact that he was more internationally-minded than many of those who worked for him. As for his humanitarianism it is clear that he was able to use his reputation as a 'humane' man in order to get support for his plan to establish a chain of stations across the Congo.

Leopold's motives for expansion. The problem of ascertaining Leopold's real motives was frequently referred to. Did he know nothing at all about the economic wealth of the Congo before he decided to try to establish a state there? Was he not concerned, at least in part, to promote a form of 'social imperialism' designed to cope with the splits caused in Belgian society by industrialisation? Was there not a contradiction between Stengers' assertion that Leopold was seeking grandeur for Belgium and the fact that he was said not to mind who owned a particular territory provided he himself was allowed to operate there? In reply Stengers said that Leopold's sole source of information about the Congo was the explorer, Stanley, who had noted the lush vegetation on each side of the Congo river, that he had only argued in favour of 'social imperialism' in his youth at a time when he still believed (wrongly) that the Belgian state might be persuaded to take some colonies of its own, and that his main purpose, at all times, was to provide money for the Belgian people regardless of whether or not he was able to push them into obtaining overseas possessions for themselves. It was profit he was after, pure and simple. And he was willing to get it anywhere.

Leopold: king or capitalist? In answer to a question about Leopold's conception of his role as a king, Stengers made the point that he was quite content to act as a constitutional monarch in Belgium itself. Moreover, it was not true, as some have asserted, that he used the Congo as a kind of 'safety-valve', a place where he could exercise his authority outside parliamentary control. In Africa and elsewhere he considered himself less of a king than a kind of capitalist/promoter, even though he was not particularly concerned with his own personal profit. Belgium always came first.

XII

French expansion in Africa: the mythical theory

A. S. Kanya-Forstner

Historians of imperialism often profess to be puzzled by the fact that the European powers pursued expansionist policies in Africa and elsewhere when there seemed to be little hope of any real economic or strategic gain. Kanya-Forstner provides two examples of such policies, the creation of a French empire in the western Sudan and the attempt to push this empire eastwards towards the Nile. In each case, in his words, the drive for new territory was based on an 'illusion', on the pursuit of 'hopelessly unrealistic objectives'.

The question then becomes—how was it possible for France's African policy to be influenced so decisively by myths and illusions? Here the answer is found mainly in the way in which decisions were made by officials in Paris; in the shared assumptions of the policy-makers, in the activities of pressure groups and in the general lack of coordination and control exercised by the politicians. In addition, some weight is given to the role of the men used to execute these policies, notably the members of the French colonial army who had interests of their own which were often very different from those of their political masters.

General theories of imperialism are concerned with the broad processes of European expansion; they may illuminate underlying trends, but they cannot fully account for the expansionist activities of any one European power over a limited period of time. The case of French expansion in Africa during the last two decades of the nineteenth century bears out this obvious point. Industrial and technological developments, it is true, determined the scale of empire-building, and changes in the European balance of power undoubtedly provided an incentive for the French to regain overseas the status and prestige which they had lost on the Continent. But these factors were the conditions rather than the positive causes of imperialism. French traders and investors, for example, showed little interest in African empire; most of their needs could be satisfied in Europe itself.[1] And if the disasters of the Franco-Prussian war contributed to the colonialist revival after 1870, they also reinforced preoccupations with continental security which militated against the diversion of resources to African expansion. Nor does any general theory take into account the most striking feature of the French experience in Africa: the enormous disparity between the hopelessly unrealistic objectives of French policy-makers and the actual results of their policies.

1. The myth of the Western Sudan

The apparent absurdities of French African policy are relatively easy to demonstrate. By any rational calculation of power, profit or even prestige, French energies should have been concentrated north of the Sahara. The security of Algeria and the western Mediterranean necessitated the establishment and maintenance of French influence in the whole of the Maghreb. The balance of power in the eastern Mediterranean and the security of communications with a growing empire east of Suez made it equally important to maintain influence in Egypt. North Africa and the Levant were also traditional areas of economic, cultural and technological penetration. France protected the Holy Places in Palestine; French *savants* had begun the nineteenth-century intellectual revival in Egypt; French engineers had built the Suez Canal, and French investors helped to satisfy the voracious appetites of modernising Egyptian Khedives and profligate Tunisian Beys. The interests at stake in West Africa were negligible by comparison, and there seemed no reason why scattered French possessions there should ever be expanded into a vast territorial empire.

Yet for most of the period French policies did not reflect these priorities. The occupation of Tunisia was not followed by an attempt to establish paramountcy over Morocco, the next logical area of French expansion. Semi-official efforts to replace the Sultan with a pro-French rival were brought to a sudden end in 1884, and for the next fifteen years successive French governments committed themselves to the maintenance of Moroccan independence and territorial

1. See H. Brunschwig, *Mythes et réalités de l'impérialisme colonial français* (Paris, 1960), pp. 84–101; H. Feis, *Europe, the World's Banker* (New Haven, Yale Univ. Press, 1930), pp. 49–57.

integrity. There were of course good reasons for such prudence. By 1881 Tunisia, as Bismarck had already pointed out, was a pear ripe for the plucking. Its corrupt Mamluk oligarchy had squandered its resources and amassed an impossible burden of debt. Beylikal authority had been sapped; the administration was breaking down, and European intervention was generally recognised as inevitable. France, the most influential European power in the Regency since the 1850s, was the obvious candidate. She could rely on the wholehearted support of Germany and the more grudging approval of Great Britain. Only the opposition of Italy and Turkey had to be reckoned with, and they were minor actors on the diplomatic stage. Morocco was a different matter. Its energetic Sultan, Mulay Hassan, withstood the temptations of rapid economic development and concentrated on the humbler task of strengthening central government. His cautious reforms had the full support of Britain, the Sultanate's major trading partner, principal adviser and chief defence against the ambitions of other European powers. Given the atmosphere of tension created by the British occupation of Egypt, France could not lightly risk another serious confrontation in North Africa. But the decline of French interest in the Maghreb also reflected a more fundamental change in her African priorities. By 1880 her attention had already begun to shift to West Africa as she embarked upon the creation of an empire in the Sudanese interior.[2] The unlimited economic potential of such an empire was the first of the myths on which French African policy in the late nineteenth century was based.

The myth itself was not new. Legends of Sudanese wealth had influenced French thinking ever since the occupation of Saint-Louis in the seventeenth century. By the 1850s the creation of a commercial empire, pivoted on Timbuktu and embracing both Algeria and Senegal, was a recognised if vague objective of policy. By the 1870s, largely through the initiative of the local authorities, a Senegalese base for the advance to the Niger had been prepared. But mid-century policy-makers had thought only of extending trade and influence. In 1879–80 these old notions of informal empire were discarded in favour of a more positive imperialism. The government now accepted the financial burden of expansion and the establishment

2. For French policies towards Tunisia and the diplomatic background to the protectorate, see J. Ganiage, *Les origines du protectorat français en Tunisie (1861–1881)* (Paris, 1959). The fullest account of Morocco's relations with Europe in the nineteenth century is J.-L. Miège, *Le Maroc et l'Europe (1830–1894)*, 4 vols (Paris, 1961–63): for French policies after 1885, see especially, IV, 233–55.

of political control as the precondition of economic development. Most significantly of all, it set out to create the new empire by military means. In 1879 survey parties were sent to map out possible routes for a trans-Saharan railway linking Algeria with the Western Sudan. In February 1880 plans for a Senegal–Niger railway system, to be financed partly out of public funds, were laid before Parliament. In September the military advance to the Niger, and with it the era of French imperialism in West Africa, began.[3]

This imperialist drive was to remain the dominant feature of West African policy for the next twenty years. Admittedly, the ambitious programme of railway-building was soon abandoned, while ever-increasing costs eventually undermined the government's enthusiasm for military expansion as well. Local military commanders, too, generated their own drives which often took them far beyond the limits imposed by Paris. But the interior retained its powers of attraction. Parliament ratified de Brazza's treaty with the Batéké in 1882 partly because the Congo was seen as a gateway to central Africa. French interest in the Lower Niger–Benue complex was based on the same consideration. Throughout the 1880s, the importance attached to Guinea and the Ivory Coast was directly proportionate to the opportunities they afforded for expansion inland. By the 1890s, indeed, Lake Chad had replaced Timbuktu as the focal point of the projected north-west African empire, and in 1900 three expeditions, from the Sudan, the Congo and Algeria, converged on the lake to mark the empire's symbolic creation.[4]

The expectation of future profit served as the rationale for empire-building on this vast scale. Senegalese governors in the 1850s had dreamt of an empire which might one day rival India in its wealth and magnificence. As late as 1904 a few colonial enthusiasts were still proclaiming the Chad basin to be 'une nouvelle Egypte, sinon une

3. For the origins of French imperialism in West Africa, see A. S. Kanya-Forstner, *The Conquest of the Western Sudan: a Study in French Military Imperialism* (Cambridge, Cambridge Univ. Press 1969), pp. 22–72. The nature and significance of the changes in 1879–80 are discussed more fully in C. W. Newbury and A. S. Kanya-Forstner, 'French policy and the origins of the scramble for West Africa', *Journal of African History*, **10** (1969), 260–75.
4. See Kanya-Forstner, *The Conquest of the Western Sudan, passim,* and especially pp. 151–6 [for Guinea and the Ivory Coast]; X. Blanc, Rapport, *Journal Officiel, Débats Parlementaires, Sénat,* 28 Nov. 1882, pp. 1089–91; M. Rouvier, Rapport, *J.O. Documents Parlementaires, Chambre,* no. 1406, pp. 2447–8 [for the Brazza treaty]; Newbury and Kanya-Forstner 'French policy', pp. 268–72; A. S. Kanya-Forstner, 'French African policy and the Anglo-French Agreement of 5 August 1890', *The Historical Journal,* **12** (1969), 647–50 [for the Niger-Benue complex].

plus grande Egypte'.[5] Policymakers too spoke of potential markets of 200 million people and based their policies on such optimistic forecasts: the projected cost to the State of the Senegal–Niger railway was 54 million frs. But the first proper survey, undertaken in 1890 dismissed the Sudan as 'un pays inculte, qu'habite une population clairsemée, sans besoins actuels, sans initiative, sans activité'. Economically, the empire was never worth the price of its acquisition. Its acquisition by military conquest made it an even greater liability. By 1898, after two decades of military rule, the Sudan's export trade was running at some 3 million frs. a year.[6] Fascinated by the lure of the Sudanese interior, the French built an empire not on solid economic foundations but on a grand illusion.

2. The myth of the Upper Nile

By contrast, French policy towards Egypt during the 1880s and early 1890s was a model of caution and moderation. There was no question about Egypt's importance. The humiliating circumstances of the British occupation and the consequent loss of French influence were bitterly resented. Its strategic implications for the Mediterranean balance and the security of French routes to the East were fully appreciated. To undo the effects of 1882 remained throughout the period, 'la considération qui domine toutes les autres'.[7] But the French had no desire to replace their rivals as masters of Egypt. Their objectives were to *negotiate* a British evacuation, to neutralise the country, to guarantee freedom of passage through the Suez Canal—in times of war as well as peace—and, above all, to prevent the Egyptian problem from causing an irreparable breakdown of Anglo-French relations. The pursuit of these objectives was just as circumspect. The French were determined to secure evacuation by agreement with Britain and confined their activity to the diplomatic sphere. In Egypt itself, they refrained from encouraging the nationalist opposition, and even their support for the Khedive Abbas was never more

---

5. Faidherbe, Memorandum, 1 Oct. 1858, Archives Nationales (Section Outre-Mer) [ANSOM] Sénégal I 45/a; P. Leroy-Beaulieu, *Le Sahara, le Soudan, et les chemins de fer transsahariens* (Paris, 1904), p. 353.
6. Picanon to Etienne, 1 Sept. 1890, ANSOM Soudan XIX 2; Note, n.d., ANSOM Soudan XIII 13.
7. Ferry to Decrais, 17 Apr. 1884, *Documents diplomatiques français*, I[e e] série [D.D.F.], v. no. 239; Ferry to Waddington, 14 Nov. 1884, Ministère des Affaires Etrangères [AE] Waddington MSS 4; Ribot to Cambon, 30 Jan. 1892, *D.D.F.*, ix, no. 180.

than half-hearted.[8] They consistently asserted the international character of the Egyptian question and shied away from isolated initiatives. Ferry refused to lead a campaign against the occupation in 1884, despite assurances of German support. Foreign Minister Spuller and his successor, Ribot, showed themselves equally hesitant in 1890.[9] Diplomatic pressure too was confined to periods when the British seemed open to persuasion. When the climate for negotiations was considered unpropitious, as it was after the Drummond-Wolff fiasco in 1887, the French usually did nothing.

The course of Egyptian policy was not absolutely consistent, and periods of firmness alternated with those of conciliation. In 1884 Ferry rejected the financial agreement on which a political settlement depended. In 1887 Flourens rejected the terms of the Drummond-Wolff Convention and organised the campaign which led to its destruction. But the general trend was towards greater moderation. By 1889 Spuller was hinting at his readiness to accept the indefinite British right of re-entry which Flourens had rejected two years before. He refused to approve proposals for the conversion of the Egyptian Dept unless the British reaffirmed the temporary character of their occupation, but in 1890 Ribot conceded this point as well.[10] The foreign minister and his ambassador in London, W. H. Waddington, continued to seek a negotiated settlement despite their gradual loss of faith in British promises to evacuate. Only in November 1892 did Waddington finally admit defeat and announce his intention to retire.[11]

The basic principles of Egyptian policy were now to be completely recast. Hopes for an amicable solution to the Egyptian question were abandoned in favour of exerting direct pressure through the establishment of a French presence on the Upper Nile. At the same time action shifted from the diplomatic to the colonial stage and from the Nile Delta to the Congo–Nile watershed. In the spring of 1893 the new under-secretary for colonies, Théophile Delcassé, and the President

8. Reverseaux to Develle, 8 Nov. 1893, *D.D.F.*, x, no. 421; Note on Revereaux to Casimir-Périer, 27 Jan. 1894, *D.D.F.*, xi, no. 31.

9. Courcel to Ferry, 25/6 Aug. 1884; Ferry, Note, 6 Oct. 1884, *D.D.F.*, v, nos. 377, 421; Spuller to Montebello, 2 Mar. 1890, *D.D.F.*, vii, no. 572; Ribot to Montebello, 20 Mar., 1 Apr., 6 June, 17 June 1890, *D.D.F.*, viii, nos. 2, 20, 76, 81.

10. Salisbury to Egerton, 24 June 1889, Foreign Office Confidential Print 5826, no. 132; Spuller to Waddington, 7 June 1889; Waddington to Spuller, 21 June 1889; Spuller to Waddington, 2 July 1889, *D.D.F.*, vii, nos. 395, 405, 410; Kanya-Forstner, 'French African policy', pp. 630–1.

11. Ribot to Waddington, 9 Nov. 1892 [Copy]; Waddington to Ribot, 11, 12 Nov. 1892, AE Ribot MSS 3.

of the Republic, Sadi Carnot, sent Commandant Monteil to occupy Fashoda and so 'reopen' the Egyptian question. In November 1894, after diplomatic complications with Britain and the Congo State had prevented Monteil's departure, the government ordered Commissioner Liotard of the Upper Ubangi to march on the Nile. Liotard also failed to reach his objective, but in the summer of 1895 Captain Marchand submitted new plans for the occupation of Fashoda. Foreign minister Hanotaux, previously the sternest opponent of any provocative action in the Nile Basin, now threw his weight behind the scheme and helped to secure the Cabinet's approval. In June 1896 Marchand left for the Congo, and with his departure French policy was set on collision course.[12]

For the next two years the 'Fashoda strategy' was to dominate French African policy as a whole. To safeguard Marchand's position on the Upper Nile, attempts were made to gain the active support of Ethiopia, and in 1897 the two sides signed an agreement partitioning the whole of the Southern Sudan between them.[13] Even the staunchest partisans of the 'Chad Plan' had by now accepted the primacy of the Upper Nile. West African expansion did not lose its impetus, and here too Anglo-French conflicts intensified. But by 1898, when the situation in the Niger Bend reached crisis point, most policy-makers had come to recognise the relative unimportance of West African disputes compared to the imminent confrontation at Fashoda.[14] When Marchand and Kitchener made contact, Britain and France stood closer to the brink of war than at any time since 1815.

In terms of French African priorities, the ultimate objectives of the Fashoda strategy—the evacuation and neutralisation of Egypt—were not irrational. But the assumptions behind it were even more wildly miscalculated than those on which the Chad plan rested. Marchand's presence at Fashoda was intended to frighten the British into negotia-

---

12. The best general account of the place of the Upper Nile in European diplomacy is G. N. Sanderson, *England, Europe and the Upper Nile* (Edinburgh Univ. Press, 1965). The fullest account of the Monteil expedition is J. Stengers, 'Aux origines de Fachoda: l'expédition Monteil', *Revue belge de philologie et d'histoire*, **36** (1958), 436–50; **30** (1960), 366–404, 1040–65. For the political background to the Marchand expedition, and especially the role of Hanotaux, see M. Michel, 'La mission Marchand' (Paris, doctorat de 3e cycle, 1967), pp. 36–63. The most recent study of French policy, R. G. Brown, *Fashoda Reconsidered: the impact of domestic politics on French policy in Africa, 1893–1898* (Baltimore, 1969), should be used with caution.
13. H. de Beaucaire, projet de règlement des questions pendantes dans le nord-est africain, 10 Feb. 1897, A.E. Hanotaux MSS. 10; Lebon to Hanotaux, 5 Mar. 1897; Lebon to Lagarde, 14 Mar. 1897; Convention pour le Nil blanc, 20 Mar. 1897, *D.D.F.*, xiii, nos. 137, 149, 159.
14. *J.O. Déb. Parl. Chambre*, 28 Feb. 1895, pp. 610–11 [speech by François Deloncle]; Kanya-Forstner, pp. 244–9.

tions by raising the spectre of foreign interference with the flow of the Nile. In 1893 a French hydraulic engineer, Victor Prompt, had indicated the Nile–Sobat confluence as the point where a dam could do most damage to Egypt's water supply, and President Carnot had a copy of his report when he spoke to Monteil. But Prompt had never meant his remarks to be taken seriously; he only mentioned the possibility of 'opérations dues à la malveillance' in order to strengthen his argument in favour of building irrigation barrages further downstream.[15] A dam at Fashoda was completely impracticable in any case, for the necessary equipment and material could not have been transported from the Congo: it took Marchand two years of superhuman effort to reach his objective with one river steamer and 160 men.

This was the least serious miscalculation, for the policy-makers were not planning to dam the Nile either; the mere threat of such action was supposed to bring the British to the conference table. The optimism of the French was based on a totally inaccurate assessment of the diplomatic situation. It was assumed that Marchand's arrival at Fashoda would lead as a matter of course to an international conference at which a united Europe, led by France, Russia and Germany, would oblige Britain to honour her pledges and evacuate Egypt. The assumption rested on the flimsiest possible evidence: joint action in China after the Sino–Japanese war, vague Russian encouragement in 1896, and a tentative German proposal for a common front on the question of Mozambique in June 1898. But the French remained so confident of success that they made no diplomatic preparations for the confrontation with Britain. As late as July 1898 the Foreign Ministry was still convinced that everything was bound to turn out all right in the end.[16]

Most serious of all was the failure to consider the full range of possible British reactions. The French completely underestimated the importance which British governments of the 1890s attached to the Upper Nile. They could not believe that Britain would be prepared to risk her worldwide commercial interests by actually going to war over Fashoda.[17] As a result, the French entered the confrontation quite un-

15. V. Prompt, 'Soudan Nilotique' [20 Jan. 1893], *Bulletin de l'Institut Egyptien*, **3** (1893), 71–116.
16. Hanotaux to Cogordan, 16 Nov. 1897, *D.D.F.*, xiii, no. 360; same to same, 21 June 1898; Note du Département, 18 July 1898, *D.D.F.*, xiv, nos. 236, 258.
17. Cogordan to Bourgeois, 16 Apr. 1896, *D.D.F.*, xii, no. 373; Cogordan to Hanotaux, 17 Mar. 1897, *D.D.F.*, xiii, no. 154; Cogordan to Delcassé, 21 Nov. 1898, *D.D.F.*, xiv, no. 531.

prepared diplomatically or militarily. In the humiliating withdrawal of Marchand from Fashoda and the subsequent loss of the Bahr al-Ghazal, they paid the price for their lack of judgment.

3. The making of France's African mythology

How then was it possible for myths to influence French African policy so decisively? The answer to this problem must be sought in the nature of French policy-making, and particularly in its deficiencies. The most obvious of these was the poor quality of the intelligence on which policies were based. When plans for the African empire were first drawn up in the 1850s, the interior was largely *terra incognita*, and medieval legends about its wealth were correspondingly easy to credit. When the plans were revived in the 1870s, the same exaggerated estimates of the Sudan's economic potential were still widely accepted. Thereafter, policy-makers were often supplied with deliberately misleading information by military commanders anxious to secure official approval for their own expansionist schemes.[18] Similarly, the assumptions behind the Fashoda strategy were reinforced by the confident assurances of the French minister in Cairo that Britain could be bullied into negotiations. But inadequate information was no more than a contributory factor. By the 1890s there was ample evidence, even from military reports, that the Sudan was not an Eldorado and never likely to become one. The optimism of Cairo also had to be weighed against the much more sober reports of the London embassy and the British government's repeated warnings about the consequences of French action on the Upper Nile.[19] The input of information was often less faulty than its processing.

In assessing the information available to them, the policy-makers were bound to be influenced by their own attitudes and ambitions. Charles de Freycinet (minister of public works: 1876–79; prime minister: 1880, 1882) and Admiral Jean Jauréguiberry (minister of marine and colonies: 1879–80, 1882–3), the architects of the African empire in the early 1880s, both had a personal interest in the Western Sudan. Freycinet was a technocrat, determined to make his reputation as the founder of the modern French railway system. For him, the Trans-sahara was merely part of a still more extensive programme of railway-building in Algeria. Jauréguiberry, a career officer and a

18. Kanya-Forstner, *The Conquest of the Western Sudan, passim.*
19. D'Estournelles to Hanotaux, 3 Dec. 1894; Courcel to Hanotaux, 2 Apr. 1895, *D.D.F.*, xi, nos. 303, 429.

former governor of Senegal, was temperamentally and professionally inclined to favour military solutions to the problems of expansion. Eugène Etienne, the colonial under-secretary responsible for the drafting and implementation of the Chad plan after 1889, was the most powerful of the Algerian deputies and the future leader of the whole French colonialist movement. All these men were genuine imperialists, concerned with the long-term prospects of empire and the role of government in imperial expansion. The immediate value of African territory was of less importance to them than its potential for development once the State had provided the necessary funds and established the necessary political control.[20]

The weaknesses of individual policy-makers also played their part, especially in the formulation of the Fashoda strategy. Delcassé's concern for the Egyptian question amounted to an obsession, and his excessive optimism was characteristic of his general approach to foreign policy.[21] Marcellin Berthelot, the minister who formally approved the Marchand expedition in November 1895, was totally inexperienced in foreign affairs and had been driven to the point of distraction by grief over the death of his daughter.[22] The supposedly astute Hanotaux was in fact just as unstable. His support for Marchand in 1895 represented a complete and sudden reversal of his previous policy. By 1897 his erratic conduct was becoming positively alarming. 'Je suis vraiment effrayé de voir les affaires etrangères entre ses mains', wrote President Félix Faure in January: 'il est tellement énervé qu'il est parfois inconscient et parle sans aucun souci de ce qu'il a dit la veille et sans penser au sens et aux conséquences de ses paroles.'[23]

But personal idiosyncrasies were less significant than the collective attitudes built up, largely through precedent, in the policy-making system itself. Policy-makers came to share a set of common assumptions about the value of African empire, even if they differed about its nature and the methods to be used in acquiring it. They also regarded African expansion as an aspect of Anglo-French rivalry; one of their principal justifications for empire-building after 1880 was the danger that inaction would result in the loss of the African interior to the

20. For the views of Freycinet and Jauréguiberry, see: Newbury and Kanya-Forstner, 'French African policy'. For the views of Etienne, see H. Sieberg, *Eugène Etienne und die französische Kolonialpolitik (1887–1904)* (Cologne/Opladen, 1968), especially *cap*. II.

21. C. M. Andrew, *Théophile Delcassé and the Making of the Entente Cordiale* (London, Macmillan, 1968), pp. 21–5.

22. Félix Faure, 'Le ministère Léon Bourgeois et la politique étrangère de Marcellin Berthelot au Quai d'Orsay', *Revue d'histoire diplomatique*, 71 (1957), 114–15.

23. Félix Faure, *Mémoires*, January 1897, Faure MSS XVII, p. 207.

British. The anti-British character of the Fashoda strategy was much more obvious still. Virtually all policy-makers shared these views. Even the most Anglophile ministers like Ribot accepted the inevitability of Anglo-French rivalry overseas and sought merely to keep that rivalry friendly.

The structure of French policy-making made these attitudes all the more potentially dangerous. Governments of the Third Republic, often precarious, always preoccupied with domestic affairs, rarely attempted to impose cabinet control over foreign and colonial policies. By tradition, the Quai d'Orsay acted as a virtually independent ministry; by oversight, the Colonial Department achieved the same status. The colonial under-secretary did not report to the Cabinet until 1889, and even afterwards colonial affairs were usually considered too trivial to be worth attention.[24] West African expansion was hardly ever discussed. Much more inexcusably the Fashoda strategy, with all its implications for the course of Anglo-French relations, was similarly neglected. The Marchand expedition was approved by the Bourgeois and Méline governments in the spring of 1896; it was not considered again until the summer of 1898.[25]

The absence of central control made effective coordination between the foreign and colonial spheres of policy-making impossible. The diplomatic repercussions of expansion had to be dealt with by the foreign ministry, but the decisions which precipitated international crises were often taken by the *Colonies* without consulting the Quai d'Orsay. The inordinate power of this relatively minor government department explains much of the confusion apparent in African policy. Sudanese expansion was under its control from the start. Jauréguiberry created the military command without informing any of his colleagues.[26] Etienne organised the advance to Lake Chad and into the Niger Bend against the initial opposition of the Quai d'Orsay.[27] And the same tradition was maintained throughout the 1890s. After 1893 the Pavillon de Flore (the home of the Colonial Department) gained control of Egyptian policy as well. Delcassé planned the Monteil expedition without the knowledge of foreign

---

24. See F. Berge, *Le sous-secrétariat et les sous-secrétaires d'état aux colonies* (Paris, 1962).
25. Michel, pp. 51, 55; Félix Faure, 'Fachoda', *Revue d'histoire diplomatique*, **69** (1955), p. 30.
26. Procès-Verbaux de la Commission du Budget, 4 June 1880 (statement by Freycinet), Archives Nationales C 3176.
27. Etienne to Ribot, 9 Aug. 1890; Ribot to Etienne, 19 Aug. 1890; Etienne to Ribot, 7 Sept. 1890, AE Afrique Nouvelle Série 1. (I am grateful for these references to Mr T. R. Roberts of the University of Aberdeen.)

minister Develle. He sent Liotard to the Upper Nile in 1894 against the wishes of Hanotaux.[28] The latter did play a crucial role in the organisation of the Marchand expedition, but by 1897 his authority had again been successfully challenged. Indeed, the colonial ministry was now conducting what amounted to its own foreign policy in Ethiopia. Only in September 1898, when the crisis was about to break, did the Pavillon de Flore withdraw from the scene and leave Delcassé, now foreign minister, to face the consequences of his earlier decisions.[29]

Ministerial instability added a further element of irresponsibility. The rapid turnover of governments enhanced the role of the permanent officials as the repositories of departmental tradition, the guarantors of continuity in policy-making, and the possessors of expertise. But their views tended to be narrow and specialised, and they rarely considered the full political implications of the policies they recommended. These defects were particularly apparent in the Colonial Department where the under-secretary, although a political appointment, was not politically accountable for his actions. Since the ministers of marine or of commerce who were nominally in charge usually gave their under-secretaries a free hand, the latter came in effect to enjoy ministerial powers without ministerial responsibility. Etienne and Delcassé knew how to exploit this situation to the full, and so did their civil servants. Jacques Haussmann and Jean-Louis Deloncle virtually ran the Department during the months between Etienne's departure and Delcassé's arrival, and they maintained the impetus of the advance on Chad.[30] After 1895 a series of weak ministers enabled the permanent officials—General Louis Archinard (director of defence), Ernest Roume (head of the administrative section) and later Gustave Binger (head of the *Bureau d'Afrique*) to assume greater powers still. The influence of civil servants, of course, depended ultimately on the strength and experience of their political masters. Men like Freycinet, Jauréguiberry and Delcassé were not transient weaklings, and many of the crucial decisions were theirs. But the same could not be said for Berthelot and Guieysse, the foreign and

28. Stengers, 'L'expédition Monteil', p. 449; Hanotaux, Note, 17 Nov. 1894, *D.D.F.*, xi, no. 285.
29. Trouillot to Delcassé, 15 Sept. 1898, *D.D.F.*, xiv, no. 352. The conflict between the Quai d'Orsay and the Pavillon de Flore over Ethiopian policy is discussed in G. N. Sanderson, 'The Origins and Significance of the Anglo-French Confrontation at Fashoda', to be published in P. Gifford and W. R. Louis, eds, *Britain and France in Africa*. I am grateful to Professor Sanderson for allowing me to make use of his manuscript.
30. Haussmann, Rapport au sous-secrétaire, 22 July 1892, ANSOM Afrique III 16/c; Lebon to Quai d'Orsay, 14 Dec. 1893 [draft by J.-L. Deloncle], ANSOM Afrique VI 106/g.

colonial ministers who formally approved the Marchand expedition, and who merely signed the papers which their officials, Archinard and Georges Benoît (*sous-directeur des protectorats* at the Quai d'Orsay) laid before them.[31]

No less influential were the agents of French expansion on the ground. The execution of French African policy, both in West Africa and on the Upper Nile, was often entrusted to officers of the *infanterie* and *artillerie de marine*, the French Marine Corps. Once established in their commands, these 'men on the spot' could decisively shape the course of policy. Difficulties of communication and a tradition of loose metropolitan control over military agents in the colonies gave them wide powers of initiative and enabled them to disregard unwelcome instructions with impunity. They supplied the information on which the policy-makers in Paris had to rely. On completing their tours of duty they frequently joined the ranks of the permanent officials as the Colonial Department's African experts. Colonel Gustave Borgnis-Desbordes, the first of the Sudanese commanders, held such a position in the 1880s. His friend and protégé, General Archinard, was to become the key official in the Pavillon de Flore between 1895 and 1897.[32]

As career soldiers, the *officiers soudanais* naturally advocated more aggressive policies than their civilian colleagues. They were obsessed with the problems of military security and relied on the use of force to solve them. Professionally, military expansion offered them tempting prospects of rapid advancement in a peacetime army whose regular channels of promotion were hopelessly clogged by the rules of seniority. Politically, the *officiers soudanais*, and Marchand was one of them, were anglophobic in the extreme, and their hostility to England was all the more dangerous since they too were ultimately not responsible for their actions. The consequences of their irresponsibility were disastrous. Uninterested in the economic potential of African empire, they turned the Sudan into an expensive and unproductive military preserve run entirely for their own benefit. Even the Fashoda strategy was made to serve their personal ambitions. Archinard supported the Marchand expedition not because he was particularly interested in Egypt but because he was Marchand's patron and saw the expedition as an opportunity to assert his supremacy

---

31. For the role of Benoît and Archinard, see Sanderson, *England, Europe and the Upper Nile*, ch. xii; Michel, pp. 36–63.
32. Kanya-Forstner, *passim*.

over Roume and the civilian elements in the ministry.[33] The Anglo-French confrontation was to some extent the outcome of a squalid intradepartmental conflict.

Finally, policy was also affected by pressures originating outside the decision-making network. Although African expansion never enjoyed massive popular support, visions of a new India did create brief flurries of enthusiasm, and policy-makers took such enthusiasm into account.[34] When nationalist rather than purely colonialist passions were aroused, the influence of public opinion could be decisive. In 1882 the government submitted Brazza's treaty for ratification against its better judgment and in direct response to widespread indignation at the British occupation of Egypt.[35] For the next decade, 'le vieux et inépuisable levain d'anglophobie qui va au fond de l'opinion publique' was the principal obstacle to the amicable settlement of the Egyptian question.[36] Parliament obliged Ferry to stiffen his terms for a financial arrangement in 1884. Fear of Parliamentary opposition inhibited Ribot's search for a solution after 1890.[37]

Much more important still was the influence of a small but highly determined pressure group, the Comité de l'Afrique Française. From its creation in 1890, the Comité enjoyed privileged access to the centres of decision-making. Its secretary-general, Harry Alis, was highly regarded by the Quai d'Orsay. Etienne and Delcassé at the Colonial Department both viewed the organisation with special favour. Haussmann and Binger were both members, and Deloncle was an equally reliable ally. The *officiers soudanais* were also well represented; Borgnis-Desbordes was a founder-member, and Archinard too joined in 1894. Partly in the expectation of financial gain but largely because of its fervent nationalism, the *Comité* championed the 'union, à travers le Soudan, du Congo français, du Sénégal et de l'Algérie–Tunisie', the first of its objectives. After 1892 it became an

33. Archinard, projet d'instructions, Jan. 1896, ANSOM Afrique III 32/a; Michel, *op. cit.*, 36–54. For Archinard's conflict with Roume over West African policy, see Kanya-Forstner, p. 241.
34. Freycinet, Rapport au Président de la République, 12 July 1879, *J.O.* 14 July 1879, pp. 6633–5.
35. H. Brunschwig, *L'avènement de l'Afrique noire* (Paris, 1963), pp. 143–53; J. Stengers, 'L'impérialisme colonial de la fin du XIX siècle: mythe ou réalité', *Journal of African History*, 3 (1962), 473–6.
36. Ferry to Waddington, 26 June 1884, AE Waddington MSS 4; Ribot to Waddington, 8 Apr. 1890, AE Waddington MSS 5 bis.
37. *J.O., Déb. Parl. Chambre*, 23, 26 June 1884; Lytton to Salisbury, 26 June 1890, Public Record Office, F.O. 84/2029; same to same, 27 June 1890, F.O. 84/2027.

equally committed partisan of energetic action on the Upper Nile. Its influence on both aspects of French African policy was truly remarkable. It helped to organise almost all the missions to Lake Chad and into the Niger Bend between 1890 and 1898 and many of them were launched on its initiative. It originated the plan for the occupation of Fashoda, contributed to the cost of Liotard's expedition, helped to clear the way for the acceptance of Marchand's project, and fostered the illusion that his arrival on the Nile would lead to the British evacuation of Egypt.[38] Pressure groups like the *officiers soudanais* and the Comité de l'Afrique Française were ultimately to blame for many of the follies committed in the name of France. They possessed the necessary strength of purpose, and their relations with government gave them the opportunity, to have their conception of the national interest officially accepted and so lead their nation into the desert fringes of the Western Sudan and the swamps of the Upper Nile. As President Félix Faure noted at the height of the Fashoda crisis: 'Nous avons été comme des fous en Afrique, entraînés par des gens irresponsables qu'on appelle les coloniaux.'[39] French African policy could have had no more fitting epitaph.

Beneath the chaos of policy-making, however, lay two factors of a more intangible character which made this sort of *folie africaine* possible. The first was the absence of restraint. Militarily, African expansion was an easy undertaking, and the losses incurred were remarkably light. Metropolitan troops were not used, and the issue of metropolitan defence was not involved. The fear of weakening continental defences may have kept the French out of Egypt in 1882, but it could not prevent the conquest of a West African empire by four thousand African *tirailleurs* under French command. Nor, on the whole, was the financial burden of empire-building unacceptably heavy. Military expansion in the Western Sudan was undoubtedly expensive, and governments were eventually forced to impose limits on the military advance. But annual expenditure, even in the 1890s, was less than 10 million frs. a year, a relatively insignificant amount in terms of total government spending. No such problems bedevilled the Fashoda strategy; the estimated cost of the Marchand expedition was 600,000 frs.[40] Most crucially of all, African expansion raised no

38. The origins and nature of the *Comité*, and its role in the formulation of African policy, are discussed in: C. M. Andrew and A. S. Kanya-Forstner, 'The French "Colonial Party": Its Composition Aims and Influence, 1885–1914', *The Historical Journal*, **14** (1971), 99–128.
39. Faure, 'Fachoda', p. 34.
40. Michel, p. 53. The final cost of the expedition was 1,300,000 frs.

issues of vital national importance. Not even the most fervent expansionist considered the acquisition of a Sudanese empire or the British evacuation of Egypt as matters of life or death. As a result, the French could afford to play games in Africa, and they played them according to broad but well defined rules. Territorial expansion was an acceptable policy, whether its objective was to gain an empire or to bring diplomatic pressure to bear on European rivals. But the financial and military costs of expansion had to be kept within limits, and any diplomatic crises had to be settled at the conference table. No matter what the stakes—and the stakes on the Upper Nile were high—war was the one card which could never be played. The French could hope to win these games of territorial and diplomatic bluff only so long as their opponents played by the same rules. When Britain, who did consider her vital interests to be at stake, changed the rules and called the bluff, the French had to throw in their hand.[41]

Secondly, the myths on which French policy was based were not peculiarly French. The supposedly phlegmatic and calculating British were prey to the same delusions. Legends of Sudanese wealth first gained currency in the nineteenth century through the efforts of the African Association, and they shaped the course of British policy in West Africa until the 1850s. After 1895 they did so again; Chamberlain's objectives were the same as those of Freycinet and Jauréguiberry fifteen years before him.[42] And the absurdity of the Fashoda strategy was matched by the seriousness with which the British regarded it. The French were at least playing games in Africa; by 1898 the British were not. Nor were Britain and France the only victims of the *mirage soudanais*; their enthusiasm for the Upper Nile was lukewarm compared to that of King Leopold.[43] In the 'neurotic world of the 1890s', the rational calculations of policy-makers did give way to irrational obsessions about 'running out of world space' and 'last chances of greatness in the coming century of superpowers'.[44] Perhaps myth might serve as the basis for a general theory of imperialism after all.

41. This same point is made in Sanderson, 'The origins and significance of the Anglo-French confrontation at Fashoda'.
42. A. Adu Boahen, *Britain, the Sahara, and the Western Sudan, 1788–1861* (London, Oxford Univ. Press, 1964); A. S. Kanya-Forstner, 'Military expansion in the Western Sudan—French and British style', to be published in Gifford and Louis, eds, *Britain and France in Africa*.
43. J. Stengers, 'Une facette de la question du Haut-Nil: le Mirage Soudanais', *Journal of African History*, **10** (1969), 599–622.
44. R. E. Robinson, Introduction to H. Brunschwig, *French Colonialism, 1871–1914: Myths and Realities* (New York, Praeger 1966), p. x.

DISCUSSION

Methodological objections. The main topic of the discussion was the methodology used in the paper and, in particular, the assumption that the questions raised about the nature of French expansion in Africa could best be answered by concentrating on the process by which policy was made. Three different, though related, criticisms were made of this approach. First, it was asserted that no attempt had been made to place the decision-making process in its economic and social context or to link it with the frame of mind in which the majority of European politicians viewed the question of empire—'the spirit of the age' as one questioner called it—with its emphasis on the competition for territory between the major powers and the need for some kind of 'preemptive' imperialism. Second, Kanya-Forstner was asked if he did not think he should have concentrated less attention on the motives of particular policy-makers and more on the constraints within which they operated. As it stood the paper might be said to rest on the implicit assumption that a central task of the historian was a study of the biographies of leading policy-makers. Meanwhile, the existence of constraints like the fact that the French had already created a large North African empire were ignored. Finally, it was argued that in history of this kind the nature of the explanation of events could be said to be conditioned by the type of evidence available. As a result of the existence of innumerable diplomatic notes and administrative memoranda too much weight was easily attached to the motives underlying particular decisions, while the shortage of records of other kinds (for example, information concerning the economic interests involved in overseas expansion) meant that much less attention was paid to the reasons why such decisions had to be made in the first place. Thus there was a systematic bias in favour of one model of political behaviour.

In his replies Kanya-Forstner stressed the fact that decisions were not made in a vacuum. Outside influences were important and could be studied through the use of the diaries of politicians (which told you whom they met) or of the letters from particular politicians contained within departmental minutes. But the important question was—how did they influence decisions? You moved from a study of policy to a study of the society and then back to policy again, you did not look at society first. Hence the crux of the whole business always remained the policy-making framework. This had to be kept central. He also took issue with those who talked in terms of 'the spirit of the age'. He had not found it a helpful concept. To take only one example, the principles underlying the attitude of French politicians towards Africa in 1879–80 were not the same as those of their British counterparts. If this was so how useful was an explanation based on the assumption of a common 'world view'?

Myth versus fact. Another series of questions concerned the way in which Kanya-Forstner had posed the central historical question he was trying to solve. It mattered less that the French were deluded about the possible gains from their African policies than that they actually established an empire for themselves in the Sudan. Too much time was spent discussing why this should not, or ought not to have happened when the fact was that it did. Following on from this it was suggested that expansion inland from the Guinea coast was guided by two general rules: (1) move into an adjacent area if you can easily or if some other power might be trying to get there first; (2) whatever your territorial gains and losses never allow yourself to be defeated by an African ruler or movement; once you start a war don't get beaten.

Kanya-Forstner agreed that the military aspect was important. The soldiers in the Western Sudan were constantly worried about their security. Again, whenever this led them to wish to make an advance they could always be sure that it would not be vetoed provided it was couched in the right terms. Nevertheless, it had to be remembered that it was the government who had put the military there in the first place, and it was necessary to ask why this had been done. Moreover, as a rule, the initial drive for expansion always came from Paris.

XIII

Economic imperialism
and the businessman:
Britain and Latin America
before 1914
D. C. M. Platt

British capital was more important than that of any other nation in nine-teenth-century Latin America. And yet, not only did the British government never assume formal control in any Latin American country, it seldom interfered in any way. Does this mean that the conclusions of the theory of imperialism are undermined, or did imperialism merely appear in a more informal guise? Platt argues that British financiers, traders and other economic interests, although they obtained influence and even control at various times and place, had very significant areas of weakness as well.

Their control never had the certainty or permanence associated with formal empire. On the basis of this criterion Platt claims that the area was an exception to the rules of imperialism in the rest of the world. In doing so he raises in a different form the questions of definition of imperialism and the relations between imperialism and colonialism already considered in a more theoretical context by Kemp, I, Barratt Brown, II, and Magdoff, VI, and taken up again in the Conclusion.

In an argument already so far advanced it may be unreasonable to attempt to introduce a new dimension. The debate on what influences *governments* in determining the shape of imperialism is reaching a point where the outline is clear. We can and shall continue to qualify it in detail. But, in general, most people are more sensible than they used to be about the relative shares of economic, social, and political considerations in the formulation of official policy. All the same, it does seem to me that even if we have progressed so far with a definition of the 'official mind of imperialism', the whole theory of imperialism is still incomplete for lack, at any rate on its economic front, of a thorough study of the political and economic power of *private individuals*—a study, that is, of 'informal imperialism' and 'control' by the foreign financier, investor, concessionaire, contractor, trader, and manager, operating independently of government assistance in the under-developed sector of the world.

Naturally, it is difficult in many cases to distinguish the power and influence of the entrepreneur from the pressures brought to bear by his government. Harry Magdoff has shown how closely identified the two may become in contemporary imperialism.[1] But British enter-prise in Latin America before 1914 provides a rare example—perhaps the only substantial example in modern times—of private enterprise operating on a large scale in an underdeveloped area *without* diplo-matic promotion or 'assistance. As such it acts as the most promising starting point for a general analysis of what, after all, is and always has been a main constituent of imperialism or 'neocolonialism': control by the foreign businessman.

Before examining some of the nuances of 'informal imperialism' and 'control', there are two points which I should make clear. First, most of my work so far has been on business/government relation-ships, and I have only recently become interested in business control *tout court*. For the moment, then, I am just skirmishing around the subject; the full-scale engagement is still ahead.[2] Secondly, I have said that British enterprise in Latin America before 1914 operated indepen-dently of diplomatic promotion or assistance, and the point is important for my general argument since it means that when I identify British pressures and control, I can be sure that these were derived fundamentally from private rather than government sources. This may or may not be a difficult proposition to accept, but I have discussed the whole subject of British official policy in Latin America at length elsewhere,[3] and I hope that I may be allowed at this point to take official non-intervention for granted.

1. Harry Magdoff, 'Economic aspects of U.S. imperialism', *Monthly Review*, **18**, no. 6 (1966); 'The age of imperialism', *Monthly Review*, **19**, nos. 2, 5 and 6 (1968).
2. The British Social Science Research Council is financing a three-year research project, with research assistants, under the title ' "Informal Imperialism" and "Control": British business experience in Latin America before 1930.' (Completed in 1974 and now with a publisher.)
3. D. C. M. Platt, *Finance, Trade, and Politics in British Foreign Policy, 1815–1914* (London, Oxford Univ. Press, 1968); 'British diplomacy in Latin America since the emancipation', *Inter-American Economic Affairs*, **21** (1967), 21–41; 'The imperialism of free trade; some reserva-tions', *Economic History Review*, 2nd ser., **21** (1968), 296–306.

1. British banks and the provision of credit

It is a truism to say that developments in Europe during the nineteenth century moulded the shape of Latin American economies. Rising population and expanding industry gave Latin America her export markets for certain types of foodstuffs and raw materials. The Republics turned their attention increasingly to production for export, often at the expense of the local consumer. Particular crops and the development of certain industries were sacrificed to European imports. The sheer size of foreign enterprises, particularly in the development of communications, made it impossible to avoid influencing economies; the welfare of whole provinces could depend on a simple business decision—whether by a railway company, a colonisation enterprise, or a mine—to readjust investment. The decisions were in far too many hands and depended on diverse and unpredictable factors beyond the control of individuals in a laissez-faire, unplanned age. But clearly the economic link existed. If 'imperialism' is simply the description of an automatic economic relationship between capitalist and underdeveloped countries, then Europeans were certainly imperialists in Latin America before 1914.

What can be said, however, about *deliberate* control, informal imperialism? In finance, given that British government assistance was not available, the strongest weapon of control was the denial of credit. On paper, the Listing Committee of the London Stock Exchange and the Corporation of Foreign Bondholders were formidable enemies, and Latin American governments have been known to collapse for want of their support. But in practice it was surprisingly seldom that a denial of further credit proved effective, at any rate over a number of years. In the first place, the defaulting government had to be anxious to raise new loans, and for many of the worst defaulters political crises and rivalries were so persistent that politicians had neither the time nor the inclination to turn again to world capital markets. Then, there had to be a general shortage of credit. If ample funds existed, competition first among the European stock exchanges and then between speculators and those in search of a high annual return was quite sufficient to make the money available, almost irrespective of the reputation of the borrower. Borrowers, in any circumstances, could depend on a conflict of interest among lenders. The supervision over new quotations maintained by the Committee of the Stock Exchange was often barely more than nominal; brokers stood to gain by encouraging new quotations, not by denying them. The Corporation of

Foreign Bondholders took a percentage on settlements; it received nothing when it failed to reach a compromise with a foreign government. Bonds were brought by speculators at rock-bottom prices, to be sold for a quick profit as soon as the defaulting government offered a settlement (however unsatisfactory to the original investor). There was no necessary community of interest between foreign investors in rival national loans, or between holders of national, provincial or municipal stock. In the end, what it comes down to is that when times were good on the European exchanges, virtually any government could come to an arrangement with its creditors and float a new loan; when times were bad nobody, however virtuous, could get money. In the large twilight area between, some control might, from time to time, prove effective, but it was a control which was likely to break down at short notice as conditions improved/deteriorated on a volatile loan market.

On the other hand, the direct, personal contact of the great London finance houses with Latin American governments—Rothschilds with the government of Brazil, Baring Bros with Argentina—gave rise to some degree of control. Further, the relations between the less-reputable finance houses and the smaller Republics, more particularly in the 1860s and 70s, gave a temporary ascendance before credit collapsed altogether. In general, until a local money market and banking system developed on an adequate scale—as they had for the larger Republics by the first decade of this century—all Latin American governments depended on European finance houses for short-term funding and accommodation. When an economy was in decline, international financiers—in the last century as in this—were inclined to impose drastic conditions before considering a remedial loan: the payment of customs duties direct into foreign banks, foreign-supervised destruction of paper money, agreements to restrict government expenditure. It is possible to exaggerate the influence of finance houses. They were themselves subject to competition. They had to maintain the goodwill of a rapid succession of rival politicians. They were often less than well-informed. They were unable, any more than other British business interests, to obtain diplomatic assistance against a government in default. But their position as the first link in the chain binding the Republics to the financial resources of Europe gave them advisory and admonitory functions far beyond those open to any Stock Exchange Listing Committee or bondholder pressure group.

Yet a clear distinction exists between finance houses and commercial banks. Foreign banking of every variety has an unenviably sinister reputation, in part a reflection of the genuinely powerful position of the finance houses, in part of the exceptional dividend record of the commercial banks, more particularly of the London and River Plate Bank and the London and Brazilian Bank. What is, perhaps, not so generally understood is that the conservative nature of British commercial banking practices in Latin America removed the commercial banks from the agricultural mortgages, the speculative industrial loans, the 'finance capitalism' which together would have created genuine opportunities for control over foreign economies. No banker in nineteenth-century Latin America escaped the occasional temptation to speculate on the rate of exchange. But with rare, and generally unfortunate, exceptions British institutions limited themselves to 'legitimate banking on sound and conservative principles':

> Neither trust funds, nor commercial deposits, nor capital provided for the security of such funds and deposits, should be used for any promoting, exploiting or underwriting purposes . . . there should be a clear differentiation in law and public regulation between commercial banking and exploiting of public enterprises and the management of corporations.[4]

The backbone of British commercial banking in Latin America was the traditional business in discounts, in advances on promissory notes, and in exchange operations. The banks existed fundamentally to service the import/export business on conventional, very conservative lines. The major British banks, offering security and a range of efficient services, attracted as much as a third of the banking deposits in Brazil in 1914, and a quarter of those in Argentina and Chile. As finance capitalists on the Lenin model, they might indeed have created serious political problems for the Republics. As it was, they acted simply as commercial services, prosperous, well managed, influential in normal, day-to-day market transactions, but essentially apolitical, unconnected directly with general industrial development. In any case, it should be said that the Latin Americans themselves were capable financiers. From the middle of the nineteenth century, as local capital became available, Latin Americans used their local knowledge, their expertise, their political, family and commercial connections to develop banking and insurance services. This was an area in which our competitive advantage lay simply in the security

4. Consul-General Leary, Report on Chile for 1907, *Parliamentary Papers* (Great Britain), 1908, cx, pp. 93–4.

offered by conservative banking, and in continued access to cheap capital in the United Kingdom. It was an advantage which would have been lost to British banks and insurance companies had they been other than the conservative, solid institutions which they set out to be.

2. British monopolies in Latin America

But what can be said of the power of foreign monopolies in communications, in public utilities, in exporting? To some extent criticism in this respect has always been directed at the general notion of a monopoly, while the fact that some of the monopolies were foreign simply made them more conspicuous, and more vulnerable. The 'Big Four' in Argentine wheat exports at the turn of the century, Argentines themselves, were as serious a problem for rural producers as any foreign syndicate, with the advantage, from their point of view, that as Argentines they were able to call on a great deal of direct political influence. There is no denying that foreign monopolies could and did hold a nation to ransom; the British-owned São Paulo/ Santos Railway did so for decades. But at the same time it would not be sensible to ignore the weaknesses of nineteenth-century monopolies, rings, pools, and consortia. Almost every liner route was under the control of Shipping Conference agreements after the 1880s. Yet Douglass North has shown, after a wide-ranging investigation of ocean freight-rates between 1750 and 1913, that with some notable exceptions 'the ocean freight market was competitive and both short-run adjustments and the long-run secular decline in the nineteenth century reflected the operation of an impersonal market'.[5] No agreement, Conference or otherwise, was sufficient to hold freight prices stable against the general fall in world prices, the augmented carrying capacity of modern shipping, and the improvements in engines and boilers which both increased speed and economised on fuel. Nor could new competition always be brought to heel. Time and again, whether in railway pools, shipping rings, or exporting syndicates, one partner would outgrow his share, demand more, and failing satisfaction, break the ring.

Similarly producers' monopolies were in danger either of pricing themselves out of the market, or of encouraging the development of

5. Douglass North, 'Ocean freight rates and economic development 1750–1913', *Journal of Economic History*, **18** (1958), 539.

substitutes. The interest of successive Chilean nitrate combinations, organised from 1884, in limiting production to keep up prices, clashed with the Chilean government's interest in increasing or maintaining nitrate exports to preserve essential revenue; both suffered when their monopoly position was challenged by the manufacture of synthetic nitrogen and by the competition of byproducts of sulphate of ammonia. Monopolist exporters faced producers at one end, sometimes well organised and politically influential in their own countries, and world markets at the other—the sugar market at New York, the rubber market in London, the European wheat markets—where prices were determined by factors outside their control. Even for the major export products, one of the elements so often forgotten in discussing 'control' is the size of the *internal* market. At the end of the nineteenth century the internal market for Mexican tobacco and coffee, for Argentine beef, for Brazilian sugar and cotton was quite large enough to maintain a strong influence over local prices and to cushion producers, protected where necessary by heavy tariffs, against the worst effects of wide fluctuations in world prices.

In the nature of the large-scale businesses they operated—railways, public utilities, the export of commodities requiring heavy investment in storage facilities, rapid shipment and elaborate marketing—foreign enterprises often took the shape of monopolies. But unless, like the São Paulo/Santos Railway, they had been able to tie themselves up with all kinds of legal and constitutional safeguards, they were always open to government intervention, to government-sponsored competition. Just as the moment when British railway enterprise in Argentina, undeniably influential in political and economic circles, was apparently at the peak of its power and prosperity—during the eight years after 1904—the companies were in fact on the run before a government policy of concessions for directly competitive lines, backed by French, by North American, and even by British capital.

The power of Latin American governments in their relations with foreign business enterprise in the late nineteenth century is commonly understated. In the last decades of the century it became standard practice in most of the major state contracts to include a 'Calvo Clause', by which foreign contractors renounced any recourse to diplomatic intervention and agreed to abide by the decisions of the municipal law courts. European governments, aware of the limitations of many Latin American judicial systems, were inclined to look askance at such self-denial. But in practice Calvo clauses inhibited diplomatic intervention except in cases of the most flagrant denial of justice. 'Those persons who think proper to accept such a position', J. D. Harding, a Law Officer, felt necessary to explain in a similar context back in the 1850s,

> do not appear to me to have, in point of principle, any very peculiar claims upon the formal support and interference of Her Majesty's Government. The maxim *caveant emptores* may well be applied to them. The intervention on their behalf by Her Majesty's Government must take place under very disadvantageous and embarrassing circumstances in an international point of view.[6]

British entrepreneurs in Latin America found from the beginning that they were dealing with men who knew aspects of their business as well as they did, and local conditions better. There was no shortage of 'geniuses' at Buenos Aires, 'nor men to direct others; nor schemers, nor learned men, nor subtle-men; the best of these last from England will find himself outdone by the Creoles'.[7] The professional politician was a sophisticated, knowledgeable, and often talented operator working within a context as familiar to him as it was alien to the British businessman. Ross Duffield, of the London and River Plate Bank, gave what, in the circumstances was the only sensible advice. He warned his managers in the 1890s that

> In all dealings with a Government you will require to act with the greatest circumspection and caution . . . to remember the difficulty of refusing persons in high authority, the envy and jealousy and consequent intrigues against you likely to arise among less favoured quarters, and the fact that contracts and agreements with Governments are liable to difficulties if they have to be enforced with any loss to the higher of the two contracting parties.[8]

Business negotiations between British capitalists and what were fundamentally European states were the balancing of power and advantage; they were never onesided. The Republics needed our capital and knew that we could provide it at the cheapest going rate. We wanted their business, and appreciated their local knowledge,

---

6. Quoted by Lord McNair, *International Law Opinions* (Cambridge, Cambridge Univ. Press, 1956), ii, 203–4.

7. J. A. B. Beaumont, *Travels in Buenos Ayres and the adjacent Provinces of the Rio de la Plata* (London, 1828), p. 255.

8. Quoted by David Joslin, *A Century of Banking in Latin America* (London, Oxford Univ. Press, 1963), p. 142.

expertise, and ultimate political control. A bargain was struck which took *all* these factors into account.

3. Relations between the producer and the exporter of raw materials

There remains one traditional area of control on which I have only touched so far: the relationship of the foreign exporting house to the Latin American producer. In a broad, general sense, as I have suggested, the European market determined that there should be an emphasis on certain basic export commodities—agricultural products such as sugar, cotton, coffee, tobacco, grain, beef, mutton; minerals such as silver, gold, copper, nitrates. Production for these markets, while it brought prosperity and development over large sectors of the economy, also created a trading situation dangerously dependent on fluctuating world prices. Latin Americans themselves were perfectly aware of the dangers of single crop economies. Neither the authorities of the State of Pará (Brazil) nor the landowners needed to be told that their economic position at the turn of the century, founded on rubber production alone, was insecure. But they also knew that it made slight economic sense to produce an alternative crop such as cocoa, which was restricted by a limited world market, produced elsewhere, and liable to a price fall if Brazilian production increased. Who, in this case, should have taken the initiative in diversifying? The decision was not in the hands of the foreign exporter alone. Both exporters and landowners took a deliberate gamble on maintained world demand for a commodity in the production of which they enjoyed overwhelming natural advantages. And who, at the time, could have been certain enough of himself to advise otherwise?

The point is that producers are bound to supply the most profitable market, even if the long-term prospects are not entirely clear. Without, in the nineteenth century, government incentives or direct intervention, it was in nobody's interest to diversify before the last moment, and no producer could be sure when that last moment had arrived. Similarly, it was in the exporter's interest to supply existing markets, rather than speculate in new markets of unknown value. Merely to maintain his turnover, he too was anxious to diversify at the right moment. But in this respect he was no better off than the producer. Both, indeed, suffered when the market finally collapsed. Neither, in this relationship, was genuinely in control of the other, since both were subject to factors of world demand and competition, to fluctuations in world markets supplied by many competing producers, well beyond the range of their businesses or their personal control. Control could exist where a single firm, or even a single market, handled the product: the American Sugar Refining Company (the 'Sugar Trust') and Cuban–Dominican sugar production; the Carnegie Corporation of Pittsburg and Cuban manganese; the United Fruit Company and Caribbean bananas; the Hamburg and Bremen market for Dominican and Brazilian tobacco; the London market for Argentine beef. But obviously an exporter's control became far more speculative as soon as the product reached beyond a single distributor or market, and few products, save bananas, remained in the hands of one distributor for long.

The individual relationship between the exporter and producer has attracted a great deal of unfavourable attention. Yet it is a relationship which is determined by size; one party is not automatically in control of the other. Small producers, whether peasants or miners, soon found themselves tied to merchants or their agents by traditional credit facilities; they became dependent on negotiating further credit, and virtually powerless in determining a fair price. This was true of Cuban and Colombian tobacco growers, of rubber cutters and shell fishers in Nicaragua, of Honduran mahogany cutters, of Peruvian and Brazilian rubber tappers, of Paraguayan orange growers, yerba producers and lumbermen, of Argentine 'colonists'. But the larger producers, the sugar and coffee planters of Brazil, the Argentine cattlemen, the major nitrate producers of Chile, themselves had the whip-hand. Their political and economic position was too strong to be undermined or overthrown by foreign export houses. When British companies attempted to recreate in Brazil the central sugar factory system—so successful in Europe in gaining total control over the output of the small, beet producers—they found themselves at the mercy of the *fazendeiros*, owners of the land (which they refused to sell to the central factories) and producers on a large enough scale to be able either to look for alternative processors, or to process their own sugar for themselves by traditional methods. The contrast is illustrated in the case of the two principal Argentine export commodities, beef and wheat. Argentine small-scale wheat producers, the 'colonists', fell into the hands of the Big Four, the export firms at Buenos Aires. The beef producers, on the other hand, headed by the leaders of Argentina's landowning oligarchy in total political control at Buenos Aires, showed that in any conflict of interest sufficiently critical to unite local breeders and fatteners against foreign meat packers, it was the packers, ultimately, who went to the wall.

4. The limitations of British business control of the South American economy

While something which could be described as a controlling relation-ship undoubtedly existed in particular areas of contact between British entrepreneurs and Latin Americans, it is clear that we should be careful in defining 'pre-eminence', 'hegemony', 'supremacy', 'in-formal imperialism', 'control' before such blanket terms are used in the context of British financial and commercial activity in Latin America before 1914. So much in the literature of economic imperial-ism has always been taken for granted that it is worth making some effort to distinguish the factors operating on both sides. My own impression is that when the study of simple, legitimate business enterprise, on the small scale common in the nineteenth century, is taken further, the emphasis is more likely to be on the limitations to the discretion and authority of the foreign entrepreneur than on the breadth of his 'control'. He was refused the assistance of his govern-ment except in cases of gross denial of justice or personal assault. He had no political voice or expertise. He was constantly outmanoeuvred by experienced politicians. He was too often a child in the hands of his local agent. He had no secure remedy through the national tribunals. He was the obvious target of criticism in economic disaster. As a foreigner his malpractices, no better no worse than average, were doubly obvious. His trade, through import taxes, bore the major part of the cost of government. His only real safeguard was his indispens-ability, and when local competitors and substitutes developed he was soon displaced.

Ultimately, real control depends both on the size of the business organisation and on its ability to enlist government support, and it may be helpful at this point if I were to emphasise the distinction between the presentday situation and the conditions existing before 1914. Harry Magdoff has recently described, most plausibly, the extent to which U.S. business interests now depend on overseas markets and sources of raw materials to maintain and expand profitability. He has explained, too, the wide range of responsibility accepted by the U.S. government in safeguarding investments and markets.[9] In some respects the position of the U.S. government is not unlike that of

9. In the articles cited in the first footnote to this chapter.

the British government before 1914, when the Foreign Office accepted a responsibility to maintain a 'fair field and no favour' for British trade and finance in all overseas markets, developed and under-developed. But there are significant differences, quite apart from the absence of an international bogey on the scale of Communism, which transformed the real position before 1914:

(*a*) *All* governments today recognise a much greater responsibility for promoting their financial and commercial interests overseas. The promotional activities of H.M. Government in Latin America before 1914 were limited simply to the provision of commercial information. The first real break with this tradition was the D'Abernon Agreement with Argentina in 1929, and an active identification of government services with overseas trade was for Britain a product of the 1930s.

(*b*) Few private enterprises in the last century were big enough, or co-ordinated enough, to exercise monopoly control over world markets. Apart from the great public utility companies and the commercial banks, the standard pattern of British business in Latin America, commercial or industrial, was the partnership of a few individuals, operating on such capital resources as they could raise privately among themselves.

(*c*) The 'channels of international finance', though certainly in the hands of European investors before 1914, were in a disorganised and often thoroughly competitive condition. It is difficult, for example, to speak realistically of 'control' during any of the long periods of 'optimism'. Furthermore, except for a few negotiations of political importance (none of which were relevant to Latin America), there was no British government direction or control over foreign investment.

(*d*) No equivalent exists, for Britain and Latin America in the nineteenth century, of today's vital materials—copper, iron, aluminium, oil. Britain had her own fuel, coal; we found our iron elsewhere; copper was not yet an essential material. The twentieth-century preoccupation with guaranteed supplies of vital raw materials begins, so far as H.M. Government and Latin America were concerned, only with some rather inconclusive negotiations over Pearson's Mexican oil at the outbreak of the First World War. Indeed, it was only in the first three months of war that Britain realised how dependent her industries were on certain materials. The tendency was simply to buy in the cheapest market, wherever it might be. The Iron and Steel Trades Committee, when recommending a more positive attitude, explained that:

> The ore trade of Great Britain was, and still is, mainly in the hands of merchants who acted as intermediaries between the consumer and the shipper or producer of the imported ore. In some cases, users of ores had taken steps to obtain interests in ore properties abroad, but it is generally true that the connection between consumer and producer was purely commercial, and that there was no real solidarity of interest to prevent a sudden interruption of supplies.[10]

(*e*) A traditional objection existed in Britain to 'tied' loans, 'tied' contracts and concessions. British traders, contractors and managers were naturally inclined to 'buy British' if they could, so long as British products were not outrageously uncompetitive. But the close deliberate link-up between development aid and contracts for home manufacturers, which has become so much the pattern for the twentieth century, had no parallel for Britain before 1914. Finance and manufacturing in Victorian and Edwardian Britain each worked to an entirely different set of rules; they were as distinct in their business contacts as they were in their geographical location. The divorce between production and finance seriously diminished Britain's economic power over the world. Things might have been very different if Lenin's 'finance capitalism' had described the situation in Britain as well as it fitted contemporary Germany.

(*f*) Britain's hands were tied in what, for a strong market, would have been her most powerful economic weapon, the manipulation of tariffs. Britain remained a free trader until the early 1930s. Public opinion denied her the use of tariffs, and in so doing blocked the powerful position which would automatically have been hers as the most important market for Chilean copper, Brazilian cotton, Bolivian tin, Argentine beef. She had nothing to offer in return for a reduction of foreign tariffs on her manufactured goods. Naturally, there were loopholes. It has never been determined very precisely whether the prohibition of Argentine livestock imports into the United Kingdom at the beginning of this century was genuinely designed to combat foot-and-mouth disease, or whether it was a protective measure in the interests of British producers. But generally the rule stands. Magdoff makes the point that 'the energetic protection of domestic business by tariffs, quotas, and special treaties, is an

10. Report of the Committee on the Iron and Steel Trades: *Parliamentary Papers*, 1918, xiii, p. 437.

essential element of U.S. international economic policy'. This option was not open to H.M. Government before 1914.

The situation before 1914, even during the peak years of the 'New Imperialism', thus left far fewer opportunities for direct economic control than today's neocolonialism, whether on the level of the businessman or of the politician. But there is a point that has to be made specifically for Britain's 'control' or 'hegemony' in Latin America over the first century of independence. The dominant British interest was in Latin America's capacity as a market for her manufactured goods. Only later did it begin to be thought of as a profitable outlet for capital. At length, well after both of these, Britain came to look to the republics as suppliers of foodstuffs and industrial raw materials. This, of course, made a vast difference to the nature of, and the possibilities for, 'control'. As a monopoly *customer*, control is not difficult. As a *supplier*, especially of goods for which the mass of the population had no real need, Britain was in a much weaker position, subject to the collapse of markets in times of civil war, to the arbitrary raising of tariffs, to the protection of local competitive industries.

A different relationship began to develop when the republics, in and after the 1850s, became genuinely interested in attracting British capital. But the timing of British business operations in Latin America is as important for an argument over 'control' as their scale. British interests in Latin America during the first forty years of independence, during the most vulnerable period of the republics' history, were almost exclusively mercantile. The early government loans were a failure, the mining enterprises a fiasco, and even the import/export business, although it brought prosperity to a few mercantile houses, was on a small scale compared with the late nineteenth century. The development of larger enterprises and of greater sophistication in business methods, whether in international finance, commercial banking, processing and exporting, railway construction or management, coincided with the growth, in the relative peace and prosperity of the decades before 1914, of sophisticated political systems. It coincided, too, with greater diversification in exports, with the breakdown of import monopolies under fierce competition, with the creation of local capital markets, of successful national banking systems, of new industries. On the whole, British traders and investors were not interested in the smaller republics; direct contact with the markets of Central America, Ecuador, Paraguay, and Bolivia (until the age of tin) was abandoned to the newer industrial nations. In the larger republics, national resources, economic and political, developed in parallel with foreign enterprise; they acted, so far as 'informal imperialism' and 'control' were concerned, as mutual checks. While a 4 per cent short-term interest rate existed both in London and in Buenos Aires, as it did from 1903, financial imperialism was dead. A British businessman at Buenos Aires, Rio, or Santiago in the first years of this century would indeed have been surprised to learn that he was in any real sense in 'control' of the bustling, progressive, and prosperous country in which he operated.

5. Conclusion

It may be more helpful, in fact, to abandon the traditional vocabulary of 'economic imperialism', and consider in its place the categories of trades, industries, and services which have by their nature given power and control to the individuals, native or foreign, at their head. The commonsense rule to apply to any trader is that he will buy in the cheapest market and sell in the dearest. Similarly, a monopolist will charge what the trade or the traffic will bear. This was as true of the two railway companies operating out of Sheffield in the late nineteenth century as it was of the British-owned railway monopolies in Latin America—the Mexican Railway, with its monopoly over Mexico's principal foreign trade route, Vera Cruz to Mexico City; the São Paulo Railway Company, with its stranglehold on the critical São Paulo to Santos line; the Antofagasta Railway, in a unique position to handle the greater part of the traffic generated by the boom in Bolivian tin. Government control over rates and prices, the development first of alternative railway concessions and then of road traffic, broke each monopoly in time, but while it lasted the monopolist, native or foreign, could be expected to behave as a monopolist. The Tucuman sugar producers, the Colligaçao Assucareira do Brazil, the sugar syndicate in Ecuador, all unimpeachably national, behaved like any other propertied, privileged, and protected trust.

For any product for which a fixed or limited market existed, and in which an opportunity existed to restrict production, an appropriate organisation developed. The organisation might be foreign-dominated: the nitrate combinations of Chile, the international iodine syndicate, the Borate Syndicate. It might be native—the committee controlling the 'valorisation' of Brazilian coffee before 1914; the promoters of an unsuccessful attempt in 1908 to organise the cocoa producers of Brazil, Sao Thomé, and Principe for the valorisation of cocoa; parties to the discussions for the valorisation of Brazilian sugar in 1912–13. If a market, local or international, offered a fixed outlet to powerful competitors, the likelihood was that an agreement would be negotiated at the expense of the consumer, such as the arrangements between British and American tobacco companies in world markets before 1914, or the market-sharing agreements of the British Rail Makers' Association with the German and Belgian Associations in 1884, extended to the Americans and French in 1904. If an agricultural or pastoral industry found itself short of capital, of transport, of storage and sales facilities, of access to markets, of means for the rapid disposal of perishable products, production and distribution normally fell into the hands of those with the capital or resource to provide some or all of these—the sugar and wine monopolists of western Argentina, the 'Big Four' at Buenos Aires and Argentine wheat; La Industrial Paraguaya (British-controlled) and Paraguayan on yerba; the Sociedad Explotadora de Tierra del Fuego, the Sociedad Industrial y Ganadera de Magallanes, and the Sociedad Ganadera 'Gente Grande', with their great sheep-runs in the frozen territories of the south; the United Fruit Company and banana production in the tropical north.

In every case it is the nature of the trade or of the industry which determines its need to 'control' a market, and this will apply equally whether it is under native or foreign direction. Similarly, local conditions, social, political and economic, can make all the difference to the adequacy of that 'control', native or foreign. Too often in the past the coexistence of foreign financiers, investors, traders, and diplomats has been taken as sufficient evidence in itself of effective 'control', of 'economic imperialism' in action. I have tried to suggest that however true this may be on particular occasions, it cannot be assumed to be the case. Generalisations on the existence and extent of 'economic imperialism', 'informal imperialism', and 'control' must, in fact, be founded on some expertise with respect to the day-to-day operation of business, some understanding of the limitations which all businessmen in practice experience, as of the genuine powers which they often possess.

DISCUSSION

Imperialism as 'control'.   A number of questions were asked about the implication contained in Platt's paper that imperialism was synonymous with 'conscious' political (or economic) control. It was pointed out, for instance, that Marxists used the term in a very much broader sense. For them the question of control was not irrelevant but what had to be asked was why political control was important for European states in some areas of the world and not in others. The answer was, that if there was to be trade and investment outside Europe then it was also necessary that there be a political and legal system to protect it. 'In Africa in the nineteenth century it was very clear that the only way to protect these things was direct colonial control. Colonialism was necessary to establish a legal framework in which capitalist relations could operate.' In Latin America, on the other hand, there was already a legal system which was sufficiently stable for trade to continue. Platt disagreed. If there was no conscious control there was no imperialism. Again, there were never sufficient guarantees of the type mentioned. Throughout the century Britain's economic interests were constantly being damaged and it could do nothing. 'If we had been out and out imperialists we would have intervened over and over again.'

During further discussion of the question of control it was also asserted that one of the chief reasons why Britain did not intervene more directly in Latin America in the nineteenth century was fear of the United States. This had been recognised by Lenin who allowed for the fact that some countries would be able to preserve their nominal independence on account of conflict between the powers.

Relations between local and foreign capitalists in South America. Another series of questions concerned the relations between British and other foreign traders and bankers in South America and their local rivals. Why should it be assumed that their interests were necessarily in conflict? Were not the local elites closely integrated into the imperialist structure? In reply Platt said he preferred to look at the subject in another way. In his opinion Robinson's theory concerning collaborating elites (see V. 2 above) could be turned on its head in regard to Latin America. There it was a question of foreigners having to cooperate with local elites, not of those elites having to collaborate with the British or French.

How much foreign intervention in Latin America? Issue was taken with some of Platt's examples designed to show that British businessmen were often unsuccessful in their disputes with local groups. In the case of the Argentine meat industry was it not the case that the foreign packing houses always won against Argentinian producers? It was also suggested that these houses had got more support from the British government than Platt allowed. In reply Platt maintained that his reading of the evidence contained in Peter Smith's *Politics and Beef in Argentina* proved that his own point of view was the correct one.

Lastly, another critic of Platt's paper claimed that his argument about the activities of European enterprises in South America was distorted by the fact that he had talked only about the British. It was clear from the Venezuelan records that many foreign businessmen had pressed exaggerated claims against local men but that many of them were not from Britain.

Conclusion
Bob Sutcliffe

1. The ambiguities of imperialism

The theory of imperialism is at once one of the strongest and one of the weakest branches of Marxist theory. Its strength is revealed in one way in most historical discussions of imperialism by the respect with which it is treated by non-Marxist scholars. Virtually all discussions of imperialism at a theoretical level assign importance to the Marxist theory—either as an explanation which is satisfactory or one which is erroneous but requiring challenge. The Marxist theory of imperialism, as even its sharpest critics admit,[1] appears to have offered a stronger challenge to orthodox non-Marxist scholars than most branches of Marxism has yet succeeded in doing. Hardly any non-Marxist economist gives serious consideration to the Marxist theory of value, for instance; but very few historians on the question fail to acknowledge what they conceive to be the Marxist theory of imperialism.

The weakness of the Marxist theory of imperialism is revealed by the paucity of contributions to it in the decades after Lenin wrote his *Imperialism, the Highest Stage of Capitalism*. The politics of the international communist movement after the late 1920s meant that, except for a few writers outside the official communist parties, the theory froze in the position in which Lenin had left it. Yet meanwhile capitalism was passing through major fluctuations in its fortunes and structure: the interwar slump, the wartime recovery and the rapid

1. For instance, Raymond Aron, *The Century of Total War*, London 1954, p. 57.

postwar growth of the 1950s and 1960s; the emergence after 1945 of United States supremacy in the world economy and its more recent erosion; and, at a more political level, decolonisation of the third world, the Chinese revolution, the rise and fall of the cold war, and the moves towards western European integration. For many years theory failed to keep pace with these changes. When in recent years the widespread discussion of the theory of imperialism began once again it suffered from this long hiatus. Marxist writers nowadays, although united in the belief that imperialism is still in some sense alive as a major feature of the capitalist system, differ very greatly about its meaning, about its laws of motion, about the themes which should compose the discussion of imperialism at the theoretical level, and about the contemporary value of the classic Marxist texts on imperialism.

The seminar on which this book is largely based was partly designed to start a discussion on the theoretical aspects of imperialism between Marxists and non-Marxists, and among Marxists with rather varied approaches. It succeeded to the extent that many of the participants felt clearer about their own views at the end than they had been at the beginning. But in other ways it failed; on many occasions discussions of some vehemence were conducted at what were obviously cross purposes. No doubt these difficulties are common to many similar discussions.

The main cause of these problems was alluded to in the introduction: it is the deep ambiguity with which the term imperialism is imbued in practice. To political leaders in the nineteenth century, to their liberal critics like Hobson or Brailsford or Parker T. Moon, to their apologists like Seeley, to politicians and intellectuals in the colonies, to some early participants in Marxist discussions of imperialism like Kautsky, the salient features of a definition of imperialism were, first, the policy pursued by the major powers in conquering and administering colonies and, second, the political and economic relations between the advanced and backward nations in the capitalist system.

It is clear that to Lenin imperialism connoted much more than this. As he indicates plainly in *Imperialism*, he uses the word to characterise the stage which the capitalist system on a world scale entered around the end of the nineteenth century. His 'five essential features' of this stage are well known: the decisive role of monopoly, the merging of industrial and finance capital, the predominance of export of capital over export of goods, the division of the world market between competing international capitalist monopolies and the completion of the territorial division of the world. The briefest possible definition, he says, would be 'the monopoly stage of capitalism'.

So, as Tom Kemp points out in the first paper, Marxists often use imperialism in this 'technical' sense, of Lenin, which is not identical with its sense in more general usage. And a central theme of Magdoff's paper is to deny the coincidence often assumed between colonialism and imperialism.[2] Probably the most common and important misunderstanding of Lenin's position concerns the scramble for territory in the nineteenth century. This is not what he meant by imperialism. On the contrary, it was a prelude to imperialism which really began partly as a result of the fact that the division of the world .was complete. The system changed its character at the end of the century because from then on both expansion and rivalry of the major capitalist powers would have to take new forms since the chances of territorial expansion had been exhausted.

Marxists since Lenin have in fact fluctuated in their use of the term imperialism. Very often it is used to describe the whole capitalist system; just as often it refers to the relations between advanced and backward countries within the system. Sometimes it is used in both senses simultaneously, either with, or more often without, an acknowledgement of the ambiguity involved. On the whole when Marxist writers in the last two or three decades have written about the theory of imperialism they have been writing about underdevelopment and the international aspects of capitalism. This ambiguity, therefore, lies at the root of misunderstandings among Marxists and between Marxists and non-Marxists; and it leads to the failure to effect a marriage between Lenin's writing on imperialism and contemporary Marxist writing about underdevelopment. It is, therefore, much more than a semantic question.

The acknowledgement of this ambiguity and an awareness of its consequences can, however, be the key to a better understanding of the theoretical aspects of imperialism and to the solution of a number of problems. It becomes easier to assess the disagreement between Marxists and others over the historical origins of imperialism, to delineate the proper scope of a theory of imperialism today, and to

---

2. A recent review (of *Marxist Sociology in Action* by J. A. Banks) in the *Times Literary Supplement* makes two mistakes based on this false identification of colonialism with imperialism. First, it claims that Lenin's theory held that 'when colonialism was brought to an end . . . the working class would lose its social democratic illusions and turn more receptively to revolutionary marxism'. Second, the review attempts to disprove the theory by arguing that 'the highest working-class standards in Europe are to be found in Sweden, a country without colonial possessions' (*TLS*, 11 Dec. 1970, p. 1438).

identify some of the more important answered and unanswered questions of imperialism theory.

2. The argument over the historical origins of imperialism

In ignoring or misunderstanding this ambiguity, non-Marxist historians and economists have invented two myths: the 'Hobson–Lenin' theory of imperialism and, what is almost the same thing, the 'economic' theory of imperialism. The brilliant and maverick, antisemitic, liberal, proto-Keynesian Hobson, wrote *Imperialism, a study* and other books and pamphlets in an effort to expose, and if possible reverse, certain expansionist policies of the British government at the turn of the century. As is well known, Lenin was greatly indebted to Hobson for the evidence he produced of the relations between British imperial policy and capital exports. But Lenin owed scarcely anything to Hobson from a theoretical point of view. Although Hobson associated imperial expansion and capital export with underconsumption at home (the result of unequal income distribution) he hardly saw it as a special stage of capitalist development. What Lenin took over from Hobson was some evidence for one country which seemed to establish a link between two elements of his multiform definition of imperialism as a stage of capitalism. To speak of a 'Hobson–Lenin theory', therefore, is greatly to exaggerate the theoretical proximity of the two.[3] Lenin explicitly repudiated Hobson's theoretical perspective.

But Lenin did agree with Hobson about the association of capital export and the territorial division of the world in the nineteenth century ('imperialism' in Hobson's more restricted sense). Lenin in fact added little or nothing to what Hobson had said about that. Neither of them, however, held the crude mechanistic view often ascribed to them by historians under the name of the 'economic theory of imperialism'. This kind of view, that there was a simple connection between economic cause and political effect (in this case between capital export and colonial annexation) was condemned by Lenin in another context as 'economism' which he regarded as a very vulgar form of Marxism[4]. But when the twin myths, the 'Hobson–

3. D. K. Fieldhouse more or less does this in his introduction to *The Theory of Capitalist Imperialism*, (London, Longmans) 1967, though he does also emphasise the earlier theoretical roots of Lenin's ideas in Marxism.
4. V. I. Lenin, 'Two tactics of social democracy', *Selected Works*, (Centenary edition, London, Lawrence and Wishart 1970), p. 90.

Lenin theory' and the 'economic theory', are under attack, at least in relation to the nineteenth century, it is very often some form of 'economism' which is being condemned.

There are four frequently used elements in this attack, and most of them received some discussion in the seminar. The first involves taking an individual country or area which came under the colonial yoke and identifying the immediate interests (very often not economic) which led to its annexation. One of two conclusions is then often drawn—either that this disproves the 'Hobson–Lenin' theory or that, while the 'Hobson–Lenin' theory may be a correct analysis of other countries, it does not hold in the particular one being studied. (Stengers' paper on the Congo is in part an instance of this.) In fact this approach seldom succeeds in really engaging the Hobson or the Lenin approach, since both of them were asserting a *general* relationship between capital export and the need for annexation, not that there was a simple unique relationship in every case. Both Kemp (in his paper) and Wehler (in the discussion of his paper) emphasise the need to look at a theory as a whole. The particular weight to be attached to it or different elements of it in particular situations is a matter of judgment. In other words it is necessary to distinguish between theorisation (explaining the essence of a phenomenon) and generalisation, which is supposed to apply to all cases alike. The exception does not prove the rule; but nor does it disprove a theory.

Of course, in a capitalist system which was in any case expansionist, whatever the root cause of that expansionism, there were bound to be a multitude of factors—especially strategic and political ones—which would crop up constantly to justify or necessitate territorial annexations. This is not to say that these non-economic factors were not the real ones which caused annexation. They were perfectly real and were in many cases decisive. The theory merely holds that structural economic factors were behind the general expansionist posture of advanced capitalist countries in the later nineteenth century. Against the theory, however, it is sometimes argued that economic motives, while they undoubtedly existed, were either not fundamental,[5] or were systematically used as a smokescreen or façade for the basic (political) reasons.[6] Opinions of this type about the causes of ex-

---

5. D. K. Fieldhouse, 'Imperialism: an historiographical revision'. *Economic History Review*, 2nd series, **14,** 2 Dec. 1961.
6. Somewhat preposterously, Raymond Aron, for instance, argues that 'the actual relationship is most often the reverse of that accepted by the current theory of imperialism; the economic interests are only a pretext or a rationalisation, whereas the profounder cause lies in the nation's will to power' (*The Century of Total War*, p. 59).

pansion are probably affected by the kind of evidence which is being examined. It is not surprising that a full examination of diplomatic notes suggests that diplomatic and strategic motives had a life of their own.[7]

The second, and perhaps the commonest, element in the attack is on a rather more general plane. It involves saying that there was very little correlation between the countries to which the capital went on the one hand, and the countries which were being annexed in the age of imperialism on the other: countries which were annexed (especially in Africa) received very little capital; and some areas which received large quantities of capital, as Christopher Platt argues for Latin America, were not annexed and were not even scenes of major British diplomatic activity.[8] It is now firmly established that most British capital in the post 1870 period did not go to the colonies which were being annexed at the time.[9] But once again this argument can easily become a caricature of Hobson's or Lenin's approach to the link between economics and politics, though it must be acknowledged that Hobson (and Lenin by association) was very slapdash in his use of evidence of this kind. Hobson is more vulnerable on this score than Lenin, who, as mentioned above, was more interested in the consequences of the fact that the world was by about 1900 fully parcelled up between the imperial powers than in exactly how the parcelling up had been done. This second argument suffers from the same general weaknesses as the first. In addition, it can be said that in some cases annexation by European powers was ruled out for obvious political reasons (as in the United States and Latin America for instance). In any case, from the standpoint of protecting investments the need for political annexation varied according to the degree of instability of the area concerned, the extent to which the law of property and contract operated in practice, and so on. In parts of Africa for instance very little trade or secure investment was possible

7. It seems to have affected the opinions of Robinson and Gallagher, for example, in *Africa and the Victorians*, (London, Macmillan, 1961).
8. For instance, L. H. Gann and P. Duigan in *Burden of Empire* (London, Pall Mall Press, 1967), accuse Hobson of 'intellectual jugglery' in presenting the figures (p. 41). Fieldhouse makes a similar point (*The Theory of Capitalist Imperialism*, p. 189–90). A. Emmanuel states that 'there is no possible link between the accumulation of these investments from 1870 to 1914 and the territorial expansion of the imperialists during the same period' ('White settler colonialism and the myth of investment imperialism', paper for Elsinore symposium on imperialism, April 1971) also see M. E. Chamberlain, *The New Imperialism*, (London, Historical Association, 1970), pp. 21–3.
9. M. Segal and M. Simon, 'British foreign capital issues 1865–94', *Journal of Economic History*, **21,** 4, 1961.

without colonial control. Almost certainly, during the scramble for Africa at least, much of the annexation was of a preemptive kind, which Johnson describes in the case of Guinea.[10]

The third element of the attack is the claim that the economic benefits postulated by the 'economic theory' failed to materialise. Some attempts to draw up a colonial balance sheet of costs and benefits suggest that more money was put into the colonies by the colonial power than was ever taken out of them. There are a variety of reasons why this type of argument is inappropriate as a criticism of either Hobson or Lenin. First, and rather trivially, it was often true that colonialists and potential investors had dreams which never materialised of the economic benefits that a particular colony would bring or of what mineral and other wealth might be found. (Wehler and Kanya-Forstner argue that such dreams were common in Germany and France.) More fundamentally, imperialism, even in Hobson's sense, was a general phenomenon, in which the value of empire was to some extent viewed as a whole; so a separate balance sheet drawn up for each colony or even non-colony may not measure the value put on that country as part of the whole system. In any case a national balance sheet has very little meaning. Lenin and Hobson in fact both condemned the colonial system because through taxation it imposed costs (for administration and so on) on many, while it produced benefits only for a few. An administrative cost matched against the returns on an investment therefore is no argument one way or the other about the root causes of imperialism.[11]

A fourth argument against the Hobson or the Lenin view of imperialism is not so much associated with the ambiguity of the concept; but it might as well be mentioned here since it is as commonly seen as the other three. It concerns the profitability of investment. Lenin, following Marx, mentioned the falling rate of profit in the advanced countries as a factor helping to explain the export of capital overseas. This has been wrongly interpreted by critics to mean that

10. P. Sweezy has made a related point in a more general way: 'Though English capitalists may have little to gain through annexation . . . they have much to lose through annexation by others . . . The result may appear to be a net loss . . . [but] what is important is not the loss or gain compared to the pre-existing situation, but rather the loss or gain compared to the situation which would have prevailed, had a rival succeeded in stepping in ahead' (*The Theory of Capitalist Development*, (London, Dobson, 1946), p. 303).

11. Fieldhouse sees this point but uses it in a rather odd way: 'Even if the expansion of Europe brought economic advantage to investors, traders and exporters these were private interests: it does not follow that European states as a whole benefited accordingly', *The Colonial Empires*, (London, Weidenfeld & Nicolson, 1966), p. 392. Quite true: but this backfires if it is meant, as seems implied, as an argument against Hobson or Lenin.

rates of return were higher overseas than at home.[12] A comparison of rates of return is sometimes made to demonstrate, with the scanty information available, that average returns were in fact scarcely higher abroad than they were at home. This evidence is interesting for some purposes,[13] but in relation to this discussion it is all but irrelevant. This is, first, because the evidence is mostly about *average* rates of return, whereas (as Magdoff points out in his paper)[14] the point, if it is to make any sense, must relate to *marginal* rates of return (i.e. the return on the last unit of investment). As long as marginal rates are higher abroad than at home then capital will flow abroad. In a competitive situation such flows will tend to equalise the marginal (but not the average) rates of return in both places. But in fact (as Magdoff shows) in an age of monopoly, when the entry of capital to some industries is restricted, ideas of an overall rate of profit (average or marginal), or of the equalisation of rates of profit, lose much of their significance, since rates of return will tend to differ even over the long run between industries.

The effect of monopoly on relative rates of return is more relevant perhaps to the period after the Second World War when the majority of capital export has tended to take the form of direct investment by corporations in their overseas subsidiaries; it is not so relevant to the period before 1914 when capital export predominantly took the form of bonds and so the capital market may have been more competitive. But at either time the effects of capital export on the profit rate cannot be assessed simply by looking at the rate of return obtained on the foreign investment itself. It must have had some effect on the profitability of other capital overseas since many investments were complementary. It must also have affected the profitability of capital at home. Some foreign investment led to an increase in demand for home produced goods (e.g. railway locomotives and track); in the recent period investment in consumer goods production has sometimes restricted exports. More generally, if everything which is invested abroad were invested at home instead, then clearly profitability would be significantly changed. The investors in any event must expect more benefit from their foreign investment than they would get by

12. Fieldhouse does this (*The Colonial Empires*, p. 386) but later corrects himself: 'A straight comparison between dividend rates on European and colonial investments is impossible since European rates were necessarily raised by the possibility of investment overseas' (*ibid.* p. 389).
13. For example, A. K. Cairncross, *Home and Foreign Investment 1870–1913*, (Cambridge, Cambridge Univ. Press, 1953).
14. So does Richard D. Wolff in 'Modern imperialism: The view from the metropolis', *American Economic Review, Papers and Proceedings*, May 1970, p. 228.

investing elsewhere or they would not do it.

Like some of the other arguments this point is really a logical rather than an empirical one. So the evidence presented against it is hardly relevant. And this is a general feature of the debate between Marxists and non-Marxists about the driving forces of imperialism in history. Much of the empirical criticism levelled against the Marxist theory is correct but misdirected. The target is often a mirage and the weapons inappropriate. And a major reason for this appears to be the ambiguity of the term imperialism.

3. The origins and proper concerns of the Marxist theory of imperialism

The same ambiguity is also responsible for a good deal of confusion among Marxists writers about the provenance of the Marxist theory and about what are its proper concerns. One of the fundamental tenets of Marxism is that different aspects of the theory of capitalist society and development are indivisible; strictly speaking it is not possible to have a Marxist theory of imperialism, but only to look at imperialism as an aspect of the theory of capitalism. But whether imperialism is viewed as a stage of capitalism or whether it is seen as those aspects of capitalist development which have related the fortunes of advanced and backward areas, it has since Lenin occupied an important and sometimes central position in Marxian analysis. Its concerns can be divided into three:

(*a*) the development and the economic and class structure of advanced capitalist societies (especially the factors which drive them towards geographical expansion of their economies) and the relations between them;

(*b*) the economic and political relations between advanced nations and backward or colonial nations within the world capitalist system;

(*c*) the development of economic and class structure in the more backward nations of the capitalist system, especially the roots of their domination and their failure to industrialise.

A good deal of Marxist writing tries in principle to take these three concerns together and to construct a theory of the whole capitalist system. But the balance between them has shifted frequently. Marx's own major concern was, of course, the first of the three, the development of capitalism in the advanced countries. But he was also interested in the backward ones from a variety of viewpoints. He saw in them some of the sources of primary accumulation for the early industrialising countries through plunder, slavery and the activities of trading companies. Then he also foresaw the colonies and backward countries developing under capitalism in the wake of the industrialisation of the advanced countries.

From Marx's writings about the falling rate of profit, the growth of monopoly and finance capitalism (later elaborated by Hilferding), Lenin's *Imperialism* is directly descended. From that work it might appear that Lenin, even more than Marx, was primarily concerned with the first of the three concerns, to the virtual exclusion of the other two. But Lenin's work has to be seen as a whole; in fact few people did more to develop an account of the third concern, the absorption by capitalism of the backward areas and their prospects within the system. This account is found in his writings about Russia, whose situation as a backward country of the capitalist system at the end of the nineteenth century and start of the twentieth has been analysed at a deeper level than that of most similar countries since them. In addition to Lenin, the major contributor to this analysis was Trotsky. Between them, though not in concert, they developed what amounts to an implicit theory of imperialism from the standpoint of the backward countries. The common accusations that Lenin's theory of imperialism is Eurocentric arise from a failure to consider this implicit part of the theory. Rosa Luxemburg more explicitly placed her analysis of the backward countries in the context of a theory of imperialism which began with an examination (again directly descended from Marx) of the development of capitalism in the advanced countries. The tradition of Marxist writing established by these writers is one which involves discussing all three of the proper concerns of the theory of imperialism. In other words it tries to incorporate them as part of an integral analysis of the capitalist system.

In the two decades after 1930 Marxism largely failed in most parts of the world to advance its analysis of the capitalist system, even though that system was undergoing profound changes. But a certain amount of analysis did take place of the economic situation of backward countries and of their place within the system, and in particular of their political and economic relations with the advanced countries. But the theory of imperialism suffered in its development from a separation of class analysis from national analysis. In other words the theory which had its origin (in Lenin, Marx and Luxemburg) as a class theory, an extension of the Marxian analysis of capitalism into a new phase, was later elaborated as a theory of the economic relations between states, developed and underdeveloped.

In other words the emphasis shifted almost exclusively to the third of the theory's three concerns. This partly reflected changing political perspectives within the international communist movement, away from the hopes of revolution in the advanced countries, which Lenin had entertained, towards emphasis on anticolonial and national liberation struggles in the underdeveloped countries.

This change in political emphasis gave birth to an ambiguity which is the exact counterpart of that other ambiguity which is central to the misunderstanding of the historical debate about the nineteenth century. Imperialism in its modern sense came to connote *both* the capitalist system as a whole *and* the political and economic dominance of the advanced countries within it. If it is taken to mean the whole capitalist system, then one of its important concerns now must be, as it was fifty years ago, the relations of the advanced capitalist countries to each other. This remains a source of considerable confusion in discussions about the meaning of imperialism, especially between Marxists and non-Marxists.[15] A related problem is what is meant by *British* or *American* imperialism in relation to imperialism as a whole. Most Marxists would probably answer this by saying that capitalism (or imperialism) is both one system and at the same time many systems, each one of which possesses a certain amount of autonomy in relation to the others. The imperialism of a particular country would be most appropriately used in discussing either the rivalry between the advanced countries or the way in which domination over the third world operates in practice.

The contemporary debate, unlike the historical one, no longer involves many non-Marxists; belief in the usefulness of the category imperialism is now largely confined to those professing or influenced by Marxism. In other circles decolonisation has been taken to mark the end of imperialism, although theoretically more vague concepts of neocolonialism or neo-imperialism have some currency even outside socialist circles. The participants in the debate over imperialism have

---

15. A recent interchange in the United States illustrates this. Harry Magdoff condemns a recent critical article about his work because 'Imperialism [the authors claim] concerns only relations between the advanced and underdeveloped countries. . . . Narrowing down imperialism to trade with, and investment in, the Third World thus eliminates a vital sector of political and economic activity: the imperialist rivalries associated with the investment operations of advanced capitalist nations across one another's borders' (*Monthly Review,* Oct. 1970, pp. 5 and 8). Magdoff is replying to an article by S. M. Miller, R. Bennett and C. Alapatt in *Social Policy,* New York, **1,** no. 3, 1970.

changed; so has the ground from which they argue. But the legacy of ambiguity is still intact.

4. Answered and unanswered questions of imperialism

The starting point for Marx and Lenin was an analysis of capitalism in the advanced countries which then reached out to incorporate the underdeveloped ones. Marxist scholars are now engaged in an effort to advance their understanding of the structure of advanced capitalism and to reunite it with an account of the position of the backward countries about which there is much wider agreement. This means that at present, while there exists a large body of useful descriptive and analytical work on the underdeveloped countries from a more or less Marxist point of view, the level of analysis of the advanced capitalist countries remains very inadequate. It is still the issues concerning the relations of the advanced and backward countries (the second of the three concerns mentioned above) which occupy a high proportion of the discussion of imperialism: issues such as the role of foreign investment, unequal exchange, the dependence of the advanced countries on the backward countries, and the role of the international firm. It is worth saying a little about these issues in turn since they all arose in discussion during the seminar on which this book is based. In retrospect it is easier to see them more as part of a general pattern, and to see which of the questions which they raise remain unanswered.

The problem which most frequently arises in the discussion of *foreign investment* is how to reconcile two things: first, the once common view that foreign investment in backward countries was a response to lack of profitable investment opportunities in the advanced countries, and second, the now common view that foreign investment has led to a much greater return of profits back to the investing countries and so acts as a 'giant pump for sucking surplus out of the underdeveloped countries'.[16] (The second point is made in the papers by Barratt Brown, Magdoff and Sutcliffe.) This is an understandable but unnecessary confusion since there is really no contradiction. If foreign investment succeeds in finding profits, this by itself implies (except when the total of new investment is growing exceptionally fast) that over some time period the return flow of profits is going to

16. P. M. Sweezy, 'Obstacles to economic development' in C. H. Feinstein, ed., *Socialism, Capitalism and Economic Growth Essays presented to Maurice Dobb*, (Cambridge, Cambridge Univ. Press, 1967).

be higher than the original outflow of investment. It is certainly true that in Britain between 1870 and 1914, in the heyday of capital export, total profits were greater than new capital flowing overseas. And the counterpart is now true for many areas of the underdeveloped countries: the outflow of profit is higher than the inflow of capital. This flow of profits, of course, increases the surplus searching for investment outlets in the advanced countries; but in the Marxist analysis this is no more of a contradiction than that which is created by the profitability of capital no matter where it may be invested.

The question of *unequal exchange* is a trickier one which has been widely discussed only recently. The notion of unequal exchange between two different capitals of unequal bargaining power is one which exists in Marx's *Capital* where it is seen as a function of temporary monopoly or monopsony power. In a world where monopoly is widespread unequal exchange on this analysis could be expected to be the rule rather than the exception. The issue has come into prominence recently through the publication of *L'Echange inegal* by A. Emmanuel, which argues that unequal exchange systematically exists in trade between developed and underdeveloped countries, and is a means of the exploitation of the latter by the former. This view has political importance since Emmanuel has claimed that unequal exchange undermines the objective basis for international class solidarity: the working class of the advanced countries actually exploits the working class of the underdeveloped countries; and, because of the tendency for the rate of profit to be equalised, the working class has gained more than capital has from unequal exchange.[17] Bettelheim in a recent vigorous debate with Emmanuel has argued that 'the rate of exploitation' is much higher in the advanced capitalist countries than in the underdeveloped ones'.[18] In other words, he claims, the gap between productivity and wages is relatively greater in developed countries than it is in underdeveloped countries. The evidence on this is very unreliable and incomplete, but it seems at present to go against Bettelheim's view. In any case in conditions of international division of labour within international corporations, productivity is not something which can be measured in different operations of one enterprise. The enterprise's ability to set arbitrary prices for transfers of semifinished goods within the same firm means

17. ' . . . super-profits can only be temporary. Super wages, however, became automatically in the long run, the normal level of wages . . . ' (A. Emmanuel, 'International Solidarity of Workers', *Monthly Review*, June 1970, p. 18).
18. C. Bettelheim, 'International solidarity of workers', *Monthly Review*, June 1970, p. 21.

that relative productivity between different branches of the firm will take on an arbitrary value. As in a single plant where, say, production line workers are paid different wages from cleaning workers, productivity (and hence the notion of exploitation) is indivisible.[19] On the other side it can also be doubted whether the evidence bears out Emmanuel's insistence that the rate of profit does in fact tend to be equalised.

Economically, this question of unequal exchange remains unanswered. One of the problems is that trade and investment cannot be properly analysed in isolation. For one thing the export of capital can lead very directly and immediately to the export of goods, and nearly always has an indirect effect on trade patterns. Also, given a system of multilateral trade and payments, a trade surplus in one place 'finances' (i.e. earns the foreign exchange for) investment elsewhere; so it was in the nineteenth century when Britain's trade surplus with India financed investment in the United States and elsewhere. This fact partly undermines the criticism levelled against the association of imperial expansion with capital export. Now, since so much trade takes place within international firms,[20] it may take place at bogus transfer prices. Where, as in the case of oil, for example, one branch of the firm sells goods to another branch in a different country, the prices of these sales can be manipulated in lieu of capital movements and the firm can locate its income and so take its profits in whichever country it wishes. So charging a low transfer price for raw material produced in one country and exported to another within the same firm, may be financially equivalent to charging a high price and then repatriating the profits. This is one reason why the theory of unequal exchange has to be incorporated into the aspects of the theory of imperialism which deal with investment.

Politically, the debate on unequal exchange harks back to something

---

19. The theory of unequal exchange begins with K. Marx, *Capital*, i, 232–3. Later contributors are: E. Preobrazhensky, *The New Economics,* (London, Oxford Univ. Press, 1965); *A. Emmanuel, L'Echange inegal,* (Paris, 1969); C. Bettelheim, critical introduction and conclusion to Emmanuel (above); J. Palloix, *Problemes de la croissance en economie ouverte,* (Paris, 1969); E. Mandel, in *Pensamiento Critico,* Havana, no. 36; S. Amin, *L'accumulation a l'echelle mondiale,* (Paris, 1970).
20. A recent estimate by GATT suggests that about 30 per cent of the total of world trade may now be of this kind.
21. Martin Nicolaus has written: 'The labor aristocracy was not merely, for Lenin, an epithet, a rhetorical insult. . . . It was a serious theoretical explanation, based on the method of class analysis appropriate in the imperialist epoch, of the recurrent and persistent tendencies towards imperial chauvinism among workers in the metropolis' ('The theory of labor aristocracy', *Monthly Review*, April 1970, p. 91).

which Lenin regarded as an essential element in his theoretical writing on imperialism—the theory of *labour aristocracy*.[21] Sections of the British working class at the end of the nineteenth century and the beginning of the twentieth not only shared some of the gains of imperialism, but also in many instances adopted a pro-imperialist political position. And this remained true in many advanced countries today of some sections of the working class. Baran and Sweezy have argued in *Monopoly Capital* against the revolutionary potential of the American working class, though unlike Emmanuel they do not attribute this to unequal exchange.

All such views combine ideological and economic elements in different proportions. Emmanuel is exceptional in arguing that the objective economic basis for working class unity against imperialism has now vanished. His view almost certainly attaches too much importance to the notion of unequal exchange, which cannot be the whole substance of the exploitation of the working class on an international plane. It may be better to see unequal exchange as mediating different rates of exploitation in the advanced and the underdeveloped countries. It is quite possible that, because of unequal exchange, a lower than average rate of exploitation in the advanced countries is sustainable with the aid of a higher one in the underdeveloped countries. Even if this is true, however—and much more work is needed to establish it—it proves that the interests of the working class in advanced and underdeveloped countries are inconsistent only if the permanent existence of capitalism in the advanced countries is being assumed. As long as there is any exploitation in developed and underdeveloped countries then the end of capitalism would imply the end of this exploitation and in principle open the way to the improvement in the material standard of the working class in both areas at once.

This is the perspective which underlies Lenin's theory of labour aristocracy. And there is a close connection between this theory and the notion of social imperialism which, in the context of Germany and the United States, is discussed in the paper by Wehler. The idea that, regardless of objective interest, a ruling class can use imperialism to divert the attention of the ruled from domestic abuses and problems is one which many governments have been aware of. More discussion can be expected of what objective basis exists if any for social imperialism or whether it is merely a question of the political position adopted by the working class in defiance of its real interests.

It is interesting to note that 'social imperialism' is also the term used by the government of the People's Republic of China to describe the policies of the Soviet Union. In what sense, if any, imperialism can be attributed to socialist countries is a hotly debated issue at the political level. The economic aspects of the question have so far been discussed very little. They were raised in one session of our seminar and it was clear then that the economic basis for imperialism of socialist countries, if one exists at all, must be radically different from that of capitalist imperialism. Private investment and the flow of profits are irrelevant to it; the terms of official loans and the terms of trade agreements could in principle be relevant. But beyond that at present we encounter ignorance: at a theoretical and empirical level these remain unanswered questions.

The relevance of the question of unequal exchange partly, of course, depends on the amount of trade which actually takes place between developed and underdeveloped countries and on the institutional framework within which this trade occur. In this connection there has been some discussion recently of the degree to which advanced capitalism is dependent on the underdeveloped countries. One measure of this dependence is the proportions in which total trade is distributed between these two groups of countries; since the war the trade of underdeveloped countries has been growing noticeably slower than international trade as a whole; but trade between the advanced countries has been growing much faster. Looking at raw materials alone we find not only what is predictable, that food and raw materials have declined as a proportion of the imports of developed countries, but also, more surprisingly, that a growing share of the food and raw materials is coming from the advanced countries themselves. Their share in this trade is in fact well over half. There are exceptions to this—fuel (oil in particular)—where since the war a rapidly growing share of imports has been coming from the underdeveloped countries; also wood, and a number of crucial materials for the manufacture of jet engines.[22]

Such exceptions suggest that the aggregate trade figures do not necessarily reveal very much about dependence in a long-run sense. Some of the trade between advanced countries (especially that in manufactures) could in an emergency be supplied from domestic resources; some of raw materials imported from the underdeveloped countries (and from the developed countries of course) are irreplaceable. In the longer run it now seems to be increasingly feared that within the foreseeable future supplies of some important materials will

22. A point stressed by Magdoff in *The Age of Imperialism*, (New York and London, M.R. Press, 1969), p. 50.

become exhausted. And the reserves of the developed countries are in most cases likely to be used up before those of the underdeveloped countries. Hence present trends in the share of trade in raw materials may be reversed in the future.[23]

It is more revealing to look at trade and investment less in terms of movements between broad blocs of 'developed' and 'underdeveloped' countries. That distinction conceals the salient features of the world capitalist economy. The fact is that since the Second World War the world capitalist system has become increasingly interdependent and internationalised in terms of both trade and investment. Patterns of capital movement have led to a growing economic interpenetration, especially of the advanced capitalist countries. And trade has risen faster than production, so that most countries have become more dependent both on imports and on foreign markets. A particularly dramatic example of this is the import of minerals to the United States. Net imports as a percentage of consumption have risen from —3·1 per cent in 1910–19, to 5·65 per cent in 1945–49 and 14 per cent by 1961.[24]

One of the vehicles of this increasing internationalisation of the system is the *international firm*, which is becoming one of the most widely discussed aspects of modern capitalism. Since a large proportion of world trade and international investment is between branches of these firms, measures of dependence which emphasise trade or capital movements between countries will fail to understand the full meaning of this change in the structure of world capitalism. The role of the international firm in increasing concentration and international competition is obviously important. Its exact nature remains, however, an unanswered question, as does the relation of these firms to the state[25] and the sense in which they can be called international.

Most of the recent analysis of all these features of imperialism has been conducted at the level of countries, and of the political and economic relations between them. What has been lacking in comparison with the earlier Marxist tradition of imperialism theory has been an analysis of the political economy and class structure of both the advanced and the underdeveloped countries. Only this could permit the three proper concerns of imperialism theory to be reunited into an

---

23. On these points see the paper to the Elsinore seminar on imperialism by Michael Barratt Brown, *mimeo*, 1971 (these papers are to be published).
24. Magdoff, *The Age of Imperialism*, p. 47.
25. On this subject see Robin Murray, 'The internationalisation of capital and the theory of the state', *The Spokesman*, London, Dec. 1970, and *New Left Review*, **67**, London, 1971.

adequate analysis of the capitalist system as a whole. Of course, some useful work in these directions has already been done.[26] But as yet the Marxist analysis of imperialism, in the sense both of the whole system and of the relations of its component countries, does not have the coherence in relation to the modern world which it possessed at the time that Lenin, Luxemburg and Trotsky were making their contributions to it. As for contemporary non-Marxist social science, it does not accept that the concept of imperialism is a relevant one, even in its account of international trade or of international relations.

Marxist theory has always flourished in a climate of intense political struggle. And for Marxists, behind all the searching after theory lies in most cases a search for an appropriate political strategy for the current stage of capitalism. Within this there seem to be a number of comparatively futile quests. One of these is the attempt to identify what is the major contradiction of the present stage of capitalism—that between capital and the working class in the advanced countries or that between the advanced and the underdeveloped countries. Theory has here reflected political events: in an age when revolutionary struggles in the underdeveloped countries seemed more common that real political conflict within the advanced countries, most theoretical writings reflected this by concentrating on the contradiction between advanced and underdeveloped countries. In more recent years the intensification of class struggle in European countries, and in a rather roundabout form in the United States, has led to a shift of emphasis if not a change of mind. It seems virtually impossible, however, to give adequate criteria for how we may judge if one contradiction in the capitalist system dominates over another.

The continued existence of imperialism implies for most Marxists that the question of how to fight it has not been answered. It is this question which is never far from the surface in several of the contributions to this book. Kemp stresses the importance of the class struggle in the advanced countries. Hodgkin describes the emergence of theories

26. For the underdeveloped countries, especially in Latin America, the work of Andre Gunder Frank has been important: See for instance: *Capitalism and Underdevelopment in Latin America,* (New York and London 1967), and *Latin America, capitalism or revolution,* (New York and London 1969). Frank's analysis of class structure has recently come in for criticism from Giovanni Arrighi in his paper (to be published) to the Elsinore symposium of April 1971, and Ernesto Laclau in *New Left Review, 67,* London 1971. Arrighi has himself written on the relations of class structure to underdevelopment in Africa. See for instance: *The Political Economy of Rhodesia,* The Hague, 1967; International Corporations, labour aristocracies and economic development in tropical Africa, in R. I. Rhodes, ed. *Imperialism and Underdevelopment,* (New York and London, M.R. Press, 1970).

in the third world which were based on doubt that a common struggle of oppressed people in both underdeveloped and developed countries was possible. These questions will be answered in a sense by political events; they cannot be finally solved in any book.

It is our hope, however, that for Marxists this book, though it does not answer questions of this kind, may at least help to remove some of the commoner confusions in discussion and to suggest lines which future enquiry might follow. At the same time we hope that for Marxists and non-Marxists alike the book offers some object lessons in the problems, possibilities and limits of intellectual confrontation.

Annotated bibliography

This bibliography is mainly designed for those who wish to read more widely about the theory of imperialism or to conduct research of their own. For neither purpose is it anything like exhaustive, but we hope that it will, at least, provide some useful leads. We have restricted it to books either directly about theories of imperialism or with a strong indirect link with theory. The annotations consist of, for books, a list of relevant chapters or section headings and, where these do not give a reasonable idea of the contents, a brief description of subject and approach; and, for articles, a brief description. It is not intended that this should be a critical or evaluative bibliography and no judgment of the importance of a book is implied by the volume of annotation.

The titles and contents of books and articles in German and Spanish have been translated, but not of those in French.

Where there is more than one edition of a book the most recent has been given, unless the date of earlier editions seemed significant.

The bold numbers following the date of publication at the end of each title are meant to give a very rough indication of the type of argument or subject. The key to these numbers is as follows:

1. Marxist—up to 1914.
2. Marxist—1914–1945.
3. Marxist—after 1945.
4. Non-Marxist economic theories of colonialism or imperialism.
5. Non-Marxist political theories.
6. Surveys of theories.
7. Critiques of economic, and particularly Marxist, theories of imperialism.

8. Social imperialism; sociological theories and critiques of sociological theories of imperialism.
9. Empirical studies with theoretical relevance; useful statistics concerning trade and investment.
10. Linguistic analyses of the word 'imperialism'; miscellaneous.

The following abbreviations have been used:

AER	*American Economic Review*, Cambridge, Mass.
BOUIS	*Bulletin of the Oxford University Institute of Statistics*, Oxford
EHR	*Economic History Review*, London
HJ	*Historical Journal*, Birmingham
JAH	*Journal of African History*, London
JEH	*Journal of Economic History*, New York
JPE	*Journal of Political Economy*, Chicago
JRSS	*Journal of the Royal Statistical Society*, London
MR	*Monthly Review*, New York
NLR	*New Left Review*, London
PSQ	*Political Science Quarterly*, New York
QJE	*Quarterly Journal of Economics*, Cambridge, Mass.
RES	*Review of Economic Studies*, Cambridge
rev.	*revised*
pb	paperback edition

Aaronovitch, S. *Monopoly: a study of British monopoly capitalism*, London, Lawrence & Wishart, 1955. [3]
1. The rise of monopoly and its forms; 2. The growth of combines; 3. Big money and big business; 4. Imperial octopus; 5. State monopoly capitalism; 6. Monopolies and foreign policy; 7. Monopolies and state financial policy; 8. Monopolies and propaganda; 9. Monopoly capitalism—enemy of ninety-nine per cent of the British people; 10. False ideas of monopoly; 11. Against monopoly capitalism to socialism.

Aguilar, A. *Pan-Americanism, from Monroe to the Present: a view from the other side*, London and New York, Monthly Review Press, 1968 (pb), rev. edn. [3]
1. Bolivar and Monroe; 2. United States territorial and economic expansion; 3. Imperialism and Pan-Americanism; 4. From 'Big Stick' to 'Philosophy of Liberty'; 5. The Gay Twenties; 6. Depression and war; 7. The eve of a third world war; 8. From Bogota to Caracas; 9. Reform or revolution; 10. From the violence of imperialism to revolutionary violence; 11. Structural changes, progress and peace. Bibliography.

Alavi, H. 'Imperialism old and new', *The Socialist Register 1964*, London, Merlin Press, 1964. [3]
Sets out to answer two questions:
(1) What was the role of imperialist expansion in maintaining the dynamic of capitalist development?

(2) How is it affected by attainment of national independence by colonies?

Alavi, H. 'Indian capitalism and foreign imperialism', *NLR*, May–June 1966. [3]
Review of Kidron's 'Foreign investments in India' from Marxist viewpoint.

Amin, S. *L'Accumulation à l'échelle mondiale:* critique de la théorie du sous-developpement, Paris, IFAN Dakar, Editions Anthropos, 1970.
I. La specialisation internationale inégale et les flux internationaux de capitaux. II. Les formations du capitalisme périphérique: la transition au capitalisme périphérique; le développement du sous-développement; les formation sociales de la périphérie. III. Les mécanismes monétaires a la périphérie et le système monétaire mondial. IV. Le role de la périphérie dans la conjoncture mondiale. V. L'ajustement de la balance des paiments extérieurs de la périphérie.

Angell, J. W. *Financial Foreign Policy of the U.S.*, New York, Council on Foreign Relations, 1933. [9]
1. Financial policy in the American sphere of special influence; 2. Financial policy toward other countries of Latin America; 3. Financial policies in Latin America, A summary; 4. Financial policies in the Near East and Far East; 5. The direct control of American capital exports; 6. Post-war financial policies toward Europe; 7. American financial policy: summary and conclusions. Bibliography.

Arendt, H. *The Origins of Totalitarianism,* London, Allen & Unwin, 1958, 2nd rev. edn. [4, 8]
II. 'Imperialism'. 5. The political emancipation of the bourgeoisie; 6. Race thinking before racism; 7. Race and bureaucracy; 8. Continental imperialism: the pan-movements; 9. The decline of the nation-state and the end of the rights of man.

Aron, R. *The Century of Total War* trans. from French by E. W. Dickes and O. S. Griffiths, London, Verschoyle, 1954. [7]
3. The Leninist myth of imperialism. Also appears in *Partisan Review* (New York), **18**, Dec. 1951.

Avineri, S. ed. *Karl Marx on Colonialism and Modernisation: his despatches and other writings on China, India, Mexico, the Middle East and North Africa,* New York, Doubleday, 1968 (Anchor books pb. 1969). [1]
Introduction by S. Avineri; I. Excerpts from the general theoretical writings; II. Articles; III. From the correspondence.

Balandier, Georges. *The Sociology of Black Africa,* trans. D. Garman, London, Deutsch, 1970.

Balogh, T. 'The mechanism of neo-imperialism: the economic impact of monetary and commercial institutions in Africa', *BOUIS*, 1962. [9]
Shows some of the ways in which economic relations of African colonies to the metropoles have done economic damage to the colonies.

Baran, P. A. *The Political Economy of Growth* (1957), New York, Monthly Review Press, 1962, 2nd edn. [3]

1. A general view; 2. The concept of economic surplus; 3. Standstill and movement under monopoly capitalism I; 4. Standstill and movement under monopoly capitalism II; 5. On the roots of backwardness; 6. Towards a morphology of backwardness I; 7. Towards a morphology of backwardness II; 8. The steep ascent.

Baran, P. A. and **Sweezy, P.** *Monopoly Capital,* New York, Monthly Review Press, 1966. [**3**]
1. Introduction; 2. The giant corporation; 3. The tendency of the surplus to rise; 4. The absorption of surplus: capitalists' consumption and investment; 5. The absorption of surplus: the sales effort; 6. The absorption of surplus: civilian government; 7. The absorption of surplus: militarism and imperialism; 8. On the history of monopoly capitalism; 9. Monopoly capitalist society; 11. The irrational system. Appendix: Estimating the economic surplus by Joseph D. Phillips.

Baran, P. A. and **Sweezy, P. M.** 'Notes on the theory of imperialism', in *Problems of Economic Dynamics and Planning, Essays in Honour of Michael Kalecki,* Oxford, Pergamon Press, Warsaw, Polish Scientific Publishers, 1966, reprinted in *MR,* Mar. 1966. [**3**]
Mostly discussion of capital export with special reference to multinational companies, Standard Oil in particular. Big companies, not finance capitalists, now dominate ruling class.

Barnes, H. E. *World Politics in Modern Civilisation; the contributions of nationalism, capitalism, imperialism and militarism to human culture and international anarchy,* New York, Knopf, 1930. [**4, 5, 8**]
I. The origins of nationalism, capitalism and imperialism; II. Modern capitalism and national imperialism; 5. The capitalistic revolution; 6. Imperialist society and political change due to the capitalistic revolution; 9. Modern capitalism and national imperialism—the partition of Africa; 10. The penetration of Asia and Oceana; 11. The British Empire and Latin America; 12. The general results of contemporary national imperialism; III. Nationalism, capitalism, imperialism and the World War.
Imperialist expansion as result of economic, political, social, religious, psychological forces. Economic forces stem from industrial revolution.

Barnet, R. J. *Intervention and Revolution: the United States in the Third World,* New York, World Publishing Company, 1968. [**4, 5**]
1. Guardian at the gates; 2. Two worlds in collision: the national-security manager and the revolutionary; 3. The roots of revolution; 4. International communism and the export of revolution; 5. The road to world leadership: the police idea in U.S. foreign policy; 6. The Truman Doctrine and the Greek Civil War; 7. The Lebanese Civil War and the Eisenhower doctrine; 8. The Dominican Republic: to the Johnson doctrine; 9. America in Vietnam: the four interventions; 10. The subversion of undesirable governments; 11. Patterns of intervention.
Severely critical and highly documented account of U.S. interventionism since 1945.

Barratt Brown, M. *After Imperialism*, London, Heinemann, 1963; rev. edn., Merlin Press, 1970. **[3]**
I. Imperialism as it was: 1. The rise of empire—why didn't they colonise us? 2. Capitalism and empire—the success of free trade: 1824–1870; 3. The defeat of protection: 1870–1913; 4. War, stagnation and empire 1914–1945; 5. Results of empire—in the colonies; II. Imperialism as it is today; 6. End of colonial empire 1945–62; 7. What remains of empire?; 8. The new empires—of the giant corporations; 9. Capitalism without empire; III. Towards an international economy; 10. The world trade blocs; 11. Industrialisation of the world; 12. Britain in a world of equals. Bibliography.

Bellamy, R. 'The effects of imperialism upon Britain', London, *Marxism Today*, May 1971. **[3]**
Article relating the economic history of Britain in the twentieth century to imperialism; emphasises growth of rent and interest in capitalist income.

Bennett, G. ed. *The Concept of Empire, Burke to Atlee, 1774–1947*, London, A. and C. Black, 2nd edn, 1962. **[5, 10]**
Selection of 128 brief passages, mostly from writings and speeches of British politicians and historians, about the British empire.

Berque, J. and **Charnay, J-P.** eds. *De l'impérialisme à la decolonisation*, Paris, Editions de Minuit, 1965. **[3, 8]**
Articles on the theme by: G. Ardant, K. Axelos, J. Berque, C. Bettelheim, G. de Bosschère, J-P. Charnay, J. Chesneaux, P. Cot, Jean Cuisenier, Jeanne Cuisenier, J-Y. Eichenberger, J. Foray, P. Galand-Pernet, G. Gueron, J. Lacouture, H. Laugier, Le Thanh Khoi, P. Marthelot, P. Meile, D. Pepy, J. Poncet, P. Rondot, H. Sicard, J. C. Sournia, P. Vermel.

Bettelheim, C. 'Economic inequalities between nations and international solidarity', *MR*, **21,** 1 June, 1970. **[3]**
Exchange with A. Emmanuel on unequal exchange and the potential solidarity of the working class in advanced and underdeveloped countries.

Betts, R. F. *Assimilation and Association in French Colonial Theory 1890–1914*, New York, Columbia University Press, 1961. **[5]**
1. The climate of French colonialism; 2. Origins and growth of the French doctrine of assimilation; 3. Ideas from abroad; 4. Assimilation and the scientific attitude; 5. Imperialism: expression of man's will to power; 6. A new policy: association; 7. Economic needs and the policy of association; 8. Military problems and the policy of association; 9. Ideal and reality.

Betts, R. F. *Europe Overseas, phases of imperialism*, New York and London, Basic Books Inc., 1968. **[5]**
1. Over the seas and far away; 2. The early European expansion of Europe; 3. The new rush overseas; 4. Empires in transition; 5. The end of empire; 6. After empire, what? 7. European imperialism in retrospect. Bibliography.

Betts, R. F. ed. *The Scramble for Africa: causes and dimensions of Empire*, Boston, D. C. Heath, 1966 (pb). **[4, 5, 6, 9]**
I. The problem from the European historical perspective: 1. E. Banning,

The peaceful penetration of Africa; 2. Sir John Scott Keltie, The scramble after years of preliminary activity; 3. Sir Charles P. Lucas, The scramble and Franco-German national problems; 4. A. J. P. Taylor, Bismarck's accidental acquisition of African empire; 5. Sybil E. Crowe, The scramble and the Berlin West African conference; 6. R. Robinson and J. Gallagher, The scramble: effect of British Egyptian Policy; 7. The scramble; effect of French African activity; II. The problem from the African historical perspective: 1. G. Hardy, The scramble; Preconditions and postconditions in Africa; 2. R. Oliver and J. D. Fage, The newness of the scramble and problems in its realisation; 3. E. Sik, The scramble as a necessary phase in European capitalistic exploitation; 4. The development of European–West African relations and the partition of West Africa; III. Towards a new perspective: 1. J. D. Hargreaves, The partition reappraised. Bibliography.

Blaug M. 'Economic imperialism revisited', New Haven, *Yale Review*, Spring, 1961. **[7]**
Criticism of Leninist theory of imperialism.

Boggs, T. H. 'Capital investments and trade balances within the British Empire', *QJE*, **29**, Aug. 1915. **[9]**
Effects of international lending and borrowing on imports and exports: 1. British India: the debit and credit items; tabular statements; foreign capital investments and interest charges; obvious gain from productive investments; 2. Canada's heavy borrowings: halt in 1914; exports and imports; 'invisible' items; approximate balance sheet; imports from United States. Covers mainly years 1900 to 1914.

Bonn, M. J. 'Imperialism' in *Encyclopaedia of the Social Sciences*, vol. vii, New York, Macmillan, 1932. **[6, 8]**
Deals briefly with Luxemburg and Lenin, but not Hobson.

Bonn, M. J. *The Crumbling of Empire; the disintegration of world economy*, London, Allen & Unwin, 1938. **[7]**
I. Colonisation: 1. Conquest and colonisation; 2. Voluntary colonisation; 3. Types of colonies; 4. The trade empire; II. Disintegration: 1. Democracy, nationalism, liberalism; 2. Economic separatism; 3. Imperialist nationalism; 4. The rising of the nations; 5. The economic revolt; 6. Autarchy; III. Empire making or empire breaking?: 1. Inequality; 2. Equality; 3. Change; 4. Equality of opportunity; 5. The value of colonies; 6. Conquest and commerce; 7. Super-state or empire; 8. The main issue: conquest or federation.
Attack on Marxist theory.

Borkenau, F. *Socialism, National or International*, London, Routledge, 1942. **[7]**
7. Imperialism.
Criticism of Leninist theory.

Brailsford, H. N. *The War of Steel and Gold: a study of the armed peace*, London, Bell, 1914. **[4]**
I. Descriptive: 1. The balance of power; 2. 'Real politics'—diplomacy and

finance—the export of capital—the trade is war; 3. The Egyptian model; 4. Class diplomacy; II. Constructive (proposals).
Hobsonite. Struggle of the powers 'always turned on the effort to secure or obtain some field of economic opportunity beyond the seas'. Also on role of arms race in capitalism in peacetime.

Brunschwig, H. *French Colonialism 1871-1914, Myths and Realities,* New York, Praeger, London, Pall Mall Press, 1966. Translated by William Glanville Brown from *Mythes et Réalités de l'Impérialisme Colonial Francais 1871–1914*, Paris, Librairie Armand Colin, 1960. **[5, 7, 9]**
An attempt at a rebuttal of an economic interpretation of imperialism.

Brunschwig, H. 'Les origines du partage de l'Afrique Occidentale', *JAH*, **5**, 1964. **[5, 6]**
Review article of books and articles on the origins of the partition of West Africa. (1) Robinson and Gallagher, *Africa and the Victorians.* (2) Newbury, 'Victorians, Republicans and the Partition of West Africa.' (3) Stengers, 'L'Impérialisme colonial de la fin du XIX siécle: mythe et réalité.' (4) Hargreaves, *Prelude to the Partition of West Africa.*

Bukharin, N. I. *Der Imperialismus und die Akkumulation des Kapitals* (Imperialism and the Accumulation of Capital), Berlin/Vienna, 1926. **[2]**
I. Enlarged reproduction in abstract capitalist society: 1. The characteristic of the third part of the 'commodity pile'; 2. The workers as possible consumers; 3. The capitalists as possible consumers; II. Money and enlarged reproduction: 1. Definition of accumulation; 2. Machinations of the capitalists A, B and C; 3. Accumulation of capital and 'average profit'; 4. The total social capital and the total profit; 5. The last carousel of comrade Rosa Luxemburg; III. The general theory of the market and of crises: 1. Partial and general overproduction; 2. Relative and absolute overproduction; 3. Overproduction of commodities and over-production of capital; 4. Temporary and continuous overproduction; IV. The economic roots of imperialism; V. The theory of the collapse of capitalism.
The book is in part an attack on Rosa Luxemburg's *Accumulation of Capital.*

Bukharin, N. I. *Imperialism and World Economy* (with an introduction by V. I. Lenin), 1st English edn. New York, International Publishers and London, Martin Lawrence, 1929 (written 1915, published 1917 in Russian). **[2]**
I. World economy and the process of internationalisation of capital: 1. World economy defined; 2. Growth of world economy; 3. Organisation and forms of world economy; II. World economy and the process of nationalisation of capital: 4. The inner structure of national economies and the tariff policy; 5. World sales markets and changed sales conditions; 6. World market for raw materials, and change in the conditions of purchasing materials; 7. World movement of capital, and change in the economic forms of international connections; 8. World economy and the 'national' state; III. Imperialism as the reproduction of capitalist competition on a

larger scale: 9. Imperialism as an historic category; 10. Reproduction of the processes of concentration and centralisation of capital on a world scale; 11. Means of competitive struggle, and state power; IV. The future of imperialism and world economy: 12. 'Necessity' of imperialism and 'ultra-imperialism'; 13. War and economic evolution; 14. World economy and proletarian society.

Cady, J. F. *The Roots of French Imperialism in South-East Asia,* Ithaca, Cornell Univ. Press, 1967. **[5, 9]**
1. French activities in the Far East 1661–1830; 2. France under Louis Philippe; 3. The revival of French political interest in the Far East to 1884; 4. The Lagrené Mission, first phase 1844; 5. The Lagrené Mission, second phase 1845; 6. French activities in the Far East 1846–51; 7. French policy under Louis Napoleon 1848–53; 8. The Taipings Treaty revision and Shanghai, 1853–4; 9. The effectiveness of the Anglo-French alliance, 1854; 10. Competition: Bowring, Montigny and Parker; 11. Origins of the joint intervention 1856–7; 12. French policy and the expedition of 1857–8; 13. British leadership: Tourane, Saigon and Taku 1858–9; 14. Objectives and preparations for the China War 1859–60; 15. The French role in the war with China 1860; 16. Imperialism takes root in Indo-China. Bibliography. Maps.

Cairncross, A. K. *Home and Foreign Investment 1870–1913,* Cambridge, Cambridge Univ. Press, 1953. **[9]**
1. Capital accumulation in the Victorian age; 2. Fluctuations in the Glasgow Building industry 1865–1914; 3. Investment in Canada 1900–13; 4. Internal migration in Victorian England; 5. The Victorian capital market; 6. The state of investment 1870–1913; 7. Fluctuations in home and foreign investment 1870–1913; 8. Investment and migration; 9. Did foreign investment pay? 10. The Victorians and investment.

Chamberlain, M. E. *The New Imperialism* (pamphlet), London, The Historical Association, 1970, pb. **[6, 7]**
Brief account of the scramble for empire in the late nineteenth century; a survey of critiques of imperialism and of recent assessments by historians. Repeats standard objections to Lenin and Hobson but more inclined to rate economic motives than most.

Clark, G. *A Place in the Sun,* New York, Macmillan, 1936. **[7, 9]**
I. The Record of expansion; II. The population fallacy; III. The trade fallacy; IV. The raw materials fallacy; V. The way out.
This book is the result of an attempt to get from the actual records an answer to the question: Do colonies pay? Most emphatically the answer is: no.

Clark, G. *The Balance Sheets of Imperialism,* 2nd edn. New York, Columbia Univ. Press, 1967, (originally published 1936). **[9]**
Statistical support to argument in *A Place in the Sun.* List of tables. I. Territorial holdings; II. Colonial data; III. Migration; IV. Trade; Foreign and colonial; V. Trade by commodity classes; VI. Trade in commodities;

VII. World production percentages. Extensive bibliography.

Conant, C. A. *The United States in the Orient*, Boston, Houghton, Mifflin, 1900. [**4**]

1. The economic basis of imperialism; 2. Russia as a world power; 3. The struggle for commerical empire; 4. Can new openings be found for capital? 5. The new economic problems; 6. The U.S. as a world power — nature of the economic and political problems; 7. The U.S. in the Orient—their advantages in the competition for commercial empire.

'The U.S. have recently assumed serious responsibilities in the Orient. While the manner of their assumption has something of the appearance of an accident, this country has only followed other civilised states in the general move to find markets for their surplus capital and the produce of their labour. The U.S. have actually reached, or are approaching, the economic state where such outlets are required outside their own boundaries, in order to prevent business depression, idleness and suffering at home.'

Conant, C. A. 'The economic basis of imperialism', Boston, *North American Review*, **167**, Sept. 1898, 326–40. [**4**]

A precursor of Hobson—accumulation of capital leads to imperialist expansion.

Court, W. H. B. 'The Communist doctrines of empire' in W. K. Hancock, ed., *Survey of British Commonwealth Affairs 1942*, ii, Part i, Problems of Economic Policy 1918–1939, London, Oxford Univ. Press, 1940, pp. 293–306. [**6, 7**]

A sympathetic treatment of Lenin and Luxemburg. But considers that economic interpretations of imperialism are inadequate.

Crouzet, F. 'Commerce et Empire: L'expérience britannique du libre-échange à la première guerre mondiale, Paris, *Annales*, **9**, 2, 1964. [**4**]

Aim: to determine if possession of a huge empire was 'un factor essentiel' for the prosperity of Victorian and Edwardian Britain. Concludes that it was development of old colonies—Canada, Australia, India and Latin America (informal) which contributed to 'enrichessement' of Britain, not creation of an African empire.

Crowder, M. *West Africa Under Colonial Rule,* London, Hutchinson, 1968 (pb). [**4**]

I. 2. The origins of European imperialism and the rise of militant Islam.

Interrelation of commercial and humanitarian factors in origins of British colonialism in West Africa.

Davis, H. B. 'Capital and Imperialism: a landmark in Marxist theory', *MR,* **19**, 4, Sept. 1967. [**1, 3**]

Shows Marx and Engels were in favour of colonialism (as a vehicle of modernisation) and against self-determination for small groups (as a barrier to progress) in their early days and views only changed in early 1860s.

Davis, H. B. 'Conservative Writers on Imperialism', New York: *Science and Society*, **18**, 1954. [**3, 6**]

Review of main conservative writings on imperialism. Strongly critical of all non-economic interpretations.

Davis, H. B. 'Imperialism and Labour: an analysis of Marxian views', New York, *Science and Society*, **26**, Winter 1962. [3]
Theoretical discussion whether labour in imperialist countries benefits from imperialism.

D'Encausse, H. C. and **Schram, S. R.** *Marxism and Asia*, London, Allen Lane, 1969. [1, 2, 3, 6]
1. Marxist views of the non-European world prior to the October Revolution; 2. Problems of revolution in the East in the days of the comintern; 3. Towards Asiocentric communism. Texts by Marx, Engels, Lenin, Trotsky, Stalin, Mao Tse-Tung, Ho Chi Minh etc. and extracts from proceedings of congresses and conferences.

Dobb, M. H. *Political Economy and Capitalism*, London, George Routledge, 1937. [2, 6]
7. Imperialism.
Debt of Marx to Ricardo and Smith. Mercantilism compared to modern imperialism. Imperialism as a counter to the tendency of the profit rate to fall. Imperialism as a reactionary force in underdeveloped countries. The restrictive and monopolistic aspects of imperialism. Critique of Hobson's theory.

Dobb, M. H. *Studies in the Development of Capitalism*, London, George Routledge, 1946. [3]
Chapters 7 and 8 give some treatment of imperialism in the development of capitalism.

Dos Santos, T. 'The structure of dependence', Cambridge, Mass, *American Economic Review, Papers and Proceedings*, May 1970. [3]
1. What is dependence?; 2. Historic forms of dependence; 3. The export economies; 4. The new dependence; 5. Effects on the productive structure; 6. Some conclusions: dependent reproduction.
Attempt to show that: the dependence of Latin American countries on other countries cannot be overcome without a qualitative change in their internal structures and external relations.

Du Boff, R. B. 'Pentagonism or imperialism' *MR* **20**, 11, April 1969. [3, 7]. A review of J. Bosch's book *Pentagonism: a substitute for imperialism*.

Dutt, R. P. *The Crisis of Britain and the British Empire*, new rev. edn. London, Lawrence & Wishart, 1957. [3]
1. Britain's crisis of empire; 2. What the empire is today; 3. How the empire developed; 4. Price of empire; 5. Crisis of the colonial system; 6. Crises of 'Western civilisation'; 7. America and the British empire; 8. New tactics of imperialism: India; 9. New dreams of empire: Africa; 10. Myths of colonial development; 11. Empire and war; 12. Labour and empire; 13. Path of colonial liberation; 14. Britain in chains; 15. Liberation of Britain; 16. Reconstruction of Britain; 17. The future of Britain and the British empire.

Earle, E. M. *Turkey, the Great Powers and the Baghdad Railway, (A study in imperialism)*, London, Macmillan, 1923. [**4.9**]
Imperialist expansion seen as being for raw materials and foodstuffs for growing population.

Eckert, C. *Alter und Neuer Imperialismus* (Old and New Imperialism), Jena, 1932. (pamphlet). [**2.5**]
Imperialism is 'a type of politics, characterised by the striving for the extension of political, economic and intellectual power of a nation of people and its culture over areas which lie outside its political boundaries'. Three types of imperialism since beginning of Middle Ages: feudal or elite imperialism; bourgeois imperialism; popular or people's imperialism in which broad masses of the people participate. Imperialism derives from the hunt for profits and the fear of a domestic crisis in capitalism; capitalism and imperialism will die together; they will pass away when crises can no longer be evaded.

Edwardes, M. *The West in Asia 1850–1914*, London, Batsford, 1967. [**5**]
II. Aspects of imperialism; 1. Imperial challenge and colonial response; 2. Was imperialism profitable? Retrospect: the age of imperialism. Claims that while British motives were in large part economic those of other countries were not.

Elton, G. R. *Modern Historians On British History 1485–1969: a critical bibliography 1945–1969*, London, Methuen, 1970 (pb). [**10**]
'The Empire', pp. 130–34.

Emmanuel, A. *Unequal Exchange: a study in the imperialism of trade*, London, New Left Books, 1972 (translated by Brian Pearce from *L'échange inegal*, Paris, Maspero, 1969).
1. Equilibrium prices in internal exchanges; 2. Equilibrium prices in external exchanges; 3. Wages; 4. Limits and implications of unequal exchange; 5. The international equilibrium price with more than two factors; 6. Comparative costs. Bibliography.

Emmanuel, A. 'The delusions of internationalism', *MR*, **22**, 1, June 1970. [**3**]
Exchange with Bettelheim on whether the benefits of unequal exchange have undermined the basis for international solidarity of the working class between imperialist and underdeveloped countries.

Esprit 'L'impérialisme', Paris, n.s. April 1969. [**3, 4, 5, 7**]
J. Boissonnat, L'économie dominante; C. Furtado, Les 'conglomerats' et l'Amérique latine; E. Denis, C. Furtado, P. Hassner, S. Hurtig, P. Jalée, J.-W. Lapierre, 'Enquête'; S. Hoffman, Critiques américaines; C. R. Kindleberger, Investissements et matières premières; J.-M. Domenach, L'empire américaine; J. Berque, Vers une humanité plénière.

Fann, K. T. and **Hodges, Donald C.** eds. *Readings in U.S. Imperialism*, Boston, Porter Sargent, 1971 (pb). [**3**]
Bertrand Russell, Peace through resistance to American imperialism; C. C. O'Brien, Contemporary forms of imperialism; T. Harding, The

new imperialism in Latin America: a critique of Conor Cruise O'Brien; J. O'Connor, The meaning of economic imperialism; P. A. Baran and P. M. Sweezy, Notes on the theory of imperialism; L. Marcus, The third stage of imperialism; H. Magdoff and P. M. Sweezy, Notes on the multinational corporation; W. A. Williams, The vicious circle of American imperialism; H. Magdoff, Militarism and imperialism; H. Dean, Scarce resources: the dynamics of American imperialism; S. Bodenheimer, Dependency and imperialism: the roots of Latin American underdevelopment; F. Castro, On underdevelopment; J. de Castro, Colonialism, hunger and progress; E. Galeano, Latin America and the theory of imperialism; T. Dos Santos, the structure of dependence; A. G. Frank, On the mechanisms of imperialism: the case of Brazil; D. Tobis, Foreign aid: the case of Guatemala; E. Mandel, Where is America going?; M. Nicolaus, Who will bring the mother down?; P. Irons, On repressive institutions and the American empire; R. Wolfe, American imperialism and the peace movement; R. Aronson, Socialism: the sustaining menace; S. Carmichael, Black power and the third world; E. Guevara, Create two, three, many Vietnams; Lin Piao, Defeat US imperialism by people's war. Bibliography. Selection of articles first published elsewhere.

Fanon, F. *Blacks Skins White Faces*, London, MacGibbon and Kee, 1968 (trans by C. L. Markmann from *Peau Noire, Masques Blancs*, Paris, Editions du Seuil, 1952). **[3, 8]**
1. The negro and language; 2. The woman of colour and the white man; 3. The man of colour and the white woman; 4. The so-called dependency complex of colonised peoples; 5. The fact of blackness; 6. The Negro and psychopathology; 7. The Negro and recognition; 8. By way of a conclusion.

Fanon, F. *The Wretched of the Earth*, London, MacGibbon and Kee, 1965 (trans by C. Farrington from *Les Damnés de la Terre*, Paris, Maspero 1961) (pb 1967). **[3.8]**
1. Concerning violence; 2. Spontaneity: its strength and weakness; 3. The pitfalls of national consciousness; 4. On national culture; 5. Colonial war and mental disorder.

Feis, H. *Europe: the World's Banker, 1870–1914: An Account of European Foreign Investment and the Connection of World Finance with Diplomacy before the War*, New Haven, published for the Council on Foreign Relations by Yale Univ. Press, 1930. **[4, 9]**
I. The record of capital movement: 1. British foreign investment; 2. French foreign investment; 3. German foreign investment; II. Relations between finance and government in the lending countries; 4. In Great Britain; 5. In France; 6. In Germany; III. Studies in lending and borrowing: 7. Introduction; 8. Non-intercourse between France and the central powers; 9. The financing of imperial Russia; 10. The financing of Italy by rival alliances; 11. The financing of Portugal—a debtor with a noble past; 12. Financing of the Balkan states; 13. Financing of the Balkan railways;

14. The Turkish empire and European investors; 15. The financing of railroads in Asiatic Turkey; 16. The financing of Persia: between two imperial ambitions; 17. Finance and fate in North Africa; 18. Japan is helped to become a great power; 19. The financing of the Chinese government.
Comprehensive study of the outward flow of European surplus capital 1870–1914. Deals mainly with Europe, North Africa, the Balkans and Japan.

Feis H. *The Diplomacy of the Dollar 1919–1932*, Baltimore, Johns Hopkins Univ. Press, 1950; New York, W.W. Norton, 1966 (pb). [4]
1. Ideas, interests and attitudes; 2. The effort of government to guide investment; 3. Some special experiences: Germany, Japan, the oil of Mosul; 4. Reflections and comparisons to the present era of dollar diplomacy.

Fieldhouse, D. K. *The Colonial Empires: a comparative study from the eighteenth century*, London, Weidenfeld & Nicolson, 1966. [5, 7]
II. Colonial empires after 1815; 16. 'Myths and realities of the modern colonial empires' including 'The myth of economic exploitation'.

Fieldhouse, D. K. *The Theory of Capitalist Imperialism*, London, Longmans, 1967 (pb). [6.7]
I. The roots of the theory: the economists and the declining tendency of the rate of profit; II. Adaptation and modification: the historicists; III. Dissection and evaluation: the critics; IV. Application of the theory: the historians; V. Some conclusions: the historian and the historicists. Further reading.
The introduction is a review of various theories of imperialism. The book is a collection of key writings on the theory of *capitalist* imperialism, i.e. it is concerned specifically with the Leninist concept. The evolution of this theory is traced from the seventeenth century up to the present. The main interest of the book centres on the historian's question: is the theory a correct explanation of the events it attempts to explain?

Fieldhouse, D. K. 'Imperialism; an historiographical revision', *EHR.*, 2nd ser, **14**, 2, Dec. 1961. [6.7]
Summary of arguments against Hobson's theory and review of the literature.

Ford, A. G. 'The transfer of British foreign lending 1870–1913', *EHR.*, 2nd ser, **2**, 2, Dec. 1958. [9]
Challenges the view that the growth of British foreign assets 1870–1913 resulted mainly from a reinvestment abroad of income from abroad.

Frank, A. G. *Capitalism and Underdevelopment in Latin America: Historical Studies of Chile and Brazil*, New York and London, Monthly Review Press, 2nd ed. 1969. [3]
1. Capitalist development of underdevelopment in Chile; 2. On the 'Indian problem' in Latin America; 3. Capitalist development of underdevelopment in Brazil; 4. Capitalism and the myth of feudalism in Brazilian agriculture; 5. Foreign investment in Latin American underdevelopment.

A critique of the 'dualist model'.

The book consists of four studies. 'Each of them is in its own way intended to clarify how it is the structure and development of capitalism itself which, by long since fully penetrating and characterising Latin America and other continents, generated, maintained and still deepen underdevelopment.'

Frank, A. G. *Latin America: underdevelopment or revolution: essays on the development of underdevelopment and the immediate enemy*, New York and London, Monthly Review Press, 1969. [3]

III. Economic imperialism: 8. Aid or exploitation; 9. The mechanisms of imperialism (on Brazil); 10. Latin American economic integration; 11. Invisible foreign services or national economic development; 12. The economics of military government; 13. The strategic weakness of the Johnson doctrine.

Frankel, S. H. *Capital Investment in Africa*, London, Oxford Univ. Press, 1938. [9]

1. The problem and its background; 2. A continent of outposts; 3. The economic revolution in South Africa; 4. The economic structure of the Union; 5. Africa joins the world economy; 6. Conclusion. Bibliography.

Freymond, J. *Lenine et l'impérialisme*, Lausanne, Librairie Payot, 1951. [5, 7]

1. Le débat sur l'impérialisme; 2. La critique socialiste de l'impérialisme jusqu'à 1914; 3. La prise de position de Lenine et ses conséquences; 4. Etude critique de la thèse leniniste; 5. L'influence des oligarchies financières. En guise de conclusion. Bibliography.

Critique of Lenin's theory—imperialism is not simply a historical phase produced by monopoly capitalism. It occurs at other times and economic motives alone do not fully explain it.

Furtado, C. *Economic Development of Latin America: a survey from colonial times to the Cuban revolution*, Cambridge, Cambridge Univ. Press, 1970 (pb). [4]

1. From the conquest to the formation of nation-states; 2. Entry into the system of international division of labour; 3. The traditional structural pattern; 4. Characteristics of the industrialisation process; 5. Growth and stagnation in the recent period; 6. International relations (traditional forms of external dependence; new forms of external dependence; towards the restructuring of the international economy); 7. Intra-regional relations; 8. Structural reconstruction policies.

Galbraith, J. S. 'The "turbulent frontier" as a factor in British expansion', The Hague, *Comparative Studies in Society and History*, **2**, 1960. [5]

The role of the man on the spot in imperialism.

Galeano, E. 'Latin America and the theory of imperialism', *MR*, **21**, 11, April 1970. [3]

Attempt to update Lenin, especially concerned with changing form, pattern and direction of foreign investment.

Gallagher, J. and **Robinson, R.** 'The imperialism of free trade', *EHR*, **6**,

1, 1953. [**4, 5**]
Argue that there was a continuity in British policy towards the empire
throughout the 19th century. Defines Victorian imperialism as a sufficient,
though not necessary, function of integrating new regions into the expanding British economy. Only when the politics of these new regions fail to
provide satisfactory conditions for commercial or strategic integration are
they incorporated within the formal empire.
Gallagher, J. and **Robinson, R.** *Africa and the Victorians,* see Robinson
and Gallagher.
Gann, L. H. and **Duignan, P.** *Burden of Empire: An appraisal of western
colonialism in Africa south of the Sahara,* London, Pall Mall Press, 1967. [**5, 7**]
I. Concepts and realities of imperialism (including imperialism—the
highest stage of nationalism, Lenin's view of imperialism, communism,
colonialism and neo-imperialism); II. Colonial rule (including development
or exploitation?); III. Decolonisation. Bibliography. Maps.
An attack on Marxist theories and apology for imperialism.
Gann, L. H. and **Duignan, P.** (eds.) *Colonialism in Africa, 1870–1960.*
vol. i. *The History and Politics of Colonialism 1870–1914;* vol. ii. *The History
and Politics of Colonialism 1914–1960,* Cambridge, Cambridge Univ. Press,
1969, 1970. [**5.9**]
Volume i contains fifteen articles and Volume ii fourteen by political
scientists and historians on various aspects of colonial rule in different
African countries.
Gastrell, W. H. S. *Our Trade in the World in Relation to Foreign Competition 1885–1895,* London, Chapman & Hall, 1897. [**9**]
1. Introduction; 2. Comparison of trade of principal nations; 3. Foreign
competition; 4. Growth and present state of British commerce; 5. Trade of
Great Britain with her colonies; 6. Textile industry and cotton trade;
7. Metals and their manufacture; 8. German industrial progress; 9. Trade
with Japan and China.
Large number of documentary and statistical appendices. Factual account
of Britain's loss of share of world trade in face of competition.
Gillman, J. R. *The Falling Rate of Profit: Marx's law and its significance to
twentieth century capitalism,* London, Dennis Dobson, 1958. [**3**]
Subjects Marx's law of the falling rate of profit to 'extended historical and
statistical tests. . . . 'These results show that whereas for the years before
World War I the historical statistics seem fully to support these theories of
Marx, after that war the series studied appear generally to behave in con-
tradiction to Marxist expectations.'
Gollwitzer, H. *Europe in the Age of Imperialism, 1880–1914,* London,
Thames & Hudson, 1969. [**5, 8**]
1. The imperialist age; 2. The demographic situation and the technical
revolution in natural science; 3. The world political constellation; 4.
Nationalism; pan movements; empire ideologies; 5. Economics in the age
of imperialism; 6. The social structure in the age of imperialism; 7. Organ-

346

isations of the imperialist movement; 8. The anti-imperialist front; 9. Imperium et liberator; 10. Social imperialism; 11. Imperialism as reflected in literature and art; 12. Imperialism and learning; 13. Imperialist welt-anschauung and attitudes to life; 14. The end of an epoch and its significance. Bibliography.
Economies secondary, nationalism more important: 'We regard the age of imperialism . . . as an epoch of positive significance for the attainment and the future of one world.'

Grabowsky, A. *Der Sozialimperialismus als Letze Etappe des Imperialismus* (Social Imperialism in the Last Stage of Imperialism), Basle, 1939. [**4. 7**]
1. Imperialism and capitalism; 2. The statist, rationalist and nationalist factor in imperialism; 3. The three stages of imperialism; 4. Imperialism and social stratification; 5. Total mobilisation; 6. Social imperialism as third imperialist stage; 7. Social imperialism and socialism.
Survey of the discussion as to whether imperialism is or is not an integral part of capitalism. Own view: rise of imperialism inherent in development of capitalism but cannot be explained fully in economic terms.

Greene, F. *The Enemy: Notes on imperialism and revolution,* London, Jonathan Cape, 1970. [**3**]
1. The face of capitalism; 2. How it began; 3. The anatomy of imperialism; 4. Imperialism's home base; 5. The great hang-ups; revolution.
Popular account of Marxist ideas on the origins and operations of imperialism with examples.

Greene, M. 'Schumpeter's imperialism—a critical note', New York, *Social Research*, **19**, Dec. 1952. [**8**]
Sharply criticises Schumpeter's narrow definition of imperialism.

Greene, T. P. ed. *American Imperialism in 1898*, (Problems in American Civilisation series), Boston, D.C. Heath, 1966. [**4, 5, 6, 8**]
1. J. A. Hobson, Imperialism; 2. W. Langer, A critique of imperialism; 3. C. A. Beard, Territorial expansion connected with commerce; 4. J. W. Pratt, American business and the Spanish-American war; 5. J. E. Wisan, The Cuban crisis as reflected in the New York press; 6. R. Hofstadter, Manifest destiny and the Philippines; 7. H. Cabot Lodge, The Philippine Islands; 8. C. Schurz, American imperialism; 9. S. F. Bemis, The great aberration of 1898; 10. T. Dennet, The Philippines.
Readings concerning American imperialism in 1898.

Grossman, H. 'Eine neue Theorie über Imperialismus und die Soziale Revolution' (A new theory on imperialism and the social revolution) in *Archiv für die Geschichte des Sozialismus und der Arbeiterbewegung,* **13**, pp. 141–92. [**2**]
I. Sternberg's 'facts' and Marx's method of research; II. Sternberg's conclusions, or how one makes revolutions; III. The economic arguments.
Marxist attack on Sternberg's *Der Imperialismus*.

Halévy, E. *Imperialism and the Rise of Labour 1895–1905*, London, Benn, 1929; 1961 (pb.) [**4, 5**]

1. Imperialism: 1. Chamberlain and Lord Salisbury; 2. The Boer War.
Hall, A. R. ed. *The Export of Capital from Britain 1870–1914*, London, Methuen, 1968 (pb). **[9]**
A collection of articles concerned with the export of capital. Mostly at global level. Some statistics.
Hallgarten, G. W. F. *Imperialismus vor 1914. Die Soziologischen Grundlagen der Aussenpolitik europäischer Grossmächte vor dem ersten Weltkrieg*, (Imperialism before 1914. The sociological origins of the foreign policy of the European great powers before the First World War), Munich, 1950, rev. edn. 1961. **[8]**
I. Origins of imperialism and its development in the West: 1. Capitalism and imperialism before 1914; 2. The sociological origins of England's expansionist policy in modern times; 3. The social origin of French foreign policy since the French Revolution; II. The sociological substructure of the German National State: 4. The formation of nationality and foreign policy; 5. The sociological origins of Bismarck's foreign policy; III. The social origins of world politics: 6. Internal and foreign politics of both . . . and'; 7. The internal origins of the foreign policy direction; 8. The internal hinderances to foreign improvements; IV. 9. The sociological causes of the World War of 1914: 10. Ideas, people, powers. Extensive and detailed bibliography.
Hammond, R. J. 'Economic imperialism: sidelights on a stereotype', *JEH.*, **21**, 4, 1961. **[5, 7]**
Opposes economic interpretation of imperialism as instance of economic historians accepting 'a striking and colourful first approximation'.
Hancock, W. K. *Wealth of Colonies*, Cambridge, Cambridge Univ. Press, 1950. **[5, 6, 7, 8]**
Critical of Lenin, economic and uni-causal theories. Some sympathy for Schumpeter but prefers to '. . . take leave of "imperialism". It is a pseudo-concept which sets out to make everything clear and ends by making everything muddled; it is a word for the illiterates of social science, the callow and the shallow who attempt to solve problems without mastering a technique.'
Hashagen, J. 'Marxismus und imperialismus' (Marxism and imperialism), *Jahrbücher für Nationalökonomie und Statistik*, **113**, July 1919.
Outline and critical assessment of 'neo-Marxist' writing on imperialism. Includes useful bibliography of German works on imperialism.
Hawtrey, R. *Economic Aspects of Sovereignty*, 2nd edn, London, Longmans, 1952. **[5, 7]**
1. Sovereignty and property; 2. Sovereignty and economic development; 3. Communications and population; 4. Economic power; 5. Economic causes of war; 7. The future.
Conservative contribution to theory of imperialism; opposes 'uni-explanatory' theories; believes in mixture of motives and causes.
Hayes, C. J. H. *A Generation of Materialism 1871–1900*, New York,

348

Harper, 1941. [5]
See chapter 6, section IV: 'Basically the new imperialism was a nationalistic phenomenon.' 'It expressed . . . an ardent desire to maintain or recover national prestige.'

Hazlewood, A. D. 'Colonial external finance since the war', *RES*, Dec. 1953. [9]
Account of external sterling balances. 'Thus the colonies have been exporting capital not importing it.'

Heimann, E. 'Schumpeter and the problems of imperialism', New York, *Social Research*, 1952. [8]
Supports Schumpeter.

Henderson, W. O. 'British economic activity in the German colonies 1884-1914', *EHR.*, **15**, 1945. [9]
About Germany's lack of capital for export and British contribution to development of Germany's overseas possessions 1884–1914.

Hilferding, R. *Finanzkapital: eine Studie über die jüngste Entwicklung des Kapitalismus* (Finance capital: a study of the most recent development of capitalism), first published Vienna 1910; further editions Moscow 1912, Berlin, 1947, 1955. [2]
I. Money and credit: II. The mobilisation of capital: III. Finance capital and the restriction of free competition: 11. Obstacles to the evening out of rates of profit and how they are overcome; 12. Cartels and trusts; 13. Capitalist monopolies and trade; 14. Capitalist monopolies and banks. Transformation of capital into finance capital; 15. The price-fixing of capitalist monopolies; IV. Finance capital and crises: 16. The general condition of the crises; 17. The causes of the crisis; 18. Credit relations in the course of the conjuncture; 19. Money capital and productive capital during the depression; 20. Changes in the character of the crisis. Cartels and crises; V. On the economic policy of finance capital: 21. The change in trade policy; 22. Capital export and the struggle for economic territories; 23. Finance capital and classes; 24. The struggle for the work-contract; 25. The proletariat and imperialism.

Hobson, C. K. *The Export of Capital*, London, Constable, 1914. [9]
1. Methods of foreign investment; 2. Causes of foreign investment; 3. Effects of foreign investment; 4. The growth of foreign investment; 5. The period of British predominance; 6. British and continental investments; 7. Capital investments and the balance of trade; 8. Capital exports, industry and emigration. Appendices.

Hobson, J. A. *The War in South Africa: its causes and effects*, London, James Nisbet, 1900. [4]
II. 1. For whom are we fighting?; 2. The political methods of the outlanders; 3. A chartered press; 4. For what are we fighting?
The war brought about by 'a small confederacy of international financiers working through a press'. A case study for Hobson's theory.

Hobson, J. A. *Imperialism—a study* (first published 1902, rev. 1905),

3rd rev. edn., London, Allen & Unwin, 1938, (pb 1965). [4]
I. The economics of imperialism: 1. The measure of imperialism; 2. The commercial value of imperialism; 3. Imperialism as an outlet for population; 4. Economic parasites of imperialism; 5. Imperialism based on protection; 6. The economic taproot of imperialism; 7. Imperialist finance; II. The politics of imperialism: 1. The political significance of imperialism; 2. The scientific defence of imperialism; 3. Moral and sentimental factors; 4. Imperialism and the lower races; 5. Imperialism in Asia; 6. Imperial federation; 7. The outcome.

Hobson, J. A. *International Trade: an application of economic theory*, London, Methuen, 1904. [4]
1. The importance of external trade; 2. The alphabet of free exchange; 3. Exchange between 'non-competing groups'; 4. Nations or trading groups; 5. Non-protective import duties; 6. The incidence of protective and preferential duties; 7. How the balance of imports and exports is achieved; 8. What a nation buys and what it pays with; 9. Can protective countries 'suck' a free-trade country? 10. The mystery of dumping; 11. Protection as a remedy for unemployment; 12. Protection and socialism. Written as straight textbook for people to judge the free trade controversy sensibly. Chapter 11 indirectly relevant to his theory of imperialism.

Hobson, J. A. *Confessions of an Economic Heretic*, London, Allen & Unwin, 1938. [5, 7]
Hobson's renunciation of his theory as too simplistic in Chapter 5: '[involvement in controversial causes and movements] led me for a time to an excessive and too simple advocacy of the economic determination of history'.

Hobson, J. A. 'Free trade and foreign policy', London, *Contemporary Review*, Aug. 1898. [4]

Hobson, J. A. 'Capitalism and imperialism in South Africa', London, *Contemporary Review*, Jan., 1900. [4]

Hobson, J. A. 'The testimony from Johannesburg', London, *Contemporary Review*, May 1900. [10]
A reply to an article previously in the same journal by Hosken arguing that the war will secure liberty for the natives. Hobson disagrees!

Hobson, J. A. 'The economic taproot of imperialism', London, *Contemporary Review*, Aug. 1902. [4]
Exposition of Hobson's theory.

Hobson, J. A. 'The scientific basis of imperialism', *PSQ.*, **17**, 3, Sept. 1902. [8]
Attack on 'biological sociology' in history—the idea that war contributed to the survival of the fittest nations.

Hobson, J. A. 'The economic interpretation of investment', London, *The Financial Review of Reviews*, 1911. [4, 9]
1. The origin of joint-stock enterprise; 2. How financial capital works; 3. The distribution of capital through investment; 4. The development of

foreign investments; 5. The distribution of foreign investments; 6. Foreign investments and home employment; 7. Political and social influences of capital; 8. The probable future of investment.
Contains some reference to the link between imperialism and foreign investment. Useful in helping to understand Hobson's theory of imperialism.

Hopkins, A. G. 'Economic imperialism in West Africa: Lagos 1880–1892', *EHR*, Dec. 1968. **[4]**
Attempt to rehabilitate economic theories of imperialism after Robinson/Gallagher attack. Considers economic motives and aspects of West African imperialism. Economic crisis led Britain to move into West Africa; depression hit certain economic interests (manufacturing and commercial) and they supported partition to prevent occupation by other imperialist nations.

Horowitz, D. ed. *Containment and Revolution: Western Policy towards Social Revolution 1917 to Vietnam*, London, Anthony Blond, Studies in Imperialism and the Cold War 1, 1967 (pb). **[3]**
Bertrand Russell, Preface; D. Horowitz, Introduction; Isaac Deutscher, Myths of the cold war; William A. Williams, American intervention in Russia 1917–20; John Bagguley, The world war and the cold war; Henry H. Berger, A conservative critique of containment; Senator Taft on the early cold war program; Todd Gitlin, Counter-insurgency: myth and reality in Greece; John Gittings, The origins of China's foreign policy; Richard Morrock, Revolution and intervention in Vietnam.
Cold war largely brought about by United States policy of maintaining *status quo* in world (i.e. supressing revolutions). Cold war latest stage of imperialism.

Horowitz, D. *Imperialism and Revolution*, London, Allen Lane, The Penguin Press, 1969. (pb. 1971). **[3]**
I. Bolshevik Marxism: a perspective: 1. Introduction; 2. Marxism and revolution; 3. Imperialism and revolution; II. Containment and revolution: 4. Open door empire; 5. Capitalism and the cold war; III. The Russian revolution and its fate: 6. The modern revolutionary framework; 7. Uninterrupted revolution: from Lenin to Stalin; 8. Uneven and combined development: the Stalin era; IV. Coexistence and revolution: 9. Russia, the Comintern and the West; 10. World war and cold war; V. 11. International revolution; 12. The epoch and the crisis.
Partly theoretical analysis, partly history.

Horowitz, D. 'The corporations and the cold war', *MR*, **21**, 6, Nov. 1969. **[3]**
Marxist interpretation of contemporary (and recent) U.S. imperialism. Dominant, powerful and expansionist-minded class control foreign policy —the corporations.

Hovde, B. J. 'Socialistic theories of imperialism prior to the Great War', *JPE*, **36**, Oct. 1928. **[1, 2, 6]**

Examination of pre-1914 views on imperialism of the Marxists (Lenin, Luxemburg, Hilferding and others) and the revisionists (Bernstein, Van dervelde and others); and the evolution of the conflict over imperialism in the second international.

Howe, F. C. 'Dollar diplomacy and financial imperialism under the Wilson administration', *Annals of the American Academy of Political and Social Science,* **68,** Nov. 1916, 312–20. **[4]**

'Dollar diplomacy means that the relations of the U.S. with the outside world are determined by the pecuniary interests of a small group of financiers who now control the credit of the country and whose prospects are menaced by surplus capital seeking investment at home'.

Huberman, L. and **Sweezy, P. M.** 'Foreign investment', *MR,* Jan. 1965. **[3, 9]**

The relation between foreign investment and imperialism. A case study of the Cyprus Mines Corporation.

Hyam, R. 'The partition of Africa', *HJ,* **7,** 1, 1964. **[5, 10]**

Review of R. E. Robinson and J. Gallagher, *Africa and the Victorians* (below). Also of Hargreaves *Prelude to the Partition of West Africa.*

A survey of the main criticisms levelled against *Africa and the Victorians* by other reviewers.

Imlah, A. H. *Economic Elements in the Pax Britannica: studies in British foreign trade in the 19th century,* Cambridge, Mass., Harvard Univ. Press, 1958. **[9]**

1. Distinctive elements in the pax Britannica; 2. Real values of British foreign trade, 1796–1853; 3. British balance of payments and export of capital, 1816–1913; 4. The terms of trade of the United Kingdom, 1796–1913; 5. The failure of the British protectionist system; 6. The success of British free trade policy.

Jalée, P. *L'Impérialisme en 1970,* Paris, Maspero, 1970. **[4]**

1. Retour aux sources; 2. L'impérialisme et les matières premières; 3. L'impérialisme et le commerce international; 4. Les exportations de capitaux; 5. La nouvelle révolution technologique; 6. Les concentrations; 7. L'oligarchie financière et industrielle; 8. Le capitalisme monopoliste d'état; 9. L'impérialisme, le tiers monde et le monde socialiste; 10. Contradictions et intégration impérialiste. Le super-imperialisme américain; 11. La contradiction principale. Perspectives politiques.

Jalée, P. *Le Tiers monde dans l'economie mondiale: l'exploitation impérialiste,* Paris, Maspero, 1968. **[3]**

I. 1. Donnés de base; 2. Production agricole et pêches; 3. Production du sous-sol—energie; 4. Industrie manufacturière; 5. Echanges et transports; 6. Mouvements de capitaux—l'aide au tiers monde; 7. Perspectives; II. Fiches économiques signalétiques par principaux pays.

Jalée, P. *The Pillage of the Third World,* New York, Monthly Review Press, 1969 (rev. edn. of *Le Pillage du Tiers Monde,* Paris, Maspero, 1965). **[3]**

1. A world sliced in two; 2. Imperialism and the third world: production relations; 3. The trade of the third world; 4. Imperialism and the third world: investments of capital; 5. A typical neo-colonialist contract: association with the European Common Market; 6. Conclusion.

Jenks, L. H. *The Migration of British Capital to 1875*, New York, Knopf, 1923; London, Nelson, 1963. **[9]**
1. Financial society at the end of the 18th century; 2. Foreign investment after war; 3. The collapse of Anglo-American finance; 4. Migration of capital at a stand; 5. The railway revolution; 6. Cosmopolitan enterprise; 7. The stakes of empire; 8. From bill-broker to finance company; 9. The government loan business; 10. The bankruptcy of the Near East; 11. At the end of the surplus. Bibliography.

Journal of Contemporary History (London), 'Colonialism and decolonisation', **4,** 1, 1969. **[5, 6, 9]**
R. Emerson, Colonialism; R. von Albertini, The impact of two world wars on the decline of colonialism; G. Leduc, The balance sheet of colonialism; P. T. Bauer, The economics of resentment: colonialism and underdevelopment; M. S. Rajan, The impact of British rule in India; W. B. Cowen, The lure of empire: why Frenchmen entered the colonial service; P. Alexandre, Francophonie: The French and Africa; H. Baudet, The Netherlands after the loss of empire; A. Bennigsen, Colonization and decolonization in the Soviet Union; K. Gladdish, Evolving systems of Government in Africa; K. J. Twitchett, The colonial powers and the U.N.; I. Geiss, Pan-Africanism.

Kautsky, K. 'Ultra-imperialism', *NLR*, **59,** Jan.-Feb. 1970. **[1]**
Translation of theoretical article from *Die Neue Zeit*, September 1914, expressing views which Lenin contested in *Imperialism* and elsewhere that in response to dangers of colonial revolution and the burden of the arms race, capitalist countries would unite in an ultra-imperialism.

Kemp, T. *Theories of Imperialism*, London, Dobson Books, 1967. **[1, 2, 3, 6]**
1. Introduction; 2. Marx and theory of imperialism; 3. Hobson and the radical democratic critique of imperialism; 4. Capital accumulation and imperialism; Rosa Luxemburg; 5. Lenin and the contradictions of capitalism; 6. Schumpeter; capitalism versus imperialism; 7. Epigones of Lenin and 'orthodox' Marxism; 8. Imperialism as a purely political phenomenon; 9. Theories of imperialism: objections and a re-statement. Detailed Marxist survey and evaluation of theories of imperialism.

Kidron, M. *Foreign Investments in India*, London, Oxford Univ. Press, 1965. **[9]**
I. Empire and decline; II. Indian and foreign capital; III. The foreign sector today; IV. Conclusions.
Concerned with the direction and outcome of changes in private foreign investment since independence. Part I deals with position at independence and factors which make change necessary. Part II. Changes in relation of private foreign, private domestic, public domestic capital since indepen-

dence. Part III. Private foreign capital as it is evolving. Part IV. Economic and social results.

Kidron, M. 'Imperialism. Last stage but one', London, *International Socialism*, **9**, Summer 1962, 15–20. [**3, 7**]
1. Introduction; 2. Monopoly; 3. Finance Capital; 4. Capital exports; 5. Colonialism; 6. End of empire.
Marxist critique of Lenin: how relevent is his portrait of capitalism today? Contains facts, figures, references. Argues that his analysis nowadays is not applicable as a description of capitalism. 'The truth of Lenin's reasoning stands or falls by his picture of capital flows: do they really shun developed countries and rush to backward ones? They do not.'

Kiernan, V. G. 'Farewells to Empire: some recent studies of imperialism', *Socialist Register 1964*, London, Merlin Press, 1964. [**6**]
Review article on A. P. Thornton's *The Imperial Idea and its Enemies*, R. Robinson and J. Gallagher, *Africa and the Victorians*, J. Strachey, *The End of Empire* and M. Barratt Brown, *After Imperialism*.

Kiernan, V. G. 'Marx and India', *Socialist Register 1967*, London, Merlin Press, 1967. [**1**]
A survey of Marx's views on the impending industrialisation of India.

Kiernan, V. G. *The Lords of Human Kind: European Attitudes to the Outside World in the Age of Imperialism*, London, Weidenfeld & Nicolson, 1969. [**10**]
1. Introduction; 2. India; 3. Other colonies in Asia; 4. The Islamic world; 5. The Far East; 6. Africa; 7. The South Seas; 8. Latin America; 9.·Conclusion.

Kittrel, E. R. 'The development of the theory of colonisation in English classical political economy', Chapel Hill, NC: *Southern Economic Journal*, **31**, 1965. [**6**]

Knorr, K. E. *British Colonial Theories 1570–1850*, Toronto, University of Toronto Press, 1944; London, Frank Cass, 1963. [**6**]
Uncritical survey of theories of colonisation including chapters on Adam Smith, James Mill and Ricardo.

Koebner, R. *Empire*, Cambridge, Cambridge Univ. Press, 1961. [**10**]
1. 'Imperium'—the Roman heritage; 2. From imperium to empire; 3. The emergence of the British empire; 4. The problem of the American colonies; 5. Revolutions and empires; 6. The imperial problem of Ireland; 7. Empire in the Napoleonic period.
Study of the change in the concepts of imperialism and empire from Roman times.

Koebner, R. and **Schmidt, H.** *Imperialism: the story and significance of a political word 1840–1960*, Cambridge, Cambridge Univ. Press, 1964. [**6**]
1. Imperialism of Louis Napoleon; 2. The name of the British empire in the first decades of Queen Victoria's reign; 3. Colonial crises and the new meaning of empire; 4. The rise of empire sentiment 1865–72; 5. The significance of Disraeli's impact—legend and reality; 6. The establishment of imperialism as a slogan in British party strife; 7. Imperialism—the

national desire for Anglo-Saxon union; 8. The incorporation of Africa into the imperial idea and the climax of popular imperialism; 9. The revulsion against imperialism; 10. From sentiment to theory; 11. Hate—Word of world struggle against Anglo-Saxon domination; 12. The slogan of imperialism after the second world war; 13. Self-determination and world order.

Claims that semantic approach to 'imperialism' reveals much about its nature in different time periods. Chapters 10, 11, 12 are concerned with history of the development of theories of imperialism.

Koebner, R. 'The concept of economic imperialism', *EHR*, 2nd ser. **2**, 1949. [**5, 6, 7, 9**]
Analysis of how concept of economic imperialism grew up and gained credence. Concludes that motives of political morality most important of those motives which brought empire into being.

Koebner, R. 'The emergence of the concept of imperialism', *Cambridge Journal*, **5**, 1952. [**10**]
The linguistic history of 'imperialism'—its meaning has reflected attitudes to its object.

Kohn, H. *Nationalism and Imperialism in the Hither East*, London, Routledge, 1932. [**5**]
4. Imperialism and nationalism—the function of nationalism—the example of Cyprus—recent British imperial policy—social forces—the civilising mission—the methods of imperialism—the capitulations—new methods in the ancient dispute.
Supports multicausal explanation of imperialism.

Kolko, G. *The Roots of American Foreign Policy: an analysis of power and purpose*, Boston, Beacon Press, 1969. [**4**]
1. Men of power; 2. The American military and civil authority; 3. The United States and world economic power; 4. The United States in Vietnam 1944–66; Epilogue—on reason and radicalism.

Kruger, D. H. 'Hobson, Lenin and Schumpeter on imperialism', New York, *Journal of the History of Ideas*, **16**, April 1955, p.252. [**2, 6, 8**]
Brief statement of the positions of three theoreticians of imperialism.

Laclau, E. 'Argentina—imperialist strategy and the May crisis', *NLR*, **62**, July/Aug. 1970. [**3**]
Sets the political explosion of May 1969 in context of changing nature of imperialism as it operates in Argentina.

Lafeber, W. *The New Empire. An interpretation of American Expansion 1860–1898*, Ithaca, Cornell Univ. Press, 1963. [**4, 8**]
1. The years of preparation 1860–1889; 2. The intellectual formulation; 3. The strategic formulation; 4. The economic formulation; 5. Reaction: depression diplomacy 1893–1895; 6. Reaction: the Venezuelan boundary crisis of 1895–1896; 7. Reaction: new problems, new friends, new foes; 8. Reaction: approach to war. Epilogue. Bibliography.
American expansion in 1890s based on general assumption that 'additional

foreign markets would solve the economic, social and political problems created by the industrial revolution'.

Lambert, R. *Modern Imperialism*, London, Longmans, 1928. [4]
1. The old and the new; 2. The partition of Africa; 3. Imperialism in Asia; 4. Dollar diplomacy in America; 5. The League of Nations and imperialism; 6. A balance sheet of imperialism.

'In conclusion then modern imperialism represents an adaptation of the economic structure in response to certain needs, which have so far been only very partially met by the means employed.' Empire marks a stage in the age-long search for self-sufficiency which began with the medieval manor, continued through the nation-state and is yet seeking its realisation. But just as an industry the trust may be regarded as a half-way house from competition to community controlled cooperation, so too empire may be a stepping-stone between nationalism and internationalism.'

Langer, W. L. 'A critique of imperialism', New York, *Foreign Affairs*, **14,** Oct. 1935. [5, 6, 7]
Attack on Hobson and neo-Marxist writing on imperialism; but produces grudging economic explanation nonetheless.

Langer, W. L. *The Diplomacy of Imperialism 1890–1902*, 2nd edn., New York, Knopf, 1965. [5, 6, 7]
3. The triumph of imperialism.
This chapter alone has some discussion of theories of imperialism and economic factors in the imperialist drive.

Lenin, V. I. *Against Imperialist War*, Moscow, Progress Publishers, 1966. [2]
Contains about 60 2–3 page passages from various sources originally but all to be found in *Collected Works*, 43 vols., Moscow, Progress Publishers; London.

Lenin, V. I. *British Labour and British Imperialism*, London, Lawrence & Wishart, 1969, earlier edn. under title *Lenin on Britain*. [2]
1. Industrial capitalism in England: 1. The rise of capitalism; 2. Marx and Engels on the British labour movement; II. Pre-war British imperialism: 1. Special features of British imperialism; 2. The British imperialist state; 3. The colonial policy of British imperialism; III. The working class of imperialist England: 1. The social roots of opportunism; 2. Liberal–Labour politics and the turn of the masses; 3. For or against British imperialism; IV. British imperialism and the war of 1914–1918: 1. 'Social chauvinism is consummated opportunism'; 2. Imperialist war is being transformed into civil war; 3. British imperialism and the Russian revolution; V. The post-war crisis of British imperialism: 1. The results of the war; 2. Intervention in Soviet Russia and the British labour movement; 3. The problem of power and councils of action; 4. Driving out the social imperialists, a condition of the victory of the proletariat; 5. The British labour movement and the national and colonial questions; 6. The tasks of the Third International; 7. The formation of the Communist Party in Great Britain.

A selection of brief extracts from speeches, letters and other writings.

Lenin, V. I. *Imperialism, the Highest Stage of Capitalism, A popular Outline,* (first published 1917), 13th edn., Moscow, Progress Publishers, 1966. [2] Preface to French and German editions (1920); I. Concentration of Production and Monopolies; II. Banks and their new role; III. Finance capital and the financial oligarchy; IV. Export of capital; V. Division of the world among capitalist associations; VI. Division of the world among the great powers; VII. Imperialism as a special stage of capitalism; VIII. Parasitism and decay of capitalism; IX. Critique of imperialism; X. The place of imperialism in history.

Lenin, V. I. *Notebooks on Imperialism, Collected Works,* vol. 39, Moscow, Progress Publishers, 1968. [2] Twenty-one notebooks and some miscellaneous notes used by Lenin in working on *Imperialism, the Highest Stage of Capitalism.*

Lenin, V. I. *On Imperialism, the eve of the proletarian social revolution,* Peking: Foreign Languages Press, 1960. [2, 3] 1. Imperialism is monopolistic, decaying, moribund capitalism; 2. All capitalist contradictions have become immeasurably more acute in the epoch of imperialism; 3. The U.S.A. represents the most ferocious and brazen imperialism; 4. State-monopoly capitalism has not changed the nature of capitalism but intensified its contradictions; 5. The fight against imperialism must be inseparably bound up with the fight against opportunism; 6. The October Revolution broke the chains of imperialism. Composed of one paragraph quotes from various works of Lenin.

Liberalism and the Empire, London, R. B. Johnson, 1900. [4, 8] Three essays: F. W. Hirst, Imperialism and finance; G. Murray, The exploitation of inferior races in ancient and modern times; and J. C. Hammond, Colonial and foreign policy.

'The first paper is an attempt to explore the finance of imperialism, and to show how militarism and excessive expenditure upon armaments both feed and are fed by calculated games and inevitable wars which serve at the same time another purpose—that of preventing reforms at home. The second attempts by the help of an historical parallel to analyse one part of the relation of the British to the subject races. . . . In the third and last a contrast is drawn between the leading ideal of liberalism in foreign policy and the teaching of modern imperialism: the morality, the tendencies and the fruits of imperialism are discussed, and an attempt is made to show that the desertion of our great trade is inconsistent with the greatness and safety of the empire.'

Lichtheim, G. 'Imperialism Parts 1 and 2', New York, *Commentary,* **49,** 4 and 5, April and May 1970. [6, 7] Explores the genesis and growth of those political structures that have called themselves, or have come to be known as, empires, and offers a critical analysis of the specific ideologies which have provided those structures with a sense of value and purpose. Part I begins with the Roman

Empire and traces the course of imperialism up to the eve of World War I. Part II deals with the phenomenon of imperialism in this century. Critical of many Marxist writers (Baran, Sweezy, Magdoff).

Lichtheim, G. *Imperialism*, Harmondsworth: Allen Lane the Penguin Press, 1971. **[6, 7]**
Revised version of articles in *Commentary* (above). 1. Introduction; 2. Imperium; 3. The rise of Europe; 4. Empire of the sea; 5. Liberal imperialism; 6. Imperialism and nationalism; 7. Imperialism and revolution; 8. From Marx to Mao; 9. The Third World.

Liska, G. *Imperial America*, Baltimore, Johns Hopkins Univ. Press, 1967 (pb). **[5]**
1. The setting defined: the cold war and after; 2. Empire and imperial politics: in the past and in theory; 3. The past and present kings: aspects and features of empire; 4. The world today: multistate and imperial orders; 5. The world today and tomorrow: interempire and interstate relations; 6. Leadership and independence: Europe facing herself and America; 7. Alliances and intervention: America facing her hemisphere and Afro-Asia; 8. Conclusion. Bibliography.

Luxemburg, R. *The Accumulation of Capital*, trans. Agnes Schwarzschild, London, Routledge, 1951 (pb. 1963), (first published 1913). **[3]**
III. The historical conditions of accumulation: 25. Contradictions within the diagram of enlarged production; 26. The reproduction of capital and its social setting; 27. The struggle against natural economy; 28. The introduction of commodity economy; 29. The struggle against the present economy; 30. International loans; 31. Protective tariffs and accumulation; 32. Militarism as a province of accumulation.

McCormick, T. J. *China Market, America's Quest for Informal Empire, 1893–1901*, Chicago, Quadrangle Books, 1967. **[4, 8]**
1. Exporting the social question; 2. The frustration of laissez-faire; 3. In the eye of the storm; 4. A dose of insular imperialism; 5. A fair field and no favour; 6. The dilemmas unfold; 7. The future in microcosm. Bibliography. Leaders used foreign policy as a way of alleviating strains in the *status quo* and their attempts at social analysis were based on economic interest groups.

MacDonagh, O. 'The anti-imperialism of free trade', *EHR*, **14**, April 1962; also in A. G. L. Shaw, ed. *Great Britain and the Colonies 1815–1865* (below). **[4, 5]**
Criticism of Gallagher and Robinson thesis, especially that free traders were aware of and approved of informal empire. He argues they opposed it very strongly. Most of the evidence from Cobden.

McIntyre, W. D. *The Imperial Frontier in the Tropics 1865–1875*, London, Macmillan, 1967. **[5, 9]**
Introduction. The imperial frontier in the tropics; I. The formulation of colonial policy; II. The dilemma; III. The new experiments; IV. The frontier in perspective; Conclusion. Mid-Victorian imperialism: a pragmatic approach to Empire.

358

Anti-unitary theories. Essential political, but pragmatic theory.

Magdoff, H. *The Age of Imperialism: the Economics of U.S. Foreign Policy*, New York and London, Monthly Review Press, 1969 (pb). **[3]**
1. Introduction; 2. The new imperialism; 3. The financial network; 4. Aid and trade; 5. The American empire and the U.S. economy. Appendix A. U.S. Defense commitments and assurances; B. U.S. involvement in international political crises and critical situations, 1961 to mid-1966.
Documents the existence of an American empire. Argues that 'Imperialism is not a matter of choice for a capitalist society; it is the way of life of such a society'.

Magdoff, H. 'Economic aspects of U.S. imperialism', *MR*, Nov. 1966 and included in *The Age of Imperialism*, New York, Monthly Review Press, 1966. **[3]**

Magdoff, H. 'Is imperialism really necessary?' *MR*, **21**, 5 and 6, Oct., Nov. 1970. **[3]**
Imperialism and relations between developed countries; investment in underdeveloped countries; raw materials and the third world; fundamental changes?

Magdoff, H. 'Militarism and imperialism', *MR*, **21**, 9, Feb. 1970, also in Cambridge, Mass. *American Economic Review, Papers and Proceedings*, May 1970. **[3]**
An explanation of the interaction between capitalism and militarism in the U.S. historically and today. And an attack on bourgeois economics for ignoring it.

Mandel, E. *Europe versus America? contradictions of Imperialism*, London, New Left Books, 1970. **[3]**
1. Europe and America; 2. International concentration of capital; 3. The relative superiority of American firms; 4. Interpenetration of capital in the E.E.C.; 5. The nation state today; 6. Britain's entry into the E.E.C.; 7. The division of the world market; 8. The international monetary crisis; 9. The future of the supranational institutions; 10. The working-class and inter-imperialist competition; 11. The socialist alternative. Bibliography.

Mandel, E. *Europe versus America? Contradictions of Imperialism*, London, Merlin Press, 1968. **[3]**
13. Imperialism: capitalism and inequality among nations; the world market and industrial capitalism; from export of goods to export of capital; colonialism; colonial super-profits; the world-wide division of labour; international trusts and cartels; private trusts wield sovereign rights in under-developed countries; economic structure of the under-developed countries; imperialism as an obstacle to the industrialisation of under-developed countries; neo-imperialism.

Mandel, E. 'The laws of uneven development', *NLR*, **59**, Jan.–Feb., 1970. **[3]**
Mandel's defence against attack by M. Nicolaus in same issue of same journal. And an enlargement of ideas on inter-imperialist rivalry, the

prospects of United States capitalism today and the fallacy of ultra-imperialism. These themes related to political prospects.

Mandel, E. 'Where is America going', *NLR*, **54**, March–April 1969. [3]
On the forces undermining the social and economic equilibrium of the United States and prospects for revolution. The decline of unskilled labour and the social roots of Black radicalisation; the social roots of the student revolt; automation, technicians and the hierarchical structure of the factory; the erosion of real wages through inflation; the social consequences of public squalor; the impact of foreign competition; the wage differentials enjoyed by American workers.

Marini, R. Mauro. 'Brazilian "interdependence" and imperialist integration', *MR*, Dec. 1965. [3]
Imperialist integration; integration and underdevelopment; autonomous capitalist development?; integrated development; the doctrine of interdependence; Latin American integration.
Argues that since the military coup of 1964 Brazil has been becoming more economically integrated with U.S.A. and that the integrated imperialism of these two will produce 'antagonistic cooperation' between the bourgeosie of South American countries.

Marini, R. Mauro. *Subdesarollo y Revolucion* (Underdevelopment and Revolution). Siglo xxi, Mexico, 1969. [3]
I. Underdevelopment and revolution: the link to the world market; the imperialist integration of productive systems; the struggle for autonomous capitalist development; the collapse of the bourgeoisie; integrated capitalist development; the future of Latin American revolution; II. The dialectics of capitalist development in Brazil: politics and class struggle; ideology and praxis of sub-imperialism; the character of the Brazilian revolution; III. Vanguard and class: sub-imperialism and capital accumulation; the super-exploitation of labour; mass struggle; the bankruptcy of reformism; renewal and tradition on the left; the assumptions of armed struggle.

Marx, K. *Capital*, vol. iii, London, Lawrence & Wishart, 1962 (first English edn. 1887). [1]
III. The law of the tendency of the rate of profit to fall: 13. The law as such; 14. Counteracting influences; (i) increasing intensity of exploitation; (ii) depression of wages below the value of labour-power; (iii) cheapening of elements of constant capital; (iv) relative over-population; (v) foreign trade; (vi) the increase of stock of capital; 15. Exposition of the internal contradictions of the law.

Marx, K. and **Engels, F.** *On Colonialism*, London, Lawrence & Wishart, 1960. [1]
A series of articles and letters written by Marx and Engels 1850–88, together with extracts from *Capital*, dealing with China, India and Ireland.

Mathew, W. M. 'The imperialism of free trade', *EHR*, Dec. 1968. [4, 5]
Examination of Britain's economic and political relation with Peru 1820–70

to see if it conforms to the Gallagher and Robinson view of imperialism. Concludes that 'there is little in the historical record to justify viewing Peru as the victim of British imperialism, as part of Britain's invisible empire of informal sway. It may also be observed that there is no special factor operating in the Peruvian case to account for the restraint which characterised British policy.'

Mill, J. S. *Principles of Political Economy*, 2 vols, London, John W. Parker. 1844. [4]
Book III. 25. Of the competition of different countries in the same market; Book IV. 4. Of the tendency of profits to a minimum.

Mommsen, W. J. 'Nationale und Ekonomische Faktoren im Britischen Imperialismus vor 1914', (National and Economic Factors in British Imperialism before 1914) Munich, *Historische Zeitschrift*, **206**, 1968. [4, 5, 9]
Multicausal explanation of imperialism—economic forces are one among many causal factors. A long article that includes graphs illustrating British exports and new capital investment overseas 1870–1913.

Moon, P. T. *Imperialism and World Politics*, New York, Macmillan, 1947. [4]
1. Significance of imperialism—world conquest and world unrest; 2. Two changes of mind; 3. Why Europe shouldered the white man's burden; 4. Dynamics of imperialism—men and motives; 5. Clothes, culture and caoutchouc in Congo; 6. Five decades of business and diplomatic bargaining in West Africa; 7. The conquest and exploitation of East Africa; 8. A climax —in the Sudan; 9. The legacy of Cecil Rhodes; 10. North Africa and the great powers; 11. Near Eastern questions old and new; 12. Anglo-Russian rivalry in the Middle East; 13. Imperialism in Southern Asia; 14. The battle of concessions in the Far East; 15. Fortunes of war and profits of peace in Pacific islands; 16. The policy of the U.S. towards Latin America; 17. Nationalism versus imperialism in Europe; 18. The League and its mandates; 19. Conclusions.

Moore, R. J. 'Imperialism and Free Trade Policy in India 1853–4', *EHR*, **17**, 1964, also in A. G. L. Shaw ed., *Great Britain and the Colonies 1815–1865*, (below). [4, 5]
Criticism of MacDonagh 'Anti-imperialism of free trade' (above).

Morgenthau, H. J. *Politics Among Nations: the struggle for power and peace*, 3rd edn., New York, Alfred A. Knopf, 1960, (first published 1948, rev. 1954). [5, 6, 7]
II. International politics as a struggle for power: 15. The struggle for power: Imperialism (i) What imperialism is not; (ii) Economic theories of imperialism; (iii) Different types of imperialism; (iv) How to detect and counter an imperialistic policy.

Nadel, H. and **Curtis, P.** eds., *Imperialism and Colonialism*, New York, Macmillan, 1964. [4, 5, 6, 7]
H. Luthy, Colonisation and the making of mankind; D. K. Fieldhouse,

The new imperialism: the Hobson–Lenin thesis revised; J. Gallagher and R. Robinson, The imperialism of free trade; H. Brunschwig, The origins of the new French empire; M. E. Townsend, Commercial and colonial policies of imperial Germany. Bibliography.

Nearing, S. and **Freeman, J.** *Dollar Diplomacy: a study in American imperialism*, New York, Monthly Review Press, 1966, (pb 1969). (first published 1925). [2, 4]
Introduction: Recent imperial experience; A. The economic background of American imperialism; I. American economic expansion; B. American imperialism in action; II. Economic penetration; III. Spheres of influence; IV. Political 'regulation'; V. Armed intervention; VI. Acquisition without annexation; VII. Conquest and purchase; VIII. War debts and settlements; C. The growth of imperial policy; IX. The evolution of American imperial diplomacy. Bibliography, maps and charts.

Neisser, H. 'Economic imperialism reconsidered', New York, *Social Research*, **27**, 1960. [5, 7]
Introduction. The nature of imperialism, its meaning; 2. Is economic imperialism inherent in capitalism? 3. The role which investment in the so-called non-capitalist countries has played in the secular development of capitalism; 4. Under-consumption in a capitalist system; 5. Did foreign investment show a tendency to increase during the downswing of the business cycle, to take the place of lagging home investment, and to decrease during the upswing? 6. Conclusion: pre-World War I, the restoration of cyclical prosperity was not, in general, conditioned by capital exports. At times, however, a rise of investment opportunities abroad, or a better utilisation of existing opportunities abroad, assisted in ending a depression. This is all that appears to be left of the theory of economic imperialism.
A brief attack on the theory of economic imperialism.

Newbury, C. W. 'Victorians, Republicans and the Partition of Africa, *JAH*, **3**, 1962. [5, 7]
Attacks Gallagher and Robinson argument (*Africa and the Victorians*) that there existed in the 1880s a causal relationship between British intervention in Egypt and the timing and pattern of the subsequent 'scramble' for tropical Africa. Suggests that 'the theory of economic imperialism' may need modification.

Nicolaus, M. 'The theory of the labour aristocracy', *MR*, **21**, 11, April 1970. [1, 2]
Survey of Engels and Lenin on the impact of imperialism on the working class in the advanced capitalist countries.

Nicolaus, M. 'The universal contradiction', *NLR*, **59**, Jan.-Feb. 1970. [3]
Polemic on 'Where is America Going?' by E. Mandel, arguing that Mandel wrongly distinguishes internal and external elements in analysing the crisis of US imperialism.

Nkrumah, K. *Neo Colonialism: the last stage of imperialism,* London,

362

Nelson, 1965, Heinemann, 1968. [3]
1. Africa's resources; 2. Obstacles to economic progress; 3. Imperialist finance 4. Monopoly capitalism and the American dollar; 5. The truth behind the headlines; 6. Primary resources and foreign interests; 7. The Oppenheimer empire; 8. Foreign investment in South African mining; 9. Anglo-American Corporation Ltd; 10. The diamond groups; 11. Mining interests in Central Africa; 12. Companies and combines; 13. The tin, aluminium and nickel groups; 14. Union Minière du Haut Katanga; 15. Economic pressures in the Congo Republic; 16. Monetary zones and foreign banks; 17. New industries; the effects on primary producing countries; 18. The mechanisms of neo-colonialism. Bibliography.
Economic imperialism. Thesis that capitalism avoided an internal collapse by transferring the conflict to the world stage. A crisis is being provoked by the uncontrolled action of international capitalism in the developing parts of the world. Afro-centric.
Paish, G. 'Great Britain's investments in individual colonial and foreign countries', *JRSS*, **74**, Jan. 1911. [9]
Data on foreign investment up to 1910. He concludes 'I think the net total of our investments in other lands would be not much short of £3,500,000,000". Gives breakdown of where it is going. Discussion of paper also printed in journal.
Palloix, C. 'Impérialisme et mode de production capitaliste', Paris, *L'Homme et Société*, **12**, April-May-June 1969. [3]
Qu'est-ce que l'impérialisme? Impérialisme et mode de production capitaliste; l'impérialisme économique, solution aux contradictions du mode de production capitaliste; mode de production capitaliste à dominante concurrentielle et impérialisme; domination économique et mode de production capitaliste; fonctions de la domination économique vis-à-vis du mode de production capitaliste; mode de production capitaliste à dominante monopoliste et impérialisme.
Palloix, C. 'La question de l'impérialisme chez V.I. Lénine et Rosa Luxemburg', Paris, *L'Homme et Société*, **15**, Jan.-Feb.-Mar. 1970. [1, 2, 3]
La problématique Léniniste: la question du marche extérieur dans le mode de production capitaliste au stade concurrentielle; la question de l'impérialisme au stade monopoliste. La problématique de Rosa Luxemburg: La détermination des contradictions du mode de production capitaliste dans l'unité du procés de production et du procès de circulation; l'impérialisme, solution aux contradictions du mode de production capitaliste. Conclusion: l'unité théorique de la question de l'impérialisme chez Rosa Luxemburg et V. I. Lénine: Génération-réalisation de surplus produit; génération absorption de surplus accumulé.
Pares, R. 'The economic factors in the history of the empire', *EHR*, **7**, May 1937. [4, 5]
'To sum up, it is pretty clear that imperialism is above all a process—and to some degree a policy—which aims at developing complementary relations

between high industrial technique in one land and fertile soils in another. These relations are pre-capitalist relations, they are also capitalist relations. Not all the Marxist teachings apply to all the facts, but many of them open the eyes of colonial historians to things which they ought to have seen before.'

Perlo, V. *The Empire of High Finance*, New York, International Publishers, 1956. [3]
III. Politics: 17. Wall Street abroad and foreign policy, oil, investment in Europe and the Morgans, corporate foreign policy and its instruments, Standard Oil foreign policy, the Morgans and foreign policy, conflicts in interests and policies.

Platt, D. C. M. *Finance, Trade and Politics in British Foreign Policy 1815–1914*, London, Oxford Univ. Press, 1968. [4, 5]
1. H.M. Government and overseas finance; 2. H.M. Government and overseas trade; 3. Finance, trade and British foreign policy. Bibliography. Study of the relationship between finance, trade and politics in the conduct of British foreign policy. A multi-causal analysis.

Platt, D. C. M. 'Economic factors in British policy during the "New Imperialism"', London, *Past and Present*, **39**, April 1968. [4, 5]
Defence of economic imperialism v. Fieldhouse etc. Argues that competition for Britain (from newly industrial Germany etc.) and fear of loss of world trade (tariffs etc.) was a major factor in the 'new imperialism' of the 1880s.

Platt, D. C. M. 'The imperialism of free trade: some reservations' *EHR*, **21**, 1968. [4, 5]
Criticism of Gallagher and Robinson's 'Imperialism of Free Trade' thesis, especially of the continuity Gallagher and Robinson claim to find between mid and late Victorian imperialism and their picture of official (British) policy to overseas trade and investment.

Porter, B. *Critics of Empire: British radical attitudes to colonialism in Africa 1895–1914*, London, Macmillan, 1968. [4, 7]
1. Introduction: the nineteenth-century legacy; 2. The imperial challenge 1895; 3. Liberals and the empire; 4. Labour and the empire; 5. The new knowledge; 6. The new radicals; 7. Imperialism: a study; 8. Liverpool and Africa; 9. The twentieth century: radicals and Africa. Bibliography.
Although they were a very small minority and hardly heeded at the time, they were very important in influencing the direction of later anti-imperialist thought (e.g. Hobson). Detailed examination of Hobson included.

Renner, K. *Marxismus, Krieg und Internationale*, Stuttgart, 1917. (Marxism, War and International Relations). [2]
I. The new society: 1. Social and political upheaval; 2. The change in basic social relations; 3. The change in class stratification and structure; 4. The combination of the nationalised economy in the economic region; II. The new state: 5. The imperialist state; 6. Imperialism and foreign relations. The

unity of the international economy; 7. The contradictions in the international economy; 8. The struggle between economic regions and the world war; 9. Possibilities and guarantees of a lasting peace; III. New tasks of socialism; 12. Socialist imperialism?

Rhodes, R. I. ed., *Imperialism and Underdevelopment: a reader*, New York and London, Monthly Review Press, 1970. (pb). [3]

I. Imperialism in contemporary and historical perspective: A. G. Frank, The development of underdevelopment; H. Magdoff, The American empire and the U.S. economy; D. Horowitz, The alliance for progress; H. Alavi and A. Khusro, Pakistan: the burden of US aid; P. Reno, Aluminium profits and Caribbean people; A. G. Frank, On the mechanisms of imperialism: the case of Brazil; J. O'Connor, The meaning of economic imperialism. II. The underdeveloped economy and economic policy: T. K. Hopkins, On economic planning in tropical Africa; D. Seers, The stages of economic growth of a primary producer in the middle of the twentieth century; C. E. Rollins, Mineral development and economic growth; T. Balogh, Agricultural and economic development; G. Arrighi, International corporations, labour aristocracies and economic development in tropical Africa; H. O. Schmitt, Foreign capital and social conflict in Indonesia, 1950–58. III. Politics, class conflict and underdevelopment: P.A. Baran, On the political economy of backwardness; F. Fanon, The pitfalls of national consciousness—Africa; J. Nun, The middle class military coup; P. Ehrensaft, The politics of pseudo-planning in a primary-producing nation; M. Caldwell, Problems of socialism in Southeast Asia. Bibliography.

Selection of articles mostly published elsewhere but some (e.g. Arrighi) original.

Ricardo, D. *On the Principles of Political Economy and Taxation*, London, John Murray, 1817; Dent, Everyman, 1955. [4]

19. Effects of accumulation on profits and interest; 23. On colonial trade.

Rippy, J. F. *British Investments in Latin America, 1822–1949: A case study in the operations of private enterprise in retarded regions*, Minneapolis: University of Minnesota Press, 1959. [9]

Introduction. Recent problems in private international investment; 1. The crisis and British experience in Latin America. I. General survey of British investments in Latin America: 2. Early imprudence and vexation 1822–1880; 3. Two decades of British investment and an intervening depression; 4. An analysis of investments at the end of 1913; 5. British investments at their peak, 1928; 6. A decade of rapid contraction; II. Country by country inspection of the British investment: chapters 7 to 14 on Mexico, the Small Caribbean countries, Northern South America, Paraguay, Bolivia and Peru, Chile, Uruguay, Brazil and Argentina; III. The crux of the matter in global setting: 15. A comparative sample of British overseas companies; 16. A recent decade of income from British overseas investments; 17. Some British views on foreign investments; 18. Views of the Latin American recipients.

Rippy, J. F. 'Background for Point Four: samples of profitable investments in the underdeveloped countries', Chicago, *Journal of Business of the University of Chicago*, April 1953. **[9]**
Useful statistical tables for the benefits from U.K. investment in Latin America.

Robbins, L. C. *The Economic Causes of War*, London, Jonathan Cape, 1939. **[5, 6, 7, 8]**
1. Introduction. The means of modern war—the object of the essay—the plan of inquiry; 2. The Marxian theory of imperialism—the economic interpretation of war—general characteristics of the Marxian theory—the underconsumption theory—the logical significance of the underconsumption theory—the Leninist theory of imperialism; 3. The Marxian theory tested—criteria of verification—examples of capitalist imperialism—more alleged cases further examined—finance and diplomacy in the modern period—the inadequacy of the Leninist theory; 4. The economic causes of war—national power and economic factors—non-economic motives of war—sectional interests and war—historical observations: England and Germany; 5. The ultimate cause of international conflict—the final task—the concomitants of dollar diplomacy—the causes of economic nationalism—the wars of a national socialist world—the root cause of international conflict—the United State of Europe. Appendix. The meaning of economic causation—introduction—the notion of a historical cause—motives as causes—the nature of an economic cause—the rules of historical explanation—social structures as causes.
Very critical of economic interpretations.

Robinson R. E. and **Gallagher, J.** (with Alice Denny) *Africa and the Victorians, the official mind of imperialism*, London, Macmillan, 1961 (pb 1965). **[5]**
1. The spirit of Victorian expansion; 2. Moral suasion over Guinea and Zanzibar 1815–80; 3. The revolt of the Afrikaner 1877–81; 4. The Suez crisis 1882; 5. Gladstone's bondage in Egypt; 6. Repercussions south of the Sahara; 7. Rhodes' counterpoise 1887–91; 8. Cairo or Constantinople? 1885–90; 9. New frontiers of insecurity; 10. Salisbury's watch on the Nile, 1890; 11. Uganda, the root of liberalism; 12. The way to Fashoda; 13. 'Imperialist' beginnings in West Africa; 14. South Africa: another Canada or another United States? 15. Nationalism and imperialism.
Britain's African empire was not obtained for economic or domestic political reasons. Main aim was to safeguard Britain's position in the world by maintaining the route to India. Safety of this route was threatened in early 1880s by nationalist crises in Africa. From start to finish the partition of tropical Africa was driven by the persistent crises in Egypt.

Rochester, A. *Rulers of America: A study of finance capital*, London, Lawrence & Wishart, 1936. **[2, 9]**
20. Wall Street's foreign empire—colonies and protectorates—Mexico,

Columbia and Venezuela—other South American countries—imperialism and the colonial workers—China—Canada—World war; a new stage in U.S. imperialism—Wall Street and the stabilisation of post-war Europe— role of capital export in American capitalism.
Investment data to support the Marxist theory in the case of America. Used directly to support theory so difficult to classify—more theory content than straight investment information but data rather than pure theory.

Rodbertus, J. K. *Die Handelskrisen und die Hypothekennot der Grundbesitzer* (The Business Crisis and the Credit Restrictions of the Property Owners), Berlin, 1858. [4, 8]
'Each new market opened up therefore represents a postponement of the final settlement of the social problem.' 'From this point we can take a rapid glance at the importance of the opening up of Asia, and in particular of China and Japan, the richest markets in the world, and the maintenance of India under English Rule. As a result of these factors the social problem is given a respite.'
Imperialism stops wage stagnation and class antagonism.

Rodney, W. 'The imperialist partition of Africa', *MR*, **21**, 11 ('Lenin Today' issue), April 1970. [3]
Defence of Lenin's theory in relation to the scramble for Africa.

Salz, A. *Das Wesen des Imperialismus*, Leipzig and Berlin: 1931. (The Nature of Imperialism). [5, 7, 8]
I. The problematic of imperialism; II. State constitution and imperialism; III. Imperialism and capitalism; IV. The roots of imperialism; V. The future of imperialism.
Book version of 1930 article (below).

Salz, A. 'Der Imperialismus der Vereinigten Staaten,' (The Imperialism of the United States), Tübingen, **50**; *Archiv für Sozialwissenschaft und Sozialpolitik*, 1923, 565–616. [4]
The specifically modern form of imperialism is found where the state puts its means of power at the disposal of expansive economic interests. American imperialism is that of finance-capitalism. Traces development of American imperialism from Hawaii 1893–98. Some details of American finance's activities abroad in first two decades of the twentieth century. Individual studies on: Nicaragua, Haiti and San Domingo, Mexico and Guatemala, Samoa and Liberia.

Salz, A. 'Die Zukunft des Imperialismus' (The Future of Imperialism), Jena, *Weltwirtschaftliches Archiv*, **32**, Oct. 1930. [5, 7, 8]
Analysis of inadequacy of pre-1914 ideas about progress towards peace through increasing trade as well as of socialist theory of imperialism. Believes that imperialism is in decline. Also that imperialism has become more conciliatory, less brutal, through being influenced by capitalist rationalism.

Saul, S. B. *Studies in British Overseas Trade, 1870–1914*, Liverpool,

Liverpool Univ. Press, 1960. [9]

2. Problems of an international economy; 3. The pattern of settlements—(i) the structure of world trade; 4. The pattern of settlements—(ii) the export of capital; 5. Trends and fluctuations; 6. Tariffs and commercial policy: 7, 8, 9. British trade with the empire—Canada, India. General conclusions.

Saul, S. B. 'The economic significance of "constructive imperialism",' *JEH*, June, 1957. [4, 5, 8]

On the social, economic and political foundations of Chamberlain's ideas on imperialism and other late 19th century British imperialist feeling. 'Concern for trade and social problems sowed the seed but ["constructive imperialism"] blossomed forth into much wider interests.'

Schatz, S. P. 'Economic imperialism again', New York, *Social Research*, 28, 1961. [4]

A comment on Hans Neisser, 'Economic imperialism reconsidered' (above). Schatz takes issue with the conclusion "At times this is all that appears to be left of the theory of economic imperialism".

Schumpeter, J. A. *Capitalism, Socialism and Democracy*, 3rd edn, London, Allen & Unwin, 1950. [7, 8]

This book only contains brief treatment of imperialism (pp. 49–54), but this demonstrates how the concept fits into Schumpeter's system.

Schumpeter, J. A. *Imperialism*, Oxford, Blackwell, 1951; New York, Meridian, 1955, first published in German in 1919. [7]

1. The problem; 2. Imperialism as a catch phrase; 3. Imperialism in practice; 4. Imperialism in the modern absolute monarchy; 5. Imperialism and capitalism.

The essay is a critique of the Bauer-Hilferding theory and an alternative theoretical framework into which war and its antecedents could be appropriately fitted. Follows usual Schumpeterian line.

Seeley, J. R. *The Expansion of England*, London, Macmillan, 1883. [5]

I. 1. Tendency in English history; 2. England in the eighteenth century; 3. The empire; 4. The old colonial system; 5. Effect of the new world on the old; 6. Commerce and war; 7. Phases of expansion; 8. Schism in Greater Britain; II. 1. History and politics; 2. The Indian empire; 3. How we conquered India; 4. How we govern India; 5. Mutual influence of England and India; 6. Phases in the conquest of India; 7. Internal and external dangers; 8. Recapitulation.

Segal, H. and **Simon, M.** 'British foreign capital issues, 1865–94', *JEH*, 21, 4, 1961. [9]

Data for the understanding of the causes of capital migration and its effects upon economic development.

Semmel, B. *The Rise of Free Trade Imperialism: classical political economy, the empire of free trade and imperialism, 1750–1850*, Cambridge, Cambridge Univ. Press, 1970. [4, 8]

1. Introduction; 2. Theory and politics of free trade empire in the eighteenth

368

century; 3. The agrarian critique and the emergence of orthodoxy;
4. The third school: Wakefield and the radical economists; 5. The Wakefield program for middle-class empire; 6. Parliament, political economy
and the workshop of the world; 7. Cobdenism and the 'dismal science';
8. Mercantilist revival; 9. Classical political economy, the empire of free
trade, and imperialism. Bibliography.
By an historian about the intellectual origins of nineteenth-century British
imperialism. Argues that in almost every particular the justifications and
analysis of the free trade empire up to 1850 anticipated the later descrip-
tions and critiques of imperialism of the generation before 1914.

Semmel, B. *Imperialism and Social Reform: English social-imperialist
thought 1895–1914*, London, Allen & Unwin, 1960. **[8]**
1. Social-Imperialism; 2. Social-Darwinism: Benjamin Kidd and Karl
Pearson; 3. A party of national efficiency: the Liberal-Imperialists and the
Fabians; 4. Joseph Chamberlain's 'squalid argument'; 5. The Social-
Imperialism of the Tariff Reform League; 6. Fabianism and Liberal-
Imperialism, 1903–1914; 7. The two imperialisms; 8. Sir Halford Mack-
inder: theorist of imperialism; 9. Viscount Milner: Social-Imperial
Idealist; 10. William Cunningham: national economies; 11. Sir William
Ashley as 'Socialist of the chair'; 12. Lord Roberts and Robert Blatchford;
13. Conclusion. Bibliography.

Semmel, B. 'The philosophical radicals and colonialism', *JEH*, 1961. **[4]**
There were Benthamite colonial reformers but in general Benthamite
radicals had a positive programme of empire—including ideas about need
for capital export.

Shaw, A. G. L. 'A revision of the meaning of "imperialism"', Brisbane,
Australian Journal of Politics and History, **7**, 1961. **[5, 7, 10]**
Shallowly disguised attack on Marxist theory, in guise of linguistic type
approach.

Shaw, A. G. L. ed. *Great Britain and the Colonies, 1815–1865*, London,
Methuen, 1970. **[1, 4, 5, 6]**
1. J. S. Galbraith, Myths of the 'Little England' era; 2. E. R. Kittrell, The
development of the theory of colonisation in English classical political
economy; 3. B. Semmel, The philosophic radicals and colonialism; 4. D. N.
Winch, Classical economics and the case for Colonisation; 5. R. N. Ghosh,
The colonisation controversy; R. J. Wilmot-Horton and the classical
economists; 6. G. S. L. Tucker, The application and significance of theories
of the effect of economic progress on the rate of profit, 1800–1850; 7. J.
Gallagher and R. E. Robinson, The imperialism of free trade; 8. O.
MacDonagh, The anti-imperialism of free trade; 9. R. J. Moore, Imperialism and free trade policy in India, 1853–1854; 10. H. O. Pappe, Wakefield
and Marx. Select bibliography.

Simon, M. and **Novack, D. E.** 'Some dimensions of the American
commercial invasion of Europe, 1871–1914: an introductory essay', *JEH*,
December, 1964. **[2, 4, 9]**

Concerned with U.S.A. trade with Europe in late 19th century. Not really directly relevant but authors stress the methodological importance of disaggregating trade figures—as they do—for testing Hobson-Lenin theses.

Smith, A. *An Inquiry into the Nature and Causes of the Wealth of Nations*, London, Dent and New York, Dutton, 1954, 2 vols. (first edn, 1776) [4] Book IV. 7. Of colonies.

Snyder, L. L., ed. *The Imperialism Reader* (Documents and Readings on Modern Expansionism), Princeton, New Jersey, Van Nostrand, 1962. [4, 5, 6, 7, 8]
Introduction. Modern imperialism: nature, causes, incentives; I. The meaning of modern imperialism; II. Characteristics, mechanics and techniques of modern expansionism; III. Pro-imperialism: advocates and proponents; IV. Anti-imperialism critics and opponents; V. The conquest and exploitation of Africa; VI. The spoliation of the Far East and Southern Asia; VII. Imperialism in the Near and Middle East; VIII. U.S. imperialism at the turn of the century; IX. Twilight of Western imperialism; X. The emergence of communist imperialism.
A 'textbook' for modern (mid-nineteenth-century onwards) imperialism. Comprehensive in coverage, worldwide—does not settle for any single explanation for imperialism. 'The editor has sought to avoid the rigidity of problem studies while seeking a balanced picture of political, diplomatic, economic, social and psychological elements of a great changing historical movement' (Preface).

Sombart, W. *Der Moderne Capitalismus*, (Modern capitalism), 3 vols, Berlin, 1916–27. [7]
Vol. iii contains small section on imperialism (pp. 64 ff). Marxist theories false, or at least one sided.

Stalin, J. *Problems of Leninism*, Moscow, Progress Publishers, 1945. [2]
Report on the work of the central committee to the 18th congress of the C.P.S.U. (B) 10 March 1939. I. The Soviet Union and international affairs. Stalin attacks 'capitalist expansionism' as vicious and backward while defending Soviet expansionism.

Stedman Jones, G. 'The specificity of U.S. imperialism', *NLR*, **60**, March/April, 1970. [3]
Characterisation of special nature of U.S. imperialism; draws on recent U.S. historical research.

Stengers, J. 'L'Impérialisme colonial de la fin du XIXème siècle: mythe ou réalité?', *JAH*, **3** 1962. [4]
Review article, critique of Robinson and Gallagher. 'Le marche intérieur de l'Afrique commençait a être livré à une compétition commerciale qui eut en tout état de cause engendre le scramble. Et cela même si l'Egypte n'avait pas existé.'

Sternberg, F. *Capitalism and Socialism on Trial*, New York, John Day, 1950, London, Gollancz, 1951. [4]

I. The rise of capitalism; 1. Capitalism conquers the world; 2. European annexation and imperialism; 3. The crises during the rise of capitalism; 4. U.S. capitalism conquers its own land; 5. Class stratification and the rise of capitalism; 6. Imperialist expansion led to war. II. The epoch of the First World War; III. The period of capitalist stagnation between the two world wars: IV. The Second World War; 5. The world today.

Sternberg, F. *Der Imperialismus* (Imperialism), Berlin, 1926. [**1, 2, 3**]
1. Surplus population under imperialism; 2. Wages under imperialism; 3. The economic crisis under imperialism; 4. The self-superceding of revisionism; 5. The imperialist war; 6. The sociological sphere of the materialist view of history; 7. The socialist revolution: the Russian revolution; 8. The capitalism of the British Empire—India; 9. German capitalism; 10. The capitalism of the United States; Note 1. Surplus value and surplus population; Note 2. Rodbertus' theory of crises.
Examines the implications of the non-capitalist world for capitalism and for social change. Partly critical of Marx. Implicit attack on Lenin's theory of imperialism in Chapter 3. Goes back to some extent to Rosa Luxemburg's *Accumulation of Capital*.

Sternberg, F. *The Coming Crisis*, London, Gollancz, 1947. [**1, 2, 3**]
I. 3. Imperialist expansion.
Marxist, but critical of Luxemburg and Lenin, Marx and Engels.

Stokes, E. 'Late nineteenth-century colonial expansion and the attack on the theory of economic imperialism: A case of mistaken identity?' *HJ*, **12**, 2, 1969. [**2, 4, 6**]
Reviews several theories of imperialism—summarises the 'peripheral' theory of Robinson and Gallagher; separates the Hobsonian from the Leninist account of imperialism; defends Lenist economic imperialism from attacks that gain strength by misrepresentation. Examples to show that economic factors must play some part in any explanation of imperialism. Sympathetic to the Leninist explanation of imperialism.

Strachey, E. J. *The End of Empire (Principles of Democratic Socialism,* vol. ii*)*, London, Gollancz, 1959. [**2, 4, 6**]
I. Empire; 1. How an empire is built; 2. '. . . Such a prize in solid money . . .'; 3. What happened to India; 4. What happened to Britain; 5. The new imperialism; 6. The Hobson-Lenin explanation; 7. The explanation; 8. The explanation considered; The Relaxing grasp; II. In place of empire; 9. The dissolution of the empires; 10. Do empires still pay? (1) In terms of trade; 11. (2) The empire of oil; 12. (3) Summary; 13. Non-colonial empires; 14. The close shave; 15. Britain without an empire; 16. By bread alone? 17. The Commonwealth; 18. An economic basis for the Commonwealth; 19. New empires for old? (1) An American empire? 20. New empires for old? (2) A Russian empire? 21. My brother's keeper? III. Towards a theory of imperialism.
Equates imperialism with empire. Empire defined as attempt of one nation to dominate another. As ever present throughout history. But we may

now be entering a period when empires are no longer necessary.

Sulzbach, W. *Imperialismus und Nazionalbewusstsein* (Imperialism and national consciousness), Frankfurt, 1959. [**5, 7, 8**]
I. National consciousness; 1. Fatherland and nation; 2. Times without national consciousness; 3. National characteristics and other factors; 4. The origin of nations; 5. Continuity and discontinuity; II. Imperialism; 1. Static and dynamic imperialism; 2. Dynasties and democracies; 3. National imperialism; III. The prospects.

Suret-Canale, J. *Afrique Noire, l'ère coloniale 1900–1945*, Psris, Editions Sociales, 1964. [**3**]
I. Le mise en place du système coloniale (1900–1919); 1. L'économie de traite; 2. Les conséquences sociales; 3. Le système administratif; 4. La pacification; 5. Les rivalités impérialistes; II. L'apogée coloniale (1919–1945); 1. L'exploitation économique; 2. L'Opression politique et administrative; 3. L'evolution sociale et politique. Bibliography.

Suret-Canale, J. *Afrique Noire, Occidentale et Centrale: Géographie, civilisations, histoire*, Paris, Editions Sociales, 1961. [**3**]
1. Le cadre géographique; II. Les hommes; III. L'Histoire: (1) Prehistoire et antiquité; (2) Le moyen age; (3) L'ére de la traite (XVIe siècle—seconde moitié du XIXe siècle) (*a*) L'accumulation primitive et la traité; (*b*) La désagrégation des vieux empires; (*c*) Les hegemonies peules; (*d*) El Hadj Omar; (4) La conquête coloniale (*a*) La libre concurrence et les premières explorations; (*b*) L'impérialisme et la colonisation moderne; (*c*) La percée vers le Niger; (*d*) La pénétration pacifique dans le Sud; (*e*) La conférence de Berlin et la partage de l'Afrique. Destruction des empires soudanais; (*f*) Les méthodes de la guerre; (*g*) La conquête du Dahomey; (*h*) La consolidation; (*i*) La course au Tchad.

Sweezy, P. M. *The Theory of Capitalist Development: principles of Marxian political economy*, London, Dennis Dobson, 1946, New York, Monthly Review Press, 1956. [**3**]
I. Value and surplus value; II. The accumulation process; III. Crises and depressions; IV. Imperialism: 1. The state; 2. The development of monopoly capital; 3. Monopoly and the laws of motion of capitalism; 4. World economy; 5. Imperialism; 6. Fascism; 7. Looking forward.

Sweezy, P. M. 'Obstacles to economic development', in C. H. Feinstein, ed. *Socialism, Capitalism and Economic Growth*, Cambridge, Cambridge Univ. Press, 1967. [**3**]
The second part argues that the imperialist world trade system perpetrates raw material production in underdeveloped countries and 'foreign investment is . . . a giant pump for sucking surplus out of the underdeveloped countries and transferring control over a large part of their productive resources to the great imperialist corporations'.

Sweezy, P. M. 'Three works on Imperialism', *JEH*, **13**, 1953. [**3, 4, 6**]
Review of three works: Rosa Luxemburg, *The Accumulation of Capital*, Fritz Sternburg, *Capitalism and Socialism on Trial*, and G. W. F. Hallgarten,

372

Imperialismus vor 1914.

Thornton, A. P. *Doctrines of Imperialism*, New York, John Wiley, 1965. [6]
1. Overtones; 2. The doctrine of power; 3. The doctrine of profit; 4. The doctrine of civilisation; 5. Undertones.

Partially historical (1870 onwards), partly analytical. Sceptical of crude, simplistic explanations of imperialism. Concerned to analyse the motives and intentions of the empire-builders. 'Imperialism is less a fact than a thought.'

Thornton, A. P. *For the File on Empire, essays and reviews,* London, Macmillan, 1968. [6]
22. 'Empire and Imperialism', a review of Koebner's 'Empire'; 23. 'The Long Shadow', a review of Strachey's 'End of Empire'. ˙

Thornton, A. P. *The Imperial Idea and its Enemies, a study in British power,* London, Macmillan, 1959, (pb. 1966). [5, 7]
Introduction. A definition of terms; 1. The emergence of empire; 2. The imperial idea at its zenith; 3. The impact of war (i) The Boer War; 4. The impact of war (ii) 1914–18; 5. The impact of nationalism; 6. The impact of democracy; 7. The combined assault.

Varga, E. 'The Problem of inter-imperialist contradictions and war' in *Politico-Economic ·Problems of Capitalism,* Moscow, Progress Publishers, 1968. [3]
Although the economic reasons for inter-capitalist rivalry remain and the U.S.A. can no longer dictate so easily to its capitalist allies, the chances of intercapitalist war have declined since bourgeois statesmen are aware of the threat.

Varga, E. and **Mendelsohn, L.** eds. *New Data for V. I. Lenin's 'Imperialism, the Highest Stage of Capitalism'*, London, Lawrence & Wishart, 1939; New York, International Publishers, 1940. [2]
I. Lenin's Imperialism, the Highest Stage of Capitalism. II. Consists of a series of tables to provide 'new data' for each of Lenin's chapters; III. consists of supplementary data headed: 1. Inability of capitalism to utilise the basic productive power of society-labour power; 2. Direct and indirect destruction of labour power; 3. Growth of unproductive labour power; 4. Retarded rate of increase of production; 5. Retardation of technical progress; 6. The chronic below-capacity utilisation of means of production; 7. Destruction of fixed capital; 8. Destruction of stocks of commodities in the period of world economic crisis; 9. Increase in distribution costs; 10. Armaments, wars, increase of police force. IV. Ten further sections commenting on the new data.
Contains new data not available to Lenin when he wrote *Imperialism*. Also commentary on his data.

Viallate, A. *Economic Imperialism and International Relations During the Last Fifty Years,* New York, Macmillan, 1923. [4]
Introduction. Economic changes in the nineteenth century; I. Growth of

industrialism. Expansion. Entente and alliance. II. The war and its consequences; Conclusion. Imperialism or economic internationalism.
Nineteenth century economic changes increased national rivalries, but also led them to develop more common interests. War, the result of these rivalries, but most important result, creation of economic interdependence between nations.

Viner, J. 'Peace as an economic problem', in G. B. Huzard, ed., *New Perspectives on Peace*, Chicago, 1944; Glencoe, Illinois, The Free Press, 1951. **[5, 7]**
Anti-economic interpretation of the causes of war.

Wehler, H. U. *Bismarck und der Imperialismus* (Bismarck and Imperialism), Cologne, Berlin, 1969. **[8]**
I. Introduction; II. A time of social-economic crisis: 1. The disruptions in world economic growth 1873–1896; 2. The economic growth of Germany; III. The ideological consensus: export offensive and social imperialism as conjunctural social politics: 1. Economy and the business world; 2. Theories of conjuncture and crises; 3. Public opinion; 4. Expansion agitation; 5. Expansionist interest groups and the 'German Colonial Union' of 1882; 6. Party politicians and ministerial bureaucracy; 7. Bismarck; IV. The beginnings of expansion: 1. First steps of economic expansion; 2. Export promotion at its height; V. Increased expansion: from 'informal empire' to colonial rule in German protectorates: 1. A 'German India' in Africa; 2. Expansion in the Pacific; 3. Unfulfilled expectations; VI. Bismarck's imperialism: 1. The guessing over the motives of Bismarck's 'colonial policy'; 2. The significance of Bismarck's imperialism. Extensive critical bibliography.

Wheelwright, E. L. 'Historical appraisal: colonialism—past and present', Japan Economic Research Centre, *The Structure and Development in Asian Economies*, Tokyo, December 1968. **[1, 3, 4, 6]**
Rapid survey of evolution of Marxist and related ideas about colonialism and fuller historical treatment of economic and social effects of colonialism in Asian economies with some discussion of the neocolonialism of aid and investment patterns. Theoretically much influenced by Baran and Barratt Brown.

Williams, E. *Capitalism and Slavery*, London, Andre Deutsch, 1964. **[4]**
1. The origin of negro slavery; 2. The development of the negro slave trade; 3. British commerce and the triangular trade; 4. The West India interest; 5. British industry and the triangular trade; 6. The American revolution; 7. The development of British capitalism 1783–1833; 8. The new industrial order; 9. British capitalism and the West Indies; 10. The 'commercial part of the nation' and slavery; 11. The 'saints' and slavery; 12. The slaves and slavery; 13. Conclusion. Bibliography.

Williamson, J. A. *A Notebook of Empire History*, London, 1st edn. 1942, Macmillan; later editions entitled *A Notebook of Commonwealth History*, rev. and ed. by D. Southgate, 3rd edn., Macmillan, 1967. **[10]**

I. The old colonial empire: 1. Overseas trade in the Middle Ages; 2. Geographical knowledge at the opening of the age of discovery; 3. The discoveries of the Portuguese and Spaniards; 4. The early Tudor period 1485–1558; 5. Elizabethan expansion, 1558–1603; 6. The early Stuarts, 1603–42; 7. The interregnum and the Restoration 1642–8; 8. From the Revolution to the end of the 7 years war 1688–1763; 9. The end of the old empire 1763–83; II. The modern empire and Commonwealth: 1. The reconstruction and the last French wars 1783–1815; 2. The development of the new principles 1815–46; 3. The period of depression 1846–74; 4. Disraeli and Gladstone 1874–85; 5. Late Victorian imperialism 1885–1902; 6. The Commonwealth takes shape 1902–14; 7. The First World War 1914–19; 8. The British Commonwealth between the wars, 1919–39; 9. Empire and Commonwealth 1939–66; 10. The Commonwealth in Asia since 1939; 11. The Middle East and the Mediterranean; 12. The end of empire in Africa; 13. The Caribbean; 14. The meaning of the Commonwealth.

Chronological notes on events in the evolution of the British Commonwealth from its imperial beginnings to the present day. A good reference book.

Winch, D. N. *Classical Political Economy and the Colonies*, London, G. Bell, 1965. [**4, 6**]

1. Introduction; 2. Adam Smith and Empire; 3. Jeremy Bentham and colonies; 4. The Ricardians and the colonial system; 5. The classical attitude to emigration; 6. The case for colonisation; 7. The political economy of new countries; 8. Colonial reform in practice; 9. Classical economics and colonisation; 10. Classical liberal imperialism. Bibliography.

Winch, D. N. 'Classical economics and the case for Colonisation,' *Economica*, **30**, 1963; also in A. G. L. Shaw, ed. *Great Britain and the Colonies 1815–1865* (above). [**4, 7**]

Review of Gibbon Wakefield's writings on the colonial question and an evaluation of their influence on British classical economy.

Winks, R. ed. *British Imperialism: gold, god, glory*, New York, Holt, Rinehart & Winston, 1963. [**2, 4, 6, 7, 8**]

Introduction. The economic interpretation (Hobson and Lenin extracts and critical articles by M. Blaug and D. Fieldhouse). The Non-human factors (articles by Halevy, A. P. Thornton, G. Himmelfarb, R. Maurier, J. Galbraith and G. Bennett, W. Lechy on public opinion, pro-imperialism literature, imperial responsibility, imperial race, humanitarian impulse, rhetoric respectively). The human factors (Schumpeter sociology and critical article by M. Greene, N. Monsergh on diplomacy, strategy and imperialism, K. M. Parikhov, An Eastern view of British imperialism, and Robinson and Gallagher, a synthesis of views and a challenge for the future). Bibliography.

Anthology from Hobson and Lenin to Robinson and Gallagher.

Winslow, E. M. *The Pattern of Imperialism*, New York, Columbia Univ.

Press, 1948 (published in Great Britain by Oxford Univ. Press). **[1, 2, 4, 5, 6, 7, 8]**
1. Imperialism versus nationalism; 2. The beginnings of controversy; 3. The historians and imperialism; 4. The search for a formula; 5. Hobson and the theory of economic imperialism; 6. Socialistic theories of imperialism: Marxian background; 7. Development of the theories of capitalist imperialism: the neo-Marxists; 8. Capitalism and socialism in a new perspective; 9. Imperialism and war as political phenomena. Bibliography.
Good comprehensive survey of the theories of imperialism. Questions assumption that economic forces constitute the causes of imperialism and war. Favours Schumpeterian line of thought.

Winslow, E. M. 'Marxian, liberal and sociological theories of Imperialism', *JPE*, **39**, 1931. **[1, 4, 5, 6, 7, 8]**
1. Three general points of view; 2. The Marxian theories of imperialism; 3. The Liberal-Hobsonian theory of economic imperialism; 4. The formula of 'Economic imperialism' and the historians; 5. A sociological theory of imperialism.
Calls attention to difficulties of using and defining the term 'imperialism'. Examines previous treatment of imperialism under the three headings in the title. Argues that empire-building is competitive, but in the political realm. Questions the assumption that capitalism has some necessary and active part in carrying imperialism to the ends of the earth. Suggests that imperialism is the active agent, using capitalism for its own ends. Pro-Schumpeterian, anti-Marxist.

Woddis, J. *An Introduction to Neo-Colonialism*, London, Lawrence & Wishart, 1967. **[3]**
1. What is colonialism? 2. Why neo-colonialism; 3. Neo-colonialism at work; 4. The future of neo-colonialism. Bibliography.
As title suggests sets out to be introduction to *understanding* what neo-colonialism is: understanding necessary so it can be fought. Optimistic conclusion about future. 'Imperialism . . . can no longer decide the fate of mankind . . . the people are on the march . . . colonialism in all forms will be ended.'

Woodruff, W. *Impact of Western Man: a study of Europe's role in the world economy 1750–1960*, London, Macmillan (pb), 1966. **[4, 9]**
1. Prologue; 2. The course of empire; 3. Exodus—the dispersal of Europeans since the eighteenth century; 4. Europe—banker to the world; A study of European foreign investment; 5. The diffusion of European technology; 6. The conquest of distance; 7. The changing pattern of trade; 8. Epilogue. Bibliography.

Woolf, L. S. *Economic Imperialism*, London, Swarthmore Press, 1920. **[4]**
1. Introduction; 2. Economic imperialism in Africa; 3. Economic imperialism in Asia; 4. Causes and results.
Anti-imperialist. Argues that the world movement is not simply 'Europeanisation' *but* also economic exploitation to further European States' interests.

Attacks the doctrine of 'the white man's burden'. Economic imperialism is only the logical application of capitalism and its principles of internationalism.

Woolf, L. S. *Empire and Commerce in Africa: a study in economic imperialism*, London, Allen & Unwin, 1920; reprinted 1968. [**4, 9**]
1. International economic policy: 1. Introductory; 2. The state's range of economic action; 3. The economic imperialism of Europe; 4. The scope of the enquiry; II. Economic imperialism in Africa: 1. Europe and Africa; 2. Mediterranean Africa: Algeria; 3. Mediterranean Africa: Tunis; 4. Mediterranean Africa: Tunis and Tripoli; 5. Abyssinia and the Nile; 6. Zanzibar and East Africa; 7. The Belgian Congo; III. Reflections and Conclusions: 1. The effects of economic imperialism; 2. The future of Africa.

Woolf, L. S. *Imperialism and Civilisation*, London, Hogarth Press, 1928. [**4**]
1. Introduction; 2. The conflicts of civilisations before the nineteenth century; 3. Imperialism in Asia; 4. Economic imperialism in Africa; 5. The inverse of imperialism; 6. The League of Nations and a synthesis of civilisations.

Wolff, R. D. 'Modern imperialism: the view from the Metropolis', Cambridge, Mass.; *AER Papers and Proceedings*, May 1970. [**3**]
Historical-theoretical characterisation of imperialism (U.K. and U.S.) by examining imperatives for control by large corporations of raw material supplies, markets and opportunities to invest.

Wright, H. M. ed., *The 'New Imperialism': analysis of late nineteenth-century expansion*, Boston, D. C. Heath, 1961. [**2, 4, 5, 6, 8**]
1. J. Holland Rose, Three conditions of expansion; 2. J. A. Hobson, Imperialism, a study; 3. V. I. Lenin, The highest stage of capitalism; 4. L. Woolf, Empire and commerce; 5. J. A. Schumpeter, Imperialism as a social atavism; 6. M. Greene, Schumpeter's imperialism. A critical note; 7. W. L. Langer, a critique of imperialism; 8. E. Stanley, Foreign investment and foreign expansion; 9. C. J. H. Hayes, Bases of a new national imperialism; 10. N. Mansergh, Diplomatic reaons for expansion; 11. P. Renouvin, The politics of imperialist expansion; 12. H. Arendt, The alliance between mob and capital. Bibliography.
Collection of the most famous analytical works on imperialism.

Notes on contributors

Michael Barratt Brown Senior Lecturer, Sheffield University Department of Extramural Studies. Author of *After Imperialism* (London, Heinemann, 1963, 2nd edn. 1970) and *What Economics is About* (London, Weidenfeld & Nicolson, 1970). Contributor to *New Left Review*, *International Socialist Journal*, *The Spokesman*, etc.

Thomas Hodgkin Former Lecturer in the Government of New States, Oxford University, and Senior Research Fellow, Balliol College, Oxford. Author of *Nationalism in Colonial Africa* (London, Muller, 1956), *Nigerian Perspectives* (London, Oxford Univ. Press, 1960), *African Political Parties* (Harmondsworth, Penguin, 1961), and articles on African affairs.

R. W. Johnson Fellow of Magdalen College, Oxford. Co-editor (with C. H. Allen) of *African Perspectives: papers in the history, politics and economics of Africa presented to Thomas Hodgkin* (Cambridge, Cambridge University Press, 1970). Author of articles and papers on Guinea.

A. S. Kanya-Forstner Associate Professor of History, York University, Ontario. Author of *The Conquest of the Western Sudan: A Study in French Military Imperialism* (Cambridge, Cambridge Univ. Press, 1969) and several articles on aspects of French African policy.

Tom Kemp Senior Lecturer in Economic History, Department of Economic and Social History University of Hull. Author of *Theories of Imperialism* (London, Dobson, 1967), *Industrialization in Nineteenth Century Europe* (London, Longman, 1969), *Economic Forces in French History* (London, Dobson, 1971) and *The French Economy 1913–39* (London, Longman, 1972)

Harry Magdoff An editor of the *Monthly Review* (New York). Author of *The Age of Imperialism: the Economics of U.S. Foreign Policy* (New York, Monthly Review Press, 1969) and articles on imperialism.

E. R. J. Owen Faculty Lecturer in the Recent Economic History of the Middle East and Fellow of St. Antony's College, Oxford. Author of *Cotton and the Egyptian Economy 1820–1914* (London, Oxford Univ. Press, 1969).

Prabhat Patnaik Assistant Professor of Economics at Jawaharlal Nehru University, New Delhi. Author of articles on aspects of the Indian economy.

D. C. M. Platt Professor of the History of Latin America and Fellow of St. Antony's College, Oxford. Author of articles on imperialism, and of *Finance, Trade and Politics in British Foreign Policy, 1815–1914* (London, Oxford Univ. Press, 1968), *The Cinderella Service: British Consuls since 1825* (London, Longman, 1971) and *Latin America and British Trade, 1806–1914*, (London, A. & C. Black, 1972).

Ronald Robinson Fellow of Balliol College and Beit Professor in the History of the British Commonwealth, Oxford. Co-author (with J. Gallagher) of 'The imperialism of Free Trade' (1953) and *Africa and the Victorians: the official mind of imperialism* (London, Macmillan, 1961).

Jean Stengers Professor in the Université Libre de Bruxelles. Author of *Combien Le Congo a-t-il coûté à la Belgique* (1954), *Belgique et Congo: L'élaboration de la charte coloniale* (1963), and editor of *Textes inédits d'Emile Banning* (1955).

R. B. Sutcliffe Lecturer in Economics at Kingston Polytechnic, Kingston, Surrey. Co-editor (with P. J. M. McEwan) of *The Study of Africa* (London, Methuen, 1965). Author of *Industry and Underdevelopment* (London,

378

Addison Wesley, 1971) and articles on Southern Africa, economic development and British capitalism.

Hans-Ulrich Wehler Professor of Modern History, Bielefeld University, Author of, *Bismarck und der Imperialismus* (1969), *Krisenherde des Kaiserreichs, 1871–1918. Studien zur Deutschen Soziall-und Verfassungsgeschichte* (1970). *Das Deutsche Kaiserreich, 1871–1918* (1972), *Sozialdemokratie und Nationalstaat. Nationalitätenfragen in Deutschland, 1840–1914* (1962, 1971) and *Imperium Americanum. Studien zum Aufstieg des Amerikanischen Imperialismus, 1865–1900* (1972).

Name Index

General Index

Batéké, 280
Bechuanaland, 123
Belgium, 252, 256, 258, 261–2, 267, 271, 277
Benty, 233
Berlin, 73, 80, 267
Berlin Conference, 99
Bissau, 232
Boer War, 125
Boffa, 233
Bolivia, 307–9
Bolshevik Revolution, 27, 52, 60–1, 108, 177, 179–80, 184
Bonapartism, 77, 78, 80, 84–5, 87
Borate Syndicate, 309
Borneo, 269
bourgeoisie,
    British, 105
    comprador, 211
    Indian, 211, 214–15, 221, 226–7, 229
    national, 69, 102, 109, 183
    petty, 182, 216
    western industrial, 111, 202, 211
Boxer rebellion, 128, 132
Brazil, 66, 156, 179, 185, 227, 298–9, 301, 303, 307, 310
de Brazza treaty, 280
Britain (U.K.), 39–40, 55–7, 70, 73, 81, 85, 124, 129, 150, 213–14, 283–4, 307, 324–5
    industry, 91
    government, 3, 5
British Rail Makers' Association, 310
Brussels, 252, 256, 267–8
Budapest, 61
Buenos Aires, 302, 304, 309, 310
Buganda, 121
bureaucracy, 84, 86, 127, 204–5, 215

Cairo, 201, 285
'Calvo Clause', 301
Cameroons, 272
Canary Islands, 256, 258, 267
capital, 53, 58, 65, 71, 105, 225, 308, 310
    accumulation of, 49, 57, 59, 60–1, 63–4, 66–7, 156, 172–3, 177, 187–8, 321
    'comprador', 65

concentration and centralisation, 13, 23, 28, 35, 48, 57, 67
constant and variable, 19, 21
exports, 2–3, 9, 21, 29, 35, 39, 48, 53–7, 63–4, 70, 147–8, 149–50, 208, 296, 300–3, 306, 308–9, 318–9, 324–5
finance, 23, 25, 29
organic composition of, 14, 19
superabundance of, surplus, 9, 54, 144, 149, 155
Capital (Karl Marx), 13–14, 18–23, 35, 43–7, 180, 183
capitalism,
    British, 26, 169
capitalist crisis, 28, 58, 82
Carolina and Mariana Islands, 256, 257
cartels, 49
Catholics, 76
Central Intelligence Agency (CIA), 168
Chad, 280, 283, 286–8
chauvinism, 110
Chicago, 104
Chile, 299, 301, 304, 309
China, 40, 45, 65–6, 81, 91, 120, 177, 256–8, 267, 270, 279
    drive into, 91
    and India, 221
    and Japanese War, 131, 284
    partition of, 53
    revolution, 34, 61–2, 128, 164, 313, 322
class struggle, 21, 84, 329
Code Napoleon, 105
cold war, 221, 313
Colligacao Assucareira do Brasil, 309
Colombia, 304
colonial expansion
    British, 43
    French colonial army, 177
colonial liberation, 95
colonial peoples, 51–2, 102, 111, 113, 115
colonial rule, 42, 63, 66, 99, 122–3, 133, 137, 212, 238, 288
    Formal rule, 82
    German, 79
    Semi-colonial empire, 158
colonial settlers, 39, 235–6, 280, 290

384

390